INSIGHT GUIDES
ICELAND

APA PUBLICATIONS
Part of the Langenscheidt Publishing Group

☆ INSIGHT GUIDE
ICELAND

Editorial
Managing Editor
Tom Le Bas
Editorial Director
Brian Bell
Photographic Director
Steven Lawrence

Distribution
United States
Langenscheidt Publishers, Inc.
36–36 33rd Street, 4th Floor
Long Island City, New York 11106
Fax: (1) 718 784 0640

UK & Ireland
GeoCenter International Ltd
Meridian House, Churchill Way West
Basingstoke, Hampshire RG21 6YR
Fax: (44) 1256 817988

Australia
Universal Publishers
1 Waterloo Road
Macquarie Park, NSW 2113
Fax: (61) 2 9888 9074

New Zealand
Hema Maps New Zealand Ltd (HNZ)
Unit D, 24 Ra ORA Drive
East Tamaki, Auckland
Fax: (64) 9 273 6479

Worldwide
Apa Publications GmbH & Co.
Verlag KG (Singapore branch)
38 Joo Koon Road, Singapore 628990
Tel: (65) 6865 1600. Fax: (65) 6861 6438

Printing
Insight Print Services (Pte) Ltd
38 Joo Koon Road, Singapore 628990
Tel: (65) 6865 1600. Fax: (65) 6861 6438

©2008 Apa Publications GmbH & Co.
Verlag KG (Singapore branch)
All Rights Reserved

First Edition 1992
Fifth Edition 2008

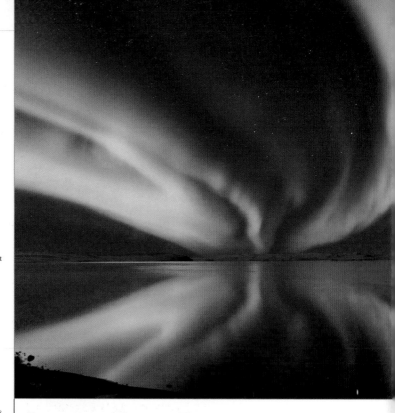

ABOUT THIS BOOK

This guidebook combines the interests and enthusiasms of two of the world's best-known information providers: Insight Guides, whose titles have set the standard for visual travel guides since 1970, and Discovery Channel, the world's premier source of nonfiction television programming.

The editors of Insight Guides provide both practical advice and general understanding about a destination's history, culture, institutions and people. Discovery Channel and its web site, www.discovery.com, help millions of viewers explore their world from the comfort of their own home and also encourage them to explore it first hand.

How to use this book

The book is structured to convey an understanding of Iceland and its culture, as well as to guide readers through its sights and activities:

◆ To understand Iceland today, you need to know something about its eventful past. Therefore, the first section of the guidebook covers the country's history, culture and environmental issues in lively essays.

◆ The main Places section provides a complete run-down of all the places worth seeing. The main sites of interest are coordinated by number with the maps. A list of recommended restaurants, cafés and bars appears at the end of each chapter.

◆ The Travel Tips listings section provides information on transport, hotels, cultural and outdoor activities, specialist tour operators and all the other practical information you'll need. Information may be located quickly by using the index printed on the back cover flap.

The contributors

Insight: Iceland was edited and co-ordinated by Managing Editor **Tom Le Bas** at Insight Guides' London office.

The text was comprehensively updated by **James Proctor**, former BBC Scandinavia correspondent, who also supplied new features on Food and Drink, Environmental Protection and Whaling. He also provided much of the new text for the tint panels and tips in the Places section, and expanded the accommodation and restaurant listings.

This new edition builds on the excellent foundations of previous editions of the book. Of particular note is **Tony Perrottet**, editor of the original edition of *Insight: Iceland*, who also wrote the chapters on The Southwest, Vestmannaeyjar, The Southeast, Akureyri and Surround-

ings, Grímsey, Lake Mývatn, The Northeast, and The East Fjords, and contributed a wide selection of colour photographs. **Rowlinson Carter** wrote the detailed coverage of Iceland's history from its murky beginnings through to the mid-20th century, while **Bernard Scudder** contributed the chapters on Modern History, Harvesting the Sea and Reykjavík. **Anna Yates** wrote Forged by Fire, Honed by Ice, the text for the photo features on Life on the Land and The Great Outdoors, A Naturalist's Paradise, and the chapters on The Reykjanes Peninsula and Snæfellsnes and the West, and the essay on Flowers among the Lava. **Alda Sigmundsdóttir**, a writer and translator living in Reykjavík, wrote the Embracing the Night essay. **Arthúr Bollason**, an Icelandic journalist and writer, contributed the photo feature on the Saga Characters, while **Doreen Taylor** wrote the photo features on Iceland's Sea Birds and Natural Wonders. **Gary Gunning** contributed the essay on the Politics of Fishing. **Birna Helga-dóttir** wrote The Icelanders, Living with the Environment, Language and Literature, and Icelandic Hauntings. The West Fjords was written by **Catherine Harlow**, and the chapters on Húnaflói and Skagafjörður and The Interior by **Julian Cremona**. **Jim Wesneski** contributed the feature on Why is Everything so Expensive?

Principal photographers include **Tony Perrotet, Bob Krist, Catherine Harlow, Bryan and Cherry Alexander, Hans Klüche, Hasse Schröder** and **Rudy Hemmingsen**.

The main places of interest in the Places section are coordinated by number with a full-colour map (e.g. ❶), and a symbol at the top of every right-hand page tells you where to find the map.

LEFT: an aurora over the interior snowfields.
BELOW: exhibit at the Á. Sveinsson Sculpture Gallery.

Contents

LEFT: Gullfoss
waterfall

Travel Tips

THE BEST OF ICELAND: EDITOR'S CHOICE

Unique attractions, fabulous landscapes, geothermal baths, outdoor pursuits and exciting nightlife ... here are our recommendations, plus some essential tips for travellers

DON'T MISS...

● **The Blue Lagoon** Bathe in geothermally-heated mineral-rich waters at this extraordinary resort in the midst of a lava field on the barren Reykjanes peninsula. *See pages 165–6.*

● **Geysir and Gullfoss** This pair of natural wonders are within relatively easy reach of Reykjavík and are most people's only encounter with the Icelandic outback. Geysir has given its name to all such water spouts across the world, although these days it is the smaller, neighbouring Strokkur geyser which draws the crowds. The dramatic double waterfall at nearby Gullfoss is awesome in its elemental power. *See pages 178–9.*

● **Central Reykjavík** Iceland's capital may be small and isolated, but it is a lively, attractive and urbane city nonetheless, with many cultural attractions. The setting, with views across to Mt Esja, is spectacular, and the nightlife is legendary. *See page 143.*

OUTDOOR ADVENTURES

See also the picture spread on pages 268–9.

● **Snow sports** Skiing, ice-climbing, skidooing, snow-boarding – options are numerous for snow enthusiasts. *See pages 334–5.*

● **Whale-watching** Catch a glimpse of one of these majestic creatures off the north or west coast. *See page 334.*

● **Horse-riding** The Icelandic horse is a sturdy breed and ideally suited to local conditions. Farms all over the country offer visitors anything from a one-hour sortie to a seven-day trek. *See page 333.*

● **Bird-watching** The sea cliffs at various points around the Icelandic coast are home to gigantic colonies of sea birds. *See page 333.*

● **Hiking** There is no better way to appreciate the dramatic, unspoiled, often extraordinary landscapes of Iceland than on your own two feet. *See page 332.*

● **The northern lights** Visit in the darkest winter months to observe this ethereal beauty in the sky at its best.

● **Swimming** Take the plunge into one of the country's geothermally-heated pools. Emerging from the heat of a hot tub into the frigid polar air is a memorable experience. *See page 333.*

TOP: hop on a skidoo.
LEFT: the Blue Lagoon.
RIGHT: the puffin, icon of Iceland.

SPECTACULAR LANDSCAPES

● **Þórsmörk**
One of Iceland's most spectacular and inaccessible wilderness areas – sealed off by a trio of glaciers, surging rivers and steep mountains. *See page 182.*

● **The coast around Vík** Black volcanic sands, pounding Atlantic surf and jagged rocks give the coastline at Iceland's southern tip a gothic majesty. *See page 183.*

● **Skaftafell National Park** Dominated by Europe's largest icecap, Vatnajökull. *See page 200.*

● **Jökulsárlón** Ethereal beauty where the glaciers of the mighty Vatnajökull icecap meet the sea in an icy lagoon. *See pages 202–3.*

● **Snæfellsnes** This mystical volcano was the entrance point to the planet's interior in Jules Verne's *Journey to the Centre of the Earth. See page 212.*

● **West Fjords** Towering cliffs and remote fjords in Iceland's sub-arctic northwest. *See page 219.*

● **Lake Mývatn** Weird volcanic landforms and fantastic birdwatching. *See page 261.*

● **Jökulsárgljúfur National Park** The impressive Dettifoss waterfall and Jökulsá Canyon are reasons to make the trip to this area in the far northeast. *See page 275.*

● **East Fjords ❧ Reyðarfjörður to Djúpivogur** Fabulous scenery with tiny coastal villages set against precipitous mountains. *See page 290.*

● **Hveravellir** In the barren heart of Iceland, these hot springs are a remarkable sight – deep pools of brilliant blue water, hissing jets of steam and outlandish coloured rocks. *See page 299.*

● **Herðubreið** This towering peak rises over the plain of the eastern interior, with the Herdubreidarlindur valley an oasis of green amid desert-like surroundings. *See page 307.*

ABOVE: the dramatic Dettifoss waterfall in full flow.
BELOW: climb high for panoramic snow views.

SIGHTS IN REYKJAVIK

● **National Museum** Recommended to anyone wishing to understand Iceland's past. *See page 153.*

● **National Gallery** A light and airy space in which to admire Icelandic and foreign art. *See page 151.*

● **Culture House** Explore the medieval past, brought vividly to life in the saga manuscripts. See also the **Saga Museum**. *See pages 151 and 155.*

● **Hallgrímskirkja** Visible from most points in the city, climb the

tower of this striking modern structure for breathtaking views. *See page 153.*

● **Árbaer Open-Air Museum** An eye-opening experience, showing how people lived in the not-so-distant past. *See page 157.*

● **Laugardalur** Reykjavík's main leisure complex features a magnificent open-air swimming pool with the full range of geothermally-heated hot tubs and plunge pools. *See page 156.*

ABOVE: a night on the town.
ABOVE RIGHT: an illustrated saga manuscript.
BELOW: razorbills, a common sight on Iceland's majestic sea cliffs.

HISTORIC SIGHTS

● **Þingvellir** The natural amphitheatre is revered by Icelanders as the site of the first national assembly back in the 10th century, and the birth of the national identity. *See page 173.*

● **Eyrarbakki** This historic port, long since declined, has two interesting museums and picturesque old wooden houses. *See page 172.*

● **Skálholt** For some 750 years from the 11th century, this was Iceland's major centre of Christianity and learning. A new church stands on the site today. *See page 177.*

● **Stöng** A reconstruction of a Viking longhouse in a remote, beautiful spot. The ruins of the original structure, excavated in

1939, is a few kilometres along the road: it was buried following the eruption of nearby Mount Hekla in 1104. *See page 180.*

● **Flatey** A perfectly preserved village on a peaceful island, this was once a major centre of learning; it remains home to a tiny library. *See page 215.*

● **Akureyri Museum** A well-presented collection of artefacts and photographs illustrating the history of the northern regions of Iceland. *See page 243.*

BEST PLACES TO SEE BIRDS

See also the picture spread on pages 228–9.

● **Lake Mývatn** Huge numbers of waterfowl and other birds in and around the lake. *See page 261.*

● **Vestmannaeyar** See some of the world's largest puffin colonies on this windswept archipelago. *See page 186.*

● **Hornbjarg bird cliffs** In the far northwest, these

spectacular cliffs are home to thousands of sea birds including guillemots, razorbills, gannets, puffins, various gulls and terns. *See page 223.*

● **Grímsey** On the Arctic Circle, this small island is known for its abundant birdlife. *See page 253.*

● **Króksbjarg** and **Bakkar cliffs** In the remote north, a haven for kittiwakes and fulmars. *See page 234.*

TOWNS AND VILLAGES

● **Akureyri** The nation's second city enjoys sunnier weather than Reykjavík, and a magnificent mountain backdrop. It makes a good base for skiing and whale-watching trips. *See page 240.*

● **Stykkishólmur** A typical small Icelandic port with brightly coloured houses, and ferry links to the West Fjords. *See page 214.*

● **Isafjörður** Remote capital of the beautiful West Fjords region, notable not just for its setting but also for its restored 18th-century timber buildings. *See page 220.*

● **Seyðisfjörður** Located within a majestic fjord, this attractive old port is the first sight of Iceland for those arriving by ferry from Denmark, Scotland and the Faroes. *See page 284.*

● **Heimaey** Almost wiped off the map by the volcanic eruption of 1973, this is a busy fishing port with an attractive harbour, situated on the Vestmannaeyjar islands off Iceland's southwest coast. *See page 187.*

ABOVE RIGHT: Austurvöllur Square, Reykjavík, lit up for Christmas.
BELOW: Seyðisfjörður

BEST FESTIVALS AND EVENTS

See pages 329–30

● **Christmas and New Year** The festive season is a colourful affair, with buildings festooned in lights to relieve the winter gloom. A huge bonfire and fireworks see in the New Year.

● **Independence Day** On June 17th Reykjavík and other places put on street parades, street theatre and music events.

● **Rettír** Festivities are held to mark the herding of sheep from their upland summer pastures.

● **Þorrablot** This ancient pagan festival is a cure for the winter blues. Held in February, towns across the country celebrate with singing and dancing, and traditional food, washed down with Brennivin, the local fire-water.

● **Sjómannadagur** (Seafarer's Day): The first Sunday in June is the greatest celebration of the year in many fishing villages. The local fishermen compete in tests of strength.

TRAVELLERS' TIPS

● **Cheap Sleeps** There are 25 youth hostels around Iceland (www.hostel.is) offering comfortable budget accommodation. Also, some hotels and guesthouses have cheap dormitories with either made-up beds or mattresses for sleeping bags.

● **Tourist Information** Local tourist offices are often located in the town hall or library. Many are closed during the winter.

● **Money-saving passes** BSÍ (www.bsi.is) offers bus passes and tickets that will save you money on longer journeys around the island. Holders of BSÍ Passport tickets are entitled to discounts on ferries, BSÍ-rented mountain bikes and campsites. The **Full Circle Passport** is valid May to September, for a circular trip on the Ring Road with no time limit. The **Omnibus Passport** is valid in 1, 2, 3 or 4 week passes and allows unrestricted travel on all scheduled bus routes. **Air/Bus Rover** tickets are good value and allow visitors to travel one way by air and return by bus.

AN EXTRAORDINARY ISLAND

Iceland offers not only a wealth of natural wonders, from glaciers to geysers, but also a rich history and literature

The reason for hereness seems beyond conjecture,
There are no trees or trains or architecture,
Fruits and greens are insufficient for health
And culture is limited by lack of wealth.
The tourist sights have nothing like Stonehenge,
The literature is all about revenge.
And yet I like it if only because this nation
Enjoys a scarcity of population...
— W.H. Auden, *Letters from Iceland*

Iceland has come a long way since the English poet Auden penned these facetious lines in 1936. From an isolated agricultural society that many people thought had scarcely progressed beyond the Middle Ages there has emerged a high-tech welfare state with one of the highest standards of living in the world. Yet at least one thing hasn't changed since Auden's visit: Iceland still has a scarcity of population (around 300,000) that leaves it with some of the greatest wilderness areas in Europe.

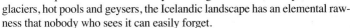

In fact, Iceland may be the ultimate nature trip. It has virtually no pollution from industry and all energy is either geothermal or hydroelectric. Drinking water comes from pure glaciers; fish, the staple food, is caught in unpolluted seas and rivers; even the lamb and cattle graze in fields untouched by fertiliser. The majority of Icelanders now live in and around the capital, Reykjavík, leaving huge swathes of the volcanically active island – one of the most recently formed on earth – quite deserted. Dotted by steaming lava fields, icecaps, glaciers, hot pools and geysers, the Icelandic landscape has an elemental rawness that nobody who sees it can easily forget.

Perhaps not surprisingly, the people who live on this extraordinary island are an eccentric breed. Speaking Europe's oldest language, little changed since the days of the Vikings, accustomed to the endless light of summer and Stygian gloom of the long winters, the Icelanders can be as extreme as their homeland. Rather shy, they will rarely be the first to talk to strangers. But once their traditional reserve is broken through, they can be among the most friendly and hospitable people in Europe.

Which may all help explain why Iceland exerts such a powerful hold over travellers – even those who have visited for only a few days – compelling them to return again and again. ❑

PRECEDING PAGES: the magnificent Hornbjarg bird-cliffs in the West Fjords; Breiðamerkurjökull glacier; Reykjavík skyline. **LEFT:** Skógafoss waterfall. **ABOVE LEFT:** the coastline near Höfn in the southeast. **ABOVE RIGHT:** the Blue Lagoon.

FORGED BY FIRE, HONED BY ICE

Iceland is one of the youngest landmasses in the world, geologically speaking. As a result, its inhabitants are used to living with change and disruption

I n geological terms, Iceland is a mere baby. No more than 20 million years have passed since volcanoes on the floor of the far northern Atlantic ocean began to spew lava, laying the foundations of what would become Iceland. Today it is still one of the most volcanically active spots on earth – giving geoscientists the chance of observing a land still in the making.

Movements of the earth's crust

According to the theory of plate tectonics, widely accepted as explaining the earth's development, the earth's surface comprises a number of rigid plates (six major and several minor plates), which "float" on the mass of magma beneath. Geographical features like the Andes and the Himalayas are evidence of massive collisions of tectonic plates, which have folded the earth's crust up to form great mountain ranges.

Plate junctions are invariably marked by narrow zones of volcanic and earthquake activity: at "destructive" junctions, the edge of one plate is forced underneath the other and part of the earth's surface is "lost", while at "constructive" junctions, two plates pull apart, allowing magma to rise from below, reaching the surface and forming new crust. This is what is still happening in Iceland.

Iceland straddles the Mid-Atlantic Ridge, where the African and American plates are being pulled apart. Thus the island is literally being torn in two, at a rate of 2 cm (nearly an inch) a year, with lava rising up from the earth's centre to more than fill the gap.

LEFT: the solfatara, or volcanic vent, of Hverarönd near Lake Mývatn.
RIGHT: on Vatnajökull, the largest icecap in Europe.

Volcanic belt

The Mid-Atlantic Ridge, running clear across the island from southwest to northeast, is marked by a belt of volcanic craters, hot springs, steam springs, solfataras (areas of high-temperature activity) and earthquakes. This belt extends to a width of about 40 km (25 miles) in the north, and up to 60 km (40 miles) across in the south, and covers about a quarter of the country.

Not surprisingly, Iceland's rocks are almost all volcanic (predominantly basalt). The country's geological history falls into four periods, evidence of each being visible from region to region. The oldest rocks, from the Tertiary pre-Ice Age period, are the plateau basalts of the East and West Fjords. Slightly inland are the younger grey basalts, from the interglacial periods. This is generally open moorland with less evidence of glaciation. Further in towards the present-day volcanic zone is the palagonite formation, from subglacial eruptions in the last part of the Ice Age. Typical of these belts are tuff ridges and table mountains, the soft rock often extensively eroded by wind and water. Iceland's youngest rocks are mainly in areas in and around the present-day volcanic zone.

The northwest and the east of Iceland are no longer volcanically active. Most of the rest of the island, however, conceals a seething mass of volcanic and geothermal activity. About 25 of Iceland's volcanic systems have been active in post-glacial times (i.e. the past 10,000 years) – 18 on land and the rest offshore – and in the past few centuries Iceland has experienced an eruption every five years on average. Some are minor and short-lived, causing minimal damage, like the photogenic eruption of Mount Hekla in 1991. They are known as "tourist eruptions", as they are popular with sightseers.

In the shadow of disaster

Despite an apparently flippant attitude towards volcanoes, Icelanders do not forget the threat they live with. The catastrophic eruption of Lakagígar in the late 18th century poured out the largest lava flow

THE BIRTH OF SURTSEY

The ultimate "tourist eruption" was the formation of the island of Surtsey, which began on the ocean floor just southwest of the Vestmannaeyjar (Westman Islands) in 1963 *(see pages 191–3)*. In addition to the familiar spectacle of lava and ash, the Surtsey eruption produced voluminous clouds of steam as cold seawater met hot lava and instantly boiled. Before the end of the eruption, the new island was 2.8 sq. km (1 sq. mile) in area – although erosion has now reduced this to about 1.57 sq. km (½ sq. mile). The new islet was a welcome gift to scientists, a natural laboratory which offered them a chance to observe the processes by which virgin land is colonised by plants.

ever produced by a single volcano in recorded history, with a volume of about 12 cubic km (3 cubic miles). As if that were not enough, it also emitted noxious gases which poisoned livestock and crops, blocked out the sun, and led to a disastrous famine. About one-third of the population died.

In 1973, the subterranean peril was brought home with a vengeance, when a new volcano flared up on Heimaey in the Vestmannaeyar. It buried one-third of the town under lava and ash *(see the panel on page 189)*.

Evidence of subterranean unrest has been felt since the mid-1970s around Mount Krafla near Lake Mývatn, an area free of volcanic activity for over two centuries. A massive eruption, which lasted from 1724 until 1729, laid waste three farms, before the lava flow halted at Reykjahlíð church, where the congregation was praying for deliverance. Two centuries later, the earth began to move when construction started on the geothermal power station below Mount Krafla; many people concluded that man's interference with the forces of nature had set off a reaction within the earth. Mount Krafla has erupted several times since 1975, most recently in 1984, although the lava has never threatened Reykjahlíð.

It has been estimated that one-third of all the lava that has erupted on earth in recorded history has come from Iceland. As any visitor will soon discover, almost all of it is of the scoria type.

AMAZING ICECAP

Vatnajökull, up to 1 km (3,200 ft) thick and 8,300 sq. km (3,200 sq. miles) in area, is not only Europe's largest icecap, it is also bigger than all the rest put together.

Although Iceland emerged from its glacial pall about 10,000 years ago, it remains a land of glaciers and icecaps – curiously, they are believed to have been formed not in the Ice Age but during a cold spell around 500 BC, reaching their largest size during the "Little Ice Age" of AD 1500–1900. Over the past 80 years or so the glaciers, with a few exceptions, have been gradually

LEFT: the 1973 eruption of Eldfell which threatened to engulf the town of Heimaey.
ABOVE: the eruption of Grímsvötn in 1996.

Loose, sharp and difficult to cross, it also creates unusual and haunting formations. A small amount is smooth, hard "ropy" lava.

Caps of ice

In spite of its subterranean heat, the island has largely been shaped by cold. Covered by glaciers in the Ice Age, Iceland has been sculpted by moving ice. Glaciation has carved out its present form, gouging the plunging fjords which cut into the coastline on north, east and west, and honing mountain ridges to knife-edges.

retreating. Ice now covers around 11 percent of the island's 103,000 sq. km (40,000 sq. miles).

Contrasts between heat and cold are nowhere so striking as in the glaciers that sit atop volcanoes. Some seem extinct: the volcanic crater on which the cone-shaped Snæfellsjökull glacier rests, for instance, has not erupted for 700 years.

Melting glaciers

Eruptions from subglacial volcanoes can cause more damage than those from open-air volcanoes. Hot lava melts the ice, triggering sudden floods – *hlaups* – with unpredictable results. Mount Katla, the volcano lying dormant under the glacier Mýrdalsjökull, is Iceland's largest caldera, at 80 sq. km (30 sq. miles). When Katla erupts, the *hlaup* can be 200,000 cubic metres (7 million cubic ft) of water a second.

In 1996 a volcano in the Bárðarbunga-Grímsvötn fissure erupted beneath Vatnajökull, melting huge quantities of ice and scattering ash over a 100-km (60-mile) area. Meltwater from the eruption flowed into a sub-glacial caldera, which began to fill. On 5 November 1996, the water in the caldera spilled over the brim, resulting in a massive flood across the sand plain south of the glacier that swept away roads and bridges. It deposited icebergs the size of apartment blocks, which, as they melted, turned the sands into pits of quicksand.

Meltwater from the glaciers flows out into winding rivers, which swell whenever warm weather melts the glacial ice or when volcanic activity begins beneath the glacier. Unlike the crystal-clear rivers fed by rain or underground streams, glacial rivers carry silt from the glacier, so they are generally brownish and murky in colour. Unbridged rivers are one of the main dangers to travellers in the highlands, as the water can rise with alarming rapidity.

Iceland is no stranger to earthquakes. The stretching and straining of the earth's crust at the junction of tectonic plates inevitably produces sudden movements under pressure. Strict build-

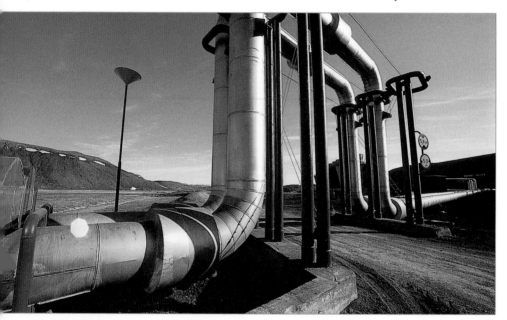

THE SOUTH ICELAND QUAKE

Every 100 years or so a major earthquake brings destruction to southern Iceland. In 1784 the South Iceland Quake, estimated at 7.5 on the Richter scale, destroyed houses, farms and a cathedral. In 1896, southern Iceland was convulsed by violent tremors and in 1912 a quake measuring 7 on the Richter scale shook the region. A set of tremors in the summer of 1998, the largest measuring 5.3 on the Richter scale, precluded the earth's convulsions in June 2000, when three earthquakes, measuring 6.5, 5.5 and 6.6, struck over the course of three days. Experts warn that although a certain amount of tension on the earth's crust has been relieved, the "big one" is yet to come.

ing regulations ensure that all man-made structures can withstand major earthquakes.

Using geothermal heat

Living on a "hot spot" implies coexistence with natural risks. Yet the heat in the earth has also brought its own inestimable benefits. In a cold climate, what could be more valuable than endless natural hot water?

All spouting springs (geysers) in the world owe their name to the Great Geysir in Iceland's southwest, which spouts to a height of up to 60 metres (196 ft). These days Geysir has given up performing, except when artificially persuaded; soap is added to the water to reduce the surface tension, which means that the spring spouts with less pressure. These induced eruptions are only carried out very rarely, but nearby Strokkur ("churn") erupts every few minutes to a height of about 30 metres (100 ft), and several more spouting geysers can be seen around the country.

Natural hot water bubbling irrepressibly out of the earth has been prized by the Icelanders ever since they settled the country. The springs Ingólfur Arnarson saw when he named Reykjavík ("smoky bay") after clouds of steam he saw rising from today's Laugardalur valley became the community's public laundry in later centuries. Housewives would trudge the 3 km (2 miles) from Reykjavík along Laugavegur ("hot spring

city. Today 85 percent of Iceland's atmospheric heating is from geothermal sources, and almost every community has its own geothermally warmed open-air swimming pool.

At Svartsengi in the southwest, superheated water (two-thirds of which is brine) from far beneath the earth's surface passes through a heat-exchange process to provide fresh water for heating, and generate electricity. A bonus is that the hot lake formed by the run-off water has developed into a popular spa, the Blue Lagoon (Bláa Lónið, *see pages 165–6*). Rich in salt and other minerals, the waters of the lagoon are reputed to be beneficial for skin diseases.

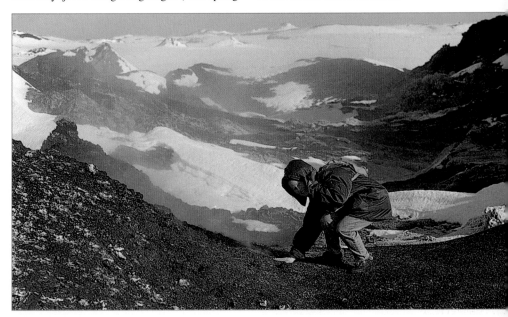

road") carrying their washing to the springs. The laundry springs (now dry) can still be seen in Laugardalur, by the Botanical Gardens *(see page 156)*. In 1930, geothermal energy was first piped from the springs to the town to heat a few dozen houses and a swimming pool. Developing technology has made it possible to look further and drill deeper for hot water, and high-efficiency insulation means that water can be piped long distances.

Reykjavík's latest source of geothermal energy is at Nesjavellir, about 30 km (18 miles) from the

LEFT: Krafla geothermal power plant near Lake Mývatn.
ABOVE: feeling the heat: one of the thousands of tourists who visit Mývatn every year.

Harnessing glacial rivers

Another valuable resource is Iceland's glaciated mountains and rivers: the water that comes tumbling over precipices means constantly renewed hydroelectric power (HEP). The first small HEP plant opened in Iceland in 1904, and today giant hydroelectric power stations supply almost all the Icelanders' own needs, and provide energy to power-intensive industries. About 15 percent of Iceland's exploitable HEP has so far been harnessed.

Whatever the changes their society is undergoing, the Icelanders still live very close to nature. They take for granted an untamed, unpolluted environment that is still growing, still changing, where eruptions and earthquakes are accepted as part of the tenor of life. ❑

Septemtrio.

Grims ey

Rauda gnupur

Langanes prom.

Refuehaffn

Fulmingauig

Sumingauig

Reida Spurd

Reidasp puut

Skanzung

Gunnelfiaur

Johanes

Grimels fiord

Midfiord

Finnafiord

Sandurg

Digranes

Q.

Olifs fiord

Huifley

Skialfandisfiord

Lundey

Hoe

Roha heyidar

Hof

Strand

Balanes

Reydar fiord

Garauig

Bern fiord

Pap ey

Oriens

Surbal dalur

Eyafiordur

Holgur dalur

NORDLEN DINGAFIOR DVNG.

Bardur dalur

Muli

Grenfted

Umiden

Munke tuere closter

Mokrufeld

Sand Iokul.

Suar tuor

Fodinæ sulphuree præstantissimæ.

Skirdu closter

Floszdallr

Austendin gafiordung

Aradal

Arnafelds Iokul.

His notis distinguitur limes inter vtramq; diœcesim.

Roaua dreyner

Langedal

Blafkoger heyd.

SVNDLEN DINGAFIOR DVNG.

Hekla perpetuis damnata igni: et ni ub horrendo boatu lapides euomit.

Fiske notn

Skalt

Hiersfeyd

Iokuls a.

Horn

SKALHOLT sedes episcopalis, cui adiuncta est schola.

Oddi

Afydals Iokul.

Eyafialla Iokul.

Solheima Iokul.

Kirke har closter

Bred

Sten Oter

Brolangs eyer

P.

Eyrarbach

Lachaus reppter

Equorum tanta hic velocitas, vt continuo cur su 20. milli aria con ficiunt.

Breidabol ftadur

Medalland.

Afburn vulpe rularum vena tio, in nidu vola trem inuestigando atque diripiendis

Ingolls hofdr

N.

O.

Porlarks haffn

Vacce marine

Corus, et falcrofnes albi.

O.

Eldor

WESTMANNA EIAR

K.

M.

L.

ILLVSTRISS. AC POTENTISS. REGI FREDERICO II DANIAE, NORVEGIAE, SLAVORVM, GOTHORVMQVE REGI, ETC. PRINCIPI SVO CLEMENTISSIMO. ANDREAS VELLEIVS DESCRIBEB. ET DEDICABAT.

DECISIVE DATES

Later Olaf Tryggvason, King of Norway sends his chaplain Þangbrand to continue conversions.

1000
Christianity is adopted as Iceland's official religion at the annual Alþingi meeting.

1163
The "Stone-Throwing Summer" of violent clashes between different groups of Vikings.

4th century BC
Pytheas, a Greek explorer, reports sightings of an island which he called "Ultima Thule".

circa 6th or 7th century AD
Irish monks *(pictured above)* start to settle on "Thule", forming small communities.

mid-9th century
A Norwegian, Hrafna-Flóki, tries to settle in the West Fjords. Foiled by the harsh winter, he calls the land Ísland (Iceland).

Viking Settlement

874
Ingólfur Arnarson (the "First Settler", *statue pictured below left)* and his brother Hjörleifur Hróðmarsson settle on Iceland on the south coast and in the southwest respectively.

930
By 930 many Norwegian chieftains and their families have followed and the population stands at about 25,000. Creation of the Alþingi parliament, a central authority presided over by a law-speaker.

10th century
Erik the Red *(pictured right)* settles on Greenland and persuades numerous Icelanders to follow.

Conversion and Feuding

984
Þorvaldur Koðránsson the Well-Travelled starts to convert Iceland to Christianity often using violent means.

Ísleifur Gissurarson

1179
Birth of Snorri Sturluson, diplomat and saga writer.

1230–64
The Sturlung Age of feuds between private armies and political factions.

1241

Murder of Snorri Sturluson on the King of Norway's orders.

1262

The Alþingi agrees to allow King Haakon of Norway to collect taxes.

Disaster and Decline

1389

A huge eruption of Mount Hekla is followed by smallpox and other epidemics.

1397

Scandinavian union of Norway, Denmark and Sweden transfers the sovereignty of Iceland from Norway to Denmark. Denmark, following Norway's example, prohibits Iceland from trading with any other countries, and agrees to send supply ships in exchange for fish.

1469

England and Denmark go to war over England's illegal trading with Iceland.

1526

Feud between Lutheran Bishop Ögmund of Skálholt and Roman Catholic Bishop Jón at the Alþingi, leading to a duel.

1541

Denmark sends two warships to impose a new church code through the Alþingi; Ögmund resists but dies on a ship bound for Denmark.

1548

Bishop Jón is summoned by the king to Copenhagen, but instead stays in Iceland and leads a rebellion against the Protestants.

1550

King Christian III of Denmark orders Jón's arrest; after being captured, he is beheaded along with his two sons.

1627

3,000 pirates land on Heimaey in the Vestmannaeyjar (Westmann Islands), killing many of the inhabitants and taking others captive.

1662

Denmark divides Iceland into four commercial trading districts which are not permitted to trade with each other, only directly with Denmark. This is reinforced by a Danish naval blockade.

1783

Eruption of Laki volcano in southern Iceland destroys communities, livestock and, for many years, the fishing industry.

1800

Abolition of the Alþingi on the orders of the Danish king.

A Revival of Fortune

1801

Battle of Copenhagen, where the British fleet detroys the Danish Navy, and confiscates the entire Danish merchant fleet.

1809

"Revolution" led by Jorgen Jorgensen, a Danishman serving in the British Navy, who liberated Iceland, declaring it independent. The revolution is quashed the same year by another member of the British Navy, and Jorgensen is jailed in England.

1811

Birth of Jón Sigurdsson, the force behind the movement for Icelandic independence from Danish rule.

1830

Iceland allowed two seats among 70 on an advisory body to the Danish crown.

1840

King Christian VIII *(pictured below)* agrees to reinstate an Alþingi of 20 elected representatives, with four to six chosen by the crown.

1854

Trade monopoly with Denmark ended.

1874

Denmark gives the Alþingi autonomy over domestic affairs, but retains a veto over all it does.

1879

Death of Jón Sigurdsson.

1881–95

Benedikt Sveinsson, a campaigner for independence, calls for real self government every year at the Alþingi; attempts to pass the proposal are foiled by the royal veto.

The 20th Century and Beyond

1904

Iceland is granted home rule.

1909

Introduction of prohibition.

1911

Founding of Reykjavík University.

1918

Denmark makes Iceland a sovereign state with its own flag, still with the king of Denmark as its head of state, and agrees to hold further negotiations on Iceland's status in 1940.

1940

With Iceland occupied by Britain and Denmark by Germany, there is no communication between them. The Alþingi announces that it has taken over the governing of Iceland.

1941

Iceland requests full independence from Denmark.

1944

Following a plebiscite at which the termination of the union with Denmark and a new constitution are approved, Iceland becomes a republic on 17 June. This date is celebrated each year as Independence Day *(pictured above)*.

1949

Iceland becomes a founding member of NATO, abandoning its "eternal neutrality".

1951

US military return to Iceland to set up an air base at Keflavík.

1952–76

Four Cod Wars (1952, 1958, 1972, 1975) with the UK over fishing rights. In 1976 an agreement is reached for a 320-km (200-mile) fishing limit off Iceland.

1955
Icelandic writer Halldór Laxness wins the Nobel Prize for Literature.

1963
The island of Surtsey is created by an underwater volcanic eruption off the southern coast.

1973
Volcanic eruption on Heimaey island *(pictured below)* threatens to destroy it; an army of volunteers and new methods divert the lava flow, preventing complete disaster.

1980
Vigdís Finnbogadóttir, the world's first democratically elected female head of state, becomes president. She is thrice re-elected, holding office until 1996.

1986
Presidents Reagan and Gorbachev arrive in Reykjavík for a summit to start talks to end the Cold War *(pictured right)*.

1989
Beer Day, 1 March, celebrates the end of the ban on strong beer *(pictured top)*.

1992
Iceland walks out of the International Whaling Commission after the country's request for a limited whaling quota is rejected. Iceland stops whaling, though does not declare itself a non-whaling country.

1994
Iceland enters the European Economic Area.

1996
The Grímsvötn volcano erupts under Vatnajökull, leading to a massive build-up of meltwater under the glacier, which floods out and sweeps away chunks of the Ring Road and several bridges on the south coast.

2000
Iceland celebrates one thousand years of Christianity and Leifur Eriksson's discovery of North America; Reykjavík is voted a European City of Culture for the millennium. Mount Hekla erupts on 26 February, and new lava stretches 3–4 km (2–3 miles). Several earthquakes hit the south of the island.

2003
Limited "scientific" whaling resumes in Icelandic waters, despite strong opposition from environmental groups around the world.

2005
The Icelandic government confirms plans to create an oil-free economy by converting all transport to hydrogen fuel by 2050.

ULTIMA THULE

Irish monks were the first to live on Iceland, but were soon outnumbered by Vikings who settled and started to farm the land

A recent visitor to Iceland overheard two farmers talking passionately in a field; they were lamenting the premature death of a young man whom they were sure would have been a great credit to the country. This sorely missed individual, it transpired, was a certain Skarphéðinn Njálsson, a character in one of the celebrated Icelandic sagas, and he had been dead for all of 1,000 years.

Various versions of this story are told by travellers to Iceland, all with the same kernel of truth: Icelanders are obsessed with their history, or at least a part of it. The period they prefer to remember is between the years 930 and 1030, with little after the 13th century on which they can reflect with pleasure. The country's current prosperity has occurred only since World War II. For the 600 or so years before, Iceland was a grim, depressing place, so much so that a 19th-century English visitor complained that he never once saw an Icelander smile.

This roller-coaster ride through history has tentative beginnings, with Irish monks looking for a quiet, isolated spot to meditate, and becomes substantive with the Norwegian Viking settlement, traditionally dated at 874. These same sword-wielding Vikings, who famously reduced hapless Europeans to prayers for the deliverance of their throats, then performed an astonishing volte-face. Within generations, they took up intellectual pursuits – without ever quite putting down their swords – and created a literary legend which scholars discuss in the same breath as Homer and the Golden Age of Greece.

These transformed Vikings not only wrote their own history as had been passed down to them, but

also collected and saved the oral prehistory and religion of the whole Germanic race. They wrote in their own tongue rather than in the scholarly language of Latin, on manuscripts made of calf-skin, one of the few commodities in Iceland which, bar fish, was always plentiful. A great number of these manuscripts were lost or cut up and reused in a subsequent period of extreme hardship. Even so, those Icelandic sagas that have survived more than make up for an almost total absence of ancient monuments in the country.

The uttermost end of the earth

The cherished history of Iceland is really quite short by European standards. As far as anyone can tell, no human had yet set foot in Iceland when,

---

LEFT: a Viking longship approaching the coast of Iceland. **RIGHT:** an early map showing the island of Thule at the world's northern edge.

for example, the Parthenon in Athens was already some 800 years old and the capital of the disintegrating Roman Empire was being moved to Constantinople.

The classical Greeks and Romans were certainly interested in what existed at the northern fringe of the known world but were invariably misinformed. The most reliable information came from Pytheas, a Greek who lived in Marseilles. He explored the north personally and returned with an account of a country situated six days' sailing north of Britain and close to a frozen sea.

This northern land was called Thule. "Iceland" only came into currency much later, apparently

monks are unlikely to have arrived before St Patrick's celebrated missionary work in Ireland, which began in 432, so evidence of an even earlier presence, like a collection of Roman copper coins, recently found at an archaeological dig, were probably booty or brought by chance visitors.

Ireland was a redoubt of Graeco-Roman learning when the Western Roman Empire crumbled. Irish chroniclers, who were familiar with earlier writers and travellers including Pytheas, tended to embellish their work with borrowed, and sometimes counter-productive, erudition. Thus the story of St Brendan's discovery of "Thule" *(see below)* is on the one hand made quite plausible by a

coined by a Norwegian named Hrafna-Flóki who attempted to settle in the West Fjords area but was defeated by the bitter winter. An earlier suggestion, which obviously did not catch on, was "Butterland" – the grass was so rich that butter dripped from every blade.

Frozen gateway to hell

Nevertheless, it was not Scandinavians who first settled on Iceland but Irish monks driven by the desire to meditate undisturbed. They set out in coracles made of hides stretched over a framework of branches and twigs. With hardly any seafaring experience, they "sought with great labour… a desert in the ocean". The Shetlands, Faroe Islands and ultimately Iceland were just the ticket. The

ST BRENDAN IN ICELAND

St Brendan and crew were bobbing about offshore in their little boat when an inhabitant appeared: "he was all hairy and hideous, begrimed with fire and smoke". Sensing danger, St Brendan made a precautionary sign of the cross and urged the oarsmen to pull harder. "The savage man...rushed down to the shore, bearing in his hand a pair of tongs with a burning mass of slag of great size and intense heat, which he flung at once after the servants of Christ... 'Soldiers of Christ', said St Brendan, 'be strong in faith unfeigned and in the armour of the Spirit, for we are now on the confines of Hell'". He was not the last visitor to believe that eruptive Mount Hekla was the entrance to Hell.

description of a volcanic eruption which could have been Mount Hekla; but on the other hand credibility suffers considerably when St Brendan discovers that "Thule" is inhabited.

Sound information about Irish activities in Iceland is contained in the works of Dicuil, author of *On Measuring the Earth*, and the Venerable Bede. Dicuil quoted priests who said that between February and August it was light enough at midnight to pick lice off one's shirt.

Since the pioneering Irish communities were exclusively male, they would not have put down roots and multiplied in the usual way. The settlements were bound to wither, but was their decline

about the fate of the Irish do not necessarily hold water. The surest mementoes of the Irish occupation are the "papa" (i.e. priest) place names.

Viking Exodus

According to Snorri Sturluson, the greatest of Icelandic saga writers, the Norwegians who chased the Irish away were themselves fugitives, in their case from the tyranny of Harald Fairhair. He became the undisputed master and first king of Norway in 872 and immediately set about mopping up the opposition, seizing the property of defeated chieftains and so forth. Of the 400 names mentioned in the *Landnámabók (Book of Settle-*

in Iceland gradual? Peace of mind would not long have survived the arrival of the 9th-century Norwegians. Ari the Learned, a 13th-century Icelandic chronicler, tells the story from the Norwegian point of view. The disembarking Vikings encountered "some Christians" who shortly afterwards "went away" because they were unwilling to live among heathens. That may be putting it mildly. Nevertheless, the Vikings were usually very candid about their atrocities, and as there is no record of anyone boasting about burying an axe in a hermit's head, scare-mongering theories

FAR LEFT: an episode from St Brendan's journey from Ireland to Thule: meeting a whale. **LEFT:** an illustrated saga manuscript. **ABOVE:** the Norsemen arrive.

ments), which lists the first settlers, 38 are known to have been previously powerful chieftains.

Some historians prefer the less dramatic impulse of poor economic conditions in Norway; others that the majority of settlers did not come from Norway at all, but were the descendants of Norwegians who had already emigrated to older colonies, particularly in the British Isles. "For the Icelanders," says one authority, "the islands west of Scotland are the cradle of their race in a much higher sense than even their motherland." This last school believes that the Norwegians may even have been outnumbered by the Irish slaves they took along, although only a small proportion of the names included in the *Landnámabók* is clearly of Irish origin.

The best-known story about these early Norwegians concerns two foster brothers, Ingólfur Arnarson (the official "First Settler" of Iceland) and Hjörleifur Hróðmarsson, who spent a winter in Iceland and were so impressed that they returned with two ships piled high with household goods. They were accompanied by family, friends and 10 slaves procured in Ireland. The two brothers parted company on reaching Iceland, Ingólfur going to the south coast (and later to the site of Reykjavík) and Hjörleifur to the west, near present-day Vík.

Hjörleifur was soon faced with a rebellion by his Irish slaves because they resented having to

dle of a meal of roast puffin. Those who escaped being killed there and then were probably mindful of the penalties meted out to slaves who rose against their masters. One Irish slave unwilling to forgive a master for castrating him (among other grievances), had tried to cut his own throat and consequently suffered the agony of a red-hot wash basin placed on his belly with gruesome results. Nevertheless, he survived – but only to be buried alive in a bog. The rebellious slaves fled to cliffs and threw themselves off. The island setting for this unpromising start to Icelandic history was Heimaey, one of the island group known thereafter as the Vestmannaeyjar (Westmann or "Irish" Islands).

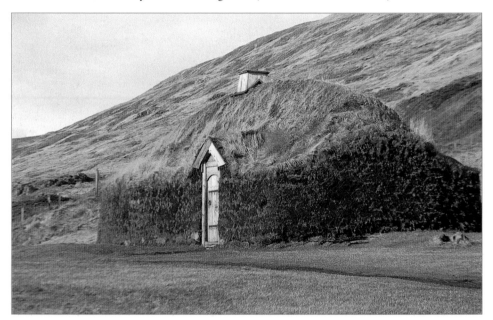

share plough-pulling duties with his only ox. Almost all the sagas carry disparaging remarks about the character of Irish slaves, and this lot were evidently no exception. They first killed the ox, blamed it on a bear and then laid an ambush to get Hjörleifur and his companions when they came looking for the bear. As the hunters fanned out, the slaves overwhelmed them one by one. They abducted the women, piled into a boat and decamped to an offshore island.

The discovery of the hunters' bodies shocked Ingólfur. Death at the hands of a slave was such a shameful fate that he could only think that his brother's Christian tendencies had caused him to neglect his pagan sacrifices. The rebels were tracked down to their island refuge and surprised in the mid-

Dividing up the island

The Age of Settlement (874–930) followed these pioneering efforts and soon the coastline was more or less fully occupied by settlers. Iceland had not long been settled, however, when the whole cycle of emigration repeated itself and for the same reasons: either land hunger, adventurism or falling foul of authority. Erik the Red was a prime example of the last. Already banished from Norway for murder, he was in turn banished from Iceland for more of the same. Having sailed off to the west and found somewhere else to settle, he then attempted to persuade others to join him. To

ABOVE: a reconstruction of Erik the Red's dwelling.
RIGHT: Leifur Eiríksson sights the coast of America.

succeed, he needed an attractive name for his new land, and in this he set a precedent for estate-agency hyperbole ever after. It was such a lush paradise, he told prospective settlers, that only one name would do: Greenland. Enough people believed him to fill 25 ships, but only 14 ships survived the voyage to the promised land.

Vikings in America

Erik's son, Leifur, is credited with discoveries even farther afield. Old Erik would have been a partner in this enterprise, but en route to the ship leaving Greenland he was thrown from his horse and injured a foot. Leifur's first port of call was a

place so dismally useless that there was no point in stretching his imagination beyond "Helluland" ("Stoneland" – northern Labrador).

Conditions to the south improved, hence it was dubbed "Markland" or "Woodland". Further still, he came across a climate so mild that it seemed not to require winter fodder for cattle. It was clearly a worthy contender for settlement, the more so when Leifur's German foster father returned from a sortie jabbering and "rolling his eyes in all directions and pulling faces". The fellow was understandably overcome by what he saw. The 10th-century Vikings were in the habit of consuming between 10 and 18 pints of powerful mead per day, along with the odd

LAYING CLAIM TO LAND

The first Viking settlers laid claim to as much land as they thought they could manage, usually by throwing the pillars of the wooden high seats (a symbol of their authority) from their longboats and making their homes wherever they washed ashore. This tradition supposedly allowed the god Thor to choose the location.

The steady influx of new settlers meant rationing the remaining land by a process known as "carrying the fire". The owner of the ship bringing a group of immigrants was a chieftain or man of substance. The rest of the party would be families and attendant slaves or "thralls". The land they were entitled to was as much as could be encircled by a ring of bonfires, with the proviso that they

had to be lit with the same torch in one day and that, when burning, they were visible from one another. The criterion for women settlers – implying that some arrived independently – was the area that a two-year-old heifer could lap in a day.

The arable coastline was gradually settled in a similar pattern to that seen today – with most inhabitants on the coast, especially in the southwest. The interior – "nothing but ice and fire" – was out of bounds and remained so for all intents and purposes until the early 20th century. It still remains mostly uninhabited, with only a few farmers eking out a living from the starkly beautiful but barrren land.

beaker of sour milk. Leifur and the rest of the company might have been primarily mead-men, but the German recognised grapes and knew what could be done with them. It was thus that they gave the name "Vínland" to the future America.

The explorations of Freydís

Leifur's observations inspired a surge of voyages to this wonderful place, including one by his dreadful half-sister Freydís in a joint venture with two Icelanders, Helgi and Finnbogi. Freydís seems to have inherited Old Erik's worst characteristics – the sagas refer darkly to her "evil mind". She had married her husband Þorstein

killed by a stone and faced the attackers. Yanking out a breast, she gave it a resounding thump with the flat of her sword. The Indians were as alarmed by this as the Vikings had been by their catapults. They bolted to their boats and paddled off at speed.

The lure of the land of wine was strong, but repeated attempts to follow in Freydís's wake were to prove similarly unsuccessful. Although the land was excellent, they could never live there in safety, so they made ready to leave the place and return home." Attempts continued at least until 1347, which has led to the theory that Christopher Columbus was inspired by Icelandic stories about this distant land. These stories were

only for his money and despised him. Freydís fell out with Helgi and Finnbogi when they reached Vínland and, making the false accusation that they had insulted her, ordered Þorstein ("thou miserable wretch") to kill both of them and their party of 30 men and five women. Þorstein did as he was told but drew the line at killing the women. "Give me an axe," said the ghastly Freydís.

As Freydís was soon to discover, the greatest barrier to settlement in the New World was the hostility of the natives. "They were small and evil-looking, and their hair was coarse; they had large eyes and broad cheekbones." Her crew retreated in bewilderment when attacked by these tribesmen armed with catapults, a weapon new to the Vikings. Freydís snatched the sword of a man

probably still being recounted in seafaring circles when in 1477, according to his son Fernando, Columbus called at Iceland as a crew member of an English ship.

The Icelandic commonwealth

Back in 10th-century Iceland, the displaced chieftains were determined never again to be relieved of their traditional authority by a single ruler. They entrenched themselves in their respective areas, or *þings*, and were called *goðar*, a word derived from "god". The commonwealth Alþingi, created in 930, was a parliament whose history is almost continuous to the present day. Presided over by a Speaker or Law-speaker, it was an acknowledgement that certain matters required a central authority. Lesser cases were dealt with by courts in the four "Quarters" of the land.

The Alþingi met for two weeks every year at the Þingvellir, a point roughly in the middle of the most densely populated part of Iceland and with a remarkable natural amphitheatre. The chieftains – 36 to begin with, later 39 – met in formal session, but every free man was entitled to attend and the occasion acted as a magnet for the entire population. These annual reunions were a great influence in promoting the development of a distinctive culture and help to explain, for example, why the language remained uniquely homogeneous without a trace of local dialects.

on a legal technicality unleashed his private army. The plain of Þingvellir was strewn with corpses before proceedings could be resumed. Litigation abounded, but the law was so complicated, and the society so riddled with vendettas, that the due process of the courts was forever on a knife-edge.

Life in the longhouses

Settlers tried to recreate the conditions of pre-monarchical Norway as far as local conditions permitted. In Norway, farmsteads were a collection of separate wooden buildings, one for sleeping, another for cooking and so on. Timber was plentiful there; in Iceland it was always in

Although the Alþingi was the supreme spiritual and temporal authority, it was not allowed to raise a military force or to exercise police authority. Moreover, the powers of the Law-speaker were deliberately circumscribed so that the office could not be used as a springboard to monarchy; when a chieftain turned up with as many as 1,500 men to support him in a feud, there was nothing the Law-speaker could do.

The Alþingi therefore had considerable difficulty living up to its ideals. In 1012, for example, a litigant who suspected that his case was slipping away

LEFT: an image from the Icelandic film *In the Shadow of the Raven*, set in the harsh early years.
ABOVE: longship from a 14th-century manuscript.

painfully short supply. The Icelandic farmstead was therefore a single unit, a row of rooms with common walls and a turf roof. Only the framework of the walls was timber; the rest was made up of stones and sod. While the Norwegian *stofa* or living-dining quarters were often large enough to accommodate several hundred guests, the Icelanders could not heat such a space. Buildings became smaller and the windows fewer.

Larger farmsteads able to afford the luxury of timber imported from Norway maintained the tradition of large festive halls, which also served as religious temples. In the winter a fire was lit in a hearth at the centre of the hall, the smoke being left to find its way out through shuttered apertures in the roof. The chieftain occupied a high seat at one end with the guests lining benches on either side, their backs to the wall. "The flesh of the sacrificed animals, after being boiled in a large kettle over the fire," says an 18th-century study, "was served up to these rude banqueters, who frequently amused themselves by throwing the bones at one another, the manner in which they were placed on the opposite sides of the hall being very convenient for indulging in this elegant pastime."

Farmsteads were also equipped with an early version of the sauna, water being poured over a stone stove in the bath house to produce vapour. The early settlers evidently made full use of the water from numerous hot springs to luxuriate in hot baths.

Early customs

Women of the period dressed extravagantly in gold-brocaded dresses, the men in brilliant mantles and ornamented helmets. Skarphéðinn, the ill-fated young man whom we met at the opening of this history, made his entrance at one Alþingi in a blue mantle, blue striped trousers with a silver belt, and high shoes. His hair was combed back behind his ears, and round his head was a gold embroidered silk ribbon. He carried a large shield but took most pride in the battle-axe which had just despatched a certain Þráinn.

Like all young men, Skarphéðinn was addicted to what amounted to the national sports, horse-

---

A VIOLENT PASTIME

Knattleikur was a ball game described in the sagas, but it is hard to work out from commentaries on play what the rules were, if any. "Þorgrímur was unable to hold his own against Gísli, who threw him down and carried the ball away. Gísli sought again to take the ball, but Þorgrímur held it fast. Then Gísli threw him down so violently that he skinned his knees and knuckles, and blood was running from his nose... Gísli took the ball in one jump, threw it between the shoulders of Þorgrímur so that he fell forwards, and said: 'The ball on broad shoulders broke, which is not to be complained of'". At the end of the game, the two players part "not as good friends as before".

fighting (theoretically a contest between animals) and a kind of ball game called *knattleikur* (*see panel, left*).

Marriages were arranged by the male heads of families – young men could veto the decision, although brides had no say in the matter. On acceptance as a wife, the woman acquired considerable property rights and other privileges. These did not extend, however, to denying the husband his concubines. A wife could sue for divorce only if she was abused; the husband could obtain one for almost any reason that entered his head. ❑

LEFT: a Viking amulet incorporating Christian and pagan symbolism. **ABOVE:** Viking sailing equipment. **RIGHT:** Vikings on the warpath.

THE COMING OF CHRISTIANITY

Although Iceland's conversion to Christianity was at times turbulent, it ushered in a period of relative stability and a literary golden age

On the rung of government below the Alþingi, the Icelandic chieftains fought tooth and nail to preserve their individual authority. The chieftainships were in reality more like political parties than regional entities. Dissatisfied "subjects" were at liberty to switch their allegiance – and divert their taxes – to some other chieftain, even one who lived at the opposite extremity of the land. These floating constituencies acted as a slight brake on the wilder excesses of ambitious chieftains; the rough and ready equilibrium, however, was severely tested by the advent of organised Christianity.

An Irish curse

The first settlement of Irish monks was at what is now known as Kirkjubæjarklaustur, or Church Farm Cloister. In going away rather than having anything to do with the Norwegian heathens, the monks left a curse on any pagan who occupied the site. The curse seems to have delivered the desired results at least in the case of pagan settler Hildir Eysteinsson; he dropped dead as soon as he laid eyes on his new home.

The Norwegian settlers arriving from the British islands must have encountered Christianity and some may even have practised it, but on reaching Iceland they reverted to paganism, or possibly paganism with a weak dash of Christianity. Icelandic paganism was a mixture of the old Norse deity, spirits who took on the likeness of men or beasts, and fetishes which made trees and waterfalls objects of veneration. Temples were built in holy places, ritual taking the form of animal sacrifices. Only in emergencies were human sacrifices offered. Temples might have specific house rules; on the holy mountain of Helgafell at Þórsnes, for example, those wishing to enter the

temple had to wash their faces thoroughly.

One of the more concerted efforts to introduce orthodox Christianity was made by Þorvaldur Koðránsson the Well-Travelled. His travels included Germany, and in 981 he was baptised there by a Bishop Frederick. With the bishop in tow, Þorvaldur returned to Iceland with the mission to convert his countrymen. The singing, ringing of bells, burning of incense and vestments involved in Christian liturgy made a favourable impression, but the number of genuine converts was disappointing. Too many merely paid lip ser-

ABOVE: Þorgeir, the Law-speaker at the Alþingi of AD 1000, who decided in favour of Christianity.
RIGHT: a brawl between a Christian and a pagan.

vice to avoid paying the pagan temple tolls, which did not go down at all well with the chieftains for whom the tolls were a source of income.

Matters came to a head when Þorvaldur preached at the Alþingi of 984. Bishop Frederick never mastered the language and was therefore merely a consultant. Héðinn of Svalbarð, an arch-opponent of Christianity, engaged comedians to mimic and poke fun at the two of them. Forgetting himself, Þorvaldur leapt on two of the comedians and killed them. Bishop Frederick "bore all with patience" but was outlawed from Iceland with Þorvaldur. They were preparing to sail when Þorvaldur spotted Héðinn of Svalbarð sawing some wood nearby. His parting shot was to kill him. "Because of this violent and unchristian act, Bishop Frederick parted from him and returned to his native country." Þorvaldur abandoned his mission to become a merchant and do yet more travelling.

Viking converts

Christianity made greater advances under the influence of Olaf Tryggvason, the future king of Norway. Saga writer, Snorri Sturluson describes him as "the gladdest of all men and very playful, blithe and forgiving, very heated in all things, generous and prominent amongst his fellows, bold before all in battle." His early life gave no clue to the future. He was a full-blooded Viking marauder at the age of 12, terrorising the English coast with his fleet of five longships. Resting in the Scilly Isles, off England's southwest coast, after months of strenuous atrocities, he made the acquaintance of an elderly sage who put him on the True Path.

Olaf's conversion was electric and he returned to England in a different frame of mind "for England was a Christian country and he was also a Christian". Olaf applied all his former Viking energies to the conversion of his countrymen in Norway. They were, in short, given no choice. As a travelling missionary he went nowhere without a few severed heads.

News of Olaf's missionary zeal reached Iceland: "It was rumoured that the people of Norway had changed religion, that they had discarded the old faith, and that King Olaf had Christianised the western colonies; Shetland, the Orkneys and the Faroe Islands." Olaf was clearly heading their way as if Iceland were just another Norwegian colony, an offensive presumption to those who had developed a strong sense of separate identity and

pointedly referred to themselves as "Icelanders".

It was one such proud Icelander, Kjartan Ólafsson, who was cajoled into entering a swimming gala while on a visit to Trondheim. He found himself racing a powerful swimmer who was not content merely to beat him but ducked him repeatedly until he was on the point of losing consciousness. The graceless victor introduced himself as Olaf Tryggvason and suggested baptism. Kjartan thought it prudent to agree, as did other Icelanders who happened to be in Trondheim at the time. "When they accepted baptism," however, "it was usually for some ulterior motive, or because they regarded it as an interesting adventure."

One of these cynical converts, the *skáld* (poet) Hallfreð, poked out the eye of a reluctant convert and ravished a certain Kolfinna to teach her hesitant husband a lesson. The saga's verdict on Hallfreð is unambiguous: "In all his conduct there is not a trace of Christian spirit."

Brutal methods

The personal history of Þangbrand, the chaplain to whom Olaf entrusted the conversion of Iceland, was not reassuring. "His knowledge of the Christian doctrine might have made him a valuable man had not his violent temper and vicious habits rendered him unfit for so sacred a calling. He not only squandered the income of his parish, but he organised piratical raids to replenish his depleted stores, an unchristian conduct for which the king finally called him to account. Due repentance saved him from banishment, but he was sent instead as a missionary to Iceland."

Relying on his patron's proven formula of exemplary terror, Þangbrand managed to win a few converts in the two years he spent in Iceland, but on returning to Norway in 999 he had to admit to Olaf that the mission had not been a total success. Olaf was furious and ordered the seizure and execution of all heathen Icelanders in Trondheim. The expatriate colony was then quite large and, freshly baptised, they were ordered to Iceland to spread the word. They timed their return to Iceland to coincide with the Alþingi of the year 1000.

Olaf was actually using Christianity as a cloak for his territorial ambitions on Iceland, and he first had to usurp the Christian party which had been developing in Iceland of its own accord. There had even been talk of the home-grown Christians setting up an alternative government, and the arrival of the Trondheim contingent in full battle array threatened to tip the country into civil war.

A crucial decision

Þorgeir, the current Law-speaker, asked for time to think. He spent a day and a night completely covered by the hide of an undefined species of animal, eventually to throw it off and make what has been described as "perhaps the most important oration ever delivered in Iceland": "It seems to be advisable that at this juncture..." he intoned, before coming down on the side of the Christians. Still, his oration was a masterpiece of compromise. His advice was that all parties back down and acknowledge that the law, and not any of them, was supreme. "It will prove true that when we sunder the law we end the peace."

The adoption of Christianity as the official religion in 1000 banned the worship of heathen gods in public, but not in private. Nor were the population required to give up their practices like exposing unwanted infants and eating horseflesh. Olaf's further plans for Iceland were never revealed because he died in battle at Svolder the same year. Olaf's Christian zealotry was his undoing. The war was the result of a grudge nursed by the wealthys Queen Sigrid of Sweden ever since Olaf first asked her to marry him and then withdrew the proposal when she declined his pre-condition: baptism as a Christian. "Why should I wed thee, thou heathen bitch?" he shouted, giving her a slap in the face to reinforce the point. "That," she replied icily, "may well be thy death." And so it proved.

Olaf Haraldsson, the future patron saint who succeeded to the Norwegian throne in 1016, appealed to Iceland's Christian leadership to tighten the loopholes which allowed pagan practices to continue, and he was so pleased with the response that he sent not only timber and a bell for a church to be constructed at Þingvellir but also an English bishop, Bernhard the Book-wise, whose aim was to speed up the conversion of the country.

One of the remaining obstacles to the establishment of orthodox Christianity was a shortage

SNORRI STURLUSON

The violence of the Sturlung Age was chronicled by Snorri Sturluson, whose family gave the Age its name. They were descendants of the saga hero Egill Skallagrímsson, and Snorri may well have written *Egils Saga*. Born in 1179, Snorri married an heiress and became a Law-speaker at the Alþingi twice. He was despatched to Norway as a diplomat, and when he returned to Iceland in 1241 against the King of Norway's wishes, he was murdered on his orders. Snorri's undisputed epitaph is the *Heimskringla*, a monumental history of the kings of Norway whose breathtaking scope is reflected in the first words: "The face of earth inhabited by man...".

of priests. The chieftains regained a measure of authority by putting up themselves or equally unqualified nominees as candidates. As the choice of bishops had to be ratified by the Alþingi, the church was for a while fully integrated in the social system, and one chieftain at least "did everything in his power to strengthen Christianity". New bishoprics were set up at Hólar and Skálholt and these gradually became known as centres of learning.

The Golden Age

Iceland enjoyed almost a century of relative peace after 1030, as if the country were quietly digesting its stormy beginnings and putting them into a narrative sequence. Long hours of darkness indoors encouraged story-telling, and the people as a whole were remarkably adept at it. An unusually large proportion of the population could read; the introduction of the Latin alphabet instead of clumsy Runic encouraged them to write as well. The Dark Ages elsewhere in Europe were characterised by clerics copying religious tracts in Latin. In Iceland people wrote in their own language – and about themselves.

Intellectual activity outstripped politics and law. The Alþingi of 1118 served as a reminder that government was still a hostage to the selfish machinations of chieftains. Proceedings against a notorious murderer named Mar degenerated into a bloody trial of strength between two chieftains which disrupted the Alþingi year after year. The general assembly passed numerous resolutions outlawing the culprits; they were laughed off.

The flaw in the legal system, as we have seen, was that the Alþingi could not initiate prosecutions nor force its decisions on spirited opposition. A complicated web of murder led in 1163 to violent clashes in what became known as the "Stone-Throwing Summer". The combatants were said to have been driven to such rage that they were hurling stones so heavy that normal men, when they tried to clean up the aftermath, could not lift them at all.

In the course of the 12th century, the country was divided between bishops aligned with the seat of Trondheim and half a dozen clans in a state of perpetual internecine warfare. At the same time

LEFT: saga hero Gunnar of Hlíðarendi.
RIGHT: opposing sides lined up for confrontation at the Alþingi of AD 1000.

ÞORGEIR'S LEGACY

Today, the phrase "að leggjast undir feld", loosely translated as "to lie down under a hide" is used when someone chooses isolation to think something through.

economic conditions deteriorated and, as the Icelanders had no timber for shipbuilding, they were increasingly dependent on Norwegian suppliers and shippers. Matters came to a head in the so-called Sturlung Age (1230–64), with a combination of horrific violence and, ironically, an intellectual flowering, which has been called the Icelandic Renaissance.

The Alþingi's impotence in the face of feuds that were tearing apart the land's most powerful families underlined the fact that anarchy had taken over. The king of Norway was as ever ready and eager to step in and the papal legate approved saying "it was unreasonable that (Icelanders) did not serve a king like every other country in the world."

In 1262 the Alþingi submitted to King Haakon by granting him the right to collect taxes. In practice, submission left the Icelandic chieftains in control of their own affairs as before except that they were forbidden to wage war on one another. The people won a respite from constant upheaval, but by the end of the 13th century it was apparent that Iceland had started an unstoppable decline. ❏

THE DARK AGES

A combination of absolute foreign rule, trade restrictions and a series of natural disasters led to the darkest period in Iceland's history

The terms of Iceland's submission to Norway were contained in the "Ancient Covenant" and every taxpayer was obliged to pay an annual royal tribute in the native wool. Royal officials replaced the *goðar*, and Snorri's murderer Gissur's reward was to be made the earl of Iceland. Even the weather served as a portent: it turned colder, and all over Scandinavia men dispensed with kilts and put on trousers. Temperatures continued to drop, necessitating underwear.

Gissur's "character and previous record", says Knut Gjerset, the eminent 20th-century Icelandic-American historian, "rendered him unfit to maintain peace and order, which was his principal official duty". In 1264, his enemies stormed his daughter's wedding, killing 25 guests while Gissur hid in a tub of whey. His revenge was to lay waste the Rangárvellir district and then invite his enemies to a peace conference. Their leader was executed, whereupon Gissur announced his retirement to a monastery. The Norwegian king decreed that Iceland would try to survive without any earls.

Imposing the law

Iceland clearly needed a new framework of government, starting with a new legal system. The "Code of Magnús Lagaboter" proved so efficient that it served with very few amendments until the 19th century. The crown, which was seen at the time as part of the divine order of things, was made the supreme legal authority, and lawbreakers were answerable to it, not to the injured party as previously. Murder, robbery, rape, counterfeiting,

forgery and seduction became capital offences, but judges were supposed to administer the law dispassionately. "For we are to hate evil deeds," the judge's manual advised, "but love men by natural instinct as our fellow Christians, but most of all their souls."

For the first time Iceland acquired a national army rather than dozens of private armies, although it was only 240 strong and the men were sent to Norway in defence of the realm against Danish and Hanseatic threats. The power of the church was strengthened, but rested increasingly in the hands of foreign bishops. Church reforms required clerical celibacy; even subdeacons who had been married for years and had several children had to give up their wives.

LEFT: dried fish, a staple of the Icelandic diet and a key element in trade for centuries.
RIGHT: an early depiction of Mount Hekla erupting.

Public dissatisfaction in a generally peaceful era was provoked by something that would haunt Iceland for centuries to come: the control of trade. Iceland had to trade to survive, and with no merchant fleet of its own the country was at the mercy of Norwegian merchants. The king was supposed to ensure that a certain number of ships called reg-

ularly to deliver essential supplies and take away the exports which paid for them. All too often the ships never came, particularly when they were most needed because of famine and natural disasters. Even supplies of altar wine dried up and the celebration of mass had to be suspended.

Years of disaster

The 14th century presaged a run of calamities almost beyond belief. Hekla erupted repeatedly; each time a pall of darkness settled over southern Iceland for days on end and the following winter was unusually severe. Heavy snowfalls thawed to become devastating floods. Hekla's 1389 eruption could be felt and heard all over the island, according to contemporary accounts: "Fire arose

not only from the mountain but from the woods above Skarð, the eruption being so violent that two mountains were formed with a chasm between them. In the neighbourhood hot springs welled up, forming lakes of boiling water." Smallpox and other epidemics added to the misery.

The industrious Hanseatic merchants – by then well-established on Norway's west coast – undoubtedly could and would have traded with Iceland, but the Norwegian king set a precedent later to be slavishly followed by the Danes, declaring that trade with Iceland was a crown monopoly. Iceland thus went through the extremes of either being completely neglected or facing demands for greater quantities of the prized codfish than the population could afford.

The Scandinavian union of Norway, Denmark and Sweden effected at Kalmar in 1397 transferred the sovereignty of Iceland from Norway to Denmark. The Danes were even more remote and less interested in Iceland than the Norwegians, and, in the country, conditions deteriorated accordingly: "Our laws provide that six ships should come hither from Norway every year, which has not happened for a long time," reads a plaintive message to the Danish king, "a cause from which Your Grace and our poor country has suffered most grievous harm. Therefore, trusting in God's grace and your help, we have traded with foreigners who have come hither peacefully on legitimate business, but we have punished those fishermen and owners of fishing-smacks who have robbed and caused disturbances."

Smugglers and pirates

The unauthorised foreign traders were mostly English and their activities would be Iceland's main access to the outside world for centuries to come. They provided essential commodities in exchange for fish, which would probably have been acceptable to the Icelanders had the English not decided that they were better equipped to catch the fish themselves. This fundamental conflict of interest would continue – all the way to the notorious "Cod Wars" between Iceland and England in the 1960s and 1970s.

The activities of the English traders were therefore a mixed blessing as far as the Icelanders were concerned, but to King Eric of Denmark,

LEFT: rough seas were braved by traders around Iceland. **RIGHT:** monsters were said to be an additional hazard.

who held the trade monopoly with Iceland, they were an unmitigated outrage. Eric protested to King Henry V of England over the illegal trade, and his royal commissioners in Iceland did their best to stop it, but the mainland fleets had fallen into disrepair and there was no way of enforcing the prohibition.

Pirates among the English merchants – the distinction between them and merchants could not have been finer – were quick to recognise the opportunities presented by an undefended coast, and their looting of Icelandic churches was an echo of what the Vikings had done in England. King Eric made attempts to stop the pirates but much

of his strikeback was in vain. On one occasion, a couple of royal commissioners with orders to arrest the offenders were themselves bundled into a ship and sent off to the dungeons of England.

Eric's successor, King Christian I, also tried to defend his kingdom, sending out the chieftain Björn Þorleifsson to arrest the pirates. Just like the commissioners before him, Þorleifsson was captured and despatched to England, along with his wife Olaf. However, the determined chieftain managed to escape and make his return to Iceland. He tried his hand again at defeating the pirates, but this time he was killed and his son captured.

WHALES, SERPENTS AND LOBSTERS

In addition to the hazards of rough seas, pirates and slave-traders, stories abounded of huge whales and other mysterious creatures to be found in the remote seas around Iceland. The country was so cut off at this time that there were few foreigners who were able to contradict the account of 16th-century German writer and cartographer Sebastian Münster, a mixture of fact and fantasy. "In the mountain of Hecla," he wrote, "there is a great abyss which cannot be sounded and here appear often people who have recently drowned as though they were alive. Their friends beg them to come home but they reply with great sighs that they must go into Hecla and then vanish forthwith." Münster went on to describe

whales "as big as mountains... which capsize large ships and are not afraid of the sound of trumpets or of empty barrels thrown at them with which they gambol. It sometimes happens that seamen encounter a whale and if in distress cast anchor upon it thinking it to be an island... Many people in Iceland build their houses out of bones and skeletons of these whales". He also described sea serpents "200 or 300 feet long" which wound themselves around ships and "a fearful beast like unto a rhinoceros with a pointed nose and back (which) eats crabs called lobsters twelve feet long". These hefty lobsters, moreover, were said to be easily capable of seizing and strangling a man.

TRADING PRODUCTS

Cod was Iceland's main trading commodity; others included sulphur, tallow and sheepskin, as well as the pure white Icelandic falcon, by far the best for falconry.

Olof paid a ransom to get her son back and then recruited an army to deal with the English. Some English were killed, and the affair escalated into a full-blown war between England and Denmark in 1469 although, ironically, the illegal traders and their customers on the spot seem to have continued their prickly but profitable dealings without even noticing.

The English traders did, however, run into stiff competition from the Hanseatic League, and the Danish kings at last found an effective weapon – to play off one against the other in what amounted to an auction for limited trading concessions.

The long decline

The auctions lined royal pockets but did nothing for Iceland. The cumulative effect of natural disaster and stifled trade was simply too much. The most conclusive evidence of national lethargy was that literary activity ceased. The only creativity, which did not amount to much, was the lightweight ballad of wandering minstrels.

LIVING CONDITIONS IN THE DARK AGES

Impoverished following years of disaster, life was harsh for most Icelanders. Jón Jónsson brings conditions into focus: "The living room of the common peasant farmstead was usually not covered with boards on the inside. One could see between rafters to the grass-covered roof, which soon looked like ordinary sod, and from which mildew and cobwebs were hanging. The floor was uncovered, consisting only of earth trampled hard. But during heavy rains when the roof was leaking water dripped down, and it soon became a pool of mud through which people waded. The walls along which the bedsteads were nailed fast were covered with a grey coat of mildew, and green slime was constantly trickling down the walls, especially in the winter. Bed clothes were very scarce among the poor people. Old hay, seaweed or twigs did service as a mattress, and a few blankets constituted the covering."

To make life even more wretched, there was a crippling shortage of firewood. In some houses the family slept on a platform with calves and lambs occupying the space underneath; this at least provided some heat which was conserved by keeping windows to a minimum both in size and numbers. A thin membrane – part of an animal's insides – served as glass, but it only allowed through a dim light, adding to the overall sense of living in dingy squalor.

The extent to which Iceland became dispirited and defenceless is revealed by an invasion in 1627 by 3,000 Barbary pirates commanded by a "Rais Murad" who was actually a Dutchman named Jan Janezen. Having run wild through Grindavík, Faxaflói and the East Fjords, the pirates then descended on Heimaey, one of the Vestmannaeyjar (Westmann Islands) "and overran the whole island with loud yells, massacring the terror-stricken and helpless inhabitants". The youngest and strongest of the population were herded into their ships; the others into a warehouse which was then put to the torch. The local priest, a composer of hymns named Jón Þorsteinsson, was struck

Heimaey never recovered from the decimation of its population, and it was set even farther back by the colossal volcanic eruption in 1783 which poured so much poisonous lava into the ocean that the fishing industry was put out of action for many years. A British traveller in the early 19th century related tales of a dwindling population of barely 200 souls, whose children were dying of malnutrition because they ate nothing but the oily flesh of seabirds.

A dismal outpost

Iceland was almost oblivious of the Reformation in Europe. The people were contentedly, if for-

dead while kneeling in prayer; his wife and children and a second priest were taken to the ships, making a total of 242 captives bound for Africa.

The surviving priest was released the following spring to present the ransom demand to King Christian IV. He reported that many of the captives were already dead. The girls had been sold off to harems and the young men committed to lives as galley slaves. Some of the men had become pirates themselves. It took five years to raise funds to secure the release of 37 captives, but in the end only 13 got back.

LEFT: spartan living conditions from the Dark Ages.
ABOVE: an artist's impression of Iceland's turbulent fall into decay.

lornly, Roman Catholic, and the Reformation arrived not as an intellectual awakening or rebellion against the old order but as a series of dimly understood royal decrees from Copenhagen backed by military threats.

The Church in Iceland had slipped back into old habits. "Although priests were not allowed to marry," says one of the sagas, "holy and godfearing fathers would permit them (I know indeed not with what authority) to have concubines instead of wedded wives... It was easy for the priests to get women, so that they often got the daughters, sisters and relatives of chieftains for their helpmates. Proper and lawful agreement was entered into by both parties, so that nothing was lacking of real marriage but the name."

Feuding bishops

The old habits affected bishops too. Bishop Ögmund of Skálholt, whose sympathies were Lutheran, confronted the Roman Catholic Bishop Jón at the 1526 Alþingi with a force of 1,300 men against the latter's 900. Full-scale battle was averted by an agreement to let the issue be settled by a duel between champions. The duel was fought on an island in the Öxará. Ögmund's man was declared the winner, but the next day his cathedral at Skálholt was mysteriously destroyed by fire. This ironically softened his feelings towards Jón because he believed the latter could only have got away with arson with God at least slightly on his side.

In Denmark and Norway, the Reformation was primarily a dynastic struggle with many nobles waiting anxiously for a pretext to despoil the rich estates of the Roman Catholic Church. That ambition extended to Church possessions in Iceland too, and in 1541 two warships were despatched to Iceland with orders to use force if necessary to push a new Church code through the Alþingi.

Bishop Ögmund, now 80 years old and blind, still mounted a spirited defence. He was dragged from his bed into a Danish ship. His captors offered to release him on payment of a ransom which amounted to his sister's money and deeds to all his property. Both were handed over but the ship sailed with Ögmund still in it. He is thought to have died on the voyage.

That left Bishop Jón, Ögmund's adversary and by now an old man himself. King Christian III, an arch-Protestant king, took grave exception to Jón's continuing defiance and in 1548 – two years after Luther's death – summoned him to Copenhagen. Jón chose instead to raise a rebellion. The geriatric bishop led 100 men down to the Protestant stronghold of Skálholt and ordered the defenders to surrender on pain of excommunication. The ultimatum brought jeers from within; Jón turned around and built himself what would be, if necessary, a last bastion at Hólar on Iceland's northern coast.

King Christian may have heard that Jón had sent a request for military assistance to Charles V, Holy Roman Emperor. In any event, he moved decisively against the stubborn bishop. Another military force was sent to Iceland but he was not to be intimidated. On 27 June 1550 an exasperated Christian outlawed him and ordered his arrest.

Demise of the rebel

Bishop Jón's path of glory ended in his eventual incarceration. For several days his captors debated what to do with him. A priest suggested over breakfast one morning that he knew how the prisoner could most safely be kept. Asked to elaborate, he replied that an axe and the earth would do the trick. This suggestion was at first received as a joke, but on reflection the idea commended itself. On 7 November 1550 Bishop Jón, and two sons captured with him, were beheaded at Skálholt, providing Scandinavian Catholicism with its first and last martyrs.

News of the executions aroused bitter resentment. Three masked men carrying coffins presented themselves at Skálholt and asked for the bodies. The request was granted, bells were attached to the coffins, and the cortège moved through the countryside to the chiming of church bells. The bishop was buried at Hólar and still remains something of a national hero.

The overthrow of the Catholic party soon followed Jón's death, and the king moved in quickly on its properties. He considered using the income from the confiscated lands to build schools, but decided to keep the money himself. Thereafter, one quarter of the tithes payable to the Church were to be diverted to the royal purse, as were all fines imposed in law suits. Other reforms were progressively introduced. Adultery became punishable by death, although only on the third offence: men were hanged, women drowned. The eating of horseflesh was banned, and persistent absence from Lutheran services was punished by flogging.

The crux of the matter was that the confiscation of Church property, the imposition of new taxes, and alterations to the law were all carried out without reference to the Alþingi or with any regard for the existing Icelandic procedure. The country was, in short, feeling the draught of absolute monarchy in Denmark, and things were to get a lot worse.

Crushed by foreign rule

Trade was always Iceland's Achilles heel, and absolute rule in Denmark heralded a tyrannical monopoly from 1602 worse than anything that had preceded it. Iceland was obliged to buy everything it needed exclusively from court-appointed Danish trading companies at prices fixed by the company. It was a case of paying what the company demanded or doing without. With Iceland thus held to ransom, it was no surprise that the price of imports rose by 500 percent over a period in which the prices paid for home-grown products remained static. The purchase price of Icelandic fish was barely a fifth of what foreign buyers would readily have paid.

In 1662 matters were made worse by the division of the country into four commercial districts. These were prohibited from trading with one another; they could deal only with Danes and on the same Danish terms. Clandestine deals with foreign vessels were made more difficult by a Danish naval blockade and more dangerous by draconian penalties. A certain Páll Torfason took a couple of fishing lines from an English ship in return for some knitted goods which the Danish merchants had previously declined, and lost the entire contents of his house. Holmfast Gudmundsson was flogged for selling fish to a near neighbour who was technically in another district.

The colonial administrators were nothing if not an extension of the arrogant court officials in Denmark. If they needed a horse, the first peasant they asked had to provide one. If it was a question of crossing a fjord, the nearest farmer was required to drop everything and get his boat out. A grumble meant a sound flogging.

Unsurprisingly, the authority of the ancient Alþingi was undermined and in 1800, on royal orders, it was abolished. The new law court which took over its political functions and the surviving

bishoprics were concentrated in Reykjavík, the population of which was a mere 300. The sense of separate identity was all but lost. "Up till 1800," says one of the annals, "the Icelanders, both men and women, dressed according to their national style, but after that they gradually adopted Danish styles."

Litany of wretchedness

The volcanic eruptions and earthquakes which had caused havoc in 1618, 1619, 1625, 1636, 1660 and 1693 continued practically unabated in 1727, 1732, 1755 and 1783. The last in the series, the eruption of Lakagígar (Laki), is still regarded as

the worst in world history, scattering ash to every corner of the globe. The Icelanders' personal losses included 11,461 cattle, 190,448 sheep and 28,013 horses. Following the human casualties of the eruption there was famine due to the haze of smoke and ash, and a smallpox epidemic. Fully one-third of the population died as a result of the eruption and ensuing disasters.

Summing up the misery of the 18th century, the historian Magnús Stephensen says Iceland experienced "forty-three years of distress due to cold winters, ice-floes, failures of fisheries, shipwrecks, inundations, volcanic eruptions, earthquakes, epidemics and contagious diseases among men and animals, which often came separately, but often in connection with and as a result of one another". ❑

LEFT: en route to a funeral.
RIGHT: 18th-century tombstone kept at Skálholt.

THE PUSH FOR INDEPENDENCE

Upheavals throughout Europe put pressure on Denmark to loosen its hold over Iceland; by 1944 Iceland had become a republic

Iceland, like Scandinavia in general, missed out on the impact of the American War of Independence and the French Revolution. It did not even feel the whiff of liberalism which passed through Denmark towards the end of the 18th century under the auspices of Dr Johann Struensee.

Struensee was a German physician who was engaged to treat the half-witted King Christian VII and contrived to run Denmark personally. He introduced freedom of the press and personal liberties including the decriminalisation of adultery. His vested interest in this particular reform was the clandestine affair he was enjoying with the young Queen Caroline Matilda, sister of England's King George III, who was also mad. The affair was discovered, the law repealed, and Struensee's severed head was posted on a pole to advertise that the old absolutist order was back in charge.

Denmark's misfortune, broadly speaking, was to choose the losing side in the Napoleonic Wars. The British fleet destroyed the Royal Danish Navy at the Battle of Copenhagen in 1801 and then bombarded Copenhagen itself in 1807. The entire Danish merchant fleet (some 1,400 ships) was confiscated, which of course left poor Iceland more isolated than ever. British merchants were eager to take over Icelandic trade themselves, and this provided the backdrop to the most bizarre chapter in Iceland's history, the "revolution" of 1809.

An unlikely liberator

The central figure was Jorgen Jorgensen, born in Copenhagen in 1780, a son of the royal watchmaker. A brilliant but unruly student, he found

himself serving in the British Navy almost by accident as "John Johnson". His early career was chequered, to say the least, and he was actually in prison in England for gambling debts when he was taken on as an interpreter for an opportunistic and unofficial English trade mission to Iceland.

After one abortive trip, the traders landed in Reykjavík to discover that the governor, anticipating their return, had plastered the town with notices prohibiting any trade with foreigners under pain of beheading. The governor, Count Trampe, was not simply enforcing Copenhagen policy; he happened to own the one Danish ship still trading with Iceland. With a warship in the background, the English traders tried to reason with Trampe but he was adamant.

LEFT: 18th-century travellers stopping at a village.
RIGHT: a portrait of Jorgen Jorgensen, leader of the 1809 "revolution".

Jorgensen then came up with a bright idea: depose Trampe, reconvene the Alþingi (abolished nine years previously), declare Iceland's independence from Denmark, and make a treaty of alliance and trade with England. Some, but not all, of the English traders thought this an excellent idea. To cries of "Traitor, you'll hang for this", Trampe was marched out of his office and locked up in one of the English ships. Jorgensen could now properly begin.

Issuing proclamations under the self-appointed title of "His Excellency, the Protector of Iceland, Commander-in-Chief by Sea and Land", Jorgensen promised the Icelanders "peace and hap-

thetic to revolutionary activity. Jones suspected that the British government might also have certain reservations.

The "revolution" squashed

The Hon. Alexander Jones's enquiries into what was going on – the flag was new to him, and he noticed that Jorgensen was building a fort at Arnarhóll – brought Iceland's "independence" to an end as perfunctorily as it had been created. "All proclamations, laws and appointments made by Mr Jorgen Jorgensen, since his arrival in this country, are to be abolished and totally null and void…"

piness little known in recent years" and their own national flag – three white codfish on a blue background. His Excellency was just 30 years old. Backed up by 12 armed sailors, Jorgensen "liberated" Iceland by seizing the property of Danish merchants. The Icelanders were not sure how to react. The fearsome Trampe was locked up in the ship's cabin but they could not be certain that he would remain there: the price of collaboration with the English if ever he regained office did not bear thinking about.

The new regime had been in existence for a little more than a month when a second British warship, *HMS Talbot*, hove into view under the command of Captain the Hon. Alexander Jones, the younger son of an Irish peer and not sympa-

In his memoirs, Jorgensen described the manner of his departure. He stepped into a fishing-boat and was rowed out to the departing warship by a crew of Icelanders: "So I went on board quietly, many of the poor natives shedding tears at my departure. It is true, indeed, that I left the island with regret. I had established liberty and freedom there without a drop of blood being spilt, or a single person committed to prison. "

He was jailed in a convict hulk on returning to England, released, imprisoned again for more gambling debts, did some sterling work for British Intelligence (at one point disguised as an Irish pilgrim), dashed off books on such weighty topics as the geography of Persia and Afghanistan, was sentenced to the gallows for selling the bedclothes off the bed he was using in his London lodgings, was instead transported to Australia – and there served with distinction in the police force. He died in Hobart, Tasmania in 1844.

A revival of spirit

The real price of Denmark's ultimately half-hearted alliance with Napoleon was paid at the postwar Vienna congress. Pressure from the victors forced Denmark to grant Norway its independence, albeit in a lopsided union with Sweden, and expectations rose in Iceland of a similar concession in the near future.

Visitors began to notice changes, and the foundations of Iceland's modern "cradle-to-grave" social security system particularly caught the attention of English reformers. "We have no hesitation in saying," they reported, "that in respect to the poor, an Icelandic parish was, to say the least, equally as well managed as an English one."

Care for the poor

The basic principle was that any person incapacitated by age, infirmity or "misfortune" should in the first instance be maintained by the next of kin according to their ability to pay, the criterion being the value of their property. If circumstances required a pecking order, priority was given to a distressed mother followed by the father, children, brothers and sisters. If supporting some or all of these demonstrably exceeded a person's resources, the parish authorities stepped in.

While parishes might keep a storehouse of emergency provisions for the destitute, the responsibility for actually looking after them was generally passed directly to the rate-payers, the number of paupers allocated to each depending on the value of the property owned. If the alimentor (i.e. he who paid alimony, before the term became bound up with unhappy marriage) failed to provide adequate support, the pauper could complain to the district Þing. The alimentor who left a parish to escape the burden was liable to the kind of house-arrest known as exclusion.

The English observers thought the Icelandic system clearly superior to the English in one respect. "The Icelanders... do not charge themselves with the support of the poor without taking especial care to keep the number of paupers within

due limits; a care which we have grossly neglected, and are now enduring the fearful consequences of our want of foresight."

The number of paupers was controlled by, for example, not allowing a man to marry until he had the means to support a family. Nor was a slave to be freed unless the owner could provide him with an adequate plot of land. If a freed slave became destitute through the former owner's neglect, he retained his freedom but was entitled to alimony.

"Very stringent regulations were also passed to keep the poor within their respective parishes," the English observers also noted.

ROMANTICS VS RATIONALISTS

The 18th and 19th centuries saw a revival of intellectual activity in Iceland. The rationalists, under the forceful leadership of Magnús Stephensen, railed against the lack of foreign influence in the language, which had remained virtually pristine Old Norse, saying that it smacked of darkness and superstition. They advocated an intellectual *Aufklärung* which welcomed the best that the rest of the world could offer. The romantics, on the other hand, glorified Iceland's history and language. Their champion in the 19th century, Bjarni Thorarensen, wrote the hugely popular *Eldgamla Ísafold* to the tune of *God Save the King*, and his poems were mostly about heroic saga figures.

LEFT: turf houses at Laufás, on Eyjafjörður north of Akureyri.
RIGHT: detail of the gable of a turf house.

"Clothes and shoes might be given to a pauper of another parish, but any parishioner who furnished such a pauper with victuals, except he was merely passing through the parish to go to his own, rendered himself liable to the punishment of exclusion. The Icelanders also took care to make able-bodied paupers work for their living. Begging was not tolerated, especially at the Alþingi. If a beggar entered a booth on the Þingvellir plain, the booth-man might forcibly eject him, and every one who furnished such a beggar with meat, was liable to be punished with exclusion. All persons who wandered about the country for fifteen days and upwards were to be regarded as vagabonds… and punished accordingly. Besides other punishments to which they were liable, any one who thought proper might mutilate them in the manner practised in the East to qualify a man for the service of the seraglio" – in other words, castration.

Unsteady steps towards freedom

Some of these comments must have been out-of-date by the time they were written. Swift social progress was obviously being made, but Iceland still had to wait until 1830 before the ripples of Norway's 1814 independence reached its shores. Even then, the concession was merely two seats

A NATIONALIST HERO

Born in Hrafnseyri in the West Fjords in 1811, Jón Sigurðsson, an Icelandic scholar and patriot, was educated at the University of Copenhagen. He has been called the greatest figure in modern Icelandic history. Curiously, in view of his fame, he made his home in Copenhagen for the rest of his life. From 1849 he merely spent alternate summers in Iceland during which time he presided over the Alþingi. It was his very considerable stature in Denmark as archivist of the Royal Norse Archaeological Society – and as an authority on Icelandic history and literature – that gave his nationalist movement weight and credibility in Danish eyes. He died in 1879, 25 years before the advent of Home Rule, and a further 14 from independence.

among 70 on an advisory body to the Danish crown. Prominent Icelanders such as the jurist Baldvin Einarsson protested that such feeble representation in a body based in Copenhagen and knowing next to nothing about Iceland was worthless. The romantics wanted the Alþingi restored. In 1840 the newly crowned King Christian VIII agreed to reinstate an Alþingi consisting of 20 representatives chosen by a qualified electorate and four or six royal nominees. The assemblies were not to be held at the old Þingvellir, as the romantics wished, but at Reykjavík, which would formally become the new capital.

As usual in such circumstances, radical elements felt that these gentle reforms did not go far enough. They insisted on holding the Alþingi at Þingvellir, on lower franchise qualifications and on the exclusive use of the Icelandic language in government. The nationalist cause was championed by the eclectic scholar Jón Sigurðsson, whose statue stands in Austurvöllur, the old town square in Reykjavík, facing Parliament House. The nationalist movement demanded a totally independent national legislature and the ending of Denmark's final say over Icelandic judicial decisions.

Progress towards more substantial independence was delayed by Denmark's preoccupation with the Schleswig Holstein nightmare, a dispute with Prussia over the sovereignty of the frontier provinces, each with a divided population whose

ironically in the 1870s that the only chance Icelanders had of tasting freedom was to emigrate en masse to Brazil or North America. As it was, Icelanders were soon leaving in such numbers that the newspaper changed its tune. People were asked to postpone their departure for a year or so in case things changed, and at the same time a number of teetotal societies sprang up. The aim was not so much a campaign against alcohol as to deny Denmark the revenue from the tax on drinks.

Under this kind of pressure, the king apparently bowed to the inevitable in 1874 by giving the Alþingi autonomy over domestic affairs,

minorities refused to give in. Moreover, the Danish royal commissioner in Iceland was obstructive. The incumbent, still, was Jorgen Jorgensen's *bête noire*, Count Trampe, and he was suspected of applying for a private army to exorcise what he considered unlawful, pseudo-patriotic nonsense. While Denmark continued to turn a deaf ear to the fundamental issue of Icelandic independence, the trade monopoly was ended in 1854.

The Icelandic exodus

With true independence still apparently unattainable, the newspaper *Norðanfari* suggested

---

LEFT: Reykjavík in the early 19th century.
ABOVE: a 19th-century engraving depicts Icelandic life.

including finance. It was not quite what it seemed because he retained an absolute veto over everything the Alþingi did, but for the moment it was enough to celebrate, especially as the date coincided with the 1,000th anniversary of Iceland's settlement.

King Christian IX attended the festivities and heard the first performance of *Iceland's Thousand Years* by Matthías Jochumsson, the present national anthem. Jón Sigurðsson was pointedly not invited, but it was said that in a private conversation afterwards the king asked him if Icelanders were satisfied with the new constitution. "As their chief wish had not been granted," he replied, "how could they be?" Sigurðsson recognised full independence or nothing.

The first breakthrough

Full independence was a long time coming. Icelanders and Danes were generally talking at cross purposes. As far as the Danes were concerned, Iceland was inconceivable except as an integral part of the kingdom, although they were willing to tinker with semantics. One proposal would have made Christian IX "King of Denmark and Iceland" instead of just Denmark, with Iceland taken for granted. Iceland was in no mood for cosmetic compromise, and talk turned to secession, or what in the 20th century became known as a unilateral declaration of independence. After Sigurðsson's death, his successor, Benedikt

Icelanders could not agree on their relationship with Denmark, however, and the impasse continued until the whole question of national sovereignty in Europe was brought under microscopic scrutiny in the peace negotiations after World War I. The Danish government then took the initiative and on 1 December 1918 Iceland became a sovereign state with its own flag, linked to Denmark by virtue of having a common king. The arrangements were ratified by a plebiscite with 12,040 votes in favour and only 897 against. This was agreed to be valid until 1940, when Iceland's status would again be open to negotiation.

Sveinsson, submitted to the Alþingi a proposal calling for real self-government every year from 1881 to 1895. It was twice passed, in 1886 and 1894, only to encounter the impenetrable stumbling block of the royal veto. The breakthrough eventually came in Denmark with the election of a liberal government in 1901. On 1 February 1904 Iceland received home rule.

The saga-writers would have felt at home in the first years of Icelandic home rule as the country fragmented into a political free-for-all, various factions feuding with seemingly no greater purpose in mind than advancing self-interests. Prohibition was introduced in 1909, a move that was unpopular, especially in Spain, which had traditionally paid for Icelandic fish imports with surplus wine.

"Occupation"

The end of 1940 was of course the worst imaginable time for Denmark and Iceland to enter into delicate constitutional negotiations. There was no contact whatsoever between them, Denmark having been occupied by Germany and Iceland by Britain. In the latter's case, strategic considerations had taken priority over the policy of "perpetual neutrality" which had been declared in 1915. Hitler's troops had marched into Norway and thus gained control of its immensely long Atlantic-facing coastline and ports. Iceland was a logical next step, its mid-Atlantic position being of inestimable strategic value for submarine operations and for aircraft not yet able to cross the ocean in one hop. Iceland had no military defences of its own, so Britain stepped in and "occupied" the country to pre-empt any German moves in that direction, a role later taken over by the Americans.

The British and American forces, who at times amounted to one-third of the population, were not always popular, but resentment was softened by the unprecedented prosperity that the war years brought in Iceland. The national income shot up by 60 percent on the twin strengths of construction work on American airfields and free-spending US personnel. Fish exports fetched record prices and, since they were generally paid for in dollars, Iceland had the means to import large quantities of American goods.

the right to a complete breaking off of the union with Denmark, since it has now had to take into its own hands the conduct of all its affairs." It added that Iceland would become a republic as soon as it was possible to terminate the union with Denmark formally.

The termination of the union and a new constitution were submitted to plebiscite in 1944 and both were approved by overwhelming majorities. The date chosen for the formal establishment of the republic at Þingvellir was, not by accident, the birthday of the great nationalist Jón Sigurðsson, 17 June.

Denmark was then still under German occupation, and many Danes felt that what amounted to

Not being able to communicate with Denmark to negotiate on constitutional changes, the Alþingi took a decision to act unilaterally: "Seeing that the situation which has been created makes it impossible for the king of Iceland to exercise the powers assigned to him by the constitution, the Alþingi announces that for the present it commits the exercise of these powers to the government of Iceland."

An Alþingi resolution made the following year went even further: "The Alþingi resolves to declare that it considers Iceland to have acquired

a secession had been brought to fruition while they were hardly in a position to do anything about it. King Christian X sent a telegram of good wishes – it was only received after a ceremony which attracted no less than 20,000 people to Þingvellir on a cold and blustery day. The first president of the new republic, who was elected to a four-year term, was Sveinn Björnsson.

Iceland's neutrality did not save 352 seamen from death as a result of German actions at sea, but it was adhered to on principle when Iceland turned down an offer to declare for the Allies in the final months of the war. One of the first actions of independent Iceland was, on the cessation of hostilities, to demand the immediate withdrawal of the American forces. ❑

LEFT: poet Grímur Thomsen reads to Danish King Christian IX at the 1874 National Festival.
ABOVE: a brass band greets British troops during World War II.

MODERN ICELAND

Since World War II Iceland has come of age as a prosperous, hardworking, modern society enriched by a healthy respect for its past

Iceland today has all the trappings of an industrialised nation, with a sophisticated, consumer-orientated society, comprehensive welfare system and one of the highest standards of living in the world. It is almost impossible to imagine that, before World War II, many visitors thought Iceland to be barely out of the Middle Ages. The leap into the modern world has been fast and furious: greater changes have taken place in the past 50 years than in the more than 1,000 years of settlement beforehand.

Joining the modern world

The transformation occurred almost overnight. Even so, Icelandic society did not abandon its long past, but rather adapted it to the present, replanting an ancient heritage in modern soil where it has more or less flourished since. The Icelandic language has been the bridge of centuries: the history of the Old Republic had been written down in the Middle Ages using a language which modern Icelanders can and very often do read *(see page 91)*.

The presence of first British and then American troops in Iceland during the war, although not exactly welcome, had its brighter sides. A frenzy of road-building and development created an economic infrastructure for the postwar period. Few Icelanders can deny that the prosperity brought by the war meant that national independence, declared in 1944, could be consolidated in peacetime.

More controversial was what to do after the war. Iceland's old stand of "eternal neutrality" was abandoned in 1949 when it became a founding

member of NATO. The US military left Iceland but returned in 1951 with a vengeance to set up a permanent marine air base at Keflavík – a base that is still in use today. The fact that this made Iceland a major target in the event of nuclear war hardly endeared the US presence to the majority of Icelanders; nor did Icelandic men appreciate rich American servicemen floating around the countryside. But the economic argument was powerful: Keflavík provided jobs. And strict controls on marines' movements, rarely allowing them out from behind a huge wire fence, meant that not too many ran off with Icelandic wives.

Even so, Iceland never established an army of its own and also managed to maintain good trade relations with the Eastern bloc during the chilliest

---

LEFT: staircases reflected in the "Pearl", one of Reykjavík's most striking modern buildings.
RIGHT: US servicemen at Keflavík NATO base, 1951.

The Politics of Fishing

Ever since Iceland gained full independence in 1944 the country's foreign policy has been moulded more by the international politics of fishing than by its role as a strategically crucial, albeit army-less, component of the NATO defence pact. Indeed, the level of dependence on seafood earnings runs to such an extent that Iceland's determination to repel any perceived encroachments on its fisheries resources has brought the country into a series of long-running conflicts with even its NATO allies.

The classic example of Iceland "getting tough" with an ally are the four Cod Wars with the UK between 1952 and 1976 (*see pages 113–14*), centering around the extension of the fishing zone around Iceland's coast. A more recent dispute has strained relations with Norway. At issue is the fishing by Icelandic vessels of the Barents Sea "loophole", international water bounded by Norway and Russia. Norway, claiming that the fishing damages cod stocks within its own waters, has on occasion seized Icelandic vessels and levied fines on Icelandic trawler owners.

Iceland has also been involved in squabbles with Norway, Russia and the EU over catch quotas on migratory species such as redfish and herring – indeed fisheries issues have also loomed large

in Iceland's decision to remain outside the EU. Most leading politicians have ruled out joining, and of the mainstream political parties, only the Social Democrats have come out in favour of considering applying for membership. Opponents of membership cite Iceland's 1994 entry into the European Economic Area – a free-trade bloc between the EU and EFTA – as proof that Iceland doesn't need Brussels. In the opinion of Iceland's largest political camp, the centre-right Independence Party, the Economic Area treaty gives Iceland all the benefits of EU membership without any of the drawbacks.

There are however fears that Iceland is being left out in the cold. Even traditionally close ties to the other Nordic countries are coming under pressure; apart from the fisheries disputes with Norway, EU members Finland, Sweden and Denmark are becoming increasingly integrated into the New Europe. With their survival as a nation still deeply dependent on seafood exports, Iceland's foreign policy seems destined to be shaped by the fishing industry.

Meanwhile, the controversial return of commercial whaling in 2006 puts an issue that has long been a thorn in the side of Iceland's international relations right back under the spotlight. Having halted the practice back in 1989, Iceland walked out of the International Whaling Commission in 1992: after this it always seemed likely that whaling would resume at some point – although environmentalist pressure and the concerns of the tourist industry (whale-watching trips grew ever more popular in the 1990s and early 2000s) delayed this until "scientific" whaling resumed in 2003. *For more on whaling and the issues that surround it, see page 115.* ❏

LEFT: washing down the boat after a fishing trip.
ABOVE: cod still form an important part of the catch.

spells of the Cold War. Anti-Keflavík feeling flared up from time to time during the Vietnam war and was a popular cause on the political Left – but by the late 1970s it had become a principle which was costing rather than winning votes.

As a non-nuclear base, Keflavík kept its nose clean during the arms race against Brezhnev, and its role largely involved escorting "stray" Soviet aircraft back out of Icelandic airspace – there were up to 200 violations some years – and monitoring submarine movements in the area. Always keeping a low profile, the US military effectively disappeared from view when a civilian passenger terminal was finally opened at Keflavík Airport in 1987. Until

Riches of the sea

After World War II, the Icelandic government – with economic foresight – channelled its wartime cash-in-hand into modernising the fishing fleet, laying the foundation for a powerful industry which has held firm right up to the present day. Soon Iceland would be producing more income per head from fishing than Saudi Arabians did from oil.

Rich on cod income, Iceland's government grew, building an impressive system of schools, public health and social security. At the same time, Iceland's regulation of the economy had few parallels in the developed Western world. During the 1950s and 1960s, import tariffs were thrown up to

then, all visitors who arrived in the country by air had to land at the US military base before treading Icelandic soil (including Mikhail Gorbachev when he arrived for the 1986 summit, *see page 65*).

However, in March 2006, things changed for good when the US ambassador to Iceland announced that the United States had decided to substantially reduce the size of their defence force on the island. Over the proceeding months, military operations at the Keflavík base were wound down and it finally closed on 6 September. The closure was a major blow to Iceland's defence since the country has no armed forces of its own.

ABOVE: the Icelandic coastguard taking on the British Navy in the Cod Wars.

protect industry, but they gradually served to foster inefficiency and higher prices for everything from fruit to toothbrushes.

It was not until the 1980s that Icelandic governments became committed, in the spirit of the times, to free-market policies. Yet throughout all of these policy changes, fishing remained the mainstay of the economy. Unfortunately, no amount of government regulation could sidestep its unpredictable nature, and fluctuations in both catches and market conditions have from time to time dealt severe blows to the virtually one-track economy.

Whenever fish catches or market prices deteriorated, the government's reaction was to devalue the Icelandic króna. This triggered an inflationary spiral in the 1970s. Wages were indexed to

HARD WORK

The average working week in Iceland – about 46–49 hours – is the longest in Europe.

price rises, so that Icelanders joked that no news was better than a foreign disaster: for example a flood in Brazil which ruined the coffee-bean harvest could push up prices in Iceland which would result in wage rises all round.

Today, wage indexation has been outlawed, although pay deals commonly include an inflation "ceiling" which grants some compensation if prices rise above a certain level. Loans, however, are still indexed, which has put an end to one of the

of the most consumer-orientated countries on earth, a hangover from the high-inflation days when it paid to spend and cost a fortune to save. Icelanders are among the world's leading owners of consumer durables such as video players, cellular phones, cars, personal computers, foot massagers and, basically, any other piece of wizardry that promises high-tech comfort.

Icelandic society is one of the most literate in the world. Education levels are very high for both sexes: more than one-third of all 20-year-olds complete secondary grammar school, there are around 5,500 students at the University of Iceland, and another 2,000 Icelanders at foreign universities

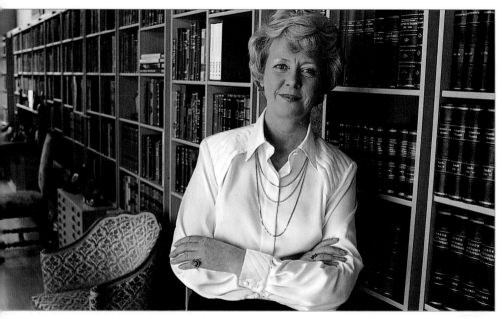

most popular national pastimes of the 1960s and 1970s: owing money. Before indexing, it was possible to take on huge debts and pray that inflation would go up enough to enable you to pay them back again. Generally it did, and whole generations bought or built the impressive apartment blocks and detached houses that decorate streets everywhere. Icelanders still live in the most spacious housing of all the Nordic countries – when they are at home and not out working to pay for it.

The affluent society

Today inflation has been brought under control and, with a fish-led recovery, Icelanders have a standard of living that few other countries enjoy. Despite gripes about the economy, it remains one

(not bad for a total national population of only 296,000). More books are published and bought per head here than anywhere else in the world.

Icelanders also have one of the longest life expectancies in the world. Traditionally, Icelandic women have vied with the Japanese for first or second place, with an average life expectancy at birth of 81.3 years. Icelandic males are also high up in the world longevity stakes with a life expectancy of 76.4 years. Doctors say that the reasons include an unpolluted environment and the pure food that this offers; the outrageously fresh air of an Atlantic island on the rim of the Arctic Circle; a healthy fish-based diet; and exemplary public health care. Infant mortality in Iceland is, at 3.1 deaths per 1,000 children, among the lowest in the world, and certain aspects of preventitive medicine, such as early detection of female cancers, are unmatched.

Moments of glory

Iceland has rarely hit world headlines, but some key landmarks stand out. In 1980, Icelanders chose Vigdís Finnbogadóttir as the world's first democratically elected woman head of state. Following a neck-and-neck race, the former theatre director, French teacher and tourist guide took the Presidency – an office outside party politics whose function is to provide a figure of national unity very similar to Western European monarchies and

which does not include any involvement in day-to-day government. Vigdís was re-elected three times to the presidency, holding office until 1996 when she announced that she would not be running for a fifth term. In the early 1980s, Icelandic women produced the world's first purely feminist parliamentary party, The Women's Alliance.

On a different front, Iceland was invaded by foreign journalists in 1986 when it became host to the historic Reagan-Gorbachev summit. As the mid-point between Moscow and New York,

LEFT: Vigdís Finnbogadóttir, president of Iceland betwen 1980 and 1996. **ABOVE:** Reagan and Gorbachev in Reykjavík, 1986. **RIGHT:** beer was finally legalised on 1 March 1989.

Reykjavík seemed a reasonable symbolic meeting place for the leaders of the superpowers to discuss nuclear disarmament and begin the eventual ending of the Cold War. Over 2,000 foreign journalists, who had little hard news to cover for much of the time they were in Reykjavík, set about informing the rest of the world about the more eccentric aspects of this little-known fishing nation.

Lifting a ban

An event that brought almost as much attention to Iceland was "Beer Day" 1989, when a long-standing ban on strong beer was finally abolished. Total prohibition had gone into effect in 1915, but wine was legalised again in 1921. A national referendum of 1935 came out in favour of legalising spirits too, but beer was not included in the vote, as a sop to the temperance lobby – which argued that because beer is cheaper than spirits, it would lead to more depravity. When the growth in international travel brought Icelanders back in touch with the forbidden drink, bills to legalise beer were regularly moved in parliament, but inevitably scuttled on technical grounds.

The absurdity of the beer ban came fully to light in 1985 when the teetotalling Minister of Justice prohibited pubs from pepping up legal non-alcoholic beer with legal spirits to make a potent imitation of strong beer. Finally beer approached legalisation in parliament – the debate and knife-edge vote were televised live and watched by huge audiences. Now well into the 21st century, a thriving bar scene exists in Reykjavík and Icelanders are accustomed to drinking beer like other nations.

Keeping traditions alive

The concern at maintaining tradition does not always seem so frivolous. An ancient and homogenous culture of relatively few people is always at risk of being swallowed up wholesale by the outside world.

Symbolic of the changes wrought in Iceland has been the growth of the capital, Reykjavík – with only 5,000 inhabitants in 1901, by 2007 the figure was about 193,000 in the greater Reykjavík area, or some 60 percent of all Icelanders. The shift from country to city has completely altered Icelandic society: the generation of Reykjavík folk now around retirement age was largely born and brought up in the countryside, on farms or in fishing villages. Their children, now middle-aged, were born and bred in the capital, but retained some links with the outside; and the generation now at or leaving school is thoroughbred urban, most of them brought up in the "concrete lava fields" of new residential suburbs such as Breiðholt and Árbær – whose populations alone outnumber those of the largest towns outside the capital area.

These are the first Icelanders to drift away from the "classical" colloquialisms of their ancient language, which is firmly rooted in the agricultural society of yesteryear. And they are the first to have no intimate knowledge of the mainstay industries of fishing, fish processing and agriculture – hands-on experience which in the past had given Iceland's managers and technocrats a telling edge over their international competition. This lack of basic manual skills poses a threat to Iceland's few industries, a threat whose consequences few can guess.

Recognising that language is on the front line, Icelanders' defence of their ancient Norse tongue is fierce (*see panel on page 91*). The same technological advances that are welcomed so warmly also pose the biggest threats. Satellite TV, for example, comes outside the jurisdiction of Iceland's legions of subtitlers, dubbers and professional and amateur word-coiners. Linguists say that the threats are becoming more subtle: borrowed words from foreign languages stand out instantly, but "hidden" foreignisms such as Anglo-Saxon syntax and thinking patterns are easier to slip into and more difficult to detect, yet undermine the very fabric of the language all the same.

And more remains of Iceland's past in today's materialistic world than the language that records it. Social scientists were astonished to discover in an opinion poll that a large majority of Icelanders still claim to believe in the existence of elves and spirits (*see* Icelandic Hauntings, *pages 248–9*). Almost all Icelanders still believe in God. Even though only a small fraction go to the Lutheran church they are all still registered at birth. At one stage during the 1960s, the Norse pagan religion was revived, although in truth it never really caught on again. Nowadays a sizeable congregation of some 280 people gathers to hear the arch-priest read from ancient mythological poems on special ceremonial occasions.

But perhaps the real achievement of modern Iceland has been to remain essentially democratic in a personal as well as a political sense. Iceland is at once a modern technological nation and a small village writ large – a place with little crime, few class distinctions and where everybody, thanks to the old Scandinavian patronymic system still in use (*see panel on page 76*), addresses one another by their first name. ❑

ABOVE AND RIGHT: celebrating Independence Day.

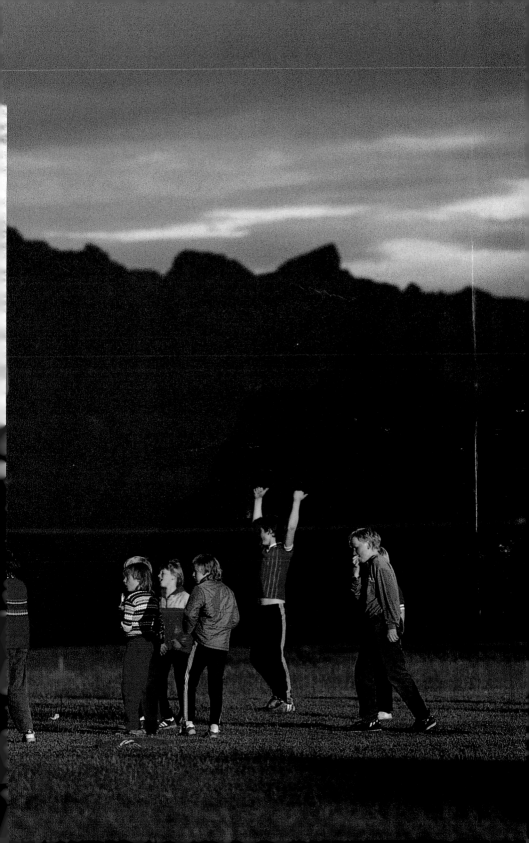

THE ICELANDERS

Today's Icelanders, a product of their landscape and history, are looking to the future with creativity and determination

"Somewhere, in all these rocks and stones, is my home."
– Nationalist poet Pétur Gunnarsson

Probably the first thought that occurs to many visitors as they drive through the desolate lava plain that separates Keflavík airport from the capital, is: "Very impressive – but why would anyone want to live here?"

The inhabitants of a country often tend to reflect their environment. The Danes, for example, live in a flat, fertile country, and are by and large an easy-going, laid-back bunch. Their Icelandic cousins, however, do not really know how to relax and enjoy life. The visitor may be puzzled at how they can be brash and completely uninhibited one minute, yet stubbornly taciturn the next, and may wonder how a nation so obsessed with the benefits of good honest labour can produce so many poets and writers.

But in these tendencies towards extremes, excess and unpredictablity, the Icelanders are only reflecting their homeland. Anyone would be a little crazy after centuries of long cold winters and a struggle for survival against a hostile environment – and managing to come out at the other end with one of the highest living standards in the world.

Icelanders have a reputation for being rather dour – but this quality does not go too deep. When the country enjoys one of its very infrequent long sunny summers, the entire nation can be seen to undergo a metamorphosis. Out come the pavement tables outside the cafés, the bottles of red wine and barbecues. Some people even manage to stop working overtime.

Medieval to modern

Icelanders have an extremely strong national identity, and a cultural heritage of which they are very proud. The constant suspicion that the outside world thinks them small and insignificant, coupled with having been isolated for so many years, sometimes makes them seem insular and absurdly patriotic. They are prone to harp on the nation's illustrious past, "cashing cheques on deeds committed 700 years ago," as writer and scholar Sigurður Norðal put it.

Yet no-one can deny that the Icelanders are a resilient bunch, having survived all sorts of calami-

PRECEDING PAGES: playing soccer in the light of the midnight sun. **LEFT:** displaying a family portrait. **RIGHT:** downtown Reykjavík café.

ties – both natural and induced – throughout the centuries. When the independence struggle began in the 19th century, Iceland was still deep in the Dark Ages. There were no roads and very few stone-built houses. But in a single generation, around the time Iceland gained self-government in 1918, the society moved, with no apparent difficulty, straight into the 20th century.

One of the most oft-cited reasons for the speed of this transition was the high standard of education in the country. While the people were poor, they were never ignorant. Nearly all of them could read and write, and quite a few could speak foreign languages.

Another is the strong sense of national identity and community. They have had to learn to stick together through necessity and overcome impossible odds. Thus, in the so-called Cod Wars with Britain in the 1960s and 1970s, this country without an army took on and defeated a world power that was threatening its interests and livelihood. A similar motivation lies behind the stubborn stand on whaling (*see pages 62 and 115*). It is not so much the importance of the whale-hunt, but the questioning of Iceland's right to self-government that raises the national hackles.

Social changes

Their fierce patriotism can give Icelanders a rather inflated view of the country's importance on the world stage. They are very sensitive to slights to their national pride, and react strongly to any real or imagined threats to the community. This characteristic can sometimes manifest itself in an unpleasant way – such as the ban on black servicemen which the Icelandic government secretly insisted on imposing when the NATO military base was established at Keflavík during the 1950s.

Iceland's racial make-up was, and still is, mostly homogenously Nordic, with a dash of Celt. Today people are much more cosmopolitan, but before the 1960s a black person walking down the street in Reykjavík was invariably followed by a crowd of excited children. In the pre-war years Hitler and his Nazis assiduously courted the Icelanders as an example of a "pure Aryan colony"; to the country's credit few people took any notice of this dubious flattery.

In fact, Icelanders are generally free of racism. In 1989, when 5,000 foreign citizens were already resident in the country (making up 2 percent of the population) a survey showed that a vast majority supported the idea of people of different races settling in Iceland. A large number of Icelandic couples adopted Vietnamese orphans during the Boat People crisis, and few of these children have experienced anything but a warm welcome into the community.

Recently an until-now-unexplored advantage of the homogenity of Iceland's population has been brought to the fore: unique opportunities for genetic research. In 1996, the first firm specialising in such research, DeCode Genetics, was founded. In its first two years DeCode grew exponentially, attracting foreign investors and generating considerable attention within the international medical community.

The genetic research discussion has been met with a mixture of awe and suspicion by the Icelanders. While DeCode's efforts and vision have been applauded, there has also been much controversy surrounding the company. This has mostly to do with questions such as whether a single company should have exclusive rights to medical information – though other companies are now being founded in addition to DeCode – and fears that the confidentiality of medical records might be violated.

Looking to foreign shores

It is one of the many paradoxes typical of Icelanders that they are, at the same time as being insular, insatiably curious about the outside world, even to the most obscure detail. The only epic poem that has ever been written in honour of the medieval Albanian hero Count Skanderbeg was composed by an otherwise unknown Icelandic clergyman in 1861.

Icelanders lay great store by being cosmopolitan and well-travelled – "sailed", as they put it. This dates back to the days of the sagas when every self-respecting Viking started off his career by journeying abroad, returning home laden with renown and gifts from European royalty. Modern-day young Vikings and Valkyries also have the community's blessing to quit the nation's shores and try their luck at seeking fame and for-

A NEW DICTIONARY

The world's first Basque dictionary was written by a farmer in a desolate part of Northwest Iceland – he had learnt the language from Basque sailors who came to fish off the nearby coast.

launched her international solo career in the UK 1993 and has since won the widespread acclaim and respect of fans and critics alike for her unique sound and experimental style. Along the way she has done more to promote her home country than any amount of advertising ever could. In May 2000 Björk added another string to her bow and heaped yet more honour on Ice-

tune in foreign lands. They are said to be *að gera garðinn frægan*, "winning renown for the old homestead."

And certainly no-one has done that with as much panache as Björk Gudmundsdóttir. Björk became a household name in Iceland at age 11, when she released her first solo record. During her teens and early twenties she sang with a handful of bands before becoming a founding member of The Sugarcubes. The Cubes were catapaulted to stardom all over the world in 1988 with their quirky song *Birthday* – largely on the strength of Björk's inimitable vocal style. Björk

LEFT: post-clubbing, 7am.
ABOVE: shops in Reykjavík.

land, when she won the award for Best Actress at the Cannes Film Festival. The newcomer to acting won the award for her role as Selma in director Lars von Trier's *Dancer in the Dark*, which stars Catherine Deneuve and also took the award for Best Film.

Björk's success in the international arena has flung open the doors for other Icelandic musicians to become better known internationally. Talent scouts from every corner of the globe have made their way to this tiny north-Atlantic island to see what other talent might be hiding among the ice and lava. Evidently, their efforts have paid off, for a number of musicians and bands, notably Indie band Sigur Rós, have since landed deals with foreign recording companies. The orgy of pop and kitsch that is the Eurovision Song Contest is taken extremely seriously in Iceland since it's regarded as an opportunity for Iceland to make its musical mark on the wider European continent.

In the classical sector, Icelanders have also excelled. The Iceland Symphony Orchestra has been winning great critical acclaim in the recent past, not least for their recordings of the works of the composer Jón Leifs. Leifs, who died in 1968 and whose unconventional – but decidedly Icelandic – sound was shunned by the establishment for decades, has recently been "discovered" by Icelanders and foreigners alike. Meanwhile, the

named one of the most influential filmmakers in Europe and his Reykjavík-based production company is a major player in Icelandic film production, in conjunction with film makers both in Iceland and abroad.

Icelanders are also terribly proud of their two Miss Worlds. As if to give credit to the common notion that Icelandic women are among the most beautiful in the world, two Icelandic women were awarded the Miss World title within three years of each other: Hólmfríður Gísladóttir in 1985 and Linda Pétursdóttir in 1988. Other Icelandic women have received other more minor titles on the beauty circuit.

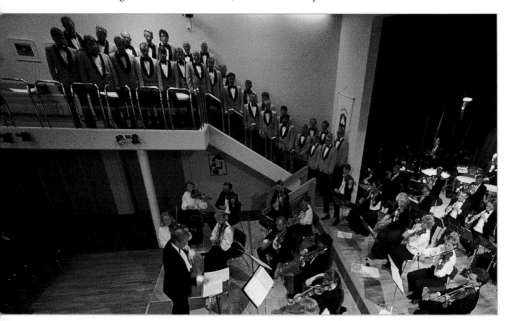

opera singer Kristján Jóhannsson – a former Akureyri native and ex-motor mechanic – today resides in Italy and boasts a schedule packed with singing engagements in the world's top opera houses, two to three years into the future.

Another heavyweight figure on the Icelandic cultural scene is filmmaker Friðrik Þór Friðriksson. His film *Children of Nature*, written in collaboration with Iceland's literary golden boy Einar Már Guðmundsson, was nominated for an Academy Award in the Best Foreign Film category, in 1992. Although it did not win, it helped pave the way for Friðriksson abroad. His subsequent films have been met with overwhelmingly favourable reviews and have won awards at numerous festivals throughout the world. Friðriksson has been

Sports and business

Two Icelanders have taken the title "Strongest Man in the World" four times each: Magnús Ver Magnússon and Jón Páll Sigmarsson, who died in 1993. Hjalti Ursus Árnason, won top prize at the World Strongmen Championships in Montreal in 1988 and Árnason and Magnússon, working together as a team, won the Scottish Pure Strength Championships in 1989.

A few other Icelanders have made the transition into the international sphere, most notably footballers, such as Eidur Gudjohnsen – who had a distinguished career at Chelsea in the English Premiership before moving on to Barcelona, and Ágúst Sigurvinsson who had a successful career in Germany. It was cause for public lament in the

German press that Sigurvinnson refused to give up his Icelandic citizenship in order to become a naturalised German and play with the German national team. Iceland established an unlikely influence in the English game, with the £85-million takeover of West Ham United by Eggert Magnusson in 2006 Earlier, in 1999, Stoke City was bought up by a consortium of Icelanders, spearheaded by fruit-and-vegetable distributor Thor Gislason. The former Icelandic national coach, Gudjon Thordarsson was appointed as manager.

A handful of Icelandic companies have been excelling in the international business arena in the recent past. As well as DeCode Genetics *(see page*

larger-than-life status in their home country; never mind that they may be queueing in front of you at the supermarket. President Ólafur Ragnar Grímsson, for instance, won office in 1996 partly on the strength of his previous experience in the international arena. The ex-parliamentarian is a former chairman and president of the organization Parliamentarians for Global Action, with which he worked actively towards disarmament and peace. Prior to his election he had done a great deal to open doors for Icelandic businesses in Asia and America and had been granted numerous international awards for his work. He was re-elected in 2004.

72)*, the brainchild of ex-Harvard professor Kári Stefánsson, there is Össur, which has been carving out a name for itself as a leading researcher and producer of prosthetics. Another is Marel, a top developer and producer of high-technology scales and software for the fishing industry. Oz, a producer of internet software and applications, sprung from nowhere in the early 1990s, led by a couple of twentysomething computer geniuses; the company now has its headquarters in San Francisco.

Whenever an Icelander "makes it" on the international level the entire Icelandic nation basks in his or her success. These people often achieve

LEFT: the Iceland Symphony Orchestra.
ABOVE: street art in a Reykjavík suburb.

My people and your people

Icelanders often claim theirs is a classless society. This claim has some basis: there is certainly a lot of class mobility. But there exist, like everywhere else, disparities of income, and some families are considered older and more "aristocratic" than others. Icelanders are obsessed with their genealogy and most can trace their ancestry back at least six or seven generations. Some even have family tables that go back beyond the age of Iceland's settlement into the realm of legend – perhaps with a Norse god or two sitting proudly at the top of the family tree. The common enquiry "who are his people?" is not just snobbery, however. It is a relevant question in a society where everyone is related to everyone else in the tenth generation.

The national inferiority complex also comes into play – and it has obviously been around for some considerable time. The author of the 12th-century *Landnámabók (Book of Settlements)*, which charted the progress of the first pioneers who came to Iceland, stated his purpose in writing as follows: "so we would better be able to answer foreigners who upbraid us for our descent from slaves or scoundrels if we knew our true origins for certain."

Small-scale society

Despite remnants of old snobberies, modern-day Iceland is on the whole an informal, egalitarian and familiar society. Everyone from the President down is addressed by their first names. Jón the doorman greets Jón the eminent politician with a cheery hello – they come from the same fishing village and are probably second cousins. As you shower after an early-morning dip in the local swimming baths there might be a famous pop-star getting changed in the cubicle next to you.

Icelanders do not identify easily with the idea of fame, with its paraphernalia of bodyguards and exclusiveness. They are used to everyone being accessible. The President grants interviews to any member of the public who wishes to see him. Top sportsmen and pop-stars usually have to keep their

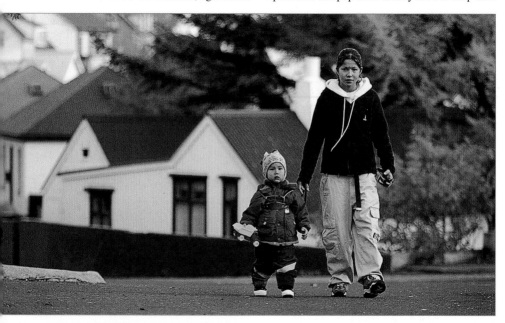

ICELANDIC NAMES

The continued widespread use of the patronymic system, whereby a surname is derived from the father's (or mother's) christian name, is in accordance with ancient Scandinavian custom. "Son" or "daughter" is tacked on; thus Björk Gudmundsdóttir is Björk, daughter of Gudmundur. Her brother would be Gudmundsson. Some families do have family names, but they are often of foreign origin: Zoega, Schram, Richter and Petersen. In the past it was possible for family names to be bought for cash by up-and-coming parvenus who considered them smarter and more aristocratic; now it is not permitted to take a new family name. The tradition makes things a lot easier for anyone seeking to trace their family roots.

day jobs, as few can afford to go professional.

And it is very easy to be famous yourself. Anyone with application and talent can stand for parliament, present a television programme, set up an art exhibition or play in a football team. Anyone can be a published author – and usually is. One in 10 Icelanders publishes something in the course of their life and writing a book is considered almost a form of National Service. If you fail to hit the headlines in your lifetime you will at least do so after your death. Even the most obscure person can be sure of at least one long obituary, with a photo, in the newspapers on the day of their funeral. Pillars of the community may run to several pages over many days.

The concept of being a participating member

of society is very strong. As a Japanese academic who settled in the country noticed: "Everyone is equal, so everyone is important. Everyone is a participant in society, it isn't possible to opt out, to deny your responsibility." Just as being a member of the community is an honour, being excluded from it is the worst possible dishonour. In the Saga Age, criminals were not killed or imprisoned, but outlawed – made outcasts from their society.

Every individual matters and in return is obliged to participate. Iceland supports three daily newspapers, six TV channels, a national theatre and opera plus dozens of orchestras, art galleries, theatre companies, radio stations and museums. None of these could hope to survive unless individuals made sure they visited the theatre at least once a year, took two newspapers, went to concerts, galleries and so on.

Spending power

Surveys have shown that in many areas Icelanders are closer to the US in their attitudes than to Europe. Icelanders are firm believers in market forces. In their personal tastes, they have a slight tendency towards ostentation, glamour and display of wealth. But this materialism is partly a matter of economic survival. Importers and retailers would go out of business unless every household found it an absolute necessity to purchase a television, a video recorder and a compact disc player.

The spend, spend, spend mentality has been encouraged by an economy plagued through the years by soaring inflation. Today, high interest rates and inflation at last brought down to single figures may dampen the spirits of some shopaholics, but most seem to carry on in their spendthrift ways regardless. Icelanders tend to be compulsive in their spending habits and are renowned for scooping up the latest gadgets. Moreover, "keeping up with the Joneses" is a national pastime and one must, of course, keep earning accordingly.

The "shopping trips" organised by Icelandair to the Scottish city of Glasgow became legendary amongst the retailers of that city, and when similar trips were organised to Newcastle in the north of England they made headline news locally. No

LEFT: going for a walk in the residential suburbs that sprawl to the east of Reykjavík. **RIGHT:** enjoying a pipe on a sunny afternoon.

wonder – a small but determined army of 50,000 Icelandic tourists manages to spend £23 million (US$37 million) each year in Britain.

As the late Nobel-prize winning author Halldór Laxness once declared, "it is, in general, expensive to be an Icelander." And to finance the expense, the nation is gripped by a collective compulsion to work all the hours that God sends. Ice-

landers are fierce devotees of the Protestant work ethic – no doubt a throwback to the days when a person's worth was measured in the number of hours of hard labour they could deliver per day.

Moonlighting is extremely common, and many people manage to hold down two or even three jobs at the same time. (As a result, they are always doing things at the last minute and are late for everything. Unpunctuality is one of the country's vices.)

Since the late 20th century there has been a budding awareness that this absolute devotion to the work ethic is turning into a national malaise. The accepted standard in the majority of companies is that employees – particularly men – must be on hand whenever required. Consequently, the strain on family life has become great and, ironically, the bottom line is that the number of hours put in does not necessarily deliver higher productivity – in fact often the reverse is true. Some companies have recognised the problem and taken steps to counter it; others lag further behind.

Working hard

It often puzzles foreigners why Icelanders devote so much time, money and effort to building palatial houses equipped with state-of-the-art furnishings when they are always at work and therefore never at home to appreciate them. However, work only for layabouts and degenerates. The reason seems to have been because it was too easy and well-paid.

But at the same time many Icelanders have a secret fascination for a more bohemian lifestyle. Hard-nosed yuppies will occasionally take the time to hang out philosophising with the regulars in one of Reykjavík's innumerable coffee-bars, and even publish a book of poems on the quiet.

Prime Minister Davíð Oddsson is a prime example of one who devotes himself to writing in his spare time: a collection of short stories written by him was, impressively, at the top of the best-seller lists in the 1997 Christmas book season.

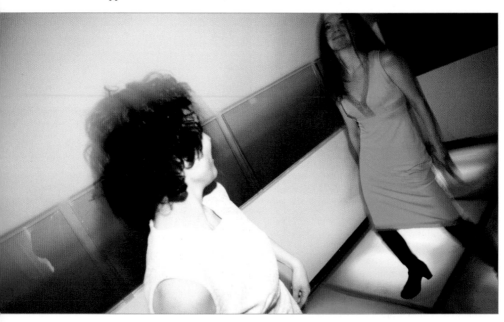

is not just a way of getting money, it is seen as an end in itself, a means of gaining self-respect. Although the Icelandic welfare state is not as highly evolved as those of some of its Scandinavian neighbours, it is still fairly comprehensive. Nevertheless, few people would ever dream of claiming money off the state. "The comprehensive ability to work is the hallmark of the Icelander, whether a desk-bound intellectual, a farmer or a fisherman," comments anthropologist Finnur Magnússon.

This extreme devotion to the Protestant work ethic was demonstrated during the World War II. "British work" – employment that was offered by the English military forces occupying the country – was despised by the Icelanders as fit

In Iceland, poets and artists command begrudging respect and seem to have a special dispensation to lead a ramshackle, layabout lifestyle. As Laxness put it ironically, "since time immemorial, the Icelandic nation has had to battle with men who call themselves poets and refuse to work for a living."

However, it must be admitted that in most cases the old Protestant work ethic tends to win out. Back in the 1960s, Icelandic hippies, although they were quite adept at tuning in and turning on, never really got the hang of dropping out. The real diehards had to head over to Copenhagen if they wanted to bum around in style – back home in Reykjavík they would have been too embarrassed not to have a job.

Playing harder

Icelanders may take their work seriously but they are equally single-minded about their play. An inability to do anything in moderation is in fact one of the most characteristic national traits, as is demonstrated by a trip to downtown Reykjavík on a Friday or Saturday night (*see* Embracing the Night, *page 150)*. This excess, however, is also partly explained by the high price of alcohol – it is too expensive to indulge in every day so many people prefer to save up for one almighty binge at the weekend.

Most Icelanders are also very quick to latch onto new trends, which can sweep across the entire nation with lightning speed. Video recorders had only been in the country for a couple of months before there were film-rental shops established on every street corner. It has been the same story with aerobics, sunbeds and new-age crystals. Aerobics teacher Sóley Jóhannsdóttir began her career in Denmark, where people would come for once-a-week dancing sessions. When she opened up a studio in Reykjavík it was a different story. She recounts: "Icelanders never do anything by halves – it's four times a week for most of my regulars with additional circuit-training lessons as well."

Non-violent society

The Icelanders are intrinsically a gentle people, and, despite having a fair share of the prevailing 21st-century social plagues – including drugs, porn, latch-key kids and so on – society is essentially non-violent, and Reykjavík is one of the safest capitals in the world. Even boxing is banned – Icelanders prefer the far more elegant ancient sport of *glíma* (which resembles sumo wrestling).

The lack of serious crime means that society can be rather at a loss as to how to treat its more anti-social and violent elements. Even the most vicious of criminals rarely gets sentences of more than seven years, and the lenient sentencing in sexual abuse and incest cases – in which the perpetrator often escapes any sort of rehabilitation – has been criticised in recent years. Progressive and forward-looking as it may be, Iceland still seems to prefer to turn a blind eye to some of the more "sensitive" issues.

The other side of the coin is that, in general, Icelanders are broad-minded and tolerant about

LEFT: partying on the dancefloor at a Reykjavík club.
RIGHT: praying to Thor.

most things. Single mothers, for example, are admired rather than frowned upon. Besides, everyone loves children and is happy to welcome them into the world whether they have two resident parents or one. Although a few moralists have predicted imminent destruction of the social fabric from such a lax set-up, marriage, which for many years was seen as irrelevant, is coming back

into fashion – even though many bridal couples have their own offspring acting as bridesmaids and pageboys.

Above all, Icelanders also have a greater respect for family ties than most other societies. They take care of each other – there are few neglected grannies and grandpas left to fend for themselves in high-rise blocks. A recent survey showed that Icelanders put family as their top priority – above friends, free time and even their beloved work.

Iceland's Valkyries

In recent times the Icelandic woman has become somewhat of an archetype, combining Nordic beauty with physical and spiritual strength. While probably a variety of factors contribute to the popularity of this image at this particular time, it undoubtedly received a boost through the two Miss World titles and the election, in 1980, of Vigdís Finnbogadóttir to the office of President. At the time of her election Vigdís was a single mother with an adopted daughter and, as such, represented a new era. She was also a survivor, having triumphed over breast cancer. In short, she combined femininity with strength, and common sense with strongly held personal views, albeit ones that she was not permitted to voice publicly by virtue of her office.

But the election of Vigdís was only the beginning: in 1983, Iceland became the first country to elect a

to appeal to women voters, was harshly criticised, both by the general public and by women from within its ranks. Bowing to public opinion, the Independent-Progressive coalition assigned four cabinet ministries to women in the following term.

Despite these problems, the women of Iceland are veterans of mould-breaking feminist activity. They first hit the international headlines in 1975, when they marked the beginning of the United Nations Women's Decade by going on a one-day mass strike to remind their menfolk of the essential role they played in society. Secretaries downed note-pads, bank-clerks and teachers stayed at home, mothers handed babies over to bewildered fathers

women-only party to parliament. The Women's Alliance (WA), a grass-roots radical movement with no leaders and an economic model based on the concept of "the thrifty housewife," had three of its members elected only a couple of months after the party was formed – and doubled its support at the following election. Support for the WA went down in the 1990s, however, mostly due to internal disagreements and the party formally disbanded before the 1999 elections; its remaining members joined the movement that became The Alliance.

The feminist movement in Iceland also suffered a backlash in the 1995 federal elections, when just one of the ten cabinet ministries was assigned to a woman. Subsequently the ruling Independence Party, which had specifically tailored its campaign

– and the country was brought to a standstill.

When the Women's Decade drew to a close in 1985, they staged another walk-out. Then-President Vígdis joined the protest, causing a constitutional crisis by refusing to sign a decree that would force striking air stewardesses back to work. Male government ministers eventually forced her to sign, but her stand was much appreciated by her female compatriots.

In fact, women have always played a forceful role in Icelandic society. The sagas and old tales are full of strong, matriarchal figures – from Aud the Deep-Minded, one of the greatest of the pioneers, to the irascible Bergþora, Njáll's wife – while ancient lawbooks indicate that the medieval Icelandic woman enjoyed a great deal more emancipation than the majority of her European counterparts. She had equal rights in marriage, could own property and even hold a *goðorð*, or chieftainship.

Feminist advances

Iceland was one of the first countries in the world to introduce female suffrage: women were given the right to vote in municipal elections in 1908 and general enfranchisement in 1915. The Women's Alliance party also has a historical precedent. Between 1908 and 1922 a number of women-only panels of candidates were put forward for municipal and parliamentary elections, with considerable success.

FEMALE FIGUREHEAD

The nation's symbolic figurehead is the Woman of the Mountains, a quasi-supernatural persona who plays a similar role in the national psyche to Marianne in France and John Bull in England.

the sea. "Icelandic women are strong because the wives of seafarers have to be," says former President Vigdís Finnbogadóttir.

Indeed, this tradition of holding the fort stretches right back to the Viking era, when women would be left in control of the farms while the men went pillaging and raiding. Today, women play a more vital role than ever in the

What has made this remote island in the North Atlantic such a hot-bed of feminist activity? Dr. Guðrún Agnarsdóttir, a founding member of the WA, says the low population is highly relevant. "A small community expects a lot from each individual, and each individual's contributions are also more likely to be noticed and appreciated." Supreme Court judge Guðrún Erlendsdóttir considers very important the fact that women in Iceland have always kept the old Norse tradition of retaining their natal surnames when they marry. But the factor that all eminent women in Iceland mention when asked about their emancipation is –

economy – as they have demonstrated through their national strikes. Over 70 percent of women work outside the home in either full or part-time employment. One of their main grievances is that their salaries are still on average 40 percent lower than that of men, and that like their sisters elsewhere in the world, they are still having to do most of the work in the home as well as outside it.

Svanur Kristjánsson, Social Sciences professor at the University of Iceland, concurs with the view that Icelandic women need still further emancipation. "Foreigners who hear about Vigdís and the Women's Alliance assume we must live in a matriarchy, but this is not so. The very existence of the Women's Alliance is symptomatic of the weak political position women have." ❏

LEFT: outdoor swimming. **ABOVE:** enjoying a pavement picnic in Reykjavík.

villu e aðr lagðæ hpitni þa v þa
ur zlzipadza iþiæt v þ hepr
vþ logu of ks haralld sun

A er Leiut vaz

þra hegat buird uezt
hpa iþu eþi nu hundzat
nuu ag z piriu air e þa
dlati hr hinc haup zi ob
rly air en a pytti are þ
vægihzc hpa dapr z li
pædæ alta gudhrandz
dou suei barn þey epz
er hua haþdz v ha lagu
bollat. þ vatv lunuc la
fuern iuw neptidz olapt
e h uair uairie aulni hu
rzguligr luo æt hr. bgr ob.

ICELANDIC LITERATURE

Iceland has a proud literary and linguistic heritage, most famously captured in the medieval sagas which tell of the early settlers, their lives, families and struggles.

The rich literary tradition of Iceland, in tandem with the preservation of the purity of the language, is of great importance to the national identity. Above all, the Icelandic saga is one of the world's most astonishing literary achievements and an important contribution to European culture. The anonymous 13th-century saga authors, who lived in a desolate northerly island in the midst of a raging civil war, were the first Europeans to write prose in their own language rather than in Latin. Why the sagas were written, whether they are history or fiction, who composed them, no-one knows. But the greatest of them – the romantic *Laxdæla Saga*; the thrilling adventures of the two outlaws Gísli Súrsson and Grettir; the tale of the rogue warrior-poet Egill Skallagrímsson; and above all the magnificent epic *Njáls Saga (see pages 94–5)* – can hold up their heads proudly in the midst of any literary company from Homer to Shakespeare.

Classified under the term "saga" – which in Icelandic simply means "story" – are countless historical chronicles, romances, legends, and lives of kings and holy men. Best known are the family sagas – 40 or so chronicles about the lives of various Icelandic families in the years following the land's settlement. The events they describe therefore occur around 200 to 300 years before the sagas were written, but until the 20th century they were taken as undisputed historical fact, passed down the generations orally until being finally recorded on manuscript. More recent scholarship, however, holds that they are basically works of fiction. The identity of the authors remains a mys-

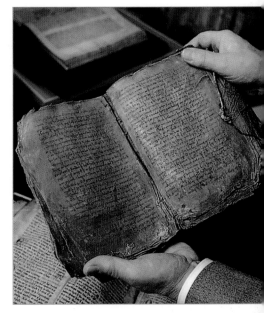

tery, although the chieftain Snorri Sturluson *(see panel on page 42)*, author of *Heimskringla*, the history of the Norwegian kings, is generally acknowledged to have written the saga of Egill Skallagrímsson.

Bloody chronicles

To summarise a saga story-line is almost impossible. They are great epic sprawls, which span many generations with dozens of characters and sub-plots. One 18th-century Icelandic scholar summed them up with the sardonic epigram "farmers at fisticuffs". He has a point – much of the action centres around blood-feuds, killings and conflict. But there is, of course, much more to them than that. They were written at a time of

---

PRECEDING PAGES: detail of a vellum manuscript of one of the sagas. **LEFT AND RIGHT:** saga manuscripts at the Árni Magnússon Institute.

social chaos, when Iceland, North Europe's first republic, was being brought back under the rule of foreign monarchs because of internal power struggles and conflicts. They contain a retrospective warning to the authors' contemporaries. As Njáll, the sage-prophet hero of *Njáls Saga*, says: "with laws we shall build our land, but with lawlessness it shall be laid waste." At the same time, there is a certain nostalgia for a heroic golden age where men fought, to be sure, but for honour rather than power and politics.

Bearing in mind that Iceland was being subjugated to the Norwegian king, there is a rather wistful recurring theme of Icelanders being feted and

society, the sagas portray the old pagan Viking morality. Oathbreaking, meanness and cowardice are the worst sins; open-handedness, courage and honour the greatest virtues. "Better to die honourably than to live on in shame," as *Flóamanna Saga* puts it.

Fate plays the strongest role in determining men's actions. Tragedy is usually the result of *ógæfa* – a near-untranslatable word, meaning more or less "ill luck."

The sagas are written in a highly distinctive terse and economic style. The dry, laconic viewpoint, both of the narrative and the characters, sometimes borders on parody. One dying Viking's

honoured at foreign courts, and being showered with gifts by, or getting the better of, various European monarchs. In the short saga of Halldór Snorrason, for example, the eponymous hero actually forces the Norwegian king Harald Hardrada at swordpoint to hand over his rightful bounty.

Morality and fate

The narrator of the sagas makes few moral judgements, but the sagas themselves are not much preoccupied with good and evil in the modern sense. Most of the characters are mixed, and unmitigated villains are rare – the cunning lawyer in *Njáls Saga*, Mörður Valgarðsson, is one of the few that spring to mind *(for more on characters, see pages 92–3)*. Despite being composed in a Christian

words, as he has a spear thrust into his gut, were "I see the broad spears are now in fashion."

The long journey home

The sagas themselves play a key role in the national psyche – they are symbolic not only of the nation's heroic past and of its literary achievements, but also of its survival. Thus it was a matter of intense national importance to have the original manuscripts returned to Iceland after centuries of "exile" overseas. Many had been taken to

ABOVE: illustrated saga manuscript dating from the 13th century. **RIGHT:** most of the manuscripts on display at the Árni Magnússon Institute have been moved to Reykjavík's Culture House.

Denmark, the ruling colonial power, by researchers who combed Iceland during the 17th and 18th centuries. The most famous and indefatigable of these researchers was Árni Magnússon (*see below*).

The Icelandic manuscripts that Árni Magnússon amassed remained at the University of Copenhagen – the undisputed centre of learning for Denmark, Norway and Iceland – for more than two and a half centuries. But as Iceland began to claim self-rule from Denmark in the late 1800s, so too did nationalists press for the return of its literary heritage. When the country became independent in 1944, the fate of the manuscripts was contested.

After years of wrangling and legal cases, Denmark finally agreed to return the bulk of the Icelandic manuscripts in 1961, hanging onto those relating to other Scandinavian countries. But it was not until a decade later that the first two books – the precious *Codex Regius* (containing the Poetic Eddas) and *Flateyjarbók* (the most important collection of sagas) – crossed the Atlantic in a Danish naval frigate. On 21 April 1971, thousands of spectators flocked to Reykjavík harbour to watch the manuscripts' arrival, carried ashore by naval officers in a solemn ceremony.

Since that day, 1,800 manuscripts have been returned by successive Danish governments. The

A LIFE'S WORK

Árni Magnússon was an Icelandic scholar who devoted his life to tracking down, saving and collating the vast number of vellum saga manuscripts that were taken away to Denmark during the days of colonial rule. Educated in Denmark, Árni returned to Iceland in 1702 to conduct a census and spent the next decade obtaining every medieval document that could be bought and laboriously copying out the rest.

Árni's almost supernatural knack of sniffing out manuscripts has become legendary: on one occasion he discovered a vellum that had been made into a template from which to cut out waistcoats! Árni took back with him no fewer than 55 cases full of manuscripts. As one of the leading scholars in Scandinavia, he was able to continue

the task from his post as Secretary of the Royal Archives in the University of Copenhagen, using his considerable influence to amass the world's best collection of Old Icelandic documents.

Tragically, fire swept through Copenhagen in 1728 and although Árni pulled most of his manuscripts from the flames, many were lost. Modern historians believe that the best parts of the collection were probably saved, but the trauma may have been too much for the ageing scholar, who died 15 months later. The research institute in Reykjavík named after him still keeps most of the manuscripts, but only a few are on public view; the Culture House in the city centre now has the largest display *(see page 151)*.

Icelandic Manuscript Institute, founded in 1961 to take on the responsibility of caring for the books, was renamed the Árni Magnússon Institute *(see page 87)* in 1972 after the great Icelandic researcher.

Sagas in modern Iceland

Numerous phrases from the old sagas spring readily to the lips of many modern Icelanders. For example, *"Fögur er hlíðin"* (how fair the slopes are), the first line of Gunnar of Hlíðarendi's lyrical speech, when he decides not to go into foreign exile but instead to stay in his beloved homeland and face his doom, has been a patriotic

actual places in Iceland. In many cases there are no remains of any buildings or features mentioned, but there are a few exceptions. Many saga readers find it fascinating to visit these valleys, hills and occasionally buildings that still resonate with the historical events portrayed. Perhaps the most well-known and best preserved saga site is Snorri's pool at Reykholt in the west of Iceland *(see page 211)*.

Also in the west are the remains of Erik the Red's farmstead. Erik married Þjóðhildur, a local farmer's daughter in Haukadalur valley, and built a farm there called Eiríksstaðir. His son Leifur, who later travelled to America, was born near

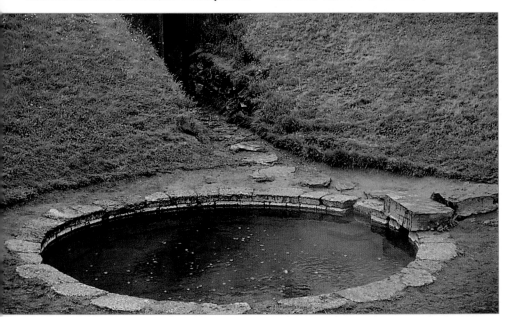

catchphrase since the days of the independence struggle in the 19th century. One of Njáll's famous sayings, *"með lögum skal land byggja"* (with laws shall we build our land) was a punning slogan of one of the leading Icelandic record companies – *"lögum"* can also mean tunes.

Heroes and villains of the sagas live on in the language. A large boulder is known as a *Grettistak* after the saga strongman's ability to lift such things, and a liar is known as a *lygamörður* after the nefarious scoundrel of *Njáls Saga*, Mörður Valgarðsson.

Visible remains of the sagas

Although the sagas are a complex mix of fact and fiction, most of their events can be located at

there. Erik went on to be exiled from Haukadalur for killing some of his enemies, and made his way to Brokey Island in Breiðafjörður, from where he was also exiled. Excavations on a site thought to be Eiríksstaðir in 1997 proved that the ruins dated from between 890 and 980. They revealed that Erik lived in a hall with a central fireplace and a ledge for seating set into the walls. The walls themselves, made of turf on a rock foundation were about 1.5 metres (5 ft) thick. The design is fairly basic, suggesting that the farm was only occupied for a few years.

The Rangárvallasýsla in the southwest is the location of many of the events in *Njáls Saga*, and a Saga Centre has been opened there which offers jeep tours to many of the sites *(see pages 94–5 and 181)*.

Keeping the sagas alive

Unlike most ancient literature elsewhere, which was both composed and enjoyed by a small and privileged elite, the sagas have, since the time of their conception, been the property of the common people. Also uniquely, because the Icelandic language has remained so little changed since medieval times, they remain accessible to the ordinary people of Iceland in their original language. The sagas are still read and enjoyed: nearly every Icelander is familiar with the characters and plots of the major works.

Other Icelandic literature: poetry

The Icelandic literary tradition extends far beyond the hallowed sagas, however. The golden age of Icelandic literature, beginning around 1100 with the historical chronicle *Landnámabók* (*Book of Settlements*), was one of the richest and most diverse in medieval Europe. Even more invaluable, for providing a feeling of the way of life, thoughts and priorities of these people, is the poetry they have left behind them. Icelanders were, from the start, poets. Between the 9th and 13th centuries there were 100 Icelandic poets working around the courts of Europe; after the end of the 10th century the position of court poet in Scandinavia was held only by Icelanders.

The poet or *skáld* had an elevated, even mystical status. He was entrusted with preserving the tribe's deeds in his poems, and raising morale with heroic verse. The Icelandic *skálds* have always been important members of society. Many, for example, took an active part in the independence struggle – and poetic talent has always been regarded as the sign of a noble personality.

The Eddic poems, like those by the *skálds*, were composed in accordance with strict rules of internal rhyme and alliteration, but are much more accessible. These works, which deal with heroic or mythological subjects, were written down at the same time as the sagas, but most of them were probably composed much earlier. Poems such as *Hávamál* give a vivid insight into the Viking mind, revealing a people preoccupied with honour, who were sociable, generous but highly pragmatic: "Cattle die, kindred die, we ourselves also die," runs one oft-quoted line, "but the fair fame never dies, of him who well deserves it".

LEFT: Snorri's pool at Reykholt, where the great chieftain used to bathe.
RIGHT: the 19th-century poet, Jónas Hallgrísson.

In the Dark Ages, Iceland's loss of independence dampened creativity, although the old language and literature remained treasured through the hard years of poverty. Since medieval times, Icelanders have always been able to read and write – children could not be confirmed until they were literate – and learning has been held in high esteem. Foreign travellers wrote of being addressed in Latin and ancient Greek by filthy half-starved natives, and taken into huts to look at priceless manuscripts.

Poetry and politics

In the 19th century, with improving social conditions and a growing independence movement, the

skáld came back into his own. The poet Jónas Hallgrímsson, born in 1807, reached the hearts of his people as no-one else has before or since. Known as "the nation's beloved son," he was the first Icelander to have a statue raised to his memory by his countrymen. A Romantic in the high tradition, Jónas was at the forefront of the struggle for independence from Danish rule, and his poetry is full of love for his native land.

He was a poetic radical – like Wordsworth, he wrote in the common tongue rather than high-flown poetic simile. He was also a highly qualified botanist, and travelled round the highlands each summer, collecting material for a comprehensive account of Iceland's natural history – a huge task he was never to complete.

Jónas, from rural North Iceland, spent much of his adult life in Copenhagen where he wrote some of his best work, including *Ísland*, a testimony to former glories and call for a better future that every Icelander knows by heart:

Iceland, happy homeland,
fortunate frost-white mother,
where is your ancient honour,
your freedom and deeds of renown…

He suffered a great deal of hardship and exposure during his explorations, and these, coupled with poverty and drink, took a heavy toll on his health. He put the seal on his reputation by dying a true poet's death – young, poverty-stricken and alone.

is Bjartur of Summerhouses, the peasant crofter hero of *Independent People*. Stubborn, infuriating but "the most independent man in the country", Bjartur represented the archetypal Icelander. His best work, *World Light,* is a trilogy dealing with the poet's role in society. He showed other writers what could be done with the language – he played around with it, changed spellings, used street language and made up or even borrowed words.

Pétur Gunnarsson, one of the first "urban novelists", innovated the use of colloquial, humorous first person narrative. Þór Vilhjálmsson makes use of fragmented language and cultural reference to come to terms with modern life, while Guðbergur

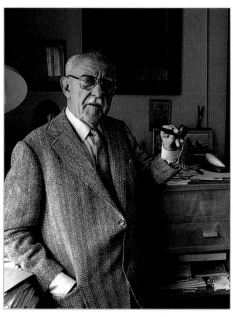

Contemporary voices

By far the most important modern literary figure is Halldór Kiljan Laxness, winner of the 1955 Nobel Prize for Literature, who died in 1998. Laxness broke away from the idealisation of peasant life prevalent in Icelandic writing, portraying the dark underside of rural life, which caused resentment amongst those who felt he was presenting Iceland in a bad light. But, in his own way, Laxness was as fervent a patriot as any. His novel *Bell of Iceland*, set in the 18th century, contains references to the contemporary independence struggle. The postwar *Atom Station,* from the time of the NATO airbase controversy, contains pointed criticism of the politicians who were ready to sign away their country's independence out of greed. His best-known creation

Bergsson criticises the American-worshipping culture of the postwar period through absurd humour. Among women writers Svava Jakobsdóttir has developed a unique brand of surreal feminism, while the lyrical narrative method of Vigdís Grímsdóttir is much admired.

There have also been great innovations in poetry. The *atomskálds* of the 1950s caused a storm when they broke all the old rules and began to write in free verse. But modern or traditional, the latter-day *skálds* of Iceland still take their responsibilities seriously. They are above all guardians of the holy trinity: language, land and nation. ❑

LEFT: reading on a long winter's night.
ABOVE: Halldór Laxness.

The Icelandic Language

To the Icelander, the mother tongue is far more than just a method of communication – it is the essence of culture, and its nurture and preservation is inextricably tied up with the survival of national identity and pride. Icelanders know in their heart of hearts that the Icelandic language is, as the poet Einar Benediktsson said, "more noble than that of any other nation."

Icelandic is one of the North Germanic family of languages, its nearest relatives still in use being Norwegian and Faroese. Thanks to centuries of comparative isolation, it is still very similar to old Norse, the language that was spoken by most of Northern Europe during the 7th to 11th centuries, and is the only language to still use the old runic symbols of ð (ed) and þ (thorn). Although no longer isolated, the language continues in its unaltered state – for Icelanders will fight to the death against any influences which might corrupt or change their beloved mother tongue.

Preserving an ancient language

What would be regarded in other countries as normal linguistic developments are seen as national disasters in Iceland. There is, for example, "dative sickness" – a debilitating contagious disease which causes sufferers to put nouns which should be in the nominative or accusative case into the dative. Like most ancient languages, Icelandic is a complex minefield of case endings, subjunctives and inflections which can catch out many native speakers, let alone foreign students. Nevertheless, any grammatical slip-ups are considered social solecisms of the worst order, and if committed by a guardian of public linguistic morals, such as a radio-show host, a grave offence.

In the spirit of individuality typical of Iceland, foreign influences on the language are kept strictly in check, and great care is taken to prevent Icelandic becoming diluted. Icelanders have no truck with such international loan-words as "radio", "telephone" or "computer", which have infiltrated many other languages. Academic committees are set up to find proper, Icelandic words for these various new-fangled phenomena. Thus, the computer was christened *tölva* – a mixture of the word *tala* ("number") and *völva* ("prophetess"). The telephone became *sími*, from an ancient word meaning

RIGHT: book shops thrive in Iceland.

"thread". A helicopter is a *þyrla* or "whirler"; a jet aircraft is a *þota* or "zoomer". The practice even extends to scientific language, which is kept as firmly non-Latin as possible. The general public joins in the fun of "word-building", and a raging debate almost always seems to ensue.

Some of these neologisms are wittily creative. Even such an eminently post-Freudian figure as the voyeur is cut down to size in Icelandic as a *gluggagægir*, the name of one of the 13 traditional harbingers of Christmas, who used to spy in through farm windows. In the 1990s, the tiny "beepers" or breast-pocket pagers used to call busy businessmen to the nearest phone, were dubbed *Friðþjófur*,

a man's name meaning literally "thief of the peace" (mobile phones have a more prosaic name – *farsími*, literally a travelling phone).

Another way in which tradition is preserved is in people's names: a surname is derived from the christian name of one's father or mother – hence Eiður Sigurdsson is the son of Sigurd, while Björk Gudmundsdóttir is the daughter of Gudmundur *(see also page 76)*.

Icelandic is known as the Latin of the North not only because the language itself has remained unchanged – it has also preserved, in its literature, the ancient Norse culture. Because it is almost unchanged since the Middle Ages, it makes the medieval sagas readily understandable to the modern Icelandic reader. ❑

HEROES AND HEROINES OF THE SAGAS

The sagas are populated with memorable and vividly drawn characters that are very human in their desires, actions and frailties.

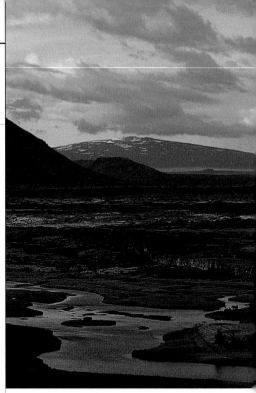

ABOVE: For centuries, the Alþingi, the national assembly of the Icelanders, took place on the plains at Þingvellir, the scene of many of the events recounted in the sagas.

One of the recurring themes of the Icelandic sagas is the difference between the fortunate "light" heroes and the unlucky "dark" heroes. The romantic Kjartan Ólafsson of Laxdæla Saga is an archetypal light hero – handsome, accomplished and brave. In a similar mould is Gunnar of Hlíðarendi in Njáls Saga: "He was a handsome man...extremely well-bred, fearless, generous and even-tempered... It has been said that there has never been his equal."

The peerless Gunnar contrasts sharply with Skarphéðinn, son of Njáll, who was "quick to speak and scathing in his words... He had a crooked nose and prominent teeth, which made him ugly round the mouth. He looked every inch a warrior." Dark heroes such as Skarphéðinn are often ugly, awkward men, at odds with society – the conventional romantic hero pales into insignificance compared with these enigmatic, tormented figures.

The saga women were no less formidable than their male counterparts. Njáls Saga contain two bloodthirsty and ruthless women – Hildigunnur and Hallgerður Long-Legs. But queen of these indomitable women is Guðrún Ósvífursdóttir, heroine of Laxdæla Saga, who marries four times in the course of her stormy career, and ends her days as Iceland's first nun.

LEFT: A Thor amulet. During the course of the sagas, the heroes converted their faith from the worship of Odin and Thor to Christianity – a cause of many disputes.

RIGHT: One of the main "light" heroes, **Njáll the Wise** is the main protagonist of Njáls Saga *(see pages 94–5)*, a sagacious man, a pacifist and a true friend.

HISTORY AND FICTION

In the Middle Ages the Icelanders were the historians of the North. The surviving saga manuscripts by anonymous authors preserve most of our present knowledge of North European history and learning during this period. At the same time they sketch the outlines of Nordic identity. In a sense, they are frontier literature, in which the descendants of the settlers reflect on their origins, legends aned back upon the settlement period as a golden age, with a well-functioning commonwealth of free chieftains.

The sagas were intended not only as a record of events but also as entertainment. Their authors therefore added a generous pinch of fiction to these tales of families and feuds. This mixture is probably what has given them their enduring appeal. Passed down through generations of Icelanders retelling saga tales ona winter's night, they are still a central part of the national consciousness.

BELOW: **Grettir the Strong** is the "dark" hero of Grettis Saga: an outlaw, strong and courageous, but quarrelsome and extremely unfortunate.

BELOW: One of the most remarkable female saga-heroes, **Hallgerður Long-Legs** is wicked, beautiful and partly responsible for her husband Hlioarendi's death.

In Pursuit of Njáll

The action of *Njáls Saga* – considered the greatest of the sagas and the most widely read today – takes place in a small stretch of the southwestern coastal plains between the rivers Rangá and Markarfljót. Written by an unknown scholar in the 13th century, *Njáls Saga* is the rip-roaring tale of a 50-year blood feud.

Njáls Saga is divided into three parts. The title character, Njáll Þorgeirsson, is the most skilled lawyer in Iceland, blessed with second sight and universally respected for his fairness and integrity. A farmer who never raises his sword in anger, he is bound by the strict codes of family loyalty and honour. Oddly, Njáll plays a small role in much of the saga, reacting to rather than shaping events.

The first part of the saga concerns Njáll's friendship with the greatest champion of the land, Gunnar. So, the best place to start a saga tour is at Gunnar's farm, Hlíðarendi. Set above the marshy Rangá plains on Route 261 (turning south from the Ring Road east of Hvolsvöllur; *see page 181*), the farm now consists of a few white buildings and pretty church among some trees in a mellow, peaceful landscape.

Gunnar could fight so skilfully that "he seemed to be brandishing three swords at once,". He was a fair-minded fellow, slow to anger and keen to avoid trouble. His problems began when he married the beautiful, manipulative Hallgerður Long-legs, who had arranged the demise of two previous husbands for slapping her face.

Hallgerður started up a feud with Njáll's equally shrewish wife, Bergþóra. Each of the women ordered the murder of the other's slaves in an escalating feud that the friends Njáll and Gunnar refused to be drawn into. Relatives of the victims became involved, until Gunnar was prosecuted at the Alþingi for butchering some assailants in self-defence. Sentenced to outlawry for three years, he was riding away from Híldarenði when his horse stumbled and he looked back. "How lovely these slopes are," he said, "more lovely than they ever seemed to me before, golden cornfields and new-mown hay. I am going back home, and I will not go away."

The decision was fatal. Gunnar's enemies soon surrounded the farm, although he kept them at bay with his bow and arrow until his string broke. Gunnar asked his wife for two locks of her hair to plait a new bowstring, but the treacherous Hallgerður – who had once been slapped by Gunnar – refused. Gunnar's reply to this death-sentence is one of the sagas' most famous lines: "To each his own way of earning fame... You will not be asked again." Although Gunnar took many of his enemies with him, he was finally slaughtered.

Skarphéðinn á Markarfljóti

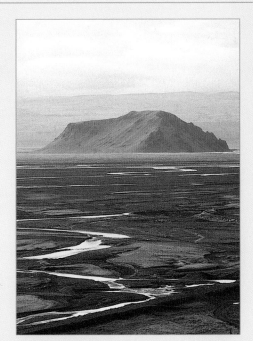

The bloodshed was far from over. Njáll's three sons – Helgi, Grímur and the eldest, Skarphéðinn – helped take vengeance on the killers of Gunnar. But they also wanted to kill Þráinn Sigfússon, a vain relative of Gunnar's who had been present at an earlier ambush. Directly south of Hildarendi, half way between Gunnar's home and Njáll's on the rough but passable Route 250 is a rounded hill in the middle of the plain. Today called Stóra-Dímon, it was in Njáll's time called Rauðaskriður, or "Red Skree" and is where the three Njálssons lay in wait one winter's morning in 995 for Þráinn Sigfússon and his friends.

The ambush was spotted, and it looked as if Þráinn would get away, but Skarphéðinn leapt onto the glassy ice of the Markarfljót, skidded downstream and sliced Þráinn over the head with his axe. The gymnastic Skarphéðinn had swooped off to safety before anyone knew what had happened.

Njáll was horrified when he heard of the killing, but organised a settlement at the Alþingi. To smooth things over, Njáll even adopted Þráinn's orphaned son, the cherubic Höskuldur. Höskuldur grew up to take over the farm Ossabær, which is now a ruined site on Route 252 heading south,

but the Njálssons grew jealous of him. One day the three sprung upon him without warning in a corn field and cut him down.

Putting the Njálssons up to this butchery was the diabolical Mörður Valgarðsson who loathed Gunnar and plotted to destroy Njáll's family. His chance came when arrangements for a money settlement over Höskuldur's murder fell through at the Alþingi. Höskuldur's kinsman, Flosi Þórðarson from the Skaftafell area, was about to accept a deal from Njáll when Skarphéðinn insulted him, suggesting that he was regularly sodomised by a troll.

Follow route 252 to the site of Njáll's farm, Bergþórshvoll. The modern farmhouse is uninspiring, but you can still see the three hills of the saga. On a clear day, the snow-covered mountains on the horizon make a spectacular sight. Having stuck by his bloodthirsty sons, Njáll spotted Flosi with 100 men bearing down on the farm. Instead of fighting, he ordered them all to retire into the house – effectively committing suicide, since Flosi promptly set the place on fire. Njáll and his wife refused an offer of mercy, preferring to die with their three sons. Only Kári Sólmundarson escaped.

Interestingly, archaeological digs undertaken at Bergþórshvoll in the 1920s and '50s have found evidence of a Saga Age burning (the accepted date is 1011), suggesting that the dramatic story may be true. ❏

LEFT: Skarphéðinn slides away on a frozen river after killing Þráinn Sigfusson. **ABOVE:** Stóra-Dímon across the plains of the Markarfljót river. **RIGHT:** a 19th-century artist's impression of Vikings at sea

LIVING WITH THE ENVIRONMENT

Iceland is a place of extremes, from long nights in winter and even longer days in summer, to heavy snow, to the threat of volcanic eruptions

The English traveller John Stanley, who visited Iceland in 1789, commented: "I pitied the poor Icelanders who could not like swallows gather themselves together for a flight to a climate less hostile to the comforts of human existence. What the Icelanders can enjoy deserving the name of happiness during the long winter I cannot imagine."

There is not so much reason to pity the poor Icelanders these days. Warm, centrally heated houses have taken the place of damp turf huts, electric light does much to compensate for the long hours of darkness, and powerful snow-ploughs mean that only the most isolated settlements are cut off during the winter months.

In fact, during winter, the inhabited areas around Iceland's coast do not experience the bitter extremes of cold that the country's name would suggest. Iceland is washed by the warm waters of the Gulf Stream and moderate south-westerly Atlantic winds, ensuring that – although summers are definitely chilly by most people's standards – the Icelandic winters are actually milder than in more southerly places such as New York or Moscow. Temperatures below -10°C (14°F) in Reykjavík are unusual.

The dreaded wind and rain

Even so, as any visitor to Iceland will quickly find out, living with the climate here is still no picnic. Iceland's real plague is wind and rain. The same Gulf Stream and mild winds that bring moderate weather run up against the Icelandic mountains and the icy polar air to create some wretched

weather. Although there are the occasional freak summers, Reykjavík normally enjoys only one completely clear day every July. In January, the average goes up to three.

The combination of gales and rain renders umbrellas completely useless, and a local joke is that Iceland is the only place where the rain falls from all directions – including horizontal. Even so, it is not uncommon to see Icelanders wandering around without any protection during quite heavy downpours. Ask them why and they might shrug: "It's rained here since I was a child. I don't even notice it any more."

The weather is worst around the southwest, improving markedly around Akureyri, the north and east. But luckily for travellers and Icelanders

---

PRECEDING PAGES: riding the stocky Icelandic horse.
LEFT: dressing up against extreme conditions at sea.
RIGHT: another rainy day in Reykjavík.

alike, the true norm for Icelandic weather is its sheer unpredictability, shifting rapidly from clear to miserably wet, then back again, several times in the course of a single day.

The polar night

Despite the blessings that the Gulf Stream brings, the Icelandic winter can still be a cold, long and miserable affair. At this high latitude, it is also particularly dark. Iceland is almost completely outside the Arctic Circle (only part of the northern island of Grímsey is within its bounds), so it avoids the true extremes of months of darkness that are associated with northern Greenland and

are reported extensively in the local press. By the middle of May the grass is turning green and wild flowers are appearing. When summer truly arrives in June, the long winter wait seems almost worth it. Although temperatures are hardly tropical, between 12–15°C (54–60°F), the sun shines almost all night.

Strictly speaking, it is only above the Arctic Circle that the true "midnight sun" occurs, whereby the sun never dips below the horizon. This can be seen on the island of Grímsey, from the mountains close to Ólafsfjörður or from the northeast coastline near Raufarhöfn (where the northernmost point of the mainland lies just 2.5km south of the

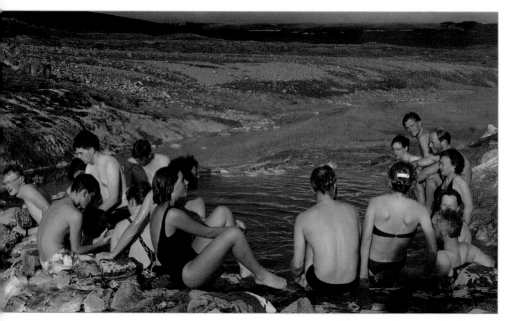

the Arctic icecap. Even so, things here are quite bad enough. During the months of December and January there are no more than five hours of daylight a day anywhere in the country.

That's when Icelanders begin to suffer from *skammdegisþunglyndi*, "short day depression". As some sort of compensation, winter is the best time to see the ghostly aurora borealis (northern lights) – shimmering green and mauve waves of astral electricity flickering in the starry sky.

Waiting for the sunshine

Across the country, Icelanders wait impatiently each year for the first signs of spring. The first sightings of migrating birds, particularly the golden plover *(lóa)* – the "harbinger of spring" –

Arctic Circle). However, even without the true midnight sun, for the rest of Iceland real night never falls during the months of June and July, with the sun only just skimming below the horizon at midnight: an extended dusk is the only sign of the passing of the day, and the stars do not come out until August.

Summer fever

Foreign visitors have often commented that Icelanders remind them of hibernating animals, sleeping in winter and letting rip in summer. June and July – and, to a lesser extent, August – are the times when Iceland's national parks are filled to overflowing on weekends and when the country's interior is criss-crossed with frantic drivers speeding around in their huge-wheeled vehicles. The *joie de vivre* is contagious and normal rules go by the board, with even very small children playing out in the street until midnight. Foreign visitors often find these endless days as difficult to cope with as the long winter nights: it's not easy to sleep when the sun is glistening through the window. However, there are advantages for the visitor. Photographers will find the golden light of the early mornings and late nights in Iceland at this time of year particularly beautiful.

At any time of year, Iceland's unpolluted arctic air makes visibility almost supernaturally clear. Far away objects often seem deceptively close:

the presence of mind to notify the National Association of Rescue Groups of their journey before they set off. This fine body of men, who work entirely on a voluntary basis, will monitor travellers and organise search-parties if they do not return to base on schedule. They do get rather annoyed, however, at having to risk life and limb rescuing people who have got into trouble through sheer foolhardiness, so it is best to use your commonsense and ensure that you take sensible precautions, such as not venturing onto a glacier alone, and not attempting to climb unknown mountains or in unfamiliar areas except with an experienced guide.

on a fine day in Reykjavík, for example, the distant icecap of Snæfellsnes looks as if it is only a few miles across a small bay.

The dangers of nature

Icelandic weather is notoriously unpredictable, and a raging storm can appear out of a clear blue sky in minutes. Temperatures can plummet to -30°C (-22°F), with wind-chill factor, in the deserted highlands of the interior.

Stranded trippers and mountaineers need not despair completely, however – as long as they had

LEFT: lounging by a natural jacuzzi at Hveravellir.
ABOVE: snatching the opportunity to soak up some of those rare summer rays.

The treacherous sea

Against some natural forces even the most careful precautions are to all intents and purposes useless. The ocean is the source of Iceland's livelihood, but it can also be a killer. Despite enormous improvements in safety aboard fishing vessels, the life of the fisherman remains a dangerous one, and there are many Icelandic women who have been widowed by the treacherous seas.

Nor is one safe on Icelandic dry land, either. Scientists at National Civil Defence monitor each tiny seismological tremor with concern. In the absence of an army, the NCD is also responsible for conducting rescue operations in the event of other natural disasters; storms, avalanches, floods and volcanic eruptions are all major threats.

On average, there is a volcanic eruption some-where in Iceland every five years. During the 20th century there were more than 20 eruptions, many of which occurred unseen, deep beneath the mighty glacier Vatnajökull. No-one, however failed to notice the two most celebrated eruptions – the one off the south coast in 1963, which formed a completely new island, Surtsey, and 10 years later, the eruption on the Vestmannaeyjar (West-mann Islands). Suddenly, in the middle of the night, what was believed to be an extinct volcano on the inhabited island of Heimaey began to erupt. Fortunately, the fishing fleet was moored in the harbour that night, and every one of the 5,300

with their environment. Nor are these the only environmental problems.

Another old enemy is erosion. Iceland was once, according to the old chronicles, heavily forested, but now there is a startling absence of trees, and most natural vegetation is scrubby tun-dra. Not only is this a shame aesthetically, but the lack of trees means there is little to bind the soil, which is bad news on a such a windswept island.

Exploiting the volcanic landscape

A natural force can occasionally be tamed and made to earn its keep. Iceland's homes have been provided with cheap and environmentally friendly

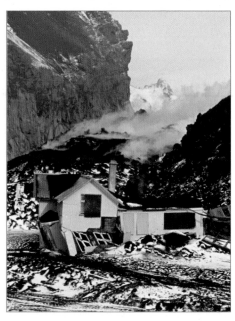

inhabitants of the island was successfully evacu-ated to the mainland *(see panel on page 189)*.

A more devastating eruption was that of Lakagígar in 1783, especially as the country's inhabitants could not then call upon modern technology to aid them. The lava flow, produced by some 100 craters in a volcanic fissure more than 25 km (15 miles) long, was the greatest ever recorded in human world history, and it eventually covered an area of 565 sq. km (218 sq. miles). It was Iceland's most cataclysmic natural disaster, and the eruption, and the Haze Famine that came in its aftermath, caused the deaths of thousands of people.

This episode, terrible though it was, is just one of many in the long saga of the Icelanders' battle

hot water and heating for the past 60 years by geothermal energy – water heated naturally under the earth's crust. This water is also used to heat the 150,000 sq. metres (37 acres) of greenhouse, used for growing fruit and vegetables, in the town of Hveragerði – the country's market-garden under glass *(see page 171)*.

And geothermal energy is also the reason that Icelanders can enjoy an open-air swim on the most bitterly cold and snowy morning – and soak after-wards in a 45°C (113°F) hot pool. Swimming in Iceland is not so much a hobby as a way of life, and the geothermal pools have a total attendance of around 1.5 million people a year. Swimming baths are one of the main focuses of social life, and many of the country's most important decisions are made in lunch-time hot pool sessions.

Icelanders have been used to regarding their geothermal water as a bottomless pit – one swimming pool, for example, uses up 1.3 million tons of water a day – but there are indications that the reserves in Reykjavík may be drying up because of overuse.

One natural resource that is in no current danger of overexploitation is hydroelectricity. With so much surplus energy, it seems logical to try to export some of it abroad. Now, with the development of ultra-low resistance wires, this scheme may soon become technologically and economically feasible, and there are already plans afoot to lay underwater cables across the ocean to Britain, and even to Germany.

Tourism is very much on the increase in Iceland, and is one of the island's most important industries, bringing in 12–15 percent of the total foreign currency earnings. However, the environment, which is seemingly so rugged and powerful, is extremely fragile – and the authorities are as a result not keen to see it grow out of control. "Iceland isn't open safari country," says Þíroddur Þóroddsen of the National Conservation Council. "We want tourists who are sensitive to the environment."

Keeping the roads open

Although Iceland does not fully merit its chilly name, winters are prolonged and snow can be heavy, but this does not discourage the Icelanders from travelling as much as possible all year round. A few decades ago, the sea was the most important route for travel between Iceland's dispersed coastal communities. Roads hardly existed, and the coastal boats transported passengers and goods alike. Today, however, the motor vehicle is king, and overland travel has become the norm.

A vastly improved road system means that land travel is possible throughout the year, if a little difficult at times. If the road network seems, to the outsider, to be a series of primitive unsurfaced tracks with the occasional stretch of tarmac, the outsider should bear in mind that it is a huge, and vastly expensive, transport network for such a small population in such a large country. The quality of the roads has advanced by leaps and bounds since

---

FAR LEFT: a geothermally heated pool in Reykjavík. **LEFT:** lava flow from Helgafjell Volcano on Heimey Island destroyed property in 1973. **RIGHT:** keeping the roads open can be a major challenge.

the 1960s, and will undoubtedly continue to do so.

Policy laid down by the Ministry of Communications aims to keep all major roads passable, as far as possible, throughout the winter months: the first priority is given to keeping open routes between centres of population within each region. These are generally cleared every working day, and even more frequently in the event of unusually heavy snow. Roads out of Reykjavík, north to Borgarfjörður and east to Hvolsvöllur, for instance, are very rarely closed to traffic for more than a few hours at a time.

The second-highest priority is placed upon keeping clear roads linking one region to the next,

such as the South to the East Fjords, or the route from Akureyri to Reykjavík. These roads are cleared two or three times weekly on average, ensuring that traffic will get through at least on those days.

Minor roads, however, are cleared less frequently, if at all. Mountain tracks across the interior, such as Kjölur and Sprengisandur, are summer-only roads and are normally closed by snow by the end of October. Although mountain roads are largely free of snow again by May, meltwater from the same snow turns them into impassable seas of mud, and they are only reopened once they are dry enough to sustain traffic, usually in late June or early July.

ROAD NETWORK

Iceland has more than 13,000 km (8,000 miles) of roads, and approximately 8,000 km (5,000 miles) of them are classified as major roads.

The Public Roads Administration assesses the state of the highland roads, decides when to open them for traffic, and closely monitors traffic on the highlands. Unauthorised travel on the muddy roads in early spring can cause havoc to the road surface, and offenders are subject to heavy fines.

Although all efforts are made to keep the road network functioning, even in severe winters, the possibilities of wintertime travelling in an ordi-

nary family car are severely limited, not least due to the unpredictable climate. The traveller may set off from home on a fine clear winter day, only to find a blinding snowstorm just over the next mountain. Ordinary saloon cars, without four-wheel-drive, are not happy with this kind of test. Icelanders have therefore taken enthusiastically to large four-wheel-drive vehicles which can operate in almost any road conditions. Wintertime travel in the souped-up giant-wheeled versions of these cars has become a popular hobby.

Alternative routes

Some major routes over highland passes – such as those into the mountainous West Fjords – are subject to such heavy snowfalls that they cannot

necessarily be kept open through the winter, and they may be closed for weeks or months. Alternative routes at lower altitudes remain open, and in some regions the sea route provides the main winter link between communities. In the West Fjords in particular, travel by sea still remains almost as important as in the past.

Air travel is of unusual importance in Iceland, and even more so in winter. It takes about five hours to drive the 389 km (243 miles) to Akureyri from Reykjavík, in good conditions. By air, you can get there in 45 minutes. In winter, with uncertain road conditions, the comparison becomes even more favourable. Flights are relatively rarely cancelled, although there can be delays, and Icelandic pilots attain great expertise in taking off, flying and landing in difficult, icy conditions.

The air route is also, of course, the emergency route into and out of most communities during the winter months. Scheduled flights operate frequently to major centres such as Akureyri, Ísafjörður and Egilsstaðir, and they run less often – although still regularly – to a host of small centres around the country, where there may be no more than a landing strip and a windsock to indicate the "airport". For convenience and security, all airport roads are cleared regularly, and invariably in connection with scheduled flights.

Icy conditions

Snow is not the only hindrance to winter travel, though. Roads are often dangerously icy, mainly because of a tendency for Icelandic temperatures to hover around freezing point for much of the winter. The temperature may be 2–3°C (35–38°F) when snow falls, then warm up to reduce the snow to the consistency of a smooth mush. The thermometer might then plummet to -10°C (14°F), and the mush freezes, smooth as a skating rink.

Winter tyres are essential from October to May, even in towns, where all roads are cleared regularly in snow, and salted to reduce ice. Many Icelanders opt for nailed tyres, which give a better grip on icy road surfaces, although braking remains a problem on slippery roads. Heavy-tread snow tyres offer better braking, but may not provide enough grip for driving up slippery slopes. If you want to learn how to handle a car in a skid, Iceland is the place. With roads this slippery, you learn fast. ❑

LEFT: dog-sledding in winter.
RIGHT: ice-climbing is a challenging winter sport.

Environmental Protection

A land of some 100,000 sq. km, and only 277,000 people, with clean air and clean water, Iceland was relatively slow to see the need for conservation. Yet in today's interdependent world, it is facing a dilemma – how can the pristine environment and outstanding natural beauty be protected from the ravages of seemingly unstoppable industrialisation and global warming? It's a problem which has vexed the Icelandic people like no other and which has attracted attention and condemnation from environmentalists the world over.

Increasing awareness has resulted in measures to reverse soil erosion, limit gravel mining in vol-

canic areas, to regulate the fishing that is essential to the economy. Other advances are stricter limits on off-road driving, and even cycling on mountain tracks.

The interior dam project

When, in 2003, the Icelandic government approved the building of a gigantic dam in an area of the uninhabited interior of the country known as Kárahnjúkar, the environmental movement gained a whole new *raison d'être*. The grand scheme, the country's biggest ever construction project, centered on a highland valley on the northeastern edge of the mighty Vatnajökull glacier, one of Europe's last areas of untouched wilderness and summer breeding grounds for the rare pink-footed goose. A graceless complex of nine dams and accompanying dykes has now been constructed to dam two rivers, the Jökulsá á Dal and the Jökulsá á Fljótsdal; the largest of the dams, fed by an artificial reservoir measuring 57 sq. km (22 sq. miles), is contained by

a 200-metre (650-ft) wall which can be seen for miles around. Hydroelectric power generated by the network of dams is channeled through a vast on-site power station to provide electricity for a new American-owned aluminium smelter just outside Reyðarfjörður in the East Fjords, which was due to start production as we went to press. Taken as a whole, the project will increase Iceland's production of hydroelectric power by 60 percent.

Not all local people are against it: in the East Fjords region, most are strongly in favour as the new plant will generate new jobs which are badly needed. Elsewhere in the country, particularly in the capital, people are less positive; in a high-profile protest even Björk's mother went on hunger-strike to express her heartfelt opposition to the construction plans. Indeed, in September 2006, the filling of the dam triggered the second biggest demonstration in Icelandic history, led by the former president, Vigdís Finnbogadóttir. Fifteen thousand people marched through the streets to gather outside the Icelandic parliament in protest. Opponents claim the Kárahnjúkur project is the first of many planned for Iceland and the government is wilfully selling off the country's pristine nature for international profit at a time when the price of aluminium on international markets is falling anyway.

Wearing away the soil

Land erosion is a problem in many countries, but in Iceland it presents a major environmental challenge. Human occupation since the time of the Settlement has caused more damage to the natural environment than in any other country in Europe. Iceland has lost 50 percent of its original vegetation and 95 percent of its tree cover; barren deserts have replaced vegetation and fertile soils, with the result that two thirds of Iceland's terrain is

---

LEFT: Iceland's glaciers are under threat from rising temperatures. **ABOVE:** much of the countryside remains unspoiled. **ABOVE RIGHT** the power station at Kárahnjúkar. **RIGHT:** grey seals in the West Fjords.

now subject to varying degrees of erosion, ranging from slight to extremely severe.

When the first settlers introduced sheep grazing to Iceland, following a well-established agricultural practice they knew from their home country, Norway, they unwittingly began the gradual destruction of entire areas of vegetation and forest. The sheep ate the fresh new shoots of plants and trees as soon as they appeared, with the result that entire forests were lost. Population growth put additional pressure on the country's natural resources and forests, which once provided shelter to smaller plants and shrubs from the heavy sea sprays, were also felled to provide fuel and much needed timber to build homes.

Efforts are now underway to reforest denuded regions and to try to manage the country's natural resources in a more sustainable manner. The soil reclamation project known as Hekluskógar (Hekla Forests) currently underway around the Hekla volcano in the south of Iceland is the biggest such programme in Europe. Its aim is to stop the spread of the desert which is occuring around the volcano and to reestablish the dense birch forest which disappeared here over two centuries ago. However the project's leader claims that without extra government funding the scheme will fail and the current desertification will continue and increase in the event of any eruption from the volcano. Environmentalists maintain that such a lack of funding and, moreover, approval of the Kárahjnúkar project, fly in the face of the government's stated aims of protecting the Icelandic countryside – and was clearly financially driven.

The marine environment

Naturally, protection of the land for an island nation, is just one area of concern. Control and regulation of the seas and fish stocks off Iceland is equally important and it was with this goal in mind that the government set a 200 mile limit for its territorial waters

following the Cod Wars with the United Kingdom in the 1970s, a standard which has since been established for international marine legislation. Part of the philosophy behind extending the fishing zone was not just to prevent foreign vessels as such, but also to be able to control how much fish was caught. After several years of bumper harvests, with the cod take nearing 508,000 tonnes (460,000 US tons) in 1982, the time came for holding back the nation's own fleet. A complex vessel quota system came into effect in 1984. In its present form, the system grants individual vessels tonnage quotas for individual species of fish based on recent catches, and the owners are free to swap or trade their quotas among themselves to maximize efficiency – and to make money. Originally aimed at the all-important cod, which is threatened with extinction, the quota system has tended to increase diversity among fishing vessels of other species, many of which are close to becoming overfished themselves now. Many skippers claim they have been transformed overnight from old-style heroic fishermen into accounts, armed no longer with nets and sea charts, but with chequebooks and spreadsheets. The government though claims the quota system should leave Iceland's main industry leaner, meaner and more able than ever to keep Iceland one of the wealthiest nations in the world. ❑

HARVESTING THE SEA

Fishing has provided food, employment and wealth for
Iceland for centuries; the challenge now is to avoid
over-exploiting the limited resources of the sea

"Life is saltfish," wrote Iceland's Nobel
Laureate, the late Halldór Laxness in the
1930s. At the beginning of the 21st century,
with the country's economy dependent on the sea
more than ever before, life is still saltfish, but it's
also canned fish, smoked salmon, frozen shrimps
and caviar.

Fish has been an important export item from
Iceland ever since the stockfish trade to Britain
commenced in the Middle Ages. But fishing only
began to outpace agriculture in economic status
with the advent of motorised fishing vessels
around the start of the 20th century.

And while improvements in vessel technology
soon made fisheries into Iceland's mainstay
national industry, at the same time they intensi-
fied the threat of overfishing by foreign deep-sea
fleets, which escalated until the famous Cod Wars
with Britain.

The first 30 years of the 20th century were a
time of intense, fisheries-led economic growth.
Iceland was gradually escaping from Danish colonial rule, and economic independence was an
obvious prerequisite for true political independence. Iceland's fishing industry has been
coloured by fierce nationalism ever since.

Salted whitefish – mainly cod, sold to Spain –
and iced whitefish and herring, sold to the UK and
northern Europe, were the mainstays of Icelandic
fisheries right up until World War II. Dependence
on those few markets had its limitations: for example, Spanish wine producers threatening to ban
imports of saltfish were able to "twist Iceland's
arm" into lifting a six-year alcohol prohibition in

RICHES FROM THE SEA

Situated in the region of the North Atlantic Ocean where
warm Gulf Stream waters merge with the cold currents
travelling down from the Arctic, Iceland's relatively
unpolluted fishing grounds offer near-perfect conditions
for an enormous variety of marine species. These include
demersal or bottom-feeding fish, led by cod, haddock,
redfish (ocean perch), saithe (pollack), ocean catfish and
flatfish such as Greenland halibut and plaice. There are
also shellfish such as shrimp, scallops and Norway
lobster (nephrops or scampi tails). Finally there are river-
migrating fish, such as wild salmon, trout and Arctic
charr, as well as pelagic (topwater) fish including herring
and capelin.

PRECEDING PAGES: the morning catch.
LEFT: fishing boat entering Heimaey harbour.
RIGHT: a fisherman at Þórshöfn in 1908.

1921. Later, the collapse of the fish market in the Great Depression devastated Iceland's economy.

The fish boom begins

Unemployment ran high right up until World War II, when Iceland suddenly became the only large fish-producer in the whole of northern Europe. Icing their catches, Icelandic fishing vessels sailed directly to Britain, often suffering fatalities from U-boat attacks. Meanwhile, superior freezing technology was developed. This would become the key to the postwar fisheries boom which was targeted at both the UK and American markets.

lation and absence of large-scale manufacturing industries keep "home-grown" pollution to a bare minimum. And Iceland has even begun exporting the technology for catching and handling fish: in some specialist areas, such as the electronic weighing of fish at sea using scales that automatically compensate for the roll of the boat, Iceland is a world leader.

Surviving in a high-risk industry

Seafood is, however, a notoriously shaky business – size of catches can never be taken for granted and prices fluctuate far more than in land-based food processing. Unstable as its economy has

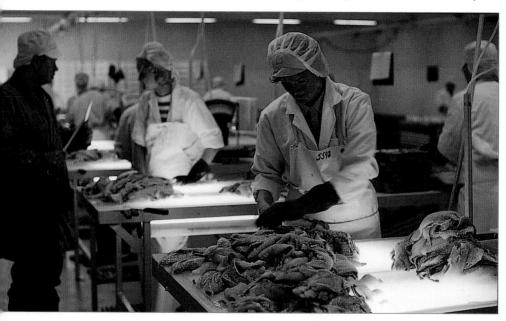

Iceland made good money during the war and allocated funds for the modernisation of the trawler fleet, and an era of larger catches and more diverse markets began. Frozen block and fillets went to both sides of the Atlantic. During the Cold War, Iceland kept good trading relations with Eastern Europe, and the Soviet Union became a major buyer of products such as salted herring. Meanwhile, the diversification began which remains the key to Iceland's survival as a specialist fish-producing nation.

Of increasing importance in this environmentally conscious age is the cleanness of Iceland's fish. The fishing grounds are far enough from the industrial centres of Europe and North America to remain very pure, while the small local popu-

been, Iceland has buffered itself against some heavy market shocks by shrewdly spreading its coverage and its product range.

The US was Iceland's main buyer of frozen fish from the 1970s to the mid-1980s, until a sliding dollar made Europe a more attractive proposition. Today, the two main European markets for both frozen and fresh (unprocessed) fish are the UK and Germany. Yet the two countries rarely compete, since the UK buys cod and haddock while the Germans prefer redfish and saithe. A north-south split in European buying trends also exists, with Portugal, Spain and Italy (which all rank among Iceland's top 10 market countries) buying almost entirely saltfish and virtually no frozen or fresh fish.

Japan, the world's largest seafood market, became important for Iceland in the 1980s, yet hardly competed with established lines sold elsewhere. The oriental taste is for flatfish, whole-frozen redfish (Europeans and Americans prefer fillets), shell-on shrimp (the British and Danes prefer peeled), and previously unexploited delicacies such as capelin roe, whole-frozen female herring, cod milt (sperm) and sea urchins. France has also shot up the market table recently, with a more catholic appetite than most other buyers.

In terms of demand, the future looks promising. Awareness of the healthiness of a protein-rich, low-cholesterol seafood diet, backed by the clean

although only 4.4 percent of Iceland's population is employed on fishing vessels and 5.6 percent in land-based processing plants.

The Cod Wars

The big problem since the start of the 1990s has been supply. Major stocks are at or beyond the maximum level of safe harvesting, and with a fleet powerful enough to vacuum-clean the ocean floor

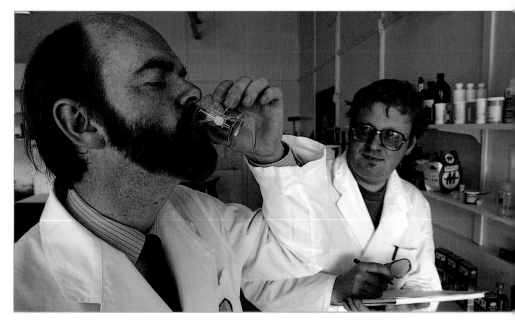

image of the waters where Iceland catches its fish, look set to keep demand buoyant well into the 21st century. An agreement negotiated in 1991 with the EC removes most remaining tariff barriers for fish from Iceland in the 19-nation European "supermarket." The onset of Creuztfeldt-Jacob and Foot and Mouth diseases has also led to an added demand for fish in important markets.

Fisheries contribute three quarters of Iceland's exports, and a seafood-led boom in 1987–88 saw the country's economy clock up one of the highest annual growth rates in Gross Domestic Product in European history, at over 8 percent. All this,

LEFT: fish-processing indoors.
ABOVE: testing cod-liver oil.

in a couple of weeks, the industry is being forced to scale down its operations. This is not a new problem. Overfishing by foreign fleets was a strong fear in Iceland in the early postwar period. The traditional 3-mile (5-km) exclusive fishing zone around Iceland's coast was extended to 4 miles (6.5 km) in 1952, and even though this seems like a drop in the ocean now, it sparked massive protests and a temporary ban on fish imports from Iceland in the UK. The first real "Cod War" began in 1959 when Iceland upped its territorial waters to 12 miles (20 km) and Royal Navy frigates were sent in to protect, unsuccessfully, British trawlers from being evicted or arrested by Iceland's tiny coastguard force.

Eventually the dispute was resolved, only to be

followed by successive extensions to 50 miles (80 km) in 1972 and 200 miles (330 km) in 1975. This renewed more ferocious clashes, although no fatalities ever occurred. While the British gunboats rammed coastguard vessels and fired shots over their bows, the ultimate deterrent in the Icelandic arsenal was the dreaded "clippers" – rather like garden shears – which were used to cut trawls from British vessels, removing both their nets and their catches. Some of these clippers are now proudly, if rather mock-heroically, on display in the National Museum in Reykjavík.

On one occasion, the world's press almost outnumbered the naval ratings when a British frigate

and Icelandic gunboat had a confrontation on the high seas. Fortunately, the opposing captains had a keen sense of occasion and the ensuing exchange was not of shots but of Biblical quotations which were delivered broadside by loudhailer. Initially taken aback, journalists managed to salvage just enough Scripture knowledge to award the result to the Icelandic team.

More considered formal arguments gradually swung international opinion over to Iceland's point of view, and a "truce" was eventually agreed in 1976 – by which time the UK itself had announced its own 200-mile limit. The territorial waters limit that Iceland established has since become a standard for international marine legislation.

Protecting the sea's bounty

In the wake of the Cod Wars, Iceland upgraded its fishing fleet. Part of the philosophy behind extending the fishing zone was not just to prevent foreign fishing as such, but also to be able to control how much was caught. After several years of bumper harvests, with the cod take nearing 508,000 tonnes (460,000 US tons) in 1982, the time came for holding back the nation's own fleet. Even as the Cod Wars were in full swing, Iceland had learned that it could overfish all by itself: the so-called "herring boom" in the Northeast collapsed in the late 1960s when the fish virtually disappeared from one season to the next.

A complex vessel quota system came into effect in 1984. In its present form, the system grants individual vessels tonnage quotas for individual species of fish based on recent catches, and the owners are free to swap or trade their quotas among themselves to maximize efficiency – and to make money.

Originally aimed at the all-important cod, the quota system has tended to increase diversification among fishing vessels of catches towards other species, most of which are also close to becoming overfished themselves now. Many skippers claim they have been transformed overnight from old-style heroic hunters into accountants, armed no longer with nets and maps but with chequebooks and spreadsheets. Unfortunately, years of poor spawning have forced the government to cut quotas regularly. Tradeable quotas have become a claim on a scarce resource and "paper fish" – the cod swimming unsuspectingly with a quota on its head – have grown in value at a rate that would draw looks of disbelief even from people who habitually play the money markets.

While the fleet's total quota for cod has been cut back, the cost of buying the rights to catch cod has jumped alarmingly. Small-boat operators claim that they are being priced out of business. Meanwhile, fish processors are finding that they can hardly make a profit on the highly priced raw fish: European processing companies are ready to pay more for unprocessed fish than domestic processors could get after salting or freezing it themselves.

Optimists say that these are just teething troubles – and that the quota system should leave Iceland's main industry leaner, meaner and more able than ever to keep Iceland one of the wealthiest nations in the world. ❑

LEFT: unloading crates of fish packed in ice.

Whaling

A long with environmental protection, whaling is one of the most hotly debated issues in Iceland today. Public opinion across the country is strongly in favour of whaling since most Icelanders regard the harvesting of the seas around their country as a virtual birthright. However, following a 20-year global moratorium on whaling introduced in 1986, Iceland continued whaling for a further three years, exploiting a loophole in the legislation and hunted whales as part of a "scientific whaling" programme. By 1989 when Iceland stopped all whaling amid a domestic political furore a further 292 fin whales and 70 sei whales had been killed for research. In the face of immense opposition from the Icelandic fishing industry and the general public, the Reykjavík government announced that it saw no alternative but to halt its whaling operations for the foreseeable future.

It was widely expected, though, that Iceland would resume whaling when the time was right. Indeed, just three years later, in 1992, the country pulled out of the International Whaling Commission (IWC), of which it had been a founding member, citing growing frustration with a protocol being drawn up which would reintroduce commerical hunting under strict international limits. It set up a rival organisation with Norway, Greenland and the Faroe Islands in the hope of challenging the power of the IWC. However, following an absence of ten years, Iceland rejoined the IWC in 2002 stating a reservation to the moratorium which, it claimed, gave the right to hunt commercially.

Amid an international outcry from conservation groups and anti-whaling nations, the Icelandic government announced in 2003 that it would catch 36 minke whales for "scientific research", later selling the meat commercially to the neighbouring Faroe Islands, whose government claimed it was exempt from a ban on importing whale meat (the Faroe Islands have self-rule under the Danish crown). This was seen as the first step towards the full resumption of commerical whaling. Sure enough, in late 2006, the government in Reykjavík announced that Iceland would resume the commercial hunting of whales and that its ships had the right to take nine fin whales (internationally

recognised as an endangered species) and 30 minke whales each year. In a statement, the Icelandic fisheries ministry claimed that the nation was dependent on living marine resources but that it would keep catches within sustainable limits. Anti-whaling nations argued that Iceland's reservation to the international moratorium was not legal and that the resumption was in contravention of the IWC; until 2006, Norway had been the only other country to hunt commerically. The aim of both countries is to export whale meat to Japan, the world's biggest market.

Prior to the 2006 announcement to resume hunting, Iceland had been gaining a reputation abroad

as one of Europe's premier whale-watching destinations. Indeed, a whole raft of companies had identified this niche in the tourist market and begun marketing whale-watching tours as part of a holiday to Iceland. Tourist leaders lost no time in pointing out to the government that butchering whales for the domestic food market was totally at odds with whale-watching and that Iceland's tourist trade would take a serious knock as a result. Indeed, Icelanders as a whole are aware that their fragile economy on the very edge of Europe can ill afford any form of international boycott, be it from tourists choosing to take their holidays elsewhere, or from anti-whaling nations refusing to import Icelandic fish and fish products which account for around 80 percent of the home economy. ❑

RIGHT: Iceland's decision to resume commercial whaling in 2006 has been deplored by environmentalists.

LIFE ON THE LAND

With a short growing season and land of variable fertility, the Icelanders have come up with inventive and successful ways of farming

In the early 20th century, Iceland's farmers still lived much as their forebears had done for 1,000 years: they kept their sheep, grazed them in summer on the highlands, cut the hay in summer, rounded up the animals in autumn. After the autumn slaughter, some of the livestock were foddered on hay through the winter, while the meat was salted, smoked and otherwise preserved. During the winter, wool was knitted and woven into clothes for the household.

Around 100 years ago, with Home Rule granted by Denmark, things began to change rapidly: aided by the cooperative movement, farming developed from a subsistence activity into a business. The countryside was transformed. Some of the most marginal regions became totally depopulated. Young people left in droves to seek education and a better life (and mechanisation meant far less labour was needed anyway). Roads and telephones made isolation a thing of the past.

There are still some 3,800 working farms in Iceland, but farmers are plagued with problems, from desertification to over-production. Over-production of lamb and milk has led to a quota system, but these have been reduced to the point where some farms have ceased to be viable. Some survive by tapping into the tourism boom, with farm-stay holidays a potentially lucrative business (and, after all, there are no quotas on tourists).

The years ahead are likely to bring greater competition. Protectionist legislation and heavy government subsidies have hitherto helped farmers survive, but these are likely to be threatened in future by Iceland's participation in the European Economic Area formed by EFTA (the European Free Trade Association) and the European Union.

ABOVE: ploughing farmland near Akureyri.

RIGHT: While the climate is too cool for growing many vegetables outdoors, inexpensive geothermal energy means that greenhouse cultivation can be profitable. Various salad crops are the mainstay, but hothouses can also produce bananas and grapes, although not usually on a commercial scale.

BELOW: Dairy farming grew rapidly in the 20th century, and is now big business. Supermarkets sell a vast range of milk, cream, cheese, butter, yoghurt and *skyr* (Icelandic milk-curd).

BELOW The roofs of rural homes were traditionally turf-clad for insulation. The memory of a time when all Icelanders lived off the land still grips the national imagination, but in reality the rural life was often one of hardship and struggle against an unforgiving environment.

SUPPLEMENTING THE DIET

Iceland's dramatic sea-cliffs, clustered with millions of birds, were once known as "pantries", and Icelanders would often have gone hungry had they not had the nourishment of these natural food stores. In all the areas where sea-bird colonies are found, men would clamber down the near-vertical cliff-faces, gathering eggs from the nests. Today sea-birds' eggs are still gathered in some quantity. *Sprang*, the art of swinging nimbly down a cliff-face on a long rope, is still a much-practised skill in the Vestmannaeyjar.

Regarded as a great delicacy by many, sea-birds' eggs are commonly eaten in coastal villages in season, and are sold in supermarkets. The eggs of the guillemot are those most often sold commercially. Other species were also hunted for food, and still are today, notably puffins and guillemots. Other than sea birds, the goose and ptarmigan are practically the only birds hunted for human consumption.

LEFT: The annual autumn sheep round-up takes place in early September, before the first snows fall on the uplands. Working in teams, the horsemen and their dogs systematically search the highland pastures for sheep. After two or three days all the sheep are accounted for, and are herded down to the lowlands and into a corral. All the local people gather to take part, and as evening falls, the festivities – *réttir* – commence.

BELOW: Iceland is too far north to grow cereal crops comfortably, as the climate is too cool and the growing season too short. A number of farmers have started to grow the hardier cereals, like rye and barley, with the help of fertilisers. These grains are used in animal fodder, replacing expensive imported cereals, and barley is also being grown for human consumption.

FOOD AND DRINK

A unique line in traditional delicacies provides variety from the ever-present, but high-quality, staples of fish and lamb. A plentiful supply of cosy restaurants makes eating out a pleasure.

Icelandic food is based on fish and lamb, the two ingredients most readily available in the country. Throughout the centuries they have been boiled fresh, and smoked, salted, pickled or dried to store for the winter months.

The fish is likely to be among the most exquisite you have ever tasted. Indeed, many Icelanders simply refuse to eat fish when they go abroad themselves because it just doesn't taste the same as it does back home. Fish generally arrives in the shops a matter of hours after it has been landed and is accordingly juicy, tender and fresh. Haddock and halibut are often boiled or grilled and served with a prawn sauce or simply with butter. Salmon and trout are served fresh or smoked – traditionally using dung. Thin slices of smoked fish are served with hot spring-baked rye bread. Try herring, smoked, pickled or the tinned variety in mustard or garlic sauce. Nothing is wasted and you will find cod's cheeks and roe alongside salmon and prawns on the fish counter.

When it comes to lamb, there's the smoked variety, often served in the home with pickled red cabbage and sugar-browned potatoes, which is mouthwateringly tender as well as regular lamb chops or steaks. Another favourite is smoked mutton, *hangikjöt*, which means "hung meat". Traditionally served with potatoes, white sauce and peas, *hangikjöt* is a festive dish, obligatory at least once over Christmas and New Year, but eagerly eaten at any time of the year and readily available in the supermarkets. In fact whatever form it comes in, Icelandic lamb, although rather expensive, is delicious since sheep are left to wander freely all summer long and graze on the herb rich pastures of the highland mountains before being rounded up in the autumn for slaughter; their meat is accordingly tasty and succulent.

Although fish and lamb are the mainstay of most restaurant menus throughout Iceland, chicken and beef are also popular. In fact, chicken has become increasingly popular in recent years since Iceland began producing its own fresh chicken meat. Before that all chicken was imported frozen. Be that as it may, chicken remains one of the most expensive meats available in Iceland.

Traditional delicacies

Whilst in Iceland look out for any restaurant serving up more traditional fare such as seabirds, particularly puffin and guillemot, which once sustained generations past but are now considered something of a delicacy. A particular favourite is smoked puffin, which has to be tasted to be believed, especially when accompanied by a delicate blueberry sauce. Seemingly Icelanders have no qualms about eating their national bird – after all, salted or smoked, puffins were one of the dietary staples of centuries past.

Many other traditional foods have survived to this day and are as popular as ever. Adventurous types in search of authentic food and blessed with a cast-iron stomach will relish the midwinter Þorrablót feast (mid-January to mid-February, although many items are available all year). The feast is largely an act of homage to the old methods of preserving food. One of the best places to

Accompanied by mashed turnips, it tastes better than it looks – even, surprisingly, the eyes. All cuts of the sheep's meat and innards are prepared in various ways, with pride of place going to pickled rams' testicles, pressed into a nightmarish cake. Not a dish for the faint of heart, but oddly digestible in small quantities.

Guts, blood, fat and a dash of meat for form's sake, nattily sown up in sheep's stomachs, create another dish appropriately called *slátur* (slaughter). *Slátur* is not confined to the midwinter feast; it is eaten regularly in Icelandic homes. The dish comes in two varieties: *lifrarpylsa*, which means "liver sausage" but isn't, and the darker, fattier

sample this traditional fare is at the Fjörukráin restaurant in Hafnarfjörður *(see page 167)*, just outside Reykjavík. Here you really can pretend you're back in Viking times and sample the strangest of dishes, washed down with generous amounts of beer or schnapps. Since almost everything a sheep can provide ends up on the Þorrablót menu, you shouldn't be surprised to spot *svið*, the sheep's head, burned to remove the wool and then boiled, staring at you from your plate. This delight is served up at the Þorrablót feast either in halves or off the bone and pressed into a kind of pâté.

LEFT: Reykjavík's Lobster House restaurant. **ABOVE:** the Þorrablot feast is a chance to sample medieval delicacies. **RIGHT:** salmon fishing estuary on the Hvitá river.

blóðmör or blood pudding, which is like Scottish haggis without the spice.

The crowing glory of a midwinter feast, and of many functions around the year, is the ceremonious intake of rotten shark *(hákarl)* and schnapps. After being buried for three months or more, shark becomes acrid and ammoniac, like the most nostril-defying of cheeses. Rubbery and rotten, it is washed down in small cubes with ample quantities of the Icelandic spirit, *brennivin* (Black Death). A few nips beforehand for courage's sake is not a bad idea! Icelanders view eating *hákarl* rather like the dark midwinter itself. It strikes an emotional chord deep within the soul and once over the joy of having survived makes life seem instantly brighter again.

Many of the specialities will not feature on the restaurant menu but can be bought at supermarkets, but should you be in the West Fjords, Cafe Riis in Hólmavík *(see page 227)* is renowned for its rotten shark – so why not pop in and tantalise your tastebuds.

Dairy products

Icelandic dairy produce is of high quality. Well worth a try as a dessert or even for lunch is *skyr*, a rich type of curd, high in calcium and low in calories, which resembles a thick, creamy yoghurt in consistency. Competition from flavoured yoghurt and ice cream has led dairy producers to create a number of varieties of *skyr* such as delicious blueberry, pear or more mainstream vanilla. However, the genuine article is still sold unflavoured, mildly sour and served with milk, or, ideally, cream stirred in. A fine topping is wild crowberries, available fresh in late summer and early autumn. You should make every effort whilst in Iceland to sample *skyr* since it is rarely available outside the country.

Súrmjólk, soured milk, is eaten at breakfast and with brown sugar. If you want normal milk, choose the cartons marked *nýmjólk* in the supermarket or *léttmjólk* which has a lower fat content. *Mysingur* is a sweet spread made from whey which is popu-

EATING OUT

Dining out in Iceland has undergone tremendous changes in the past twenty years or so. The number of restaurants has multiplied, and a diverse variety of ethnic food barely heard of in 1990 is now readily available in Reykjavík, though less so in the countryside. Also, a vast number of Icelandic chefs have sought training abroad and returned home to experiment with different ways of cooking traditional Icelandic ingredients. It has also become fashionable for restaurants to invite guest chefs to the country to concoct both their native and regional speciailties for Icelandic gourmet aficionados.

Icelandic restaurants tend to be of a high standard. And while in the past dining out in Iceland was invariably expensive, it need no longer be so. Many restaurants offer good-value special tourist menus or lunch or dinner buffets. There is usually an unlimited supply of fresh bread and butter, as well a a jug of cold tap water.

All establishments displaying a Tourist Menu sign offer a set menu during the summer months with a soup or starter followed by a fish or meat main course and coffee, for a fixed price. Prices are lower at lunch. Children under 6 usually eat free and 6–12 year olds pay half price. It is rare though to find these sorts of special offers outside the capital. Most restaurants are open for lunch 11.30am–2.30pm and evening meals 6–10.30pm or 11pm. In Reykjavík it is advisable to book ahead for evening meals, particularly at weekends.

lar with children. Icelandic cheeses, though tasty, are unlikely to overly excite the palate and there is no tradition of cheese eating after dinner found in some European countries. Cheese is generally of the mild Gouda-type yellow variety and rarely matured to develop its flavour.

Breads and pastries

Although sandwiches are generally served on familiar white, or occasionally on wholegrain sliced bread, there are several other varieties of bread you should look out for whilst at the bakery. Rye is a popular ingredient in bread making across the Nordic countries and no less so in Iceland where a particular favourite is a loaf of filling and extremely healthy rye bread, often consumed at breakfast with toppings of ham, cheese, pâté or jam. Rye is also the key ingredient in the delicious *flatkökur*, which as the name suggests are flat, rounded pancakes. These can be found in most corner shops and supermarkets across the country and are a good source of fibre and excellent for picnics. Pastries can usually be found in super-markets as well as bakeries and are similar to their equivalents elsewhere in Scandinavia, particularly in Denmark. The most common pastry, devoured with gusto over a cup of strong coffee, is a square-shaped folded pastry which contains a sweet, gooey vanilla filling. Cinammon buns are also commonly eaten with coffee and are as delicious as you might imagine.

Fruit and vegetables

Although Iceland proudly boasts that it can pro-duce its own bananas in greenhouses in the south of the country, much of the country's fruit and vegetables is still produced abroad and imported. Unfortunately, long transit times north to Reyk-javík by freighter can take their toll on the fresh-ness of the produce on offer, particularly in smaller supermarkets in the countryside. When out shopping you should be sure to carefully pick through the vegetables and fruit on sale to get the very freshest; onions, especially, can be rotten on the inside. Although vegetarianism is widely known, and respected in Iceland, it is not com-mon and vegetarians intent on holidaying in Ice-land are advised to bring vitamin supplements to enhance their diet which is most likely to consist of pizzas and uninspiring salads.

LEFT: gourmet party at a cosy Reykjavík restaurant.
RIGHT: Brennivin, the local spirit.

What to drink

Coffee is undoubtedly the national drink of Ice-land. At seemingly anytime of day people drink coffee from early morning to late at night, at home, at work or even walking down the street. In fact in recent years, there's been a vertible explosion in the coffee culture in Iceland and it's now possible to get expertly brewed espressos, cuppuccinos and lattes, just like elsewhere in Europe and the US. At lunchtime in particular the favoured drink is sim-ply a glass of water or even milk.

With dinner, beer or wine naturally are popular, though the inflated price of alcohol is often the decisive factor in determining whether diners will

order wine by the glass or the bottle in a restau-rant. Wine prices in Icelandic restaurants are sky-high. The bottle that is expensive enough at the state liquor store will invariably be around three times higher in price at a restaurant. Even house wines generally cost around ISK600 per glass.

You should reckon on paying upwards of ISK5000 for a decent bottle of wine in a good restaurant. Beer, whilst not exactly inexpensive, is generally a much more affordable ISK600–700 per half litre. All this means that most Icelanders don't eat out on a regular basis.

Iceland's local home-produced drink is Bren-nivin, a caraway-seed-flavoured spirit, drunk icy cold. It is generally referred to as "Black Death", to give you an idea of its strength. ❑

A NATURALIST'S PARADISE

Iceland is home to, or a stopping off point for, a wide variety of birdlife. And although it has only one indigenous land mammal, the arctic fox, there are a number of introduced species. Its seas are rich in marine mammals

Any traveller to Iceland with even a vague interest in birdlife should bring along a pair of binoculars and a good ornithological guide. Around 70 species of birds breed annually in every corner of Iceland (including year-round residents and those which migrate to Iceland each spring), while a total of over 300 different species have been seen in the country at one time or another.

Some species regularly winter in Iceland before flying further north to breed in summer. Others are birds of passage stopping off on a long migratory journey. Many are accidentals – individual birds which have drifted across the ocean on prevailing winds; those of North American origin are of great interest to European bird-watchers – the majority of sightings of these birds are in the south during the autumn months.

Seventy breeding species is not a great deal, although the actual bird population is numerically large: some of the commonest species, like the puffin, are present in millions. The Icelandic environment is particularly favourable to sea birds, which make up 23 of the country's breeding species *(see also pages 228–9)*, while it is less welcoming for passerines (perching birds) – with the principal food source – insects – in short supply. While about 60 percent of the world's birds are passerines, they make up only one seventh of Iceland's avian population.

Most of Iceland's birds are also found in Scandinavia and Northern Europe. Three species, however, are American: the Barrow's goldeneye, the great northern diver or common loon, and the harlequin duck, which breed practically nowhere else outside North America.

LEFT: bird-watching by the Jökulsárlón iceberg lagoon in Southeast Iceland. **RIGHT:** the great northern diver.

Heralds of spring

Both the arctic tern and the golden plover are migratory birds commonly regarded as harbingers of spring. The golden plover, which generally arrives in early April, is a particular favourite with Icelandic poets:

> Lóan er komin að kveða burt snjóinn,
> kveða burt leiðindin, það getur hún.
> Hún hefur sagt mér að senn komi spóinn,
> sólskin í heiði og blómstur í tún.

"The plover has come and she'll sing away winter / Drive off all sorrow as only she can / She says that the whimbrel soon will be coming / Sun on the valley and hayfields in bloom."

The arctic tern, which usually appears in early May, is one of the wonders of the ornithological world. It migrates each spring from Antarctica, 17,000 km (10,500 miles) away. The arctic tern is a graceful flyer, often seen hovering over water. It also makes unnerving "dive-bombing" attacks on humans who enter its nesting colonies in June and July, screeching "*kría!*" (also the bird's name in Icelandic).

The puffin is Iceland's commonest bird, with a population of 8–10 million. The comically digni-fied stance of this decorative bird has earned it the nickname of *Prófastur* (The Dean). Around the third to fourth week of May each year, puffins start flying ashore for the breeding season, after spending the winter out on the North Atlantic.

Rare birds

One of the most famous of the island's bird species is, sadly, extinct. The great auk *(Pinguinus impen-nis)* was a big, awkward, flightless sea bird, about 70 cm (27 in) high, and very tasty, according to the fishermen who hunted it for food. The last two great auks were clubbed to death on Eldey in 1844 *(see also* Iceland's Sea Birds *on pages 228–9).* The Natural History Museum in Reykjavík has on dis-play a stuffed great auk, originally part of the taxi-dermic collection of a Danish nobleman, which was bought at auction in London in 1971.

Today all rare and endangered species are pro-tected by law. An endangered species native to

Their main breeding grounds are on sea-cliffs (particularly in the Vestmannaeyjar/Westmann Islands and the West Fjords), and also on low-lying offshore islands such as Grímsey.

These unusual birds do not simply build a nest – they dig a burrow, up to 1.5 metres (5 ft) deep, where a single egg is laid. On the sea cliff, puffins are usually found nesting at the top, where a little soil and vegetation provides the space to dig. Puffin pairs will return year after year to the same burrow. After the Vestman-naeyjar on Heimaey eruption in 1973, many returned to find their burrows buried under a thick layer of lava. Rather than nest elsewhere, they tried to burrow to their old nesting places; some died in the attempt.

Iceland is the gyrfalcon, the largest of all falcons at 51–60 cm (20–23 in) long. About 200 pairs are estimated to breed each year. The gyrfalcon has a colourful history as one of Iceland's most presti-gious and valuable exports. Due to their skill and manoeuvrability in the air, gyrfalcons were prized as hunting birds and made gifts fit for kings and princes. In medieval times, up to 200 trained birds were exported each year, and in the 16th century the king of Denmark (who also ruled over Iceland) claimed a monopoly on the trade, which made a significant contribution to the royal coffers.

Although falconry largely died out in Europe by the 18th century, it continues in other parts of the world. Even today, an illicit trade in hunting falcons exists, and isolated attempts have been made in recent years to steal falcon eggs and chicks and smuggle them out of the country. The smugglers (including, on one occasion, a German "tourist" with two chicks hidden in his luggage) have been apprehended and heavily fined. Iceland's gyrfalcons enjoy special protection: their nesting places are kept secret, and carefully monitored. No-one may approach the nests, or photograph them, except by permission of the Ministry of Culture.

The gyrfalcon lives in close community with its preferred prey, the ptarmigan, although it also hunts down other birds when ptarmigans are unavailable. Humans share the falcon's taste for

aesalon. It lives mostly on passerines such as redwings, wheatears and meadow pipits.

Lord of the skies

The largest of Iceland's birds of prey is the white-tailed eagle, up to 90 cm (3 ft) long, with a wingspan of up to 2.5 metres (8 ft). This is a close relative of the bald eagle, the US national bird. It is a rare sight

ptarmigan (*Lagopus mutus*), a species of grouse. Considerably smaller at 35 cm (13 in) than its European relatives, the red and black grouse and the capercaillie, the ptarmigan adopts protective white colouring in winter. This does not stop hunters going out to shoot it in large numbers throughout the winter hunting season.

The gyrfalcon may be spotted in most parts of the country, but Iceland's most numerous bird of prey is the merlin. Smaller than the gyrfalcon at 27–32 cm (10–12 in) long, the Icelandic merlin is a unique subspecies, *Falco columbarius sub-*

LEFT: Barrow's goldeneyes, one of three American species to breed in Iceland.
ABOVE: a gyrfalcon.

today, following determined extermination. During the early 19th century, there were 200–300 breeding pairs in Iceland. The bird was accused, however, of carrying off lambs, and it certainly disturbed eider colonies by taking both eggs and chicks. A bounty was offered for eagles. They were shot and poisoned by farmers and eider breeders until, in 1920, only 10 pairs remained. Since 1913 the eagle has been protected by law, and is making a slow recovery. Today breeding pairs number 35 to 40, so prospects for the future seem promising.

By the sea

Iceland's coasts and offshore islands provide marvellous opportunities to see sea birds at close quarters. The islands of Breiðafjörður, for instance, teem with shag and cormorant, and the occasional white-tailed eagle may be seen. The grey phalarope (which is much rarer than its red-necked cousin) also breeds on the islands. On sightseeing cruises from Stykkishólmur, birdwatchers can sail in close to see the birds.

Bird cliffs are found in many places around the country, although the mixture of species nesting on the cliffs varies from region to region. The common guillemot, for instance, prefers the north, while the Brunnich's guillemot is found most commonly in the south. Sea-cliffs provide ledges and hollows not only for the ubiquitous puffin, but also for fulmars, kittiwakes, guillemots and razorbills.

Látrabjarg, at Iceland's westernmost point, is one of the world's great bird-cliffs. Sixteen km (10 miles) long, the cliffs soar 500 metres (1,600 ft) up from the sea. The cliffs that fringe Hælavíkurbjarg and Hornbjarg, in the far northwest, are less accessible, but certainly no less spectacular. Other bird-cliffs can be seen on the Vestmannaeyjar (accessible by sightseeing cruises from the main island, Heimaey), plus Krísuvíkurbjarg on the southwestern peninsula, Reykjanes. The Snæfellsnes peninsula, in the west, is also an excellent area for viewing cliff birds and other seabird species.

Grímsey island, 40 km (25 miles) off the north coast, is a must for birdwatchers, with dramatic bird-cliffs. It is also the only Icelandic habitat of the very rare little auk, which is so well protected by law that you need to obtain a permit simply to approach the nesting area. About 16,000 pairs of gannets nest on Eldey island off the Reykjanes peninsula, the fourth-largest gannet colony in the world. Casual birdwatchers, however, are not welcome as Eldey is a closely protected bird sanctuary.

Bogs, marshes and wetlands also provide important habitats for many species of birds, including the whooper swan, the greylag goose, and waders like the whimbrel and golden plover. In Þjórsárver, in the depths of the highlands, Iceland boasts one of the largest breeding sites of the pink-footed goose. About 10,000 pairs of pink-footed geese, winter residents in England and Scotland, breed here each year.

The southern coast of Iceland is a particular favourite with birdwatchers who are on the lookout for exotic "accidentals", lost birds that have

BIRDLIFE AT LAKE MÝVATN

Lake Mývatn *(see pages 261–7)*, in the north, is a unique natural phenomenon; a large lake, 37 sq. km (14 sq. miles) in area, yet with a depth of only 1–4 metres (3–13 ft). It is also fed by underground hot streams from the adjacent active geothermal and volcanic area, which raise the temperature higher than one would expect both at this northerly latitude and at its altitude of 277 metres (908 ft) above sea level. Even in severe winters, the lake never freezes completely, thanks to this input of warm water.

This benign environment means that Mývatn is a paradise for ducks, providing lavish feeding whether for divers or dabblers, and all of Iceland's duck species save the eider (which prefers life at sea) are found breeding here.

Most common is the tufted duck (with an estimated 3,000 pairs), then the scaup (1,700 pairs) and Barrow's goldeneye (700 pairs). Other common species include the common scoter, red-breasted merganser, long-tailed duck, gadwall and teal, while the mallard and pintail are less common. The goosander, shoveller and pochard are rare. The harlequin, which likes fast-flowing waters, is found on the adjacent Laxá river.

Many other bird species are also found in the unspoiled countryside around the lake. The Slavonian grebe nests at Mývatn, and the short-eared owl on nearby marshes, along with snipe and red-necked phalarope. Merlins and gyrfalcons nest in the nearby mountainous areas.

flown from North America and mainland Europe. At Skaftafell National Park, an excellent location for birdwatching, the wren is particularly common. Though the smallest of all the Icelandic birds at 12–13 cm (5 in), it is larger than wrens in nearby countries, and is defined as a special subspecies, *Troglodytes troglodytes islandicus*.

One Icelandic bird you cannot expect to see is the water rail. This extremely shy species is so wary and elusive that it has hardly ever been photographed, although its call may be heard in its typical habitat, reedbanks edging marshy lowlands. Wholesale draining of marshland has slowly but surely been destroying the water rail's

Mammals in the wild

Because Iceland was never connected to any of the ancient land masses, it's hardly surprising that it has few native animals – although a variety of marine mammals have been established on its coasts for millennia.

The only land-based Icelandic mammal which pre-dates the settlement in the 9th century is the arctic fox *(Alopex lagopus)*, a small breed found throughout the Arctic region. Two variants exist: the "blue", relatively rare in other Arctic areas, comprises about two-thirds of Iceland's fox population; it is dark brown in summer, and turns a lighter brown in winter, with a bluish sheen. The

habitat, and it is also an easy prey for the fast-moving and bloodthirsty mink, so its call may not be heard in the marshes of Iceland for very much longer.

From common-or-garden sparrows, starlings (Icelandic residents only since 1912) and redwings to the rarely glimpsed white-tailed eagle or little auk, Iceland promises the birdwatcher endless pleasure. Even those who cannot tell a hawk from a handsaw may find themselves flicking through ornithological guides in search of identifying features.

LEFT: a white-tailed eagle, one of the most spectacular species in Iceland, moves in for the kill.
ABOVE: a great skua on the lookout for prey.

"white" variety only lives up to its name when in winter camouflage; its summer coat is greyish-brown with a grey or white belly. Exceptionally well insulated, the arctic fox grows a thick and furry winter coat, including fur on the soles of its paws.

Icelandic farmers have always believed that foxes killed lambs, and retaliated by trying to exterminate them, simply going out with their shotguns, shooting to kill. Research has, however, shown that Iceland's foxes pose little threat to livestock, and today, it is no longer regarded as an unmitigated pest – fox-hunting aims only to control numbers. In recent years, a few commercial species of fox have been imported to farm for their fur. Some have, however, escaped to the wild and mated with native arctic foxes, producing hybrids.

Rodent residents

Iceland has several naturalised mammals introduced, deliberately or not, over the years. Four
rodent species have settled here, arriving as stow-
aways on ships. These are the long-tailed field
mouse or wood mouse (*Apodemus sylvaticus*),
house mouse (*Mus musculus*), brown rat (*Rattus
norvegicus*) and black rat (*Rattus rattus*). The
house mouse, brown rat and black rat are only
found in and around urban areas; of them only the
brown rat is common.

The long-tailed field mouse (a uniquely
Icelandic sub-species, *Apodemus sylvaticus
grandiculus*) certainly deserves its name, with a

rapidly to every region. The black rat has been
sighted from time to time since 1919, but is not
firmly established.

Another addition to Icelandic fauna was accidentally introduced into the wild. The American
mink (*Mustela vison*) was brought to Iceland in the
1930s for the first attempts at fur farming, but a
number of animals escaped. Within 35 years, the
species had spread all over the country except for
the central highlands, a localised area of the southeast and some islands. These blood-thirsty preda-
tors cause havoc among nesting birds such as
puffins, guillemots, ducks and eiders by taking eggs
and chicks. They also feed on fish, small birds and

tail as long as its body (8–10 cm/3–4 inches). It is
found all over the country, near human habitation
and in remote areas. The mouse lives mostly off
the land, eating plants, berries and fungi, as well
as small insects. It does not hibernate, and sometimes takes shelter in houses and outbuildings in
cold weather.

Both the house mouse and long-tailed mouse
are long-established residents in Iceland, probably dating back to the original settlement.
Some zoologists believe that the long-tailed
mouse must, like the fox, pre-date human habitation, as 1,000 years would not account for the
development of this sub-species' differences
from its mainland cousins. The brown rat is
believed to have arrived in 1840, and spread

mammals. They are hunted by farmers, although
their numbers remain high.

Imports from Lapland

Another of Iceland's wild mammals is a
reminder of a well-meaning but misguided
attempt to alter the Icelandic way of life. Several dozen reindeer (*Rangifer tarandus*) were
introduced from northern Scandinavia in the
1771–87, when the Icelanders lived in penury,
on the verge of starvation. The beasts were
imported on the grounds that some Icelanders
could adopt the nomadic herders' existence of
the Sami people, also known as Lapps, in northern Norway, Sweden and Finland. The experiment did not work and the reindeer reverted to

the wild, to add an exotic touch to the uplands, and some meat to hunters' tables.

By 1817, reindeer were widely distributed in many areas, and their growing numbers gave rise to fears that they were overgrazing the upland pastures, traditionally sacrosanct to the sheep. A royal charter of 1817 permitted unlimited hunting of the animals, except for juveniles under a year old. Half a century of indiscriminate slaughter left the reindeer stocks in a poor state by 1882, when hunting was restricted.

Thanks to a total hunting ban from 1901 to 1940, the herds made an excellent recovery, and the population is now about 3,000. The reindeer is

ox (*Ovibos moschatus*) and the snowshoe or mountain hare (*Lepus timidus*) into Iceland, but with no success.

Examples of Iceland's wild mammals, which are at times hard to spot in the wild, can be viewed at Reykjavík's zoo: fox, mink and reindeer in semi-wild open-air pens.

Mammals of the sea

A range of marine mammals have been long established around Iceland's rugged coast. Seals are most likely to be spotted. Breeding in Iceland are two species, the common or harbour seal and the grey seal – Iceland boasts about half the world pop-

protected, but in most years a limited cull is allowed to control the population.

Herds of deer are now found only in the mountains and valleys in the east of Iceland. They graze on mosses, fungi, lichens and grasses, but will also nibble shoots of shrubs and young trees. The shy creatures can rarely be spotted in summer, but in the depths of winter they sometimes descend to lowland farms and villages in search of adequate grazing.

Attempts have been made to introduce the musk

FAR LEFT: an arctic fox, Iceland's only indigenous land mammal, in its brown summer coat.
LEFT: a baby grey seal in the West Fjords.
ABOVE: a successful whale-watching trip.

ulation of harbour seals, which often can be seen sunning themselves on the black sands of remote fjords. Five other species breed on Greenland and the polar ice floes but make occasional visits to northern Iceland: they include the ringed, bearded, harp and hooded seals, and the Atlantic walrus. The walrus is probably the least frequent visitor.

Iceland was famous in the Middle Ages for the whales off its coast and these days whale-watching tours do a booming business. The most common by far is the killer whale, or orca, which hunts in shallow waters. Of the larger whale species, the sperm, fin, humpback and minke whales are probably the most common. Off the south coast, dolphins are frequently seen, especially in late spring and summer. ❏

PLACES

A detailed guide to every region of Iceland, with
principal sites clearly cross-referenced by number
to the maps

Iceland is one of the world's most spectacular destinations, its
vast empty landscapes illuminated by sparkling clear sub-arctic
air, cosy fishing villages sheltering from Atlantic storms beneath
gargantuan cliffs, a paradise for anyone with a love of nature and
the great outdoors. The whole experience is lent a surreal edge by
the presence of the restless tectonic activity beneath.

Each region has its own attractions. Reykjavík is a pleasantly
small, personable and lively capital city, the perfect base for
exploring the so-called "Golden Circle", which includes some of
Iceland's best-known natural spectacles, such as the waterfall Gullfoss, the
eponymous Geysir and Iceland's historical centre, Þingvellir. Also within easy
reach is the amazing Blue Lagoon spa resort. Beyond the black sand beach at
Vík, Iceland's southernmost point, lie Iceland's most accessible glaciers and
Skaftafell National Park, a favourite hiking spot among locals.

North of Reykjavík is the historic Snæfellsnes Peninsula, setting for many
Icelandic sagas, while further north is the remote, windswept West Fjords

region with some of the wildest (and wettest) landscapes in
Iceland. Akureyri, Iceland's only large town outside of the
capital, is the jumping-off point for exploring the North.
Nearby Lake Mývatn is Iceland's most popular tourist spot
outside the "Golden Circle", where dramatic volcanic
activity can be seen at close range. In the Northeast is
Jökulsárgljúfur National Park, an awe-inspiring series of
canyons leading to Dettifoss, Europe's most powerful
waterfall. The East Fjords region is an area of quiet fishing
villages and rugged scenery.

Finally, there is the interior – an area quite different from the rest of Iceland.
Almost all coastal roads, including the "Ring Road" that circles the country, are
passable in two-wheel drive cars; the various routes through the interior demand four-wheel drive or a specially designed touring bus. The
coast has hundreds of villages and farms offering accommodation; in
the interior, camping is the only option. Weather by the coast is relatively warm, if often wet; temperatures in the interior can plunge to
dangerous levels without warning.   ❑

PRECEDING PAGES: Jökulsárlon lagoon; Strokkur geyser in mid-spurt; Ásmundur
Sveinsson Sculpture Gallery. **LEFT:** hiking in the West Fjords. **TOP:** Austurvöllur Square
in central Reykjavík. **ABOVE:** Gullfoss waterfall. **RIGHT:** the Snæfellsnes peninsula.

Arctic Circle

G r e e n l a n d   S e a

Straumnes

H o r n s t r a n d i r

Bolungarvík

Suðureyri

Ísafjörður

Ísafjarðardjúp

Drangajökull
▲
925

Norðurfjörður

Rifsnes

S k a g a f j ö r ð u r

S k a g a h e i ð i

Malmey

Ho

76

Kópur

Þingeyri

61

A r n a r f j ö r ð u r

Bíldudalur

60

G l á m a

Hólmavík

Skagaströnd

H ú n a f l ó i

Sauðárkrókur

H a r a ð s v í t n

Patreksfjörður

B a r ð a s t r ö n d

Blönduós

Bjargtangar

Skáleyjar

Flatey

Króksfjarðarnes

Hóp

Hvammstangi

V a t n s d a l u r

B l a n d a

Blöndu

B r e i ð a f j ö r ð u r

Laugar

60

68

Borðeyri

G r í m s t u n g u h e i ð i

Blöndu

Stykkishólmur

Hvammsfjörður

Búðardalur

57

A r n a r v a t n s h e i ð i

Hellisandur

Öndverðarnes

Þjóðgarður
Snæfellsjökull

Ólafsvík

Grundarfjörður

S n æ f e l l s n e s

Norðurárdalur

Eiríksjökull

K j ö l u r

54

M ý r a r

Hvítá

LANGJÖKULL

Hvítárvatn

Borgarnes

F a x a f l ó i

52

Miðsandur

Gullfoss

Akranes

H v í t á

E s j a

Þjóðgarður
Þingvellir

Reykjavík

36

Þingvallavatn

Búrfell

Sandgerði

Hafnarfjörður

30

Keflavík

41

Vogar

Hveragerði

32

Hekla
1491

Fjall

Njarðvík

Reykjanesfólkvangur

Selfoss

26

V a t n a f j ö l l

Eldey

42

Ólfusá

Þjórsá

Grindavík

Þorlákshöfn

Hella

Hvolsvöllur

MÝRD

JÖKL

Markarfljót

Skógar

Vestmannaeyjar

Heimaey

Surtsey

Iceland

0   40 km
0   40 miles

REYKJAVÍK

The world's northernmost capital is a bright, colourful city. Rich in cultural attractions and with a vibrant nightlife, Reykjavík also has parks and wildlife areas surprisingly close to its centre

Visitors are often unsure whether Reykjavík is a scaled-down city or scaled-up village. Probably it is both. Housing around two thirds of Iceland's population, it is the undisputed political, business, cultural and intellectual centre of the country. Yet it retains a certain slow pace and almost rustic charm that makes it unique amongst the world's capitals. From the higher elevations the eye is drawn across the bay to the flat-topped mountain of Esja, often snowbound, its cold grey bulk a constant reminder of the sub-arctic location.

It was here that the "official" settlement of Iceland began, after a few false starts, in the late 9th century AD. For centuries there was little to distinguish it from any other cluster of farms elsewhere in the country, although the strands of its noble fate had already been woven: while the practical details of settlement and development were entrusted to man, the site itself was originally chosen by the pagan gods. Ingólfur Arnarson, who has been given the title First Settler of Iceland, brought with him from Norway not only his family and cattle but also the high seat that was the symbol of the homestead. Following established Viking custom, Ingólfur dutifully tossed overboard the pillars on which the high seat was mounted – wherever they washed ashore, that was where the gods willed him to live.

It took over three years for Ingólfur's slaves to find the pillars, while the Viking himself stayed temporarily in the south, but eventually they turned up on the shores of what is now Iceland's capital. One of the slaves, less than impressed with the gods' choice, snapped that "to no avail we have crossed fine districts to live on this outlying wilderness", and ran off with one of Ingólfur's maidservants. But the other slave, Vífill, was given his freedom; he lived at Vífilsstaðir, now the site of a sanatorium, between Reykjavík and neighbouring Garðabær, just to the south of the city. Ingólfur himself submitted to the gods' judgement and probably built

Main attractions
AÐALSTRÆTI
CULTURE HOUSE
NATIONAL MUSEUM
HALLGRÍMSKIRKJA CHURCH
SAGA MUSEUM
NIGHTLIFE

PRECEDING PAGES: Leifur Eiríksson by the Hallgrímskirkja. **LEFT:** the city in winter. **BELOW:** geothermally heated pool at Laugardalur.

Viðey 29 ★ Lundey

Reykjavík

0   400 m
0   400 yds

LAUGARNES

27 Safn Sigurjóns Ólafssonar (Sigurjón Ólafsson Museum)

Sundagarðar

Sundlaugarvegur

Laugarnesvegur

Dalbraut

Sæbraut

SUNDAHÖFN

Vatnagarðar

æbraut

Kirkjuteigur

Laugardalslaug (Swimming Pool)

TEIGAR

LAUGARÁS

Laugardalsvöllur (Sports Stadium)

Kleppsvegur

Efstasund

Sandsund

Skútuvogur

Sigtún

LAUGARDALUR

Laugarásvegur

Sunnuvegur

26 Ásmundarsafn (Ásmundur Sveinsson Sculpture Gallery)

Laugardalshöllin (Sports Hall)

Suðurlandsbraut

Skautasvell (Skating Rink)

25 Grasagarðurinn (Botanical Gardens)

Holtavegur

Langholtsvegur

SUND

Barðavogur

mannaskólinn vigation School)

★ Húsdýragarðurinn (Farm Animal Zoo)

Ármúli

Engjavegur

MÚLAR

Fjölskyldugarðurinn (Family Park) 24

Armeiri

Kringlumýrarbraut

Hallarmúli

Safamýri

City Centre

0   200 m
0   200 yds

Vesturgata

Geirsgata

Tryggvagata

Kalkofnsvegur

Laugarnes

Hús Verslunarinnar (House of Commerce)

Öldugata

Fischersund

3 Reykjavík Art Museum

4 Kolaportið Flea Market

Hafnarstræti

Ingólfur Statue

Lækjartorg

7 Þjóðmenningarhúsið (Culture House)

Skúlagata

Klapparstígur

Frakkastígur

Kringlan Shopping Mall

Túngata

Kapólska kirkjan

5 1 Austurstræti

Aðalstræti

AUSTURVÖLLUR

2 6 Stjórnarráðið (Government House)

Þjóðleikhúsið (National Theatre)

Borgarleikhúsið (City Theatre)

28 Árbæjarsafn (Árbær Open-Air Museum)

Hávallagata

Garðastræti

9 Alþingishúsið (Parliament Building)

Vonarstræti

Dómkirkjan

Iðnó

Lækjargata

Þingholtsstræti

Hverfisgata

18 Nýlistasafnið (Living Art Museum)

Laugavegur

Grettisgata

Listabraut

Suðurgata

11 Ráðhús Reykjavíkur (City Hall)

Skólavörðustígur

Bergstaðastræti

Ljósvallagata

† † † † †
† † † † †
† † † † †
† † † † †

10 Tjörn

Frikirkjuvegur

Fríkirkjan

8 Listasafn Íslands (National Gallery)

Bankastræti

15 Hallgrímskirkja

Hávarðsstaðir

Hafnarstræti

Tjarnargata

Skothúsvegur

Hellusund

Barónsstígur

Njarðargata

14 Þjóðarbókhlaðan (National and University Library)

Hljómskálinn (Music Tower)

16 Safn Einars Jónssonar (Einar Jónsson Museum)

Bústaðavegur

Hringbraut

13 Þjóðminjasafn Íslands (National Museum)

Sóleyjargata

Njálsgata

Bragagata

17 Ásgrímssafn (Ásgrímur Jónsson Collection)

Mímisvegur

Sjúkrahús Reykjavíkur (City Hospital)

Háskóli Íslands (University of Iceland)

12

Laufásvegur

Baldursgata

Barónsstígur

★ Keflavík

★ Keflavík

Reykjavík's climate is mild for its latitude, but the city still gets plenty of snow between November and March.

BELOW: summertime in Austurvöllur town plaza.

his house in the old city centre, with a view of the duck-filled lake, Tjörnin.

In the shadow of steam

The First Settler, Ingólfur, named his new home Reykjavík (Smoky Bay), after clouds he saw rising from the ground, probably in what is now the Laugardalur area. The "smoke" was steam from geothermal springs – ironically, the same "smoke" that today makes Reykjavík an almost completely pollution-free city. The first pipes bringing hot water to the city were laid in 1930. Today all the city's houses are heated from natural geothermal sources, removing the need for fossil fuels.

As for Ingólfur, he still has a presence in the shape of one of the statues so characteristic of the capital (by Einar Jónsson, 1874–1954). The First Settler is now perched atop **Arnarhóll hill**, at the virtual centre point of the city, next to Government House, his back turned upon the Culture House *(see page 151)*. The statue gazes across the harbour to where, on a clear day, the glacial cap of Snaefellsjökull glimmers mystically on the horizon, some 100 km (60 miles) away to the north.

Reykjavík today

For a visitor, the old city centre is definitely the most charming part of the capital. Well-to-do residential streets, with their brightly coloured corrugated-metal-clad houses and mossy lawns enclosed by picket fences, run alongside the shops, cafés and galleries of the main commercial thoroughfares. In contrast to the compact centre, Reykjavík's sprawling suburbs extend eastwards for mile after mile, all drab apartment blocks and busy roads.

The city as a whole has been undergoing a transformation of character in the past ten or fifteen years. Whereas visitors to Iceland once considered Reykjavík little more than a stopover en route to the country's undisputed main attraction – the landscape – the capital has now earned its stripes as a destination in its own right (a process encouraged by the availability of cheaper flights since the turn of the century). Its energetic and distinctive cultural scene is a constant source of fascination. After all, what other city with a population of a little over 100,000 has an internationally acclaimed symphony orchestra, two major professional theatre companies, numerous independent theatre groups, an opera company, a national ballet and both a national and municipal art gallery? On top of this, dozens of smaller independent galleries and venues offer continuous exhibitions, recitals and performances throughout the year, and a biannual arts festival attracts numerous renowned artists of international standing.

Reykjavík nightlife has also been discovered by visitors from around the world eager for something different and vibrant. The city's reputation as a "happening" place has largely grown out of the success of pop diva Björk since the early 1990s and the roster of international stars that have since taken to visiting the country. The international press has taken note, and reporters are routinely sent over to document the merriment.

Unlikely as it may sound, Reykjavík has also become increasingly popular as an attractive option for the cosmopolitan shopping enthusiast. Retailers claim that, as a result of low overhead costs and mark-up, prices for designer wares are often lower in Reykjavík than in the world's metropolises. The city also has a wide range of shops, from ultra-trendy to conservative, all within a relatively small geographical area.

Exploring the old city

The old city centre is bordered roughly by Suðurgata to the west, Hafnarstræti to the north, Lækjargata and Fríkirkjuvegur to the east and Hringbraut to the south. Street names give some hint of the way Reykjavík looked in the 19th century and before. The traffic artery of Lækjargata ("brook street"), for example, followed a stream between the shore and the lake; eels were caught here once, but it is now buried beneath asphalt and flagstones. Today's main shopping street of Laugavegur ("pools road") points the way that women followed on foot or horseback to the Laugardalur hot springs to do their washing.

Austurstræti ❶ was until recently the city's most easterly point – the street's maidens were immortalised, like distant cousins of Heine's *Daughters of the Rhine*, by Tómas Guðmundsson (1901–83), Iceland's first urban poet. The town plaza **Austurvöllur ❷** ("eastern field") is today a small park laid out around a

BELOW: New Year's pyrotechnics.

Houses clad in corrugated metal are a common sight in Reykjavík – a tradition dating back to when all houses were made of timber. Corrugated metal is a great shield against wind and rain, and allows the timber to breathe, so it is still used to cover timber houses today.

BELOW: view of the city centre from the spire of Hallgrímskirkja.

statue of the nationalist hero Jón Sigurðsson. It is said that Ingólfur Arnarson actually grew his hay here.

Parallel to Austurstræti, Hafnarstræti ("harbour street") is no longer on the harbourfront – it was superseded by Tryggvagata, built during World War I on gravel and sand dumped to extend the waterfront, then by the modern Geirsgata which is now on the harbourfront. Hafnarstræti houses the customs office, tax office and a couple of pubs, but the houses on the southern side of Hafnarstræti date back to the 19th century. At Tryggvagata 17 is the **Reykjavík Art Museum** ❸ (Hafnarhús; open daily 10am–5pm; admission charge; www.listasafnreykjavikur.is), situated in the stylishly renovated former warehouse of the Port.

Kolaportið Flea Market ❹ (open Sat and Sun 11am–5pm), situated on Geirsgata, across from the harbour, is a cheerful occasion selling clothes, books and other assorted odds and ends. The food section is a must for anyone who is curious about traditional Icelandic fare; here are featured the tasty *harðfiskur* (dried fish), *hákarl* (cured shark), *síld* (pickled herring) and the infamous pickled rams'

testicles, as well as a wide range of other culinary novelties and delights.

Aðalstræti

Reykjavík's oldest buildings are on **Aðalstræti** ❺ ("main street"). In the 18th century, Aðalstræti was earmarked by High Sheriff Skúli Magnússon (nicknamed "the Father of Reykjavík") for a crafts and trades development project. An unusual effort to catch up with the outside world, it was a scheme for creating cottage industries – wool-dyeing, knitting, weaving, etc. Although it folded, the project left not only inspiration, ambition and skills, but also the capital's earliest surviving architecture.

The most tangible signs of Reykjavík's past settlement can be seen at the **Settlement Exhibition** (Landnámssýningin; open daily 10am–5pm; admission charge), Aðalstræti 16, where you'll find the impressive remains of an oval-shaped Viking-age farmhouse just below the current street level. The layer of volcanic ash which lies just beneath the ruins has enabled archaeologists to date the structure to around 871 AD. With a hearth as its central point, the farmhouse covers

The Rise of Reykjavík

For centuries after settlement, Reykjavík remained little more than a few farmhouses. In a census taken in 1801 its population was a mere 301 souls, mainly spread between the lake and the Old Harbour where the shops and offices of the old city centre now lie. The population was presumably even less in 1786, when Reykjavík was first granted a municipal charter as an official trading post. In 1901, Reykjavík still only had 5,000 inhabitants. The sudden leap to today's 117,000 has occurred mostly since World War II, as tens of thousands of provincial Icelanders moved to the capital in search of better job prospects and a more cosmopolitan way of life. However, Reykjavík's gain has been the countryside's loss: many areas are suffering decline as a result.

around 85 sq. metres (915 sq. feet) and is thought to have been occupied until around 1000 AD.

Sandwiched between the museum and the **tourist office**, Aðalstræti 10 is the oldest surviving building in the city, built in 1764 to replace a 1752 weaver's shop that had burnt down. Its history is dotted with larger-than-life characters, including one-time owner Bishop Geir Vídalín (1761–1823). A cleric famed for his hospitality, Bishop Vídalín left an immortal dedication to the city's nightlife: "There are two places where the fires never die down – Hell and my house." Burning a hole through his wallet in the process, Vídalín won the dubious honour of becoming the only bishop in ecclesiastical history to be declared bankrupt. On show across the road, beneath a thick layer of clear plastic, is one of the old wells that used to provide Reykjavík's residents with drinking water. Relics dating back to the Settlement have been found to the right of the well, at the corner of Aðalstræti and Túngata.

Although the old centre has diminished in importance by day as the newer areas have developed and come to life,

once night falls it regains something of its former character. A plethora of pubs and restaurants lends a boisterous atmosphere to downtown Reykjavík by night, creating a beehive of activity more in keeping with a city many times the size. Nightlife begins late and lasts until early morning. Bar prices are high and most nightlifers "warm up" with a few drinks at home before taking the plunge. The "in" spots tend to change regularly; what was hip today may be passé tomorrow. Queues are quick to form when the action gets underway.

Humble beginnings

Iceland's **Government House** (Stjórnarráðið) stands on a small grassy bank overlooking Lækjartorg square, a stone's throw downhill from the First Settler, Ingólfur's statue on Arnarhóll. Built between 1765 and 1770, which makes it one of Reykjavík's oldest buildings, this unassuming whitewashed structure now houses the offices of the Prime Minister, yet it began its days less

The tourist office at Aðalstraeti 2, is open daily 8.30am–7pm in summer (1 June–15 Sept). At other times of the year it is open 9am–6pm weekdays and 9am–2pm at weekends.
See www.tourist.reykjavik.is
Tel: 590 1550
Fax: 590 1501.

BELOW LEFT: a designer boutique.
BELOW: Government House.

Embracing the Night

Something curious happened to Reykjavík nightlife at some point in the early 1990s – it became very hip, especially for foreigners with money, such as young, well-to-do Europeans. One example is the British pop star who was so taken with the scene that he returned again and again before finally purchasing a share in his favourite pub – and a flat nearby.

The initial rush of recognition may have subsided a little in the years since, but that isn't to say that the scene has diminished. Clearly, Reykjavík nightlife is still something to write home about. International media still send their people over to chronicle the festivities and wind up with exposés as colourful as a Reykjavík sunset in summer. Quite a change from the old days when tourists wearing hiking boots and cameras around their necks barely awarded the capital a second glance.

And what is so appealing? Perhaps it is the riproaring, spine-tingling Viking intensity with which the Icelanders approach their merriment. Or all those Beautiful People, packed like sardines into the small trendy cafés. Or lined up in queues outside those hot night spots, shivering in the latest Parisian fashions: never mind that it is a mere 5°C outside – that slip dress and those strap sandals will stay on!

Inside, there is pulsating action and bartenders have their work cut out. A steady stream of alcoholic beverages leaves the bar, cocktail waiters and waitresses moving with amazing agility through the crowd. The loudness of the music makes regular conversation impossible. Bodies bop up and down and should there be a shortage of space the tabletops will do just fine, thank you. Actors and actresses rub shoulders with upstart politicians who rub shoulders with inebriated bohemians who claim to have solved the riddle of life.

At closing time, typically 5, 6 or 7am, the lights go on and everyone has to leave, but the action continues out in the street. Everyone heads on down to Lækjartorg square; if it is summer and the weather is good there will most certainly be a 5,000-strong crowd there. It will be only slightly smaller if it is winter and there is a blizzard.

Navigate your way through the throng and behold anything from ecstasy to wretched misery, all within a single city block. For all this celebration is not without cost. There exists a dark side, in the form of drunken minors passed out in doorways or whacked out on illicit substances. Although the city's law-enforcement officers are doing a commendable job, Reykjavík nightlife is neither as simple nor as benign as it used to be. Now, for instance, there are more acts of random violence. And while one of the main hazards used to be traffic – the motorised kind – now there is trafficking – the highly organised kind. This, too, is a part of Reykjavík nightlife.

But for the most part, capital revellers can enjoy the absence of serious crimes and misdemeanours: it is still relatively safe to embrace the night. And this, too, may be something to write home about. ❑

ABOVE: on the dancefloor. **LEFT:** revellers congregating late at night on the streets of Reykjavík.

gloriously, as a prison workhouse. This building also housed the offices of the President of the Republic until 1996, when they were moved to premises at Sóleyjargata 1.

Behind the National Theatre on Hverfisgata is the **Culture House** ❼ (Þjóð-menningarhúsið; open daily 11am–5pm; admission charge; www.thjodmenning.is), an excellent museum where you'll find a well-conceived exhibition of Iceland's ancient sagas and other medieval manuscripts and artefacts. Displayed in sealed glass cabinets and dimly lit to aid their preservation, a visit here is a trip into a different world: swirling, flamboyant characters seemingly leap from every page telling the tale of life in the North Atlantic during the stirring Viking age. Upstairs there's an engaging multimedia exhibition recounting the birth in 1963, and subsequent development, of the island of Surtsey *(see pages 20, 191–3)*, off Iceland's southwest coast, which has been nominated for inclusion on the UNESCO World Heritage List.

Further along Lækjargata, on the same side as Government House, stands a row of houses built in the mid-19th century.

These narrowly escaped demolition some years ago and have been renovated to house two restaurants and the Iceland Tourist Board. Here is also where the well-equipped tourist information centre known as the **Kleif Travel Market** is located (the government Tourist Information office is on Aðalstræti). Further still, shortly before Tjörnin lake, the stately **Reykjavík Grammar School** (Menntaskólinn í Reykjavík) presides over the streetscape. This was the first school of its kind in the country and among its alumni are two Nobel Laureates: Halldór Laxness (literature, 1955) and Níels Finsen (medicine, 1903).

The **National Gallery** ❽ (Listasafn Íslands; open Tues–Sun 11am–5pm; free; www.listasafn.is), overlooking the lake at Fríkirkjuvegur 7 and next door to the grey and green Fríkirkjan (Free Church), is yet another historical building which has had its ups and downs. It was originally built as a cold store in which to keep ice cut from the lake which was then used for preserving fish. Later it served as a fish-freezing plant and a hot dance spot – so hot, in fact, that it once caught fire. Now renovated in a light-filled modern

Viking relics at the Culture House.

BELOW: swans on the Tjörnin Lake in front of the City Hall.

TIP

The Reykjavík Tourist Card – available for 1, 2 or 3 days – is good value if you plan to visit several museums and galleries, and unwind in one or more of the city's seven thermal pools. Bus travel is included in the price. For more information see page 317.

style, the small gallery has a fine permanent collection of work by Icelandic artists that is supplemented by changing exhibitions. There is a café on the first floor with internet access.

The grey basalt **Parliament Building** (Alþingishúsið) ❾ on Austurvöllur square was custom-built in 1880–81 to house the ancient assembly. After more or less continuous operation in nearby Þingvellir *(see pages 172–7)* since the year 930 (albeit mostly as a court, because Iceland lost its independence in 1262), the Alþingi moved to Reykjavík in 1798. The building visible today was built to house it during the tide of the 19th-century nationalist awakening.

Around Tjörnin lake

On a clear day, it is worth taking some time to stroll around **Tjörnin lake** ❿, which is still a natural breeding habitat for over 40 species of birds – most noticeably ducks. There are seats and a pleasant walkway along its eastern side (below Fríkirkjuvegur), giving views of a splendid row of houses on the opposite bank.

The **City Hall** ⓫ (Ráðhús Reykjavíkur) was built on the edge of the lake in the 1980s – an impressive postmodern edifice in its own right, but disliked by many Reykjavík residents for clashing with its serene environs. There is a huge relief map of Iceland just beyond the entrance hall which is well worth a look, and at times this is the venue for free concerts and exhibitions. There is also a pleasant coffee shop with internet access and a lovely view of the lake.

On the north bank of Tjörnin, at the end of the City Hall walking bridge, is a corrugated-metal clad structure, which is fondly known as **Iðnó**. It was originally constructed to house a craftsmen's guild but is best-known for being the home of the Reykjavík Municipal Theatre Company from 1897 to 1987. Iðnó has recently been reopened after painstaking renovation which has transformed it into one of Reykjavík's historical gems; it now serves as a venue for cultural performances and also houses a quaint little coffee bar and a fine restaurant. Iðnó is the setting for one of Reykjavík's most popular tourist shows, **Light Nights**; the drama is based on the sagas and Viking tales and is performed every Monday and Tuesday at 8.30pm from mid-July through August.

BELOW: the map inside City Hall.

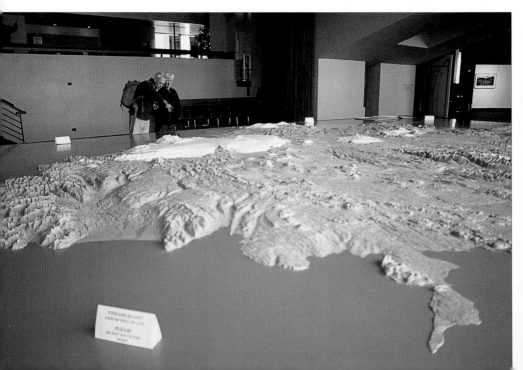

South of Tjörnin lake

A bridge across Tjörnin leads to some grassy park areas with a series of public sculptures, followed by the **University of Iceland ⑫** (Háskóli Íslands), which was founded in 1911 – although its ponderous Third Reich-style main building dates from the 1930s.

Situated just east of the university is the **Nordic House** (Norræna Húsið), designed by the highly respected Finnish architect Alvar Aalto (Sturlugata; open Mon–Fri 8am–5pm, Sat & Sun noon–5pm). Its purpose is to cultivate and strengthen ties between the Nordic countries. To that end, it has a coffee shop complete with current Scandinavian newspapers, a library and an ongoing programme of Scandinavian cultural events – many of which are free of charge.

On the outskirts of the university at Suðurgata 41 is the **National Museum ⑬** (Þjóðminjasafn Íslands; open May–mid-Sept daily 10am–5pm, mid-Sept–April Tues–Sun 11am–5pm; admission charge; www.natmus.is), which is essential viewing for anyone interested in Icelandic history and contemporary society. The museum's main exhibition, *The Making of a Nation*, is gripping stuff, tracing Iceland's history from the Settlement down to the present day. The section on the use of DNA testing is particularly interesting, detailing research work on the teeth of the first settlers in order to determine their origins. Contemporary sections relate key periods in the country's development, such as the restrictive trade monopoly and the founding of the republic. Most of the archaeological finds around Iceland over the past few hundred years have ended up in the National Museum – including the impressive medieval wooden church door from Valþjófsstaður, carved in the 13th century with the story of a knight who slays a dragon.

Across from the National Museum, on the other side of Suðurgata, is the **National and University Library ⑭** (Landsbókasafn Íslands), housed in an airy, modern structure which opened in 1994 after a prolonged construction operation that lasted almost two decades (Arngrímsgata 3; open late May–mid-Aug Mon–Fri 9am–5pm, Sat 10am– 2pm; mid-Aug–late May Mon–Thur 8.15am–10pm, Fri 8.15am–7pm, Sat 9am–5pm, Sun 11am–5pm). The library houses a manuscript collection and there are excellent research facilities for scholars, students and the general public.

Hallgrímskirkja

East from the lake, all roads climb to the imposing **Hallgrímskirkja church ⑮** (open daily: summer 9am–5pm; free), a modern basalt structure that many visitors find profoundly ugly. You can, however, climb the tower – or take the lift – for the best views of Reykjavík and the deceptively close Snæfellsnes peninsula. On a clear day, as they say, you can see forever. In front of the church is a huge and impressive statue of Leifur Eiríksson, "Discoverer of America", a gift from the US on the 1,000th anniversary of the founding of the Alþingi in 1930.

Next to Hallgrímskirkja is the studio home of Einar Jónsson, now the **Einar**

Completed in 1974, Hallgrímskirkja is designed to resemble columns of Iceland's basaltic lava. The tower, at 74.5 metres (244 ft), is the tallest structure in Iceland.

BELOW: an appreciative audience.

Hallgrímskirkja is the centre of the country's Lutheran faith, practised by some 82 percent of the population.

BELOW: city rooftops from the Hallgrímskirkja tower. **BELOW RIGHT:** Saga Museum mannequin.

Jónsson Museum (Safn Einars Jónssonar), which houses a collection of works by one of Iceland's great sculptors (Njarðargata; open June–mid-Sept Tues–Sun 2–5pm, mid-Sept–May Sat & Sun 2–5pm, closed Dec–Jan; admission charge; www.skulptur.is). Jónsson was a master of symbolism and epic, and many of his works combine a classical human form with symbols drawn from Norse, Greek and Oriental mythology.

A short walk to the south of Hallgrímskirkja, you might like to stop off at the **Ásgrímur Jónsson Collection** (Ásgrímssafn; Bergstaðastræti 74; open by arrangement; admission charge). Jónsson was Iceland's first professional painter and one of the nation's foremost landscape artists. The Ásgrímur Jónsson Collection is his donation to the Icelandic nation and is now a department within the National Gallery.

If you head north from Hallgrímskirkja, you will come to the **Living Art Museum** (Nýlistasafnið), another must-see for art connoisseurs (Laugavegur 26; open Wed–Sun noon–5pm, Thurs until 9pm; admission charge; www.nylo.is). It was originally founded as a coopera-tive in the 1970s by a group of artists who opposed what they saw as the National Gallery's shunning of experimental art. The museum stages ongoing exhibitions by artists both Icelandic and foreign and has become a permanent fixture on the artistic landscape.

Conveniently located at one of the main bus terminals is the **Icelandic Institute of Natural History** (Náttúrufræðisafnið; Hlemmur 5; open Mon, Thurs, Sat & Sun June–Aug 1–5pm, Sept–May 1–4pm; free; www.ni.is). This is a great place to learn about Iceland's geology and there are exhibits dedicated to Icelandic flora and fauna, including a specimen of the now-extinct Great Auk *(see page 229)*.

Southeast from the Icelandic Institute of Natural History is the **Kjarvalsstaðir Municipal Gallery** in Miklatún park, dedicated to Iceland's most famous modern artist, Jóhannes Kjarval (Flókagata; open daily 10am–5pm; admission charge; free on Thurs). Born in 1885, Kjarval worked on a fishing trawler until his artistically minded fellow workers ran a lottery to raise money for him to study in Copenhagen. The collection of his landscapes here is well worth seeing.

Landmark buildings

Building in Reykjavík is still taking place on a grand scale. The literally outstanding feature of the Reykjavík skyline these days is the glass-domed **"Pearl"** ❷ (Perlan) – a revolving restaurant that sits on top of the glistening silver hot-water tanks on **Öskjuhlíð** hill, offering a breathtaking view of the city on clear days. The tanks can take 24 million litres (more than 5 million gallons) of hot water and cater for almost half of Reykjavík's water consumption. An impressive man-made **geyser** spewing water at five-minute intervals has been constructed near the "Pearl", and efforts over the past two decades to turn Öskjuhlíð into a nature sanctuary have delivered impressive results.

This is also the location of Reykjavík's **Saga Museum** ❷ (Sögusafnið; open daily April–Sept 10am–6pm, Oct–Mar noon–5pm; admission charge; www.saga-museum.is), an absorbing collection of life-like wax models of characters from Iceland's medieval literature. If you're keen to get to grips with the sagas, and have children in tow, the real-life figures here are a much better option than the

manuscripts inside the Culture House. Beyond Perlan, Reykjavík's purpose-built geothermal beach, **Nauthólsvík**, is a good place to catch the rays and bathe in a sublime seawater lagoon.

Located back down near the shoreline is what is probably Reykjavík's best-known building internationally, the **Höfði House** ❷. This is the municipal reception hall behind whose clapboard exterior former presidents Ronald Reagan and Mikhail Gorbachev met in October 1986 to take their first bows before the *pas-de-deux* towards global disarmament. Now it is used for official city social functions, but is closed to the general public. At the time of its completion in 1909 to house the French consulate, Höfði was on the outskirts of the capital, and became the exclusive residence of poet and businessman Einar Benediktsson (1864–1940). This famous figure brought to the house not only his family but also a ghost. Reportedly, the ghost stayed on rent-free when the poet's fam-

The Höfði House, location of the 1986 summit between Reagan and Gorbachev.

BELOW: the figures outside Perlan.

Modern sculpture at the Ásmundur Sveinsson Sculpture Gallery.

ily sold it to the British consulate, which grew in turn so tired of being haunted that the building was eventually sold to the city.

Nature and high art

For all Reykjavík's modern expansion, the city's natural treasures remain as precious as ever. The **Laugardalur** area, a green belt situated slightly to the northeast of the old city centre by the side of one of the main roads through town, has been largely preserved from development and until recently still had sheep and horses on it. It serves as the capital's main sports area with a large open-air, geothermally heated swimming pool, soccer stadium, sports hall and artificially frozen ice-skating rink. There is also the Viking theme park rides of the **Family Park** (Fjölskyldugaðurinn) and adjoining **Farm Animal Zoo** ㉔ (Húsdyragarðurinn; both open daily mid-May–Aug 10am–6pm, Sept– mid-May 10am–5pm; admission charge; www.mu.is) with domestic animals as well as animals that are native to Iceland, plus an aquarium. The nearby **Botanical Gardens** ㉕ (Grasagarðurinn; open daily Apr–Sept 10am–10pm, Oct–Mar 10am– 5pm; free) have an impressive collection of 5,000 plants and nearly the entire Icelandic flora.

Over the road from the soccer stadium is the **Ásmundur Sveinsson Sculpture Gallery** ㉖ (Ásmundarsafn; Sigtún; open daily May–Sept 10am–4pm, Oct–Apr 1–4pm; admission charge). Sveinsson (1893–1982) drew inspiration from saga events, folklore and everyday life. His works are set in and around his bizarre dome and pyramid studio/home. The outdoor sculpture garden is impressive, and open at all hours – many tourists pass it regularly, as several hotels, including the Grand Hotel Reykjavík and Park Inn Ísland, are situated nearby.

Not far away on the shoreline is the **Sigurjón Ólafsson Museum** ㉗ (Safn Sigurjóns Ólafssonar, Laugarnestangi 70; open June– Sept Tues–Sun 2–5pm, Oct–May Sat & Sun 2–5pm; www.lso.is), dedicated to an Icelandic painter who lived from 1908 to 1982. In addition to the art collection there is a small family-run café with a lovely sea view and weekly music recitals in the summer.

The New Reykjavík

Since World War II the capital has been expanding to the east, leaving its past behind. In the 1980s, as it approached a six-digit population, more modern and grandiose architecture appeared on its skyline. A new commercial and cultural centre was built entirely from scratch some 4 km (2½ miles) east of the old centre, including not only the large indoor shopping mall, **Kringlan**, but also a complex to house the Municipal Theatre company.

As new residential suburbs sprang up – tasteless "concrete lava fields" such as Breiðholt and Árbær, each many times more populous than the largest of rural Icelandic towns – so this new part of Reykjavík has become the geographical as well as the business and commercial centre. This expansion is perhaps the most instantly visible result of Iceland's rapid shift from a traditional, rural country to a modern technological society.

Located on the edge of the Árbær suburb is the **Árbær Open-Air Museum** ❷❽ (Árbæjarsafn; open daily June–Sept 10am–5pm; admission charge; www. arbae-jarsafn.is), a living history museum that in the summer offers a schedule of events at weekends. A number of historical houses have been moved here from various locations in Reykjavík and around Iceland, and the past is re-created as accurately as possible. Household items and furnishings used throughout the centuries are on permanent display, and there is also an old turf church which is a popular spot for wedding services. The atmosphere is compromised by the busy road that runs next to it, however.

Between the suburbs of Breiðholt and Árbær, and well within the city limits, runs the idyllic **Elliðaár** river, which pays handsome tribute to the lack of pollution in Reykjavík as one of the best salmon rivers in Iceland, with annual catches of around 1,600 fish. By tradition the city's mayor opens the fishing season on 1 May every year. Angling permits, being carefully shared out, are difficult for visitors to come by, but there is no problem in buying permits during the summer season for nearby **Lake Elliðavatn**, where there is good local trout in wonderfully calm and picturesque surroundings.

KIDS

Reykjavík is a family-friendly city. The Laugardalur valley has a cluster of attractions that will appeal to children, including the Family Park and Zoo, a skating rink and a fabulous thermal swimming-pool complex.

BELOW: the Perlan revolving restaurant.

Whale-watching tours depart from the old harbour (Höfn) in the city centre from April to October.

BELOW: the solfar sun craft sculpture.

Elliðavatn borders the capital's **Heiðmörk** nature reserve to the south of the city, a popular spot for picnics and strolls, where wild patches merge harmoniously with areas reclaimed from wind erosion by the planting of trees.

Boat excursions

The island of **Viðey** ㉙, five minutes by motorboat off the north shore from the new Sundahöfn harbour, was given to the Reykjavík authorities as a birthday present in 1987 when the capital celebrated the 200th anniversary of its municipal charter (boat trips depart daily from Sundahöfn–Klettavör harbour between mid-May and September at hourly intervals 11.15am–5.15pm, with one more at 7.15pm. Today the island provides a haven for Reykjavík's inhabitants to "get away from it all".

High Sheriff Skúli Magnússon moved to Viðey in 1751 and had a residence built there, which was completed in 1755. It has recently been restored and now houses a splendid, if somewhat pricey, restaurant. The church on the island dates from 1794 and is also one of the oldest in the country; before the

Reformation, Viðey housed the richest monastery in Iceland, which owned a good part of Reykjavík and the land beyond, until it was torn down by Lutheran zealots. An ambitious scheme for a fisheries operation was launched in the early 20th century but eventually went bankrupt; remains of the "ghost town" can be visited on a pleasant walk around the eastern part of the island, which takes about an hour.

Departing from the main harbour in Reykjavík, two companies, *Elding* and *Whale Watching Centre*, offer daily **whale-watching tours** (Apr–Sept 9am & 1pm, June–Aug also 5pm, Oct 1pm only) in Faxaflói, the bay which lies between the capital and the Snæfellsnes peninsula. Minke whales and humpback whales are the most common species spotted on the tours, though there's also the chance of seeing killer whales, dolphins, sei and blue whales. En route to the whale-watching areas, the boats sail past the rocky islands of Lundey and Akurey which are home to up to 30,000 puffins, giving you a chance to see these comical birds at close quarters, though the vessels do not put ashore on the islands.

Greater Reykjavík

Reykjavík and the towns surrounding it have been growing so fast that they now form an almost continuous conurbation, known as the **Greater Reykjavík Area** and home to some 193,000 people – around two thirds of Iceland's total population. The urban area extends some 11 km (7 miles) to the east of the old city centre. Most of these towns are new and quite colourless, including Kópavogur, which has swollen in recent years to accommodate 28,000 people and is thus the second-largest community in Iceland. One of Kópavogur's claims to fame is that it is home to the country's biggest shopping mall, Smáralind, opened in October 2001. Sightseeing tours from Reykjavík take in some of the more interesting and historic places, such as Bessastaðir and Hafnarfjörður *(see pages 162–4)*. ❑

Why is Everything So Expensive?

Visitors to Iceland are often shocked by the high price of everything. It's not at all uncommon to discover that one has just paid two, three, or four times as much as one would expect to part with back home for the same item of comparable quality (with the exception of some items, such as designer goods). It all adds up. A tiny, isolated population with one of the highest living standards in the world is an expensive proposition.

Why is everything so expensive? For starters, Iceland's geographical isolation and harsh climate make it virtually 100 percent dependent on imports for everything except meat, potatoes, fish and dairy products. As a result, a web of importers, wholesalers and other middlemen has developed, supplying every corner of the land. While virtually every conceivable item is available, import tariffs and multiple layers of price markup can, and do, drive retail prices sky-high.

Imports of agricultural products are, with few exceptions, banned; at the same time, an overproducing farming sector is propped up by government subsidies which allow lamb, beef, milk, potatoes and other products to be produced at a huge loss in this highly inefficient sector. Although these subsidies should help to keep prices down, due to the lack of economies of scale to fall back on, supermarkets and other food retailers must count on huge markups to make up for the lack of volume. Throw in a 24.5 percent value-added tax on farm supplies, equipment and fuel that are already expensive – plus the VAT at the supermarket checkout – and you have a recipe for some of the highest priced victuals money can buy.

How can Icelanders afford to live here? The answer is relatively simple: almost everyone who is able to, works. Nearly 80 percent of those between the ages of 15 and 74 are employed outside the home, including seven out of 10 women; unemployment is less than 4 percent. Generally, low wages are compensated for by working weeks of 50, 60 or even 80 hours. In many instances, even this isn't enough to make ends meet. Thousands of families are heavily in debt and struggle to pay off their mortgage, car, and appliance loans, a situation compounded by Icelanders' expensive tastes.

RIGHT: an upmarket boutique in Reykjavík.

The dilemma is not limited to domestic households. Since around the 1960s, government borrowing abroad has helped create a highly developed and costly system of social services. Iceland now has one of the world's highest levels of foreign debt per capita in the world, with repayment obligations consuming one-fifth of the country's export revenues annually.

Of course, with nearly everyone working, taxes shouldn't really need to be so high. However, approximately one-quarter of the population are civil servants and as such do not contribute to the national wealth in the same way as, say, fish exporters do. The eleven Icelandic embassies in Europe, Scandinavia, Russia, China and North America – a lot for a nation barely the size of an American suburb – are also costly to run.

There is some good news, though In March 2007, in an attempt to reduce the cost of living, the government drastically reduced the levels of value-added tax (VAT) which apply to a number of services – on restaurant services VAT was lowered from a whopping 24.5 percent to just 7 percent. A similar reduction was introduced for hotel accommodation, shop-bought food, books and magazines, all formerly taxed at 14 percent but now subject to a 7-percent tax rate. As a result, prices have fallen, but it remains to be seen whether goods will remain correspondingly cheaper in the long term. ❑

RESTAURANTS, CAFÉS & BARS IN REYKJAVÍK

Restaurants

A næstu grösum
Laugavegur 20B
Tel: 552 8410
Delicious, wholesome
vegetarian food, an airy,
relaxed atmosphere and
good value for money
make this a very popular
place, particularly at
lunch time. Indian theme
on Fridays; lunch not
served on Sunday. The
entrance is on
Klapparstígúr. **$**

Apótek
Austurstræti 16
Tel: 575 7900
Owned by a husband and
wife team, this is one of
Reykjavík's most
cosmopolitan restaurants.
The menu is inspired:
traditional Icelandic
dishes such as salted cod
or scallops given an
international makeover,
with particular influence
from the cuisine of
Southeast Asia. **$$$**

Argentína Steak House
Barónsstígur 11
Tel: 551 9555
Top-quality steaks, lamb
and reindeer are served
at this justifiably popular

PRICE CATEGORIES

The price guide is
for the average
price of dinner per
person, without
wine:
$$$ Over ISK 4,000
$$ ISK 2,000–4,000
$ Under ISK 2,000

restaurant which is open
daily from 6pm. The
atmosphere is warm and
inviting but enjoying a
bottle of good wine with
your steak adds hugely to
the cost. **$$$**

Austur Indíafélagið
Hverfisgata 56
Tel: 552 1630
Unlike most other
countries, Indian food in
Iceland is expense-
account stuff. However,
at Austur-Indíafélagið, at
least, the quality of the
fare is excellent and the
service is among the
best in Reykjavík:
friendly, professional and
tactful. **$$$**

Austurlandahraðlestin
Hverfisgata 64A
Tel: 552 6007
Despite the tongue-twist-
ing name, this Indian
takeaway is a real find.
All your favourite spicy
Indian treats to take with
you or, alternatively,
there's a handful of
tables inside. **$**

Gallery Restaurant
Hótel Holt, Bergstaðastræti
37. Tel: 552 5700
Dining at this leading
restaurant inside Hótel
Holt is sure to impress.
The magical combination
of top-notch gourmet
French cuisine and
exquisite artwork
decorating the walls is
unparalleled anywhere in
the city. Menus change
frequently, but be sure to

ask if smoked puffin
breast in blueberry sauce
is available. **$$$**

Hornið
Hafnarstræti 15
Tel: 551 3340
This was the first Italian
restaurant to open in
Iceland and it has been
popular ever since. The
atmosphere is relaxed
and the pizzas and pasta
dishes are excellent.
There's also a range of
Mediterranean-influenced
fish dishes. It is almost
always packed in the
evening so a reservation
is recommended. **$$**

Jómfrúin
Lækjargata 4
Tel: 551 0100
An excellent choice for
lunch, when the
restaurant is full with
homesick Danes. A
seemingly endless choice
of filling Danish-style
open sandwiches.
Choose carefully and
lunch need not cost more
than ISK 1500. **$**

Icelandic Fish & Chips
Tryggvagata 8
Tel: 511 1118
An upmarket place
specialising in organic
vegetables and the
freshest quality fish.
They make a special
point of not using wheat
or sugar in the kitchen.
It's without question the
best place for deep-fried
fish and chips in town
and does a roaring trade

in takeaways, too. **$–$$**

Kaffivagninn
Grandagarður 10
Tel: 551 5932
Unpretentious harbour-
side place where local
fishermen come for
coffee and wholesome
home-cooked fare. **$**

Lækjarbrekka
Bankastræti 2
Tel: 551 4430
In an atmospheric timber
building dating from
1834, this cosy
restaurant with period
furniture, chandeliers
and heavy drapes is
known for its gourmet set
menus featuring lobster,
puffin or lamb. It's an
excellent choice for a
special occasion. Round
off your evening with a
drink in the snug lounge
upstairs. **$$$**

Rosso Pomodoro
Laugavegur 40
Tel: 561 0500
A good choice for Italian
food whilst out shopping
on Reykjavík's main
thoroughfare. Excellent
pizzas, pastas, salads
and fish dishes in a
pleasantly modern
atmosphere. Look out for
special lunch offers. **$$**

Siggi Hall
Hótel Óðinsvé, Þórsgata 1
Tel: 511 6677
Iceland's favourite
celebrity chef, Siggi Hall,
has now opened his own
restaurant inside Hótel

Óðinsvé. In a stylish yet informal setting, this accomplished eaterie is the place to come to enjoy top-quality seafood, including the excellent *bacalao* which is one of Siggi's trademarks. **$$$**

Vegamót
Vegamótastígur 4
Tel: 511 3040
An extremely popular bistro in the centre of town serving exceptionally good-value food: everything from fresh fish to TexMex dishes. There's a great brunch available on Saturday and Sunday. It's also a relatively cheap place for a beer. **$**

Við Tjörnina
Templarasund 3
Tel: 551 8666
Undoubtedly one of the city's finest fish restaurants located close to Tjörnin lake, as the Icelandic name suggests. A unique menu with creatively prepared fish which never fails to tantalise the tastebuds. **$$$**

Þrír Frakkar
Baldursgata 14
Tel: 552 3939
They've been serving whale steaks at this cosy neighbourhood French-style bistro for years and it's still the best place in town to sample the meat, should your conscience allow. Otherwise, an accomplished menu of fish dishes, including the traditional *plokkfiskur*, a

kind of fish and potato mash. **$$**

Cafés

Brennslan
Pósthússtræti 9
French-style café overlooking Austurvöllur square that is popular with Reykjavík's younger crowd. Good light meals at reasonable prices as well as sandwiches, coffees and a wide selection of beers.

Café Paris
Austurstræti 14
A Reykjavík institution that's been here as long as anyone can remember. Although rather cramped, its central location overlooking the parliament is unsurpassed and it's a good choice for decent coffee and light snacks. In summer there's outdoor seating.

Grái Kötturinn
Hverfisgata 16A
A basement café renowned across the city for its excellent hearty breakfasts and bagels. Small, cosy and intimate place to stop for a cup of coffee or a bite to eat.

Mokka
Skólavörðustígur 3A
The oldest coffee house in Iceland which has been plying the masses with the dark stuff since 1958. There's never any music here – it's a place to come with friends for a

chat over a cup of coffee.

Kaffi Solon
Bankastræti 7A
Half café, half bar, this airy, contemporary place overlooking the main street is a good bet for a coffee. Stylish interior, a wide selection of coffees and some tantalising cakes.

Segafredo Espresso
Lækjartorg
The Italian coffee chain has made it to Iceland serving industrial-strength espressos, lighter lattes and a tasty selection of panini and other light snacks perfect for lunch. It is small, though, so sometimes it can be difficult to find a free table.

Bars

Dubliner
Hafarstræti 4
Long-established Irish pub in the heart of town, with Guinness and a decent array of whisky.

Gaukur á Stöng
Tryggvagata 22
Another Reykjavík institution. While other places come and go, Gaukur has been here since the outset opening when beer became legal back in the 1980s. Always a good choice for an evening drink.

Grand Rokk
Smiðjustígur 6
Loud and lively British-style pub with live music,

generally at the weekends. The beer here is amongst the least expensive in town.

Hverfisbarinn
Hverfisgata 20
Another winner, this inordinately popular bar has been a Reykjavík favourite for several years now.

Oliver
Laugavegur 20A
Bar, nightclub and restaurant (in the daytime) all rolled into one, this eclectic place is a good choice for a drink and a dance and is probably the best place in town to meet young Reykjavíkers.

Q-Bar
Ingólfsstræti 3
Newly renovated and offering stylish and comfortable surroundings, this lounge-like establishment attracts gays and straights alike.

Sirkus
Klapparstígur 31
Often packed to capacity, this Bohemian bar and club is certainly one of the places to be seen. A favourite of Björk's when she's in town, Be prepared to queue at weekends.

THE REYKJANES PENINSULA

Situated just south of the capital, the Reykjanes peninsula is a compact area to visit. The undisputed highlight is the stunning Blue Lagoon, but there are also excellent bird-watching sites and nature reserves.

BELOW: the Blue Lagoon

The Reykjanes peninsula is easy to ignore – a smallish promontory south of **Reykjavík ❶**, it is undeniably overshadowed by the capital's greater pulling power. Yet most people's first glimpse of Iceland is actually of Reykjanes – Keflavík international airport is situated right in its heart.

Almost all arriving tourists simply jump aboard a bus or hire a car, and head for the mountains or the city without a backward glance. But one really should give the region a little time: the principal sights can be seen on a day tour, but hikers, whale-watchers, birdwatchers and devotees of the Blue Lagoon may find it hard to tear themselves away.

Lashed by the Atlantic

Situated in Iceland's far southwest, the peninsula bears the full force of the violent storms that regularly pile in from the Atlantic. Small, nondescript fishing villages dot the coastline, while much of the inland area consists of lava fields, some of which flowed as recently as the 14th century. In fact the peninsula is a continuation of the Mid-Atlantic Ridge which pushes apart two immense plates of the earth's crust at the rate of 2 cm (¾ inch) each year. Pillow lava and tufa formations from Ice-Age eruptions give some indication of what the submarine ridge looks like. While the broad expanses of volcanic rock may seem grey and barren at first glance, in fact they have donned a coat of Iceland's typical grey-green moss, soft and springy underfoot. The tenacious moss has paved the way for higher plants, which thrive in the more sheltered areas. Two hundred species of grasses, mosses and flowering plants have been identified, with the occasional birch or other tree.

Hafnarfjörður

The gateway to Reykjanes, only 15 minutes by bus south of central Reykjavík, is the old town of **Hafnarfjörður ❷**. This was one of Iceland's most important ports long before Reykjavík had even grown into a village: in the 15th century it was run by English traders and in the 16th century by Germans, before the Danes imposed their trade monopoly of 1602.

Situated within the craggy Búrfell lava field which covers most of the peninsula, Hafnarfjörður has a population of 24,000. It is a part of the Greater Reykjavík area but is by no means a satellite town of the capital, with its own thriving port and fishing industry, and a broadly based local economy. A pleasant public park, **Hellisgerði**, is situated in the middle of the town, in among the lava. The **Hafnarborg Arts Centre** by the harbour-side offers art shows and musical events, as well as a cosy coffeeshop. The town has two modest museums: the **Hafnarfjörður Museum**, which canters through the town's history, and **Sívertsen-Hús** – dating from 1803 – which is the oldest building in town and was once the home of local bigwig, Bjarni Sívertsen (both open June–Aug daily 1–5pm, Sept–May Sat & Sun 1–5pm; admission charge). Many Reykjavík dwellers make the short trip here to visit the several upmarket restaurants on the waterfront.

Hafnarfjörður is also well known for its "hidden population". For as long as can be remembered, people have believed that elves, dwarfs and other harmless urchins live in its lava cliffs in peaceful coexistence with other town residents. There is even a map available at the local tourist information centre, showing hidden sites where these mysterious beings live (*see also* Icelandic Hauntings, *pages 250–1*).

In addition, Hafnarfjörður has become the "Viking centre" of Iceland. The nation's only Viking restaurant, Fjörukráin, is located at the harbour, where traditional food is served in a Vikingfest atmosphere, with lively song and celebration. The best time to come here is during the ancient Viking month of Þorri (late Jan–late Feb) when traditional foods, such as preserved shark and rams' testicles, which once sustained people through the long winter months, are devoured with gusto.

Bessastaðir

At **Bessastaðir** ❸, north of Hafnarfjörður and just across the Skerjafjörður inlet from Reykjavík, is the presidential

The corrugated-metal-clad church in Hafnarfjörður.

BELOW: much of the peninsula is made up of moss-covered lava fields.

The Hafnarfjörður Museum, housed in a renovated 19th-century warehouse, recounts the history of the town, providing an insight into a close-knit Icelandic community. There is also an exhibition of children's toys.

been renovated, giving the opportunity for archaeological excavations on the site which have yielded a range of artefacts dating back to the Middle Ages. The adjacent church was built in 1780–1823. Considerable repairs were carried out in 1946–48: the original stone floor disappeared under concrete, but can still be seen in the vestibule and tower. The windows illustrate themes from Icelandic ecclesiastical history. The altarpiece, by the Icelandic artist Muggur, is a triptych, painted in 1921.

residence. Bessastaðir is first mentioned in the *Íslendiga Saga (Saga of the Icelanders)* by Sturla Þórðarson. The place then belonged to the famous Edda-author Snorri Sturluson *(see page 42)*. Later it became the first royal estate in Iceland, a possession of the king of Norway until the late 18th century. From 1805 Bessastaðir was the site of the highest educational institution in Iceland, the Lærði skólinn, for some 40 years.

Since 1941 it has been the presidential residence. The present-day building dates from the colonial period, and was originally constructed as a governor's residence in 1763. The residence has

Along the peninsula

Route 41 along the north coast of Reykjanes leads to the twin towns of **Njarðvík** (population 2,500) and **Keflavík ❹** (population 10,000). Both trading centres since the Middle Ages, they have virtually joined together in recent years. Fishing and other commercial enterprises are strong here. The closure of the American air base at Keflavík in 2006 has had little impact on the local economy as few Icelanders were employed there.

Beyond Keflavík is the outcrop known as **Miðnes ❺**, with the tiny fishing outposts of **Garður** and **Sandgerði**. Just south of Sandgerði is the small **Hvalsnes** church, built in 1887. The church's most treasured posession is a gravestone hand-cut by the poet Reverend Hallgrímur Pétursson in 1649. The stone came to light during excavations in 1964. The ruins of the village **Bátsendar** are nearby, destroyed by a freak tide at the end of the 18th century.

The dirt road Route 425 follows the coast to the peninsula's southeastern tip. There is a lighthouse and view out to a 50-metre (165-ft) rock pinnacle Karl ("man"), while pillars of steam spray from the lava fields on the horizon.

Grindavík ❻, now a typical fishing community of about 2,700 people, can look back on a long and eventful history. It was a major trading centre during the Middle Ages, and in 1532 a business rivalry between English and Hanseatic merchants led to the murder of an Englishman, John "the Broad". Barbary pirates raided Grindavík in 1627, capturing a number of Danes and Icelanders, plus two merchant ships. Today Grindavík is a quiet and unassuming town, with a statue to the families of local fishermen lost at sea.

Surreal spa

Just outside Grindavík, and a handy 15 km (10 miles) from the airport, is the **Blue Lagoon ❼** (Bláa Loníð; open daily June–Aug 7.30am–9pm; Sept–May 10am–8pm; admission charge; www.bluelagoon.com). The evocative name notwithstanding, this is not a natural phenomenon, but a recent by-product of geothermal energy usage. The Svartsengi power plant pumps mineral-laden water from up to 2 km (1¼ miles) beneath the earth's surface, at a temperature of 240°C (470°F). The superheated water passes through a dual process, on the one hand to generate electricity, and on the other to heat fresh water. The run-off water, rich in silica, salt and other elements, flows out at a lower temperature to collect in the Blue Lagoon. Psoriasis and eczema sufferers noticed some years ago that bathing in the lagoon seemed to ease their symptoms, and, once the word was out, it started developing a reputation as a health spa.

The place became so popular that a major refurbishment was deemed necessary. The lagoon itself was moved a few hundred metres from its original

*The **Reykjavegur trail** extends more than 130 km (80 miles) from the southeastern tip of the peninsula to the Nesjavellir power plant east of Reykjavík. It is possible to reach most of the trail's stage points by car, and walk from one to the next in a day (there are 7 stages). This is one of the few places on earth where you can observe the phenomenon of continental drift from marked out and accessible areas. The route is clearly mapped in a booklet available from tourist information centres.*

BELOW: enjoying the benefits of bathing at the Blue Lagoon.

The creeping thistle (Cirsium arvense), otherwise rare in Iceland, grows in Grindavík. Local tradition claims that it grew up on the spot where both Christian and heathen blood was spilt.

At the Innri-Stapi cliff near Lake Kleifarvatn, there is a bronze plate beside the road commemorating an Icelandic guide who was so fond of the area that his ashes were scattered over the lake at his own request.

BELOW: in the Blue Lagoon.

site in 1999. State-of-the-art facilities, carefully designed to complement the surrounding landscape, were then built, notably a cave-like sauna carved into the lava. There are conference facilities, a restaurant, snack bar, shop and, should you care to spend the night, a guesthouse just a stone's throw away. One thing that is slightly below standard, however, is the size of the changing rooms: on sunny days, particularly at weekends, they get very crowded and it may be worth getting up early to beat the crowds. If you're impressed by the lagoon's waters, note that their beneficial properties can now be enjoyed at home – a range of skin and bathing products are on sale across the island (*see panel, below*).

Hot spot

Geothermal power in a more natural setting can be seen east of Grindavík at **Krísuvík** ❽, within the Reykjanesfólksvangur. Here *solfataras* and boiling mud springs surround the world's largest blowing steam vent. While the intention has always been to harness the geothermal energy at Krísuvík for heating pur-

poses, nothing has yet come of this. The whole area seethes with subterranean heat, so tread carefully and keep to the paths to avoid being scalded.

Near Krísuvík is the dramatic and somewhat spooky **Lake Kleifarvatn**, reputed to be the home of an aquatic monster. If you are not put off by this, you can also fish for trout here. Permits are available in Reykjavík, Hafnarfjörður and Keflavík. On the coast beyond Krísuvík is **Krísuvíkurbjarg** ❾, one of Iceland's best-known bird-cliffs: most numerous are kittiwakes, while fulmar, razorbill, common guillemot and Brunnich's guillemot are also plentiful. Puffin, shag, herring gull and black guillemot, though less common, can be observed at Krísuvíkurbjarg, and seals can often be seen basking on the shore. Farther offshore, one may occasionally glimpse groups of whales.

About 14 km (9 miles) off the Reykjanes shore lies the island of **Eldey** ❿, a high rocky pillar standing 77 metres (250 ft) out of the sea. Eldey is home to the world's largest gannet colony – around 70,000 birds nest on the island each year. The island is a nature reserve, and a per-

Spa Benefits

There is an array of unusual health-giving salts, sprays and lotions on sale at the Blue Lagoon. Products contain a blend of minerals, silica mud and algae found naturally in the lagoon's geothermal seawater. A range of face care products is available to smooth and moisturise the skin, as well as cleansing products such as silica purifying shampoo, algae and mineral body scrub designed to cleanse and purify. The active ingredients have been proven to revitalise, nourish and protect human skin. They are particularly effective in treating certain conditions such as psoriasis. Various skin treatments are also on offer, such as a thirty-minute salt glow whereby the skin is polished with a mix of mineral salts to remove dead cells and stimulate blood circulation.

mit is needed to visit. Here the last of the great auks was clubbed to death in 1844 (*see page 229*).

Church of miracles

The little **Strandarkirkja** ⑪ church on the south coast between Krísuvík and Þorlákshöfn has a bizarre history. Tradition says that a ship on its way to Iceland ran into a storm; the crew prayed for deliverance, and promised to build a church if they were saved. An angel appeared on the shore and guided them to safety; they landed at the spot where Strandarkirkja stands today. A tradition arose that the church could work miracles: through the centuries seamen in peril have prayed and promised donations to Strandarkirkja, and they still do so today. As a result, this little church, which no longer has any parish to serve, is reputed to be one of the wealthiest in Iceland.

Near Strandarkirkja, at the small lake Hlíðarvatn, is the farm **Vogsósar**. Formerly a parsonage, the farm is well known as the home of the clergyman-magician Eiríkur (1638–1716), who is mentioned in many folktales. One such

story shows that Eiríkur was not a person to fool around with. Once travellers came to Vogsós in winter and some of them went without leave to the pastor's haystack and helped themselves to hay for their horses. The next morning they continued on their way, but when they reached the estuary, their horses began to drink, and went on drinking, however hard they tried to urge them on. Hearing that the travellers were stuck at the river, Reverend Eiríkur went down to find out what was happening, and when he came there he said, "It's thirsty, the hay of Vogsós. You should not give it to your horses again." With this they parted, each going his own way.

A little further to the west is the abandoned farm **Herdísarvík**. Above the farm is a big crag from which impressive lava streams have flowed. This was the home of the great Icelandic poet Einar Benediktsson, who died here in 1940. Herdísarvík bay may have inspired some of Benediktsson's lines from *Surf*: "I hear in thy short-lived waves weeringly rolled / The footfall of time that e'er onward must hold / And my blood surges on with the bruit of the main....". ❏

The Reykjanes coastline is dotted with lighthouses on rocky headlands.

RESTAURANTS, CAFÉS & BARS

Restaurants

Brim
Hafnargata 9, Grindavík
Tel: 426 8570
A no-nonsense, reliable restaurant popular with locals that serves the freshest of local fish dishes at reasonable prices. **$**

Fjörukráin
Strandgata 55, Hafnarfjörður
Tel: 565 1213
If you're looking for traditional Viking fare, this is the place to come: shark, dried haddock and

lamb shank are generally on the menu. During þorrablót (late Jan–late Feb), there's a Viking banquet featuring delicacies such as singed sheep's head and pickled rams' testicles, as well. **$$–$$$**

Flug Hótel
Hafnargata 57, Keflavík
Tel: 421 5222
A first-class restaurant is available inside the hotel which itself is only 10 minutes away from the international airport. A wide variety of expertly pre-

pared dishes, in particular lamb and fish, is always on the menu. **$$$**

Mamma Mía
Hafnargata 7a, Grindavík
Tel: 426 9966
A dependable choice of tasty and affordable pizzas are available at this popular pizzeria in the heart of the town. **$$**

Cafés and Bars

Blue Lagoon Café
Blue Lagoon
A pleasant place for a refreshing cup of coffee and a light bite to eat after an afternoon steaming in the Blue Lagoon. **$**

Paddy's Irish Bar & Pizzeria
Hafnargata 38, Keflavík
The best and most agreeable place for a drink in Keflavík – and popular with the locals, too. **$**

Ráin
Hafnargata 19A, Keflavík
A long-established bar-cum-eaterie with tasty fish dishes, pizzas and salads. It's also a popular place for a beer in the evening. **$**

• • • • • • • • • • • • • •
Categories are for an average-priced dinner per person, without wine. **$$$** *over ISK 4,000,* **$$** *ISK 2,000–4,000,* **$** *under ISK 2,000.*

THE SOUTHWEST

This area is full of historical sites from the time of the sagas, plus a wealth of natural wonders, all within comparatively easy reach of the capital and the Ring Road

The rich farming land of southwest Iceland has made it one of the most densely populated parts of the country since the Saga Age. Today it is also the most heavily visited: some of Iceland's most famous attractions are within striking distance of Reykjavík, tied together under the label of "the Golden Circle".

Every day, hundreds of travellers are bussed from one natural marvel to another, with scarcely enough time to draw breath between snapshots. This may be fine for anyone on a short stopover in Iceland and is probably an unfortunate necessity for those without their own transport. But others will prefer to take a more leisurely pace around the region, stopping in the more obscure valleys and farmhouses to appreciate Iceland's mellow rural atmosphere.

East of Reykjavík

The Ring Road east of Reykjavík quickly ascends to a volcanically scarred mountain pass. The moss-covered scoria lava field here, known as **Kristnitökuhraun**, was spewed up from the earth around AD 1000. The **Hellisheiði** area is a good walking destination en route from Reykjavík, with a well signposted trail network and detailed maps available.

There are panoramic views as the road descends towards the southwestern plain, with steaming crevasses and yellow sulphur markings on the slopes above **Hveragerði ❶**, a town of 1,700 people that has made a living from harnessing

geothermal activity. Greenhouses provide the bulk of Iceland's home-grown produce, including bananas and tropical fruit. Although an unashamed tourist trap, the **Eden** greenhouse is among several that are open to visitors (open summer daily 9am–11pm; winter daily 9am–7pm), while the Naturopathic Health Association of Iceland operates a clinic here for spa and mud cures. Lying just to the north of town are the hot springs of **Grýla**, named after a hungry local she-troll with a penchant for devouring small children.

Main attractions
EYRARBAKKI
ÞINGVELLIR
GEYSIR
GULLFOSS WATERFALL
STÖNG VIKING LONGHOUSE
SAGA CENTRE, HVOLSVÖLLUR
ÞORSMÖRK
SKÓGAR FOLK MUSEUM
VÍK

PRECEDING PAGES: Gullfoss waterfall. **LEFT:** Strokkur exploding at Geysir. **BELOW:** growing roses, Hveragerði.

Eyrarbakki's oldest building, dating from 1754, houses the folk museum.

BELOW: the view northeast across the Þingvellir plain, with the historic farmhouse and church in the foreground.

While Hveragerði itself is unlikely to hold travellers' attention for more than a couple of hours, it can be a base for hikes into the surrounding countryside – the nearby mountain **Selfjall** to the north of the town and the lava tube **Raufarhól-shellir** to the southwest are popular destinations.

The next town along the Ring Road is **Selfoss ❷** (population 4,000), the centre of Iceland's thriving dairy industry and a major road intersection. On the highway just before town, **Hjarðarból** (tel: 567 4203 or 864 4203) offers farmhouse accommodation.

Stokkseyri and Eyrarbakki

To the south of Selfoss lie a trio of fishing towns, including **Stokkseyri ❸**, where a **Maritime Museum** (open daily) has been set up in the house of Þuríður Einarsdóttir, a 19th-century woman who captained a local fishing boat. More atmospheric is **Eyrarbakki ❹**, set by the shores of a driftwood-strewn black sand beach. This was one of Iceland's main fishing ports from the 12th to the 19th century, and has several 18th-century buildings still intact – the oldest of which houses the **Söfnin**

Folk Museum (open June–Aug daily 10am–6pm; Apr, May, Sept & Oct Sat & Sun 2–5pm). The **Maritime Museum** (open June–Aug daily 11am–5pm; Apr, May, Sept & Oct Sat & Sun 2–5pm; tel: 483 1082) is in an adjacent building. Also, **Husid Folk Museum** (open June–Aug daily 11am–6pm; Apr, May, Sept & Oct Sat & Sun 2–5pm; www.husid.com). Across the wide Ölfusa estuary, a prime location for birdwatching, lies **Þorlákshöfn ❺**, the departure point for the twice-daily ferry to the Vestmannaeyjar (Westmann Islands), a journey that can be very pleasant in mild weather but wretched in rough seas.

Þingvellir

Route 35 turns off north of Selfoss at the hillock of **Ingólfsfjall**, where the First Settler, Ingólfur Arnarson, is said to be buried. Among a group of smaller craters is the 55-metre (180-ft) deep Kerið, blasted out 3,000 years ago and now containing a lake. Continuing north it is possible to reach **Þingvellir National Park ❻** (also accessible directly from Reykjavík).

When Iceland's unruly early settlers decided to form a commonwealth in AD

930, the site they chose for their new national assembly, the Alþingi, was the natural amphitheatre of Þingvellir ("parliament plains"). It was a grand experiment in republicanism at a time when the rest of Europe wallowed in rigid feudal monarchies, and it lasted, despite the odd lapses into chaos, for over three centuries.

Today Þingvellir is still regarded with reverence by Icelanders, its historical weight reinforced by a serene natural beauty. Declared part of a national park in 1928, the historical section is set along the north of **Þingvallavatn** – at 84 sq. km (30 sq. miles), Iceland's largest lake – and by the banks of the **River Öxará** ("axe river"). On the horizon in every direction lie low mountains, snowcapped for much of the year: to the north lies the volcano of Skjaldbreiður ("broad-shield") whose lavas created Þingvellir, flanked by the mountains Botnssúlur, Hrafnabjörg and Ármannsfell (home, it's said, to Ármann, a spirit who is the guardian of Þingvellir). To the south lies the geothermally active Hengill.

The lava plain of Þingvellir itself is covered with wildflowers in summer and sumptuous shades of red in the autumn.

This is also a spot where the two halves of Iceland – the European and American tectonic plates – are tearing apart. Aerial photographs show that the great crack of **Almannagjá** ("everyman's chasm"), on whose flanks the Alþingi was held, is just one fissure in a huge series running northeast like an ancient wound through the plains. Occasional earthquakes have reshaped the site: a quake in 1789 caused the plain to drop about 1 metre (3 ft). The plates are drifting apart at a rate of 1.5cm (⅔ inch) each year.

Journey into the past

The **visitor centre** is located on the eastern side of the Öxará River, to the north of the historic sites. From here a track heads south to the church and farmhouse, while a path veers off southwest to the Lögberg, viewpoint and educational centre on the other side of the river. The point where the latter crosses the Öxará is **Drekkingarhylur**, the famed "drowning pool" that came into use in the 16th century. Men condemned to death were beheaded, but women who committed adultery, infanticide or perjury were tied up in a sack and flung into the pool –

The Lögberg ("Law Rock"), from which the Law-speaker addressed the Alþingi at Þingvellir.

A Key Place in History

Almost every important moment in Icelandic history has taken place at Þingvellir. When the Alþingi was first held here, this was the fringe of the farm Reykjavík, which was owned by the descendents of the First Settler, Ingólfur Arnarson. It was, and remains, in the centre of of the densely populated farming areas of the land. Here the decision was made for Iceland to convert to Christianity in AD 1000. This was the place for Byzantine legal cases to be argued and voted on, although they were often finally resolved by the Viking recourse to arms and the field of Þingvellir would be soaked in blood. In time, this violence would grow out of control, and it was at Þingvellir in 1271 that Icelanders voted away their independence. The Alþingi at Þingvellir kept operating as a court until the 1760s, although with less and less relevance as first Norway and then Denmark asserted colonial control. Even so, Icelanders kept a special affection for Þingvellir, as a place where, no matter how imperfectly, the country had managed its own affairs. Poets and agitators would appeal to the saga past when they pushed for independence and, when Iceland finally did declare its nationhood again in 1944, the field of Þingvellir was the obvious place for the ceremony.

Laying Down the Law

By their own admission, Icelanders have always been rather quarrelsome, and it is true that much of their history concerns aggrieved characters choosing between taking up the sword and going to court. The annual Alþingi set up in 930 gave the best of both worlds: legal proceedings with an adjournment while the litigants fought pitched battles. They could then apologise to the court, sit down and allow the proceedings to continue.

"Icelanders", wrote an 18th-century English commentator, "have surpassed all other nations in legal chicanery. Jurisprudence was the favourite study of the rich. A wealthy Icelander was always ambitious to plead a cause before the Alþingi, and the greater skill he showed in the art of prolonging... the greater was his celebrity. A man gained as much reputation for defeating his adversary in a lawsuit as for killing him in a duel."

Law covered every contingency imaginable. Thus: "If a man holds his weapons in a peaceable manner, as a person ordinarily does when he is not going to use them, and when they are in this position another man runs against them and wounds himself, he who held the weapons is liable to the punishment of banishment if competent witnesses can prove that he held them in this apparently quiet manner, in order that the other might run against them and be wounded thereby."

This law – and a hundred like it – reflected the fine calculation that made punishment fit the crime. The case of a man who seduced a girl and was then wounded by the girl's father was considered all square. Punishment, when required, fell into three categories: death and two types of "banishment", exile or house arrest. The last normally carried the option of a fine, which was just as well because it was almost impossible not to break laws and most people would have spent a large part of their lives indoors.

Witchcraft and theft commonly carried the death penalty, murder or manslaughter rarely so. Thieves were beheaded; those convicted of witchcraft, usually men, were burnt or drowned to reduce the risk of trouble with their ghosts. Killing was shameful only if it was done in an underhand manner, like killing someone asleep. In other circumstances, which drew no distinction between self-defence and mindless butchery, it could be sorted out by the payment of a fixed penalty determined by the victim's social status.

In retaliation for effrontery or insult, killing was absolutely honourable, merely requiring a public announcement of the deed, which had to be made on the same day. After the event, care had to be taken not to conceal the body beyond a covering to protect it from scavengers. If insults were not immediately dealt with by the offended party, offenders were liable to exile. Indictable insults included throwing sand at someone, a punch, and attempting to throw a man into a mire "though he may actually not fall therein". Exile lasted 20 years and in practice was not far short of the death penalty. An exile had a price on his head and could be killed with impunity

In today's Iceland the rule of law and order is no less important. In line with the other Nordic countries, renowned for their no-nonsense approach to alcohol, Iceland operates one of the toughest drink-driving laws in Europe and alcohol limits for drivers are far stricter than in the United Kingdom, for example. The possession of even small quantities of soft drugs can lead to heavy fines and possible imprisonment. A law prohibiting smoking in restaurants, bars and public transport came into effect in June 2007 and anyone caught smoking will be asked to leave the premises. Failure to do so will lead to arrest and a fine. ❏

LEFT: Vikings in discussion.

deeper and more turbulent than it is today. A short distance upstream is the Öxarárfoss waterfall.

The path continues to what was the focal point of every Viking Alþingi: **Lögberg** , the "Law Rock", today marked by a stone and a flapping Icelandic flag, right by the Almannagjá fissure. On the smoother ground below, the Lögrétta (Legislature) took place, attended by the 36 (later increased to 39) *goðar* or chieftains who would debate new laws. All free men were welcome to listen or comment, but only the *goðar* could vote. It was also the site of the Quarter Courts, one for each section of the country. The proceedings were considered so important that farmer-warriors rode in from every corner of Iceland, some taking as long as 17 days to arrive from the East Fjords.

The whole business was run by the Law-speaker, who was elected from among the chieftans. His was a difficult job: apart from keeping the proceedings orderly, he had to recite from memory all of the Icelandic laws, one third every year, from the Lögberg. The acoustics here are still excellent.

Scattered amongst the grass and lava on either side of the Lögberg are the few remains of various **búðir** , or booths. Every chieftain set up his own personal booth for the two weeks that the Alþingi lasted (usually from the Thursday after 18 June each year), a canvas-covered place to sleep, eat, drink and meet. The stones that can be seen today all probably belong to booths from the 18th century. The **Hotel Valhöll** , built in 1898 *(see page 324)*, is on the site of Snorri Sturluson's booth, Valhöll.

The path continues up to the **educational centre** and lookout point behind the hotel at the top of the Almannagjá fissure, with great views across to the church and the Þingvellir plains.

Religious centre

On the east bank of the river is the glistening white **Þingvallabær farmhouse**

Þingvallakirkja church is a mid-19th century construction, although the pulpit dates from 1683.

BELOW: the rich colours of autumn in Þingvellir National Park.

D and **Þingvallakirkja church** **E**. A church at Þingvellir was the first in Iceland to be consecrated, probably soon after the conversion of 1000, although not at this location. The present version dates from 1859. To enter, ask at the farmhouse – the older part, built in 1930, is occupied by the park warden, who also happens to be the priest; the newer section, dating from 1974, is the summer residence of the Prime Minister. Visitors are loaned the huge, gilded church key, almost more impressive than the church itself.

Inside, there is a pulpit from 1683 and a treasured altarpiece, painted by Ófeigur Jónsson of Heiðarbær in 1834, that had been taken from Iceland and wound up in a church on the Isle of Wight in southern England. It was rediscovered only in 1974, and returned to Iceland in time for the 1,100th anniversary of the settlement, which was celebrated at Þingvellir. There are three bells in the church steeple: one dating from the Middle Ages, one from 1698, and the third called Íslandsklukkan – "Iceland's bell" – moulded to ring out for Iceland's independence in 1944.

There are two cemeteries at the church, the higher one a circular plot of ground with only two graves in it: both of poets, the illustrious nationalists Jónas Halgrímsson (1807–45) and Einar Benediktsson (1864–1940). Just to the north of the church is **Biskupabúð**, the "Bishops' booth", which is the largest ruined booth in Þingvellir and one that dates back to its earliest Viking times.

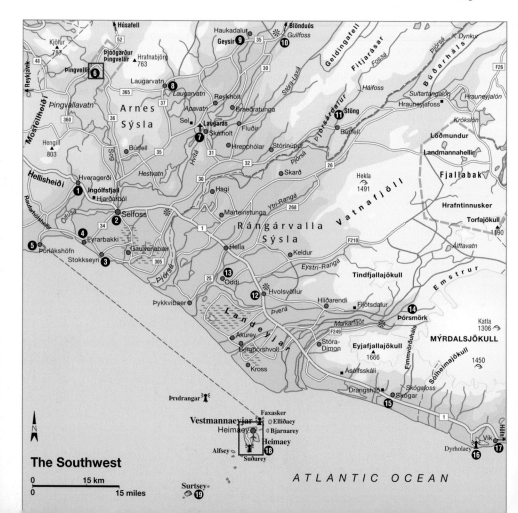

The Southwest

0   15 km

0   15 miles

ATLANTIC OCEAN

Walk back to the visitor centre from here, with a short detour to a strip of land, **Spöngin** **F**, caught between two fissures. Some historians believe that the Lögrétta was initially held on the flat land near here, but had to be moved closer to the Lögberg when the Öxará was diverted. On the opposite side of the bridge is **Peningagjá** **G** ("coin rift"), a natural wishing well. Toss in a coin and ask a yes-no question: if you can follow the coin with your eyes right to the bottom, the answer is Yes; if not, it's No.

Around Þingvellir

It is possible to take day hikes into the surrounding countryside. Almost all paths lead to the old sheep farm of **Skógarhot**, abandoned in 1936, to the west of Þingvellir. About a kilometre south is **Skógarkotshellir**, a long cave that has never been fully explored. The less energetic can enjoy a drive around Lake Þingvallavatn on the narrow dirt roads – although this can get a little hectic on summer weekends and might best be avoided. Luxurious summer houses line the whole lakeside, retreats for Reykjavík inhabitants.

From Þingvallavatn, roads cut off in every direction – west to Reykjavík, north to the deserts, east to Geysir and south to Selfoss – following the ancient routes that were once ridden by Viking farmers, every June, to their unique, quixotic assembly. The road north is the **Kaldidalur** route between Þingvellir and Húsafell. This rocky track usually opens during July when the snows melt around the Langjökull icecap, and will give a small taste of the interior. Shield volcanoes dominate the skyline, the most impressive being the evenly shaped Skjaldbreiður (1,060 metres/3,500 ft), while, on the ground, colourful tundra flowers stud ancient lava flows. River crossings are straightforward and the track runs very close to the hanging glaciers of the icecap.

Skálholt

Returning to Route 35, heading northwards, the road now enters an area that is known as Biskupstungur ("fields between rivers"), between the rivers Brúará and Hvítá. The main attraction is **Skálholt** **7**, Iceland's first Christian bishopric and for over 700 years its theological powerhouse. Skálholt's power was built by an influential dynasty of chieftain-priests. First it was the farm of Gissur the White, the browbeating holy man who had led the pro-Christian faction at the AD 1000 Alþingi. His talented son, Ísleifur, was educated in Germany to become the first properly trained Icelandic priest and, in 1056, Iceland's first bishop. Finally, Ísleifur's eldest son, Gissur, took up where his father had left off, making Skálholt the undisputed Church centre of Iceland, its many schools financed by the first tithe to be imposed in northern Europe.

Skálholt maintained its position of power even through the Reformation, but in 1797 the holy see was moved to Reykjavík and Skálholt all but disappeared. In 1953 – precisely 900 years after the ordination of Bishop Isleifur – the foundations were laid for the new church that now stands on the site. In the process, archaeologists found the remains of one

A 17th-century grave at Þingvellir cemetery.

BELOW: a bishop is consecrated in 14th-century Iceland.

Visiting Gullfoss waterfall is a dramatic experience, with the huge volume of water producing a deafening roar audible from miles away.

BELOW: the mouth of the Great Geysir.

of Skálholt's many cathedrals that had burned down in 1309. At 50 metres (165 ft) in length, it was the largest wooden church in Iceland at the time of building.

Even more oddly, excavators found the carved stone coffin of Páll Jónsson, another of the learned, tough early bishops. According to *Páls Saga*, the bishop's death in 1211 was greeted by an earth tremor and deluge. When excavators opened the coffin in 1953 – revealing the skeleton and walrus-bone bishop's crook – there was one of the biggest downpours that Skálholt had seen in years. Today Páll's coffin is in the church's crypt. The best exit from the crypt is out of the wooden door, through an underground passage that

was part of the medieval cathedral.

Within sight of Skálholt, 3 km (2 miles) away, the idyllic working farm of **Sel** offers accommodation among sheep-filled fields. Just further on is the village of **Reykholt**, which has a geyser that erupts several times an hour and a pleasant, thermally heated swimming pool. Lying south of Skálholt is **Laugarás**, a verdant, geothermally active area with a camping ground. The paved Route 37 turns off directly north of Route 35 to the spa village of **Laugarvatn** ❽ by the shores of the lake of the same name. Summer brings hundreds from Reykjavík to enjoy its pleasures, including the hot spring **Vígðalaug**, used as an all-weather baptism spot by the first bishops of Skálholt.

The land of boiling waters

Both Routes 35 and 37 finally lead to **Geysir** ❾, which has given its name to all such water spouts around the world. Sadly, the Great Geysir, which started erupting in 1294, hasn't performed well for decades: in the 20th century, eager tourists poured gravel into its mouth to lower the water level and force an explosion, but the process seems to have only made it more and more difficult. Nowadays soap is used to break the surface tension, but only on special occasions such as Independence Day. Even then, there are no guarantees that the geyser will perform. If it does, the spume can hit 60 metres (200 ft).

In the light of this, many people were stunned when Geysir suddenly erupted in June 2001, seemingly quite out of the blue. Water spouted up to 40 metres (130 ft) into the air, and the activity continued periodically over several weeks. However, this extraordinary occurence had a perfectly rational explanation: earthquakes in Southern Iceland caused subterranean pressure that gave the great Geysir renewed vitality.

For the rest of the time, visitors will have to be content with the smaller but more reliable geyser, **Strokkur** ("the churn"), which spits up its column of water every five minutes or so to a height of around 20 metres (66 ft). Meanwhile, the whole Geysir area is geothermically active, with walking trails marked out among steaming vents and glistening, multi-coloured mud formations. Never stand too near to Strokkur – an average of seven tourists are scalded every week in summer, mostly from putting their hands in water pools to test their temperatures.

The greatest waterfall

Nine km (6 miles) further along Route 35 is the big attraction of the Golden Circle tour and perhaps Iceland's best-known natural wonder: the waterfall **Gullfoss ❿** ("golden falls"). A path from the parking area leads alongside the deafening double falls, where the River Hvítá tumbles 32 metres (105 ft) into a 2.5-km (1½-mile) ravine. Trails climb past the waterfall's northern face, allowing you to get within an arm's length of the awesome flow. Wear a raincoat, or the clouds of spray that create photogenic rainbows on sunny days will douse you from head to foot.

A stone plaque near the parking area remembers Sigríður Tómasdóttir, a farmer's daughter who lived on the nearby farm Brattholt. Private plans had been drawn up to dam the Hvítá river at Gullfoss for a hydroelectric project, but Sigríður walked to Reykjavík to protest to the government and even announced that she would fling herself into the waterfalls if construction went ahead. The government instead bought the falls and made them a national monument.

Another path leaving from the parking area climbs to the top of the surrounding cliffs for a panoramic view of the falls. From Gullfoss, the road stretches ahead into the uninhabited deserts of central Iceland, and on a clear day you can see the icecap **Langjökull** ("long glacier").

The English poet W.H. Auden noted in the 1930s that Icelanders were already using liquid Sunlight soap to encourage Geysir to explode. The soap had to be imported, since the thinner local type did not work.

BELOW: Mount Hekla dominating the Þjórsárdalur valley.

Below: the serene
farmland of the
southwest.

Viking relics

For anyone even vaguely interested in
Saga Age history, it is worth making the
tortuous trip to the excavated Viking
longhouse of **Stöng** ⑪ and its re-created
twin, **Þjóðveldisbær** ("the Commonwealth farm").

Both lie in **Þjórsárdalur** ("bull river
valley"), off Route 32, formed 8,000
years ago by the biggest lava outpouring
since the Ice Age. The valley is overshadowed by the snow-capped form of
Mount Hekla. Instead of a classic
volcano cone, Hekla is part of a rather
squat series of ridges, becoming progressively squatter with each eruption;
however, even this is usually hidden
behind the thick bank of clouds that
earned Hekla its menacing name, which
means "hooded." The seafaring Irish
monk St Brendan might have been the
first to see Hekla's volcanic pyrotechnics
as he sailed past Iceland in the 8th century, and soon after settlement Hekla
showed that it was a presence to be
feared. The volcano's notoriety grew
such that, in medieval Europe, Hekla was
widely known to be one of the twin
mouths of hell. It has remained active,

with the last eruption in February 2000.

Stöng was the farm of the warrior-
farmer Gaukur Trándilsson, whose saga,
sadly, has been lost. He moved there at
the end of the 11th century, but in 1104
Mount Hekla erupted without warning,
soon covering the once-lush valley with
a thick layer of white ash. Stöng and 20
other nearby farms had to be abandoned,
and Þjórsárdalur was never resettled. In
1939, archaeologists uncovered Gaukur's
house: it was in the form of two long
rooms built end to end, with two annexes
for the dairy and lavatory. As Iceland's
best example of an early medieval home,
it became the model for the nearby
reconstruction of Þjóðveldisbær, begun
in 1974 to mark the 1,100th anniversary
of Iceland's settlement.

It's worth visiting the turf-covered
reconstruction first, designed by architect
Hörður Ágústsson using the Stöng floor-
plan and built by traditional methods
(note the irregular-shaped planks of wood
for the roof, fitted together so as not to
waste an inch of precious wood, and the
marks of axes used to plane them).

The original Stöng is hidden away
several kilometres further along a very

poor dirt road. A large wooden shed has been built over the ruins to protect them from the elements, but it is never locked. Although only the stone foundations remain, this damp, slightly overgrown set of stones is the best place in Iceland to get the historical imagination working. On a fine day, those with spare time might want to take the two-hour walk beyond Stöng to Iceland's second-highest waterfall, **Háifoss**.

Following the south coast

Back on the Ring Road, the unassuming towns of **Hella** and **Hvolsvöllur** ⓬, both with around 500 inhabitants, mark the beginning of the countryside where perhaps the most famous of the Icelandic Sagas, *Njáls Saga*, took place. The new **Saga Centre** (open June–Aug daily 9am–7pm; www.njala.is) in Hvolsvöllur, has a very accessible exhibition showing life in Iceland in the Viking Age and telling the story of *Njáls Saga (see pages 94–5)* in an easy yet comprehensive way. The centre is signposted from the main road. If you're interested in Iceland's rich literary history, consider combining the Saga Centre with a visit to the Culture House in Reykjavík *(see page 151)*, where examples of the ornately written sagas are on display. Together, the two museums help provide the visitor with a clear understanding of Viking life in medieval Iceland.

Between the two towns, Route 266 heads south to **Oddi** ⓭ which quickly became home to Iceland's most learned saga writers, including Snorri Sturluson. Oddi's first inhabitant, Sæmundur the Learned, was well known to be a wizard: the man had no shadow, since it had been stolen by the devil while he was studying at the "Black School" for satanists in Paris. Sæmundur offered his soul if Satan could take him back to Iceland without getting him wet. In the shape of a giant seal, the devil swam the North Atlantic with Sæmundur on his back, but as soon as they got near the coast, Sæmundur whacked him on the head with a prayer book. The wily wizard swam the rest of the way and, since he was soaked, kept his soul.

The church at Oddi today was built in the 1920s, but has a number of curious artefacts on display, including a silver chalice dating from the 14th century.

Ruins of the turf houses by Drangshlíð farm near Skogar.

BELOW: a glacier burrows into Þórsmörk.

Þórður Tómasson, the curator of Skógar Museum.

BELOW : the black sand beach at Vík.

Thunder god's forest

East of the Ring Road along Route 249 is the valley of **Þórsmörk** – literally, "Thor's forest", one of Iceland's most spectacular but inaccessible wilderness areas. Sealed off by three glaciers, two deep rivers and a string of mountains, Þórsmörk has received added protection since the 1920s as a nature reserve operated by the Icelandic Forestry Commission. The single dirt road into the park is impassable to everything but the specially designed high-carriage buses – some of the oversized Icelandic four-wheel drives can make it in when the glacial rivers are low, which is usually in the early morning.

Despite the difficulties, Þórsmörk often attracts well over 1,000 Icelandic campers every summer weekend and a growing number of foreigners on day trips (there are no hotels or guesthouses here, but there are two tourist huts). Visitors are rewarded with spectacular glacier views, fields of wildflowers, pure glacial streams and forests of birch and willow full of birds – particularly blackbirds, ravens and wagtails.

The Ring Road continues south along a narrow plain of farmland between the black sand coast and rugged cliffs that lead to the icecap **Eyjafjallajökull**, riddled with caves and marked by thin waterfalls. Ruins of indeterminate age crop up at intervals here, giving the area considerable atmosphere. Beside the driveway to the farm **Drangshlíð** are some collapsed turf houses built into caves.

Three km (2 miles) further east, **Skógar** is home to a meticulously managed **Folk Museum** (open June–Aug daily 9am–7pm, May & Sept 10am–5pm; admission charge), the most visited of its kind in Iceland, run since 1959 by a local character Þórður Tómasson. Apart from a 6,000-piece collection, the museum has examples of different types of Icelandic housing down through the ages. There is a summer Edda Hotel at Skógar, as well as the splendid waterfall **Skógafoss**, whose sheer fall offers one of south Iceland's best photo opportunities. The trek from here to Þórsmörk, passing between the icecaps of Eyjafjallajökull and Mýrdalsjökull over the **Fimmvörðuháls** pass, is popular with the hardy between June and September, so much so that it becomes quite crowded, particularly in July. There are two huts

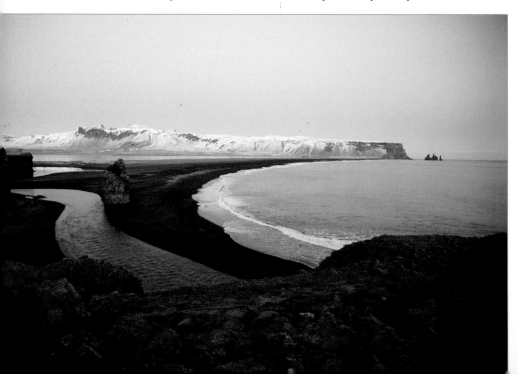

between the icecaps, one an emergency shelter, the other bookable ahead.

Six km (4 miles) east of Skógar, **Fúlilækur** ("foul river") announces itself with the overpowering rotten-egg stench of sulphur. The river emerges from beneath the **Sólheimajökull** glacier, which can be seen from the road, and originates near the volcano Katla, whose subterranean activities beneath the Mýrdalsjökull icecap have often sent glacial tides to devastate this area. Further on, Route 218 cuts south to **Dyrhólaey** ⑯, a protected nature area with a steep cliff and a much-photographed natural rock arch out to sea; this is one of the best places to photograph puffins in south Iceland. Saga hero Njáll's son-in-law Kári had his farm here.

Vík ⑰ (sometimes referred to as Vík í Mýrdal to distinguish it from other Víks), is a small town of around 400 people set along a dramatic stretch of coastline: here the North Atlantic swell hits the land, its

waves crashing dramatically on a long beach of black sand. At the end of the beach are the **Reynisdrangur**, towering fingers of black rock standing out to sea and inhabited by colonies of arctic terns. The relentless, battering wind adds to the Gothic scene – helping to make this the only non-tropical beach to be rated by *Islands*, a US magazine, as one of the world's top 10 beaches. ❏

The arch at Dyrhólaey.

BELOW: a delectable variety of seafood

RESTAURANTS & CAFÉS

Eldstó Café

Austurvegur 2, Hvolsvöllur
Excellent homemade sandwiches and cakes are available at this pleasant little café, the focal point of local life in the small town of Hvolsvöllur. **$**

Fjöruborðið

Eyrarbraut 3, Stokkseyri
Tel: 483 1550
A renowned and highly popular lobster restaurant by the sea. Well worth the drive down from Reykjavík.
$$$

Halldórskaffi

Víkurbraut, Vík
A cosy little café tucked away inside the former nineteenth century store, Brydebúð, on the main street. **$**

Hótel Geysir

Geysir. Tel: 480 6800
Everything from wholesome soups to top-notch lamb dishes at the restaurant inside Hótel Geysir. A good place to stop and eat on the Golden Circle tour. **$$**

Hótel Ork

Breiðumörk 1C, Hveragerði
Tel: 483 4700
One of the best restaurants for miles is attached to the hotel here. Accomplished cuisine featuring the likes of slow-cooked lamb, grilled *bacalao* and chicken in tarragon sauce. **$$$**

Menam

Eyravegur, Selfoss
Tel: 482 4099
A real find in provincial Iceland: a genuine Thai restaurant serving up tasty green curries and superb noodle dishes. **$**

Rauða húsið

Búðarstígur 4, Eyrarbakki
Tel: 483 3330
The grilled seafood here has to be tasted to be believed and it's one of the best restaurants for miles around. **$$**

● ● ● ● ● ● ● ● ● ● ● ● ● ●

*Categories are for an average-priced dinner per person, without wine. **$$$** over ISK 4,000, **$$** ISK 2,000–4,000, **$** under ISK 2,000.*

VESTMANNAEYJAR
(THE WESTMAN ISLANDS)

The comparatively recent volcanic origins of
this small and scattered group of islands off
the southwest coast are clearly visible in their
rugged appearance

Main attractions
HEIMAEY
FOLK MUSEUM
ELDFELL
CLIFFTOP WALK FROM
HERJÓLFSDALUR

PRECEDING PAGES:
fishermen off
Heimaey. **BELOW:**
Heimaey beneath
the ever-threatening
Elfell volcano.

I n the earliest years of Iceland's settlement, five Irish slaves ambushed and
butchered their master Hjörleifur
Hrodmarsson, brother of the first successful settler, Ingólfur Arnarson. Drag-
ging along a handful of slave women,
they commandeered a rowing boat and
– according to the ancient *Landnámabók
(Book of Settlements)* – escaped from
their farm near Vík to one of the small
green islands visible from the country's
south coast.

Not surprisingly, the slaves' new-
found freedom was short-lived. Two

weeks later, the other Viking settlers
tracked them down, stormed their camp
and mercilessly put the escapees to
death. Even so, the whole archipelago
has since been known in the slaves' honour as the Vestmannaeyjar, or, in English, the Westman Islands – the islands
of the western men.

Today the Vestmannaeyjar (pronounced, roughly, *vestman-air*) have
become one of Iceland's most popular
destinations. Comprising 16 small
islands and some 30 rocks or skerries,
they combine a seductive serenity with
raw natural beauty: the archipelago is
among the world's newest volcanic cre-
ations, and one of its islands, Surtsey,
only emerged from the ocean in 1963.

Even Heimaey – the largest of the
group and the only one with a permanent
human population – is scarred black with
fresh volcanic flow from the 1973 eruption that nearly caused it to be permanently abandoned *(see panel on page
189)*. The eruption changed the shape of
the island forever, adding 15 percent to
its area and introducing a new volcanic
peak, Eldfell, which now dominates the
main town. In parts of Heimaey the
ground still steams and is warm to the
touch, and one can easily imagine that
this is how the earth looked at the time of
its formation.

Violent birth

Although this area off Iceland's southern
coast had been the scene of underwater
volcanic activity for hundreds of thou-

sands of years, scientists estimate that the first land did not emerge from the sea here until 10,000 years ago, and most islands were not formed until 5,000 years ago – the blink of an eye, in geological terms.

As a result, most of the islands are tiny, rugged and inhospitable. Each is ringed by sheer cliffs, topped with lush vegetation and crowded with sea birds: more species gather here than anywhere else in Iceland. Most are populated only by seasonal puffin-catchers, whose huts can be seen from the sea.

For the vast majority of visitors, the point of arrival will be **Heimaey** ⓲ (pronounced *hay-may*). The name of both the largest island and its township, Heimaey can be reached by a 25-minute flight from Reykjavík or a three-and-a-quarter-hour ferry trip from Þorlákshöfn on the coast (a glorious journey when it is sunny, but when the sea is rough, one of Iceland's most dismal). Many visitors make only a day-trip to the island, although it is worth staying overnight.

Heimaey's 4,800 inhabitants are a hardy and independent breed, steeled by generations of isolation, brutal living conditions and an extensive history of disasters. After the Irish slaves' abortive attempt to hide out here, the island was first occupied by a certain Herjólfur Barðursson, a reclusive farmer who had become tired of the constant strife on the mainland. Life was relatively peaceful – if not particularly easy – on the island for several centuries, until it became a target for pirate raids.

As if to repay the islanders for the depredations of their Viking ancestors, a series of cut-throats descended on the Vestmannaeyjar: British pirates ruled the islands for almost a century, and then, in 1627, the Turks arrived. Well into the 20th century, island children were terrified by the tale of the bloodthirsty heathens who put 34 men and women to the sword and carried off more than 200 as slaves. Those who tried to hide in the cliffs were shot down like birds.

Epidemics wracked Heimaey for the next couple of centuries, while the 1783 eruption of Laki on the mainland killed off all the fish around the islands, reducing its inhabitants to living on sea birds and an edible root called *hvönn* (with plenty falling to their deaths from cliffs in pursuit of both).

View of some of the smaller Westman Islands.

BELOW: Heimaey church and the memorial to lost fishermen, with Eldfell in the background.

TIP

Ferries between the mainland (Þorlákshöfn) and Heimaey take around 2 hours 45 minutes. There are two ferries daily in each direction (for details, see page 316). Þorlákshöfn is some 75 km (45 miles) west along the coast from the Vestmannaeyjar: unfortunately, it is the closest functioning port – the area of the mainland nearest the archipelago – just 10 km (6 miles) away – is marshy and unsuitable for docking.

BELOW: Heimaey harbour.

Later, fishing accidents would take a dreadful toll: twice, when the island's population was less than 350, storms would send more than 50 men to the bottom of the sea on a single day. In the 19th century, some 100 fishermen drowned from Heimaey, a fact of life which may have accounted for the population's famous sangfroid in the face of the 1973 volcanic eruption.

Fishing capital

Today Heimaey is the most important fishing centre in the whole of Iceland – with only 2 percent of the country's population, it supplies some 12 percent of its exports. A large part of the catch is processed on the island, giving locals a healthy slice of Iceland's prosperity.

Heimaey town ⒶＡ itself is spread out around the harbour, where over 100 colourful trawlers can dock in the natural windbreak of the lava wall created by the 1973 eruption. The setting is spectacular, with rugged brown bluffs on one side and the two volcanic peaks, Eldfell and Helgafell on the other. Keep an eye out for the colourful mural painted by school children on the side of a building near the harbour, depicting the fateful morning of the eruption.

Walking away from the harbour into town along **Kirkjuvegar** (to the left of the harbour, with the water at your back), the streets run along the base of the lava wall where it was stopped in 1973 – literally, in some people's backyards. The ruins of one house still haven't been removed, as a reminder of the destruction. Steps have been built up onto the convoluted lava fields, here covered with a thin film of green moss, through which the wind whistles eerily.

With few cars in Heimaey, the streets are empty and peaceful – in fact, their utter desolation on Sundays gives them the haunting feel of a Bergman film. Points of interest include the picturesque white **church**, with a statue commemorating the island's fishermen lost at sea, and the **Folk Museum** (open mid-May–mid-Sept daily 11am–5pm, mid-Sept–mid-May Sat & Sun 3–5pm) above the library, which has a well-organised set of relics, model ships and photographs. Well worth a visit to see its extraordinary live collection of Icelandic fish is the **Aquarium and Natural History**

Heimaey

Museum (open May–Sept daily 11am–5pm, Oct–Apr Sat & Sun 3–5pm). Particularly odd are the Icelandic cod, which appear to be made of white plastic, and the horrifying Icelandic catfish, a fish that boasts piranha teeth and a bad-tempered, strangely human expression.

Exploring the island

Unless you have brought a car over by ferry from the mainland, or have the time and energy to walk, the easiest way to visit Heimaey's attractions is on one of the bus tours run by Viking Tours (tel: 488 4884).

A rough dirt road has been cut to Eldfell **B**, the 221-metre (725-ft) high peak formed during the 1973 eruption. The spectacular view from the base clearly shows how a sixth of the island is now fresh lava flow. The vista stretches across the brightly painted corrugated iron roofs of Heimaey to the harbour and, on a clear day, to the mainland. A short walk up leads to barren, steaming tephra fields. If the ground seems warm to the touch, dig a few inches down – it's hot enough to bake bread, and Heimaey housewives, in their more whimsical moments, still use the earth for that pur-

pose. Roads have also been cut into Kirkjubæjarhraun **C**, the 3-sq. km (7.4-acre) lava field spat up in 1973. Apart from a pillar marking where the oldest settlement on the island once was (now 300 metres/980 ft below ground), little disturbs the dark lava's contorted expanse besides geothermal units, heating the town's water and houses.

On the other side of the town, a road leads past a surreal monument in the shape of giant football, to the lush natural amphitheatre of Herjólfsðalur **D**. Archaeologists found the ruins of a Saga Age home here, assumed to be that of the island's first settler, Herjólfur Barðursson. These days, however, it is more famous as the camping ground where thousands of Icelanders gather around a giant bonfire for three days to celebrate the Þjóðhátíð festival in early August. The prodigious feats of drinking make this long weekend a must for many Icelanders, but most foreigners find it a good time to avoid the island.

Puffin cliffs

A path across the golf course near here leads to a splendid view of several block-

A mural in Heimaey in honour of the all-important fishing industry.

BELOW LEFT: evacuating the island in 1973.

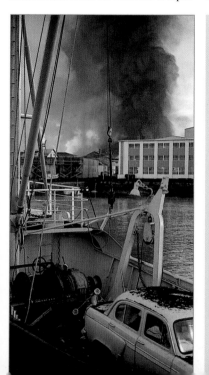

Crisis on Heimaey

Early on 23 January 1973, a mile-long fissure cracked open without warning on the eastern side of Heimaey, and a wall of molten lava poured out towards the town. Islanders were told to abandon their houses. By great good fortune, the entire Heimaey fishing fleet was in dock that night: some 5,300 people left the island on trawlers. Not a life was lost. Over the next five months, some 33 million tons of lava spewed from the fissure, threatening to devastate the island. Hundreds of tonnes of tephra (volcanic debris) hailed down on the town, smashing windows and igniting houses. By early February the greatest danger was from the 165-metre (500-ft) wall of lava moving towards the harbour – the lifeline of the local community. In an attempt to avert disaster, two commercial dredging ships equipped with water cannons pumped over 43 million litres (11½ million gallons) of water a day to cool the lava. Heimaey was covered in a blanket of steam, and the lava flow was stopped before it blocked the harbour entrance. More pumps worked around the clock for the next three months to help cool over 5 million cubic metres of lava. Scientists pronounced the eruption over in July, and the residents began returning home.

Twice daily in season, a boat sails around the main island, offering a chance to see some of Heimaey's sea caves, as well as spot birdlife and possibly whales. Book with Viking Tours, tel: 488 4884.

BELOW: the three-day Þjóðhátíð party in early August.

shaped islands including **Hæna**, **Kafhellir** and **Hani**. The cliffs here house the island's most accessible puffin colony. Although the islanders hunt puffins *(see panel on page 192)*, their attitude towards these ungainly birds is not always entirely mercenary. Late in August every year, thousands of baby puffins waddle into the township of Heimaey – lured by the bright lights in their search of food, since their parents cease feeding them in late summer. To save the puffins from a grisly end from cats, dogs and cars, Heimaey's children flock to the streets and collect them in cardboard boxes. Next day, the baby puffins are taken to the coast and ritualistically flung out to sea – and, hopefully, a successful puffin career. At least they will not end up on island dinner tables until they reach adulthood, since an unwritten law holds that the young puffins should not be eaten.

From Herjólfsðalur, precarious trails requiring mountain equipment can be taken along the cliffs to the northern promontory of **Ystiklettur**, above the harbour. An easier trail also follows the road south to **Stórhöfði E**, where a light-house looks out over the island's most exposed coastline. Winds of 250 kph (150 mph) and waves of 23 metres (75 ft) have been recorded here in storms.

Boat cruises

A visit to Heimaey would not be complete without an excursion on the waves. Regular departures in small boats leave from the harbour docks, weaving out past the salmon farm (the huge salmon can actually be seen leaping from the water) and around the island. The trip gives views of Heimaey's steep cliffs crowded with sea birds (gannets, five species of auk, storm petrels, guillemots and puffins) and usually several sure-footed sheep perched on what appear to be almost vertical green fields.

If you're lucky, orcas (killer whales) can be spotted among the smaller islands, their glistening black and white flanks clearly visible as they leap from the waves. Boats also pull in to several of the natural caves on the coast.

Klettsvík Bay F became the new home of Keikó, the world-famous killer whale, star of the film *Free Willy*. Captured off the coast of Iceland 1979, Keikó spent three years in an Icelandic aquarium. Then the whale was airlifted to Marineland in Niagara Falls, Ontario, where he was trained to perform. After spending some 10 years in an amusement park, he was flown to Oregon Coast Aquarium, where it was nursed back to health. And in September 1998 the 6.5-metre (21-ft) long animal, weighing about 4,500 kg (10,000 lb), was airlifted to a protected cove in Klettsvík bay, where he lived in a 145 million-litre (3.2 million-gallon) pen, the largest of its kind in the world. Keikó was moved on to Norway in the summer of 2002 as part of the process of releasing him back into the wild, but sadly died the following year.

The final attraction in Heimaey is the **Volcano Show** (mid-June–mid-Sept, one or two shows daily) at the local cinema, which includes a documented story that has become emblematic of the islanders' constant battle with Nature.

Half man, half seal

One night in March 1983, a fishing vessel capsized 5 km (3 miles) off Heimaey's coast. All of the crew quickly perished in the freezing winter seas, except for a fisherman named Guðlaugur Friðfljófsson. He staved off the confusion of hypothermia by talking to hovering sea birds, and set off swimming for shore. It took him six hours – about five hours longer than anyone else has ever survived in water that temperature.

As if that wasn't enough, Guðlaugur swam ashore onto some of the sharpest lava on the island, cutting his feet and losing blood as he stumbled to the town. Doctors could not find his pulse, but the fisherman survived. Later, when the London Hospital Medical College performed tests, Guðlaugur's body fat proved to closely resemble that of a seal. It's a story that islanders recount fondly, as if to steel themselves for the next skirmish with the sea, the winds or the volcanic peaks that threaten them every day.

The birth of an island

The youngest of the islands, **Surtsey** , burst from the North Atlantic in a dramatic eruption in 1963. Captured on film by airborne camera crews, highlights of its fiery, four-year-long birth were seen around the world, providing a unique glimpse of how volcanic islands are

A Reykjavík restaurant advertises a "puffin feast". Most of the puffins caught for food in Iceland are from the Vestmannaeyjar.

BELOW: Heimaey harbour entrance seen from the wall of lava that threatened it in 1973.

TIP

Since Surtsey is off-limits to all but a small number of research scientists, the only way to get close to the island, though not set foot on it, is on a boat trip organised by Viking Tours (tel: 488 4884). Departures are on request and require a mimimum number of passengers. There's a good chance you'll spot whales on the journey, too.

BELOW RIGHT: there are an estimated 8,000–10,000 puffins in Iceland.

formed and still giving scientists unique and invaluable data on how virgin habitats are colonised by plant and animal life.

The eruption began below the waves in the Mid-Atlantic Ridge, the submarine mountain chain that runs into the south coast of Iceland. Island fishermen were the first to notice smoke rising from the sea in November 1963. Molten lava spewing onto the sea floor was cooling on contact with the icy waters, but soon a pile of volcanic debris had risen the 130 metres (430 ft) to the surface to create a burning mass above sea level. A pillar of black ash, intertwined with a stream of steam, was sent 10 km (6 miles) into the air – looking menacing from nearby Heimaey and visible from as far away as Reykjavík. The first flights over the site confirmed that the Vestmannaeyjar now had a 16th member, and that eruption was continuing: fluid lava was piling up over the mound of tephra and solidifying, turning it from a giant volcanic refuse heap into a permanent presence.

A scientific laboratory

The new island was named after the fiery Norse giant Surtur, who sets the world alight at Ragnarök, the end of the world. For the next four years, until June 1967, Surtsey provided the world's scientific community with the spectacle of its ongoing formation, before finally settling down to an area of 1.57 sq. km (½ sq. mile) and 155 metres (510 ft) in height. During the same period, two smaller islands emerged from the eruption but have since eroded away and disappeared below the waves. Indeed, other islands in the archipelago, which formed in the same way as Surtsey several thousand years ago, provide a clue as to what will happen to the island in the future. They have been substantially eroded by the heavy seas and the wind since their creation and suggest that Surtsey will continue to exist for several centuries before vanishing for good, too. Since its creation Surtsey has been reduced in size by half and the pattern of volcanism in the Vestmannaeyjar indicates that any further eruption on the island which would potentially add to its size is unlikely. In line with its unique status, the Icelandic government submitted an application in 2001 for Surtsey to be included on the UNESCO

Hunting for Puffins

The appealing, stubby-winged puffin is regarded as a particularly mouthwatering morsel in Iceland, especially in the Vestmannaeyjar. The islanders' affection for the puffin as Iceland's national emblem does not discourage them from seeing it as a source of food – and one which has helped them to survive hard times. Today's puffin-catchers swing nets with 3-metre (10-ft) long handles to catch the birds on the wing – puffins are slightly clumsy in the air. On Heimaey the puffin-catchers can most frequently be seen at work on windy days on top of the cliffs by the golf course in the west of the island. Some 16,000 puffins are caught on the island every summer to make up Iceland's national dinner. The catchers are careful to avoid catching immature birds so that the colony's numbers are not endangered. The record for a single puffin-catcher is 1,202 in one day. Puffin and guillemot, usually under the generic name of *svartifugl* (the Alcidae family of birds), appear on the menus of some of the more adventurous restaurants in Reykjavík. The dark, gamey meat, with a slightly fishy taste, is sometimes served fried or boiled, often with a curry sauce, or alternatively it may be smoked. It is a great favourite with Icelandic gourmets.

World Heritage List as an example of a volcanic island and its accompanying ecosystem.

Fascinating as Surtsey's formation had been, its greatest scientific value started after the eruption had ended. Its 1,000°C (1,830°F) surface temperatures during the eruption had left it completely free of any living organism: the island became a sort of natural laboratory approximating how Iceland itself must have been when its first segments emerged from the sea some 20 million years ago.

Seeds arrived on the island in its first summer, carried by the wind, sea and passing sea birds. The first sprouting plants were noticed during the following year, 1965, even before the island's eruption had completely finished. By the end of 1967, no less than four species of plants had established themselves around the coastline.

Midges and flies were the first animals to settle the island, with seals making an appearance after the surrounding seas became restocked with fish. In 1970, black-backed gulls became the first birds to nest on Surtsey. Since that time, scientists have observed 60 bird species on

the island – some are just stopping off on their migration to other shores, while others are making this their new home.

Surtsey is still a scientific station and remains off-limits to casual visitors. Any uncontrolled intrusion might upset the island's natural development, either by damaging fragile plant life or accidentally bringing in new presences (a seed caught on a visitor's shoe, for example, might sprout into a plant). Fly-overs in light aircraft, taking about two hours, however, can be organised in Reykjavík *(contact tourist office for details, page 341).* ❏

The Vestmannaeyjar archipelago comprises 16 islands (plus a further 30 tiny islets) – only one is permanently inhabited.

BELOW LEFT: scientists recording the development of plant life on Surtsey.

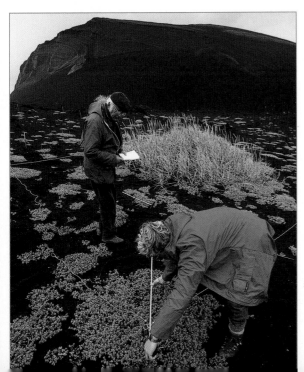

RESTAURANTS

Café María
Skólavegur 1, Heimaey
Tel: 481 3160
The most cosmopolitan place to eat in Heimaey with excellent puffin on the menu as well as an array of fish, lamb and crêpes. **$$**

Lanterna
Bárustígur 11, Heimaey
Tel: 481 3393
Huge pizzas are the speciality at this Italian restaurant, though there's also puffin and fish choices on the menu. **$$**

Kökuhús
Bárastígur 7, Heimaey
Great cakes, buns, sandwiches and coffee at this handy bakery in the centre of town. **$**

• • • • • • • • • • •

Categories are for an average-priced dinner per person, without wine. **$$$** *over ISK 4,000,* **$$** *ISK 2,000–4,000,* **$** *under ISK 2,000.*

THE SOUTHEAST

In this region overshadowed by the vast Vatnajökull icecap and precariously situated on expanses of glacial debris, the highlight is the rugged and popular Skaftafell National Park

Icelanders often say that their country was unfairly named, since it is, after all, strikingly green for much of the year – and it is an undeniably odd fact that Iceland and Greenland were christened the wrong way round. But anyone paying a visit to the southeast of the country will have ice on their minds, no matter what the season. The whole area is dominated by Europe's largest icecap, Vatnajökull, whose enormous glaciers creep down through every crack in the coastal mountains like oozing blue putty. Indeed, such is the size of Vatnajökull – as large as the entire English county of Yorkshire – that driving along its southern flank can take several hours and is one of the most memorable trips this part of the country has to offer. Snout after snout of chiselled ice and snow edges its way down from the icecap tentatively towards the Atlantic, treating visitors to some truly jaw-dropping scenery.

Volcanoes regularly erupt beneath it, devastating farmland with flows of melted ice and debris as large in volume as the Amazon River. Little wonder then if the Viking explorers – including the First Settler, Ingólfur Arnarson, who spent three years in the southeast – thought the name "Iceland" appropriate.

The damage caused by Vatnajökull's glacial flows (called *hlaups*) made much of the coast next to impassable for centuries. Until the Ring Road was finally driven through in 1974, parts of the southeast were among the remotest in Iceland. To reach Skaftafell or Höfn by land, for example, one had to drive the entire 1,100 km (680 miles) around the north of the country.

Today the highway from Reykjavík to the southeast is fully paved, and the glacier-riddled Skaftafell National Park has become the most popular wilderness area in the country. (In fact, on June and July weekends, it becomes so crowded that it is probably best avoided by travellers.) Meanwhile, the drive along the coast passes a luxuriant, haunting landscape dotted with tiny farms and historic settlements.

Main attractions
LAKI CRATERS
SKAFTAFELL NATIONAL PARK
JÖKULSÁRLÓN
VATNAJÖKULL ICECAP
GLACIER EXHIBITION, HÖFN

PRECEDING PAGES: Hiking near Höfn. **LEFT:** Skaftafellsjökull reflected in a lake in Skaftafell National Park. **BELOW:** skidooing.

Iceland's edible berries include black crowberries and blueberries.

Curse of the Irish monks

The gateway to the southeast is the town of **Kirkjubæjarklaustur** ❶ (call it "cloister" and you will be understood), a green oasis in the volcanic desert formed by the eruptions of the Laki craters in 1783 – an event that devastated Iceland and is still considered to be one of the worst natural disasters in recorded history.

Kirkjubæjarklaustur was first settled by Irish monks, who fled the Vikings but left a curse that no pagan would ever live here. A Christian Norseman named Ketill the Foolish (so named by his peers for converting from the worship of Thor) lived on the site quite happily for many years. But when another Viking, Hildir Eysteinsson, decided to move in, he no sooner clapped eyes on his future farm than he dropped down dead. Perhaps, reasoned the Norsemen, Ketill had not been so foolish after all.

Religion plays a big part in the rest of Kirkjubæjarklaustur's history. In 1186, Benedictine nuns set up a convent here (*klaustur* means cloister), which was closed in the 16th-century Reformation. It can't have been a model institution, since two of the nuns were burned at the stake: one for sleeping with the devil, the other for maligning the Pope.

Contemporaneous with the nuns' convent at Kirkjubær, there was a monastery at Þykkvibær, a short distance away. It is said that the abbot and the monks of Þykkvibær often went up to Kirkjubær to see the mother superior and the sisters. On one such occasion both the abbot and some of the monks spent the night at Kirkjubær. The story goes that in the middle of the night the mother superior went with a light to check on the propriety of the sisters' conduct. In one cell, she came upon a monk and a nun sleeping together. The mother superior was about to reprimand the nun when the latter noticed her superior's headgear and said: "What is that you have on your head, dear mother?" Then the mother superior realised that she had taken the abbot's underpants by mistake and put them on her head instead of her bonnet. As a result, she softened her voice, saying as she retreated: "We are all sinners, sister".

During the 1783 Laki eruptions, a wall of lava looked like wiping out the settlement when the local curate, Jón Stein-

The Southeast

grímsson, herded everyone into the wooden church. There he delivered the ultimate fire-and-brimstone sermon whose effect, with great chunks of ash smashing down just outside the window, can only be imagined. When the sermon had finished, the congregation stumbled outside to find that the lava had been diverted and the church saved. The modern **Steingrímsson memorial chapel** has been built on the old church's site to commemorate this neat piece of divine intervention.

Today Kirkjubæjarklaustur is a pretty but somnolent outpost of 300 people, with the waterfall **Systrafoss** spraying down from steep cliffs as its backdrop. The 1783 lava fields, dotted with pseudo-craters, can still be seen just south of town, en route to the curious **Kirkjugólf** – the name means "church floor", since Viking settlers assumed it was part of a stone floor built by the curse-happy Irish monks. It is, however, a natural formation, with the tops of hexagonal basalt colums fitting together as perfectly as tiles.

Most people stay in Kirkjubæjarklaustur as a jumping-off point to the infamous **Laki craters ❷**, responsible for

the 1783 eruptions. Over a period of 10 months, 30 billion tons of lava and three times as much sulphuric acid belched forth from the so-called "Skaftá fires". Not only were whole communities wiped out by the flow, but Laki sent up a cloud of noxious gas that began the "Haze Famine" and killed a fifth of Iceland's already much-diminished population and half its livestock – a toll so dramatic that plans were made to evacuate the island completely. Today Laki is extinct, but the craters at its base are still steaming. There are some fantastic views to be had from the peak.

The Ring Road east of Kirkjubæjarklaustur runs to the attractive farm of **Foss**, named for the thin waterfall flowing from the cliffs on the property, followed by the basalt columns of **Dverghamrar**. A sunken plain of moss-covered lava – once again created by Laki – must be crossed before finding the farm of **Núpsstaður ❸**, at the base of the imposing 770-metre (2,500-ft) cliff called **Lómagnúpur** ("loon peak"). Núpsstaður has one of Iceland's most charming 17th-century churches and a still-working antique harmonium.

 TIP

Laki can be reached only by four-wheel-drive vehicles. Tours run there daily in summer from Kirkjubæjarklaustur.

BELOW: the 18th-century chapel at Núpsstaður.

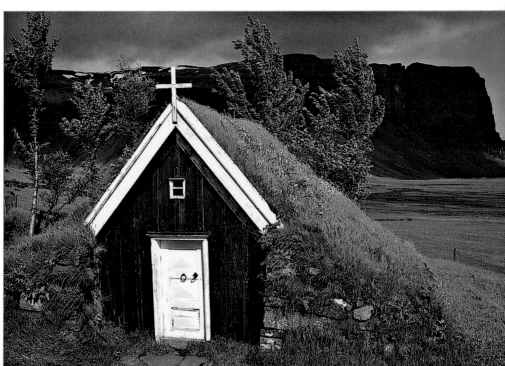

Volcanoes regularly erupt beneath the Vatnajökull glacier, melting the ice and causing torrents of floodwater to surge into the sea. Naturally, road-building in the area has been particularly problematic and it wasn't until 1974 that the Ringroad was finally pushed through, employing a complex systems of bridges and drainage gulleys, to channel the water away from the road.

BELOW: a volcanic wasteland, Skeiðarársandur.

At this point begins **Skeiðarársandur** ❹, the biggest of the southern *sandurs* – great wastelands of black sand and glacial debris carried out by volcanic eruptions from underneath Vatnajökull. Before the Ring Road was built, the only way across here was on horseback, accompanied by one of the farmers from Núpsstaður who had spent their lives learning to navigate the treacherous terrain. Today, cyclists dread this stretch of road most in Iceland: it is completely monotonous, and regular sandstorms make any open-air activity a misery.

Long bridges and flood barriers have been built to counteract any further glacial flows created by eruptions of **Grímsvötn** – although located under Vatnajökull, the most active and potentially lethal of Iceland's many volcanic craters. The last eruption under the ice began at the end of September 1996. More than two months later, on the morning of November 5th, the long-awaited glacial burst began. Large parts of Skeiðarársandur disappeared under black and muddy floodwater, electric cables across the sands were destroyed, as was the main road itself. The bridges

over the rivers Sæluhúsakvísl and Gígja were swept away, and the 906-metre (2,980-ft) long bridge over the River Skeiðará, was badly damaged. South of the road the flood carried immense amounts of sediment to the sea and the beach stretched 800 metres (2,600 ft) further out into the ocean than it had before the flood. Two days later, when the burst came to an end, a million tons of ice had broken away from the margin of Skeiðarárjökull glacier, which dominates the view on the north side of the road. Since the glacial burst, the bridges and road have been renewed and restored.

Skaftafell National Park

Approached from the west, **Skaftafell National Park** ❺ is announced by views over its rugged peaks and the three glaciers that have worked their way between them: from the left, **Morsárjökull**, **Skaftafellsjökull** and **Svínafellsjökull**. The twin glaciers of **Kvíárjökull** and **Fjallsjökull** can be seen further on. Finally, seen from the park, these are all dwarfed by **Öræfajökull** to the east, whose peak, **Hvannadalshnúkur**, is 2,120 metres (6,700

Skaftafell

0   1 km
0   1 mile

Morsárjökull

Skarð
839

Morsárdálur

Skorar

Kristínartindar
1126

706

650

Fremrihnaukur
610

B o t n

Flár

Skerhóll
526

Morsá

Stóralækur

Skaftafellsheiði

Sjónarnípa

Sjónarsker

Svartifoss

Eystragil

Hæðir

Bölti

Þjónustumiðstöð

998

Vík, Höfn

Skeiðará

SKAFTAFELLSJÖKULL

ft) high. All are fingers of the icecap **Vatnajökull** – which, like other icecaps in Iceland, is believed to have been formed not during the Ice Age but in another cold period 2,500 years ago.

The National Park was established in 1967 and expanded in 1984 to take up some 1,600 sq. km (580 sq. miles). Settlers first came here in the Saga Age, and there are still two farms in the park, one of which now operates as a guesthouse. The park service operates an **information centre** Ⓐ next to a parking area and large camping ground. On summer weekends, this becomes a cross between a particularly raucous Reykjavík pub and a refugee camp, so anyone interested in communing with nature should come on a weekday. There is also a supermarket and snack bar, which overflows with card-playing backpackers in rainy weather.

All walks into the park depart from this point. The easiest is to the snout of the glacier **Skaftafellsjökull** Ⓑ, less than half an hour away. Covered in volcanic refuse, the ice is actually a shiny grey, like graphite. You can climb onto the edge of the glacier, but be careful. It's slippery – and a fall would dunk you

straight into a near-freezing meltwater stream that soon disappears underground.

The most photographed attraction in Skaftafell is **Svartifoss waterfall** Ⓒ, a short walk along the road up to the Bölti farm/guesthouse west of the camping ground. Svartifoss is surrounded on both sides by basalt columns, giving it a grand organ-pipe effect. The path continues on to the peak of **Sjónarsker** Ⓓ, with a view disk, and then further into the mountains: the more energetic can make a day-trip to include views of Morsárjökull and Skaftafellsjökull

The beautiful Svartifoss waterfall, surrounded by basalt columns.

BELOW LEFT: admiring the view at Fjallsárlón lagoon, east of the National Park.

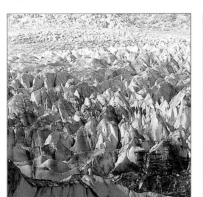

Vatnajökull Icecap

Vatnajökull covers about 8,500 sq. km (3,280 sq. miles), or one twelfth of the whole country, and is 1,000 metres (3,300 ft) thick in parts. It is the largest icecap in the world outside the countries designated as polar regions. At first sight Vatnajökull displays a general resemblance to the main polar ice sheets, but its nature is quite different. This is a so-called temperate glacier. Its temperature is at melting point, or very close to it, at any given depth, except in the top layers, where frost may remain until far into the summer, although that varies.

During the first centuries after settlement the glaciers of Vatnajökull were smaller than they are now, but towards the end of the 12th century the climate began to cool and the ice started to expand. Vatnajökull's glaciers reached their greatest extent during the 18th and 19th centuries. Since 1890 however, they have withdrawn and thinned, especially in the years between 1920 and 1960. Between 1960 and into the 1990s, Vatnajökull thickened and the recession of its glaciers slowed, although global warming is now starting to reverse this trend – the effect being exacerbated by the volcanic eruption at Grímsvötn in 1996, which caused a large amount of ice to melt.

Glacier tours offer the closest possible encounter with mighty Vatnajökull.

BELOW: perfect reflections at Jökulsárlón. Boat trips on the lagoon can be booked through Vatnajökull Travel (tel: 894 1616) who will also provide bus transportation to and from the nearby town of Höfn. There are departures several times daily in summer.

which look like twin seas of ice. In the **Morsárdalur** valley, surrounded by high mountains and huge icecaps, you will also find one of the most impressive woods of the country, with birches reaching a height of 10 metres (33 ft). It's in this area, too, that you'll find one of Iceland's many natural hot pools. Across the Morsá River and a short hike up the hillside behind, a trail leads to a sublime geothermal source which has been dammed to create a round pond where weary hikers can cast off their clothes and steam to their heart's content whilst enjoying an unsurpassed view of the unsullied expanses of the national park – a quintessentially Icelandic experience.

The information centre can give instructions for other day trips into the park. Nature lovers can spot over 200 species of plants around Skaftafell as well as Iceland's usual plethora of birds, including the largest breeding colonies of great and arctic skuas in the northern hemisphere.

The lake of ice

East of Skaftafell along the Ring Road is the farm **Svínafell**, which was the home of Flosi Þórðarson, the murderer of Njáll and his family in *Njáls Saga*, followed by **Hof ❻**, which offers picturesque farmhouse accommodation and has a small turf church. It is near here that the First Settler, Ingólfur Arnarson, lived before moving to Reykjavík – the promontory of **Ingólfshöfði** marks the site. It was here that Ingólfur spent his first winter in Iceland before setting off in search of his high seat pillars which he had tossed in the water as he approached the Icelandic coast. The posts, an important symbol of power, were later discoverd where Reykjavík is located today. In clear weather, this flat headland is the first glimpse of Iceland that most visitors get since the promontory is where Iceland-bound planes usually make landfall.

Immediately after a suspension bridge over the Jökulsá River is one of Iceland's most photographed sights: the iceberg-filled lake of **Jökulsárlón ❼**. The ice has calved from the glacier Breiðamerkurjökull, which runs into the lake, burying its snout underwater. The lake was formed only when the passage to the sea was blocked by land movements in the 20th century: geologists suggest it could come unblocked in the near future, draining the lake and making the Ring Road impassable. Boat cruises operate around Jökulsárlón several times daily in summer, weaving among the glistening ice formations. Sometimes the guide on the boat fishes out of the water a small piece of the astonishingly dense, clear ice so that you can have a closer look.

James Bond fans may get a sense of déjà vu at Jökulsárlón – the opening scenes of the film *A View to a Kill* were shot here.

Excursions on the icecap

East of Jökulsárlón, a turn-off to the left advertises trips to **Jöklaferðir** at the top of Vatnajökull. The road itself is passable only by four-wheel-drive vehicles, but those without such transport can meet the bus from Höfn on the so-called "Glacier Tour" every morning at 10am for the ride up. A small chalet has been built at the edge of the icecap, and hire of snowcats can be arranged. It's not entirely environmentally sound – so much noise and the first touches of air pollution on the pristine icecap. On a clear day, you can see for miles across the white sea of Vatnajökull, and trips usually include a stop at a ravine.

The river valleys along this part of the Ring Road are beautiful but thinly populated, while the flatlands of **Mýrar** ❽ are excellent for birdwatching. On one farm here, **Bjarnanes**, a troll woman named Ketillaug is said to have been seen taking a kettle of gold up into the multi-coloured alluvial mountain **Ketillaugarfjall**. There is one day of the year when humans can try and take the kettle from her, but those that attempt it are subject to hallucinations – typically of the farm below catching fire – and always run back to give the alarm.

Höfn

The southeast's administrative centre, with a population of about 1,600, is **Höfn** ❾ – the name literally means "harbour" – boasting one of the few in the south-

east. The town's fortunes have improved rapidly with the completion of the Ring Road in the 1970s, turning it from a one-horse town to its present, ungainly concrete self. But what it lacks in aesthetic appeal is made up for by its beautiful setting on **Hornafjörður** fjord, almost completely cut off from the sea by spits to form a tranquil lake. There is a **Folk Museum** (open July–mid-Aug daily 9am–9pm; admission charge) in town with a mixture of exhibits from around the region, but, much more interestingly, the **Glacier Exhibition** (open June–Aug daily 9am–9pm, May & Sept daily 1–6pm, Oct–Apr Mon–Fri 1–4pm; admission charge) at Hafnarbraut 30, which has an amazing film of the 1996 eruption under Vatnajökull and the ensuing flood which washed away part of the Ring Road. Upstairs you'll find a couple of short video clips from the James Bond films, *A View to a Kill*, and *Die Another Day*, which were filmed around the nearby glacial lagoon, Jökulsárlón. From Höfn it's also possible to arrange a "glacier tour" of Vatnajökull which includes snowcatting and a visit to the glacial lagoon in a single, easy trip. ❏

 KIDS

Although Höfn is a small town it does have a pleasant outdoor swimming pool (the only one for miles around) which can be a good place to entertain the kids for an hour or two. With hotpots and a regular pool, it also catches the afternoon sun making it one of the most agreeable places to relax in Höfn.

RESTAURANTS

Kaffi Hornið
Hafnabraut 42, Höfn
Tel: 478 2600.
A good choice for pasta dishes, burgers and fresh fish beside the main road. **$$**

Hótel Klaustur
Klausturvegur 6, Kirkjubæjarklaustur
Tel: 487 4900.
Fine dining inside the Icelandair-run hotel. **$$$**

Hótel Skaftafell
Freysnes, Skaftafell
Tel: 478 1945.

Fairly-priced meat and fish dishes are served every evening inside the hotel restaurant. **$$**

Ósinn
Víkurbraut 20 Höfn
Tel: 478 2200.
This pleasant restaurant inside Hótel Höfn has good value buffet dinners. **$$**

Systrakaffi
Klausturvegur 13, Kirkjubæjarklaustur.
Tasty homemade cakes and buns at

the village's one and only cafe-cum-restaurant. Also serves more expensive dinners. **$–$$**

Víkin
Víkurbraut 2, Höfn
Tel: 478 2300.
A no-nonsense fish diner tucked away on a side road heading for the harbour. **$$**

• • • • • • • • • • • • •

Categories are for an average-priced dinner per person, without wine.
$$$*** *over ISK 4,000,* ***$$
ISK 2,000–4,000, $ under
ISK 2,000.

An Ever-changing Landscape

From volcanoes to glaciers, Iceland is home to a greater concentration of nature's wonders, both hot and cold, than any other place on earth.

Above: Visitors are fascinated by the burst of water and steam that spouts from the Strokkur geyser roughly every 10 minutes.

In 1963, the island of Surtsey exploded out of the sea off Iceland in a great arch of flame and lava. It was only the latest natural wonder in Iceland's long, turbulent life. The Mid-Atlantic Ridge, which runs through the middle of the country from southwest to northeast, is the cause of the geothermal activity that has shaped much of Iceland's geology and unique landscape. Equally responsible are the thousands of years of glaciation, and the glacial meltwater, which together have modified the land.

The area close to the Mid-Atlantic Ridge has the greatest number of volcanoes: all around smoke and steam rise constantly. Here you will find spouting geysers, hot springs and craters – both active, like those near Myvatn, and inactive, solidified into fantastic lava shapes or filled with calm lakes. In some areas the ground is still very warm, and the Icelanders may even use a small covered pit as an oven to bake a delicious speciality – lava bread.

At the other end of the scale are glaciers, such as Vatnajökull, which, when it calves (when a mass of ice breaks off), fills the nearby Jökulsárlón lake with icebergs. The glaciers are bleak and dramatic moonscapes of peaks, crevasses and a surprising range of colours from dirty black to pure icy blue. Meltwater feeds many of the powerful waterfalls that are also a feature of this dramatic land.

Left: Molten lava glows red as it pours off Mount Hekla, one of Iceland's most active volcanoes. Its last major eruption was in 2000.

Right: Dettifoss is Europe's most powerful waterfall, dropping 44 thunderous metres (145 ft) into a canyon in Jökulsárgjufur National Park in the northeast.

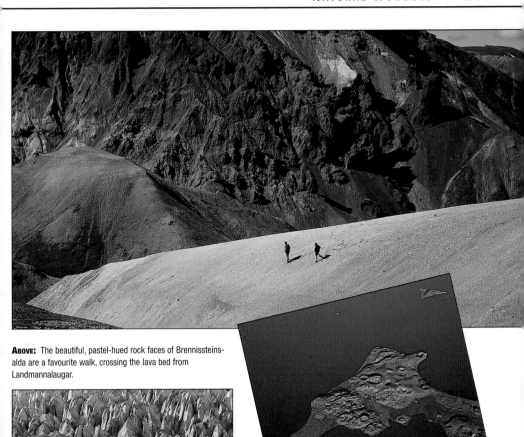

ABOVE: The beautiful, pastel-hued rock faces of Brennissteins-alda are a favourite walk, crossing the lava bed from Landmannalaugar.

ABOVE: Mývatn's pseudo-craters, of hugely varying sizes, formed when lava flowed over wetlands.

ABOVE: Viewed from afar, some of Iceland's icecaps appear smooth and white. Up close, areas are pushed into peaks or pitted with streams.

BELOW: The spectacular aurora borealis, commonly known as the northern lights, are a frequent sight in the long Icelandic winter.

SNÆFELLSNES AND THE WEST

This large area between Reykjavík and the West Fjords is easy to explore and has a variety of places to visit, from sites associated with the sagas to remote fishing villages

Icelanders, in their more lyrical moments, are apt to dub their homeland the Saga Isle. This description is particularly appropriate for the Snæfellsnes peninsula and the West, where some of the most dramatic events of the sagas took place. Names of farms, villages and towns conjure up the presence of historical characters such as the warrior-poet Egill Skallagrímsson and the chieftain and scholar Snorri Sturluson. Along these shores, constantly swept by the wind and the rain, occurred the terrifying hauntings of *Eyrbyggja Saga* and the tragic romance of *Laxdæla Saga*.

Though the West echoes with historic and literary associations, the jewel in its crown is the work of nature alone: the Snæfellsjökull icecap, at the western end of the Snæfellsnes peninsula. At 1,446 metres (4,743 ft), the glacier dominates the surrounding countryside. From as far away as Reykjavík, 100 km (60 miles) to the south across Faxaflói bay, Snæfellsjökull can be seen when the weather is clear, shimmering on the northern horizon.

North from Reykjavík

The glacier-bound traveller setting out from the capital can either follow the coast road to the north, or make the first leg of the journey through the new tunnel under Hvalfjörður. The tunnel itself is about 7 km (4 miles) long, and cuts distances between Reykjavík and points north by over 100 km (62 miles).

Taking Route One, the Ring Road, north out of Reykjavík, a detour east on

Route 36 leads to two famous farms: **Laxness** where the writer Halldór Laxness was born; and **Mosfell**, where saga figure Egill Skallagrímsson died – supposedly after ordering his slaves to bury his treasure, and then slaughtering them to ensure secrecy. Egill had intended to take the money to Þingvellir and fling it in the chieftains' faces, but was prevented from so doing by his family.

The Ring Road leads along the roots of **Mount Esja**, 918 metres (3,011 ft) high before turning into **Hvalfjörður**. In the mountains at the head of the fjord,

PRECEDING PAGES: on Snæfellsjökull. **LEFT:** the church at Buðir. **BELOW:** seals are a common sight on the peninsula's north coast.

The view looking east along the Snæfellsnes peninsula from Arnastapi.

about an hour's walk above the road, is Iceland's highest waterfall, **Glymur ❶**, at 198 metres (650 ft). The modern church at **Saurbær ❷** on the northern coast of Hvalfjörður is dedicated to the memory of Iceland's greatest devotional poet, Reverend Hallgrímur Pétursson, who served this parish in the 1600s.

On the peninsula at the northern side of the fjord lies the town of **Akranes ❸**

(population 6,000), offering hotels, guesthouse accommodation and restaurants. About a kilometre to the east in **Garður** is an interesting **Folk Museum** (open May–Sept daily 10am–6pm, Oct–Apr Mon–Fri 1–6pm; admission charge), with the emphasis on maritime history. In the ancient **cemetery** is a stone given to Iceland by the Irish government in 1974, to commemorate 1,100 years of settlement: an inscription in Icelandic and Gaelic remembers the role of Irish monks in the island's discovery.

Continuing north, the town of **Borgarnes ❹**, near the mouth of **Borgarfjörður** fjord, has grown close to the very spot, **Borg**, where Egill Skallagrímsson lived in the 10th century. The son of one of the first Norse settlers, Egill was a paradoxical figure: a fierce and often cruel Viking

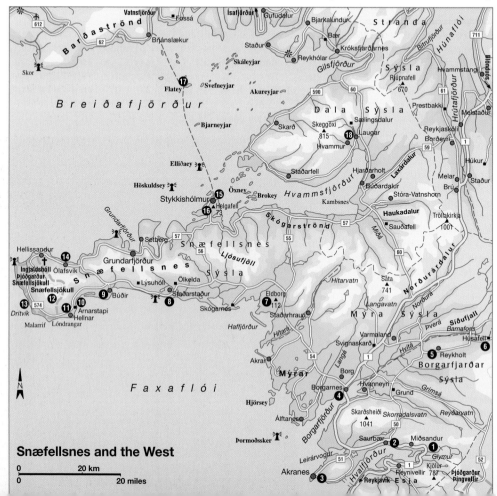

Snæfellsnes and the West

0 — 20 km
0 — 20 miles

warrior, he was also a great poet in the *skaldic* tradition of intricate word-play and metaphor. A modern sculpture commemorates Egill and his work. *Egils Saga*, which tells his story and preserves his poetry for posterity, was probably recorded by one of his descendants, Snorri Sturluson *(see panel on page 42)*. In 1241 he was ambushed and murdered by his enemies on the orders of the King of Norway at his home at **Reykholt ❺** – today a tiny hamlet some 36 km (22 miles) east of Borgarnes on Route 30.

Snorri's farmstead is long gone, but a hot pool remains where the scholar and chieftain once bathed *(see page 88)*. A tunnel (now partly restored) led from the pool to the farmhouse. A modern statue commemorates Snorri's masterly *Heimskringla (History of the Norwegian Kings)*, which saved centuries of Norwegian history from oblivion. A new church and a research centre have been built.

Lava caves and waterfalls

The green, rolling country of Borgarfjörður is at its most beautiful up beyond Reykholt. **Hraunfossar** is a multitude of tiny cascades tumbling into the Hvítá river along a 1-km (⅝-mile) stretch. A footbridge crosses the river at the churning **Barnafoss** waterfall, where the Hvítá flows through a rugged chasm. At nearby **Húsafell ❻**, summerhouses cluster in one of Iceland's largest woods. Húsafell farm is first mentioned in *Laxdæla Saga*. Its most famous occupant was Snorri Björnsson, who lived here at the end of the 18th century. Besides being a well-known sorcerer he was said to have tried his strength on the 180-kg (400-lb) boulder **Kvíahella**, which still can be seen close to the pens that he built.

The area is full of geothermal water. In Húsafell alone you will find two swimming pools, three hot pools, a water slide and a steam bath. Near the farmhouse is an open-air exhibition of the sculptures of Páll Guðmundsson, who lives and works in Húsafell, using stones from river gorges in the nearby mountains.

Hidden beneath **Hallmundarhraun** lava field lies Iceland's largest lava cave,

Surtshellir, 1.5 km (1 mile) in length. Signposted from the road, the cave is found by following a marked trail. Good shoes and torches are essential for exploring the cave. There are guided trips from Húsafell daily in July and August. Surtshellir was already known in the Saga Age, when a band of outlaws lived in the cave. It took some time for the farmers to overcome them, and place names refer to this time in history – for example Vopnalág ("weapons hollow") and Eiríksgnípa ("Erik's pike"). Ancient traces of human habitation can still be seen in the cave today. Close to Surtshellir is another cave, **Stefánshellir**, which also makes an interesting tour. To visit the third cave in the area, called **Víðgelmir**, you have to be accompanied by a guide from the nearby farm of Fljótstunga.

West to the peninsula

To the west along paved Route 54 from Borgarnes lies the Snæfellsnes peninsula and its mysterious glacier. The first landmark is **Eldborg ❼**, a crater 112 metres (367 ft) high, formed in a volcanic eruption 5–8,000 years ago. The crater, which commands magnificent views, is about

The statue of Snorri Sturlusson at Reykholt.

BELOW: early exploration of the Surtshellir lava cave, c.1860.

40 minutes' walk from the main road.

The **Kerlingarskarð** pass, over Route 55 which reaches 311 metres (1,020 ft) above sea level, was once a hazardous trail which claimed many lives in bad weather. Kerlingarskarð is a popular ski centre in winter.

A peculiarity of the Snæfellsnes peninsula is its mineral springs, producing naturally fizzy water – a rarity elsewhere in the country. Probably the most famous is on **Ölkelda** farm (the name, naturally enough, means "mineral spring") near **Staðarstaður ❽** on the south side of the peninsula. Staðarstaður is believed to have been the residence of Ari the Learned (1068–1148), author of the *Book of Icelanders*, one of the most important sources on the early history of the nation.

At **Lýsuhóll**, mineral water is found in a geothermal area: it produces hot, bubbly water, which is used to heat a swimming pool. **Búðir ❾**, once an important fishing centre, became better known for the hotel of the same name, now rebuilt having been destroyed by fire in 2001. **Arnarstapi ❿** and **Hellnar ⓫**, small fishing villages beneath the Snæfellsjökull glacier, are famed for their strange rock formations and their birdlife. Close to Hellnar is a sea cave, **Baðstofa** ("farmhouse loft"), where bizarre effects of light and colour are seen. Opposite the cave, on the beach, a small coffee-shop is run in the summer by the locals. Adjacent to Hellnar is the now-deserted farm of Laugarbakki, birthplace of Guðríður Þorbjarnardóttir, one of the heroines of the Norse discovery of Greenland around AD 1000. She emigrated to Greenland as a young girl, then later settled with her husband, Karlsefni, in Vínland, the Norse colony in North America, where she gave birth to her son Snorri, the first white child to be born in North America. Natural wonders at Arnarstapi include **Sönghellir** ("song cave"), with remarkable acoustics, and a huge stone arch. Sea birds nest on the cliffs in their thousands.

The focus of the peninsula, the **Snæfellsjökull glacier ⓬**, can be approached from several directions: the summit is four to five hours' walk from Arnarstapi. A ski lift goes to the top at weekends in winter. From Ólafsvík, north of the glacier, it is possible to drive part of the way and then walk on – again, a four- to five-hour hike to the summit. While the

Tales of ghostly apparitions have long been attributed to the Kerlingarskarð pass, and even today stories are told of travellers who sense the presence of an "extra passenger" in the car as they cross the pass.

BELOW RIGHT: the start of the descent at Snæfellsjökull in Jules Verne's *Journey to the Centre of the Earth.*

Journey to the Centre of the Earth

During the late 19th century, the book *Journey to the Centre of the Earth* by French writer and pioneer of science fiction, Jules Verne, became essential reading. Published in 1864, it tells the story of the German geologist, Professor Lidenbrock of Hamburg, and his nephew Axel (called Harry in some English translations), who discover a coded message about a path into the centre of the earth which descends from the Snæfellsjökull in Iceland. With their Danish-speaking guide (Iceland was part of Denmark at this time), the three intrepid explorers descend into the bowels of the earth and embark on a remarkable adventure. Their subterranean world is filled by an immense ocean and after encounters with unsavoury monsters, a prehistoric human and a powerful maelstrom, the book's heroes are finally swept upwards to the earth's surface, emerging on the volcanic island of Stromboli off southern Italy.

Snæfellsjökull is an extinct volcano (ie there is no historical record of it having erupted), but past activity has riddled the surface with lava formations, craters and a large number of caves – the likely inspiration for it as Verne's choice as the portal into the earth's interior. The distinctive shape, and impressive bulk, of the mountain has also imbued it with a natural mystique bound to stimulate a novelist's imagination.

highest of the three mountain peaks is difficult to scale without special climbing gear, the walk up the glacier itself is fairly easy. In summer, however, crevasses open in the ice, so a guided walk is recommended (available from Ólafsvík).

Test your strength

Farther down the coast from Hellnar, by **Malarrif**, stand two lofty pillars of rock, **Lóndrangar**. The taller, 75 metres (248 ft) high, is called "Christian pillar", and the lower is "heathen pillar". While fishing remains the livelihood of the peninsula, some communities have now disappeared, leaving only traces of the centuries of fishing seasons: 60 boats used to row out from **Dritvík** ⑬, for example, where today there is nothing left but spectacular wilderness – including the great rock formation called **Tröllakirkja** ("church of the trolls").

Those who wish to try out their muscle-power in true Icelandic tradition should stroll along the shore from Dritvík to Djúpalón where four weighty stones present an age-old test of strength. The aim is to lift them up onto a ledge of rock at about hip height. The largest,

Fullsterkur ("full strength") is 155 kg (341 lbs), the second, *Hálfsterkur* ("strong enough"), 140 kg (308 lbs), the third, *Hálfdraettingur* ("half strength"), 49 kg (108 lbs) and the last, *Amlóði* ("weakling") 23 kg (50 lbs). *Amlóði*, unfortunately, is now broken. Lifting at least *Hálfsterkur* was a requirement for joining the crew of a boat from Dritvík.

Ólafsvík and Stykkishólmur

Now a deserted farm and church just inland from Rif, **Ingjaldshóll** was once a major manor and regional centre. Just to the east, **Ólafsvík** ⑭ is one of the larger communities on the peninsula with a population of 1,200. It is also Iceland's

Snaefellsjökull looms large over the western end of the peninsula.

TIP

You can travel to the top of Snæfellsjökull by snow scooter or snow mobile, starting from Arnarstapi tourist centre.

BELOW: natural arch at Arnarstapi.

TIP

Breiðafjördur Bay, off the north coast of the Snæfellsnes peninsula, is one of the best places in Iceland to go whale-watching. Tours operate from Stykkishólmur and Ólafsvík, both within easy reach of the whales' feeding grounds. Blue whales, the largest mammals on earth, are commonly seen here. Book through Seatours, tel: 433 2254.

oldest-established trading town, granted its charter in 1687. Ólafsvík offers a guesthouse and restaurants, a swimming pool and golf course. An old merchant's storehouse from 1844 has been restored and houses the local **museum** (open June–Aug daily 9am–7pm; admission charge). Ólafsvík is also one of Iceland's best known whale-watching centres, with regular sightings of humpback, minke and blue whales in the cold waters off the peninsula.

Stykkishólmur ⑮ is the principal town on the Snæfellsnes peninsula and the starting point for those who are going to the West Fjords by ferry. Nearby is **Helgafell ⑯** ("holy mountain"), a 73-metre (240-ft) hill. According to local folklore, those who climb Helgafell for the first time will have three wishes come true, provided a few conditions are observed: you must not look back or speak on the way; you must make your wishes facing east; you must not tell anyone what they are; and only benevolent wishes are allowed. Even if your wishes are not fulfilled, Helgafell is worth climbing for the spectacular views of **Breiðafjörður** bay.

Helgafell has, in fact, always been considered to have supernatural powers. The first settler here, Þórólfur Mostraskegg, built a wooden temple to Thor at its summit. Þórólfur's son, the curiously named Þorstein Cod-Biter, claimed that on Helgafell he was able to see Valhalla, where dead Norse warriors drank with the gods.

In the 10th century, Helgafell became a Christian holy mountain with its own church built by Snorri the Priest. According to the *Eyrbyggja Saga*, a long blood-feud was sparked off when a certain family group, unmindful of Helgafell's religious significance, used it as a toilet. Helgafell is supposedly also where Guðrún Ósvífurs-dóttir, heroine of *Laxdæla Saga*, lived out her last years as a hermit.

Stykkishólmur offers a hotel, guest-house and youth accommodation. Jet-skis can be hired to skim over the harbour. The local **Folk Museum** (open June–Aug daily 11am–5pm; admission charge) is housed in a beautifully restored timber house dating from 1828. Known simply as the **Norwegian House**, it was imported in kit form from Norway. Stykkishólmur's new church overlooks the town.

BELOW: the tiny library at Flatey.

Sub-arctic archipelago

The car/passenger ferry *Baldur* plies Breiðafjörður between Stykkishólmur and Brjánslækur in the West Fjords, calling at the island of **Flatey** ⑰ *(see page 316 for details)*. Breiðafjörður is dotted with about 2,700 islands, which once supported a large population thanks to the abundant fisheries. Flatey was the site of a 12th-century monastery and a major cultural centre until the 1800s. One of the greatest treasures of Icelandic literature, *Flateyjarbók* (the Flatey Book), was preserved here for centuries before being presented to the Danish king in the 16th century. In 1971 it returned to Iceland.

The islanders gradually deserted their remote homes during the early part of the 20th century, and few remain. Flatey, though, is a delight, a perfectly preserved example of what an Icelandic village used to be. While the island is all but uninhabited in winter, many families spend their summers there renovating the lovely old timber houses of their ancestors. A triumph of painstaking restoration is Iceland's oldest, and smallest, library (4.75 metres by 3.43 metres, or 15 ft 6 in by 11 ft 3 in), built in 1844 to house the collection of the Flatey Progress Society.

Viking romance

North of the Snæfellsnes peninsula is **Hvammsfjörður** fjord, with the village of **Búðardalur** at its head. Route 59 runs along **Laxárdalur** (Salmon River Valley). This is saga country, and almost every place name strikes a chord for Icelanders. In the **Haukadalur** valley (Route 586) is the site of the farm **Eiríksstaðir**, the birthplace of Leifur Eiríksson, which has been excavated.

The farm **Hjarðarholt**, just outside Búðardalur, is the birthplace of Kjartan Ólafsson, whose ill-starred love for Guðrún Ósvífursdóttir from **Sælingsdalur**, 30 km (18 miles) to the north, is the central theme of *Laxdæla Saga*. Geothermal springs made Sælingsdalur an important centre in Ósvífursdóttir's day, when there was a hot bathing pool, of which traces can still be seen, at the farm of **Laugar** . A modern swimming pool now uses the natural hot water, while a summer hotel and a small **Folk Museum** (open summer daily 1–5pm) operate in the school. ❑

A display in the Norwegian House in Stykkishólmur.

Just east of Stykkishólmur lies the uninhabited island of Öxney, once the home of Erik the Red, discoverer of Greenland, and his son Leifur – known as "the Lucky" – who discovered North America some time around AD 1000.

RESTAURANTS & CAFÉS

Fimm Fiskar
Frúarstígur 1, Stykkishólmur
Tel: 436 1600
The cheaper of Stykkishólmur's two main restaurants – a fish-lover's paradise. **$$**

Narfeyrarstofa
Aðalgata 3, Stykkishólmur
Tel: 438 1119
Top-notch fare in this intimate restaurant specialising in tasty scallops and a good choice of fish dishes with a Mediterranean flavour. There's also a selection of burgers. **$$$**

Hótel Barbró
Kirkjubraut 11, Akranes
Tel: 431 4240
The hotel restaurant is the best place for a filling fish dinner in Akranes. **$$**

Hótel Borgarnes
Egilsgata 12, Borgarnes
Tel: 437 1119
Top-quality puffin breast in blueberry sauce is the speciality, though there is also a good choice of fish suppers. **$$$**

Hótel Búðir
Búðir. Tel: 435 6700
Reopened after a devas-

tating fire, this all-wooden hotel and restaurant once again offers superb quality dining in its oceanside restaurant. **$$$**

Hótel Reykholt
Reykholt. Tel: 435 1260
The only place to eat in Reykholt, the hotel restaurant serves an array of fish and meat dishes. **$$**

Krákan
Sæból 13, Grundarfjörður
Tel: 438 6999
A village institution which has operating for years. A heavy wooden interior reminiscent of a Bavarian beerhall. Excellent fish suppers. **$$**

Snjófell
Arnarstapi. Tel: 435 6783
A cosy diner in a solid timber building on the main street in Arnarstapi offering burgers, pizzas and some simple but tasty fish dishes. **$**

Vogur
Flatey island. Tel: 438 1413
A cosy café in the same building as the island's guesthouse. Mouthwatering cakes and a choice of freshly-landed fish. **$–$$**

● ● ● ● ● ● ● ● ● ● ● ● ● ●
*Categories are for an average-priced dinner per person, without wine. **$$$** over ISK 4,000, **$$** ISK 2,000–4,000, **$** under ISK 2,000.*

THE WEST FJORDS

This remote, inaccessible region has whole areas that are deserted, creating natural reserves of a beauty and fertility unknown elsewhere in Iceland

Reykjavík

Shaped like an outstretched paw, the West Fjords region is at first sight one of the least hospitable parts of Iceland. Lack of fertile lowlands has, since the days of settlement, forced the inhabitants to look to the sea rather than the land for their livelihood. Land travel has always been difficult or even dangerous in this area, which is characterised by rough and steep mountain slopes, shores that every now and then are cut off by the tides, and under constant threat from snow avalanches or earth slides.

Since the days of settlement the inhabitants of the West Fjords have lived their lives on isolated farms, without any regular contact with the outside world, and here, at the westernmost point of Iceland, an independent, and in many ways strange, local culture has developed. Under the rough and rocky mountains the belief in monsters, ghosts and evil spirits has become more deeply rooted than in any other part of the country.

The mechanisation of the fishing industry in the 20th century has made life more comfortable, but government-imposed fishing quotas in recent years have led to a steady stream of emigrants from the West Fjords to Reykjavík. Meanwhile, many small farms in the area have been abandoned as unprofitable – with more and more farmers giving up as the years go by.

Travellers here face a string of serious obstacles, including some of the worst roads in the country. Yet the region offers Iceland's most dramatic fjords and some of its best hiking, while soaring cliffs host literally millions of breeding sea birds. And, once the proverbial ice is broken, its self-reliant people prove to be among the most hospitable in the land.

A glacial past

Geologically speaking, the West Fjords region is the oldest part of the country, bearing the scars of intense glaciation. The area is basically a triangular plateau made up of layers of lava, most of them about 15–16 million years old. Between the layers there are, in several places, fossilised

Main attractions
ÍSAFJÖRÐUR
HORNSTRANDIR
HORNBJARG BIRD CLIFFS
ÖNUNDARFJÖRÐUR BEACH
DYRAFJÖRÐUR
DYNJANDI WATERFALL

PRECEDING PAGES: an aerial view of the West Fjords landscape. **LEFT:** an elderly couple. **BELOW:** a razorbill.

TIP

Highways 60 and 61
converge at Ísafjörður,
forming a circular route
around the West Fjords
that can be driven in
two to three days –
although if you include
a few detours it is easy
to spend a full week.

remains of luxuriant forests, which have grown between volcanic eruptions. Later, Ice-Age glaciation dug the fjords and valleys that make the area habitable today. The glacier was so powerful that it almost made an island of the West Fjords. As the crow flies the isthmus connecting the fjords Gilsfjörður and Bitrufjörður is at one point only 7 km (5 miles) wide.

A base for exploring

Most visitors start their visits at **Ísafjörður ❶**, the focal point of the region. With a population of 4,100, it is the only town of any size, with a choice of accommodation and some good restaurants. The site of a 9th-century farmstead, **Eyri** is the oldest part of town, with one of Iceland's best natural harbours. On a fine summer evening, a stroll through the old

town is an unforgettable walk through the past. The oldest buildings at the end of the sandspit are four restored timber buildings dating from the 18th century. More by accident than design, these ancient (by Icelandic standards) houses were left standing as fish factories and warehouses sprang up around them.

Oldest of the four is **Tjöruhús**, built in 1733–42, followed by the adjoining **Krambúð**, dating from 1761 and originally a shop. The meticulously restored **Turnhús** (Tower House) was built in 1744. It once housed a salt-fish plant and now contains the **West Fjords Maritime Museum** (open July–late-Aug daily 10am–5pm, May–mid-June & late-Aug–mid-Sept Sat & Sun 1–5pm; admission charge). Exhibits trace the development of the town and its fishing industry, with all

West Fjords

sorts of unusual nautical paraphernalia. Ísafjörður has excellent skiing facilities in the **Seljalandsdalur** valley above town.

Around Ísafjörður

The broad fjord of Ísafjarðardjúp, on which Ísafjörður sits, almost severs the West Fjords in two. Near its mouth to the northwest of Ísafjörður, is **Bolungarvík** ❷, the second largest town in the region. Between here and **Hnífsdalur** is the steep mountainside Óshlíð, where avalanches and landslides have often occured. In Bolungarvík is Ösvör, an old fishing hut from the rowboat-era, which has been restored and turned into an interesting **Maritime Museum** (open May–mid-Sept daily 10am–5pm; admission charge). There is also a **Natural History Museum** (open summer daily 9am–6pm). A jeep track continues to **Skálavík** where those seeking solitude will find plenty at a remote, uninhabited bay facing the Greenland Sea.

Route 61, which hugs the southern shore of Isafjarðardjúp, southeast from Ísafjörður, was completed in 1975. Súðavík is the only village in these parts, developing from a Norwegian whaling-station *circa* 1900. Of the 70 houses in Súðavík 22 were completely destroyed by the 1995 avalanche.

Further along, close to the tip of the Ögurnes peninsula is **Ögur**, an impressive farmstead – built in the 19th century, it was at the time one of the largest in Iceland. At Mjóifjörður is the Djúpmannabúð roadside cafeteria, and the only petrol station along this stretch of coast. Another ancient farm site is at **Vatnsfjörður**, in its heyday a wealthy estate that produced several pastors of note. The village of **Reykjanes** ❸, at the head of Ísafjarðardjúp is one of the few places in the West Fjords with geothermal water. There is a summer hotel, swimming pool and greenhouses here.

The road continues as Route 635 along Ísafjarðardjúp's northern shore to **Kaldalón** ❹, a sheltered beauty spot. A small glacier here tumbles down from Drangajökull, the only large ice-field in the north of Iceland. At the head of the valley there are some grassy islets, then moraine brought by the descending glacier tounge. Accommodation is available at the farm Ármúli nearby.

Beyond Kaldalón, the road comes to

With an intensely convoluted coastline, road journeys in the region are long and winding. Most villages are connected by ferry.

BELOW: Ísafjörður from the air.

Cycling by the brightly coloured houses of Ísafjörður.

BELOW RIGHT: a sign of the times – an abandoned farm in the West Fjords.

an abrupt halt at Unaðsdalur valley, where the uninviting Snæfjallaströnd ("snow mountain coast") begins. The snow line is lower here than anywhere else in the country – even in mid-summer, some snow lies at sea level.

Islands and wilderness

Two of Ísafjarðardjúp's islands are inhabited: **Vigur** and **Æðey** ("eider island"). There are regular boat tours from Ísafjörður in the summer. A walk around Vigur gives the visitor an opportunity to enjoy the rich birdlife in its natural environment. Thousands of eider ducks, arctic terns, puffins and other sea birds can be found on the island. There is also a small and homely coffee-shop in the mid-19th century farmer's house, as well as a mini post office, where guests can mail their cards and letters. Æðey is the biggest island in Ísafjarðardjúp and, as its name suggests, also has an impressive bird population.

Ísafjörður is also the jumping-off point for trips to the uninhabited nature reserve of **Hornstrandir ❺** to the north. The Reserve includes the whole area north of Skorarheiði from the end of Hrafnfjörður

to the end of Furufjörður. Abandoned by its farming community during the first decades of the 20th century and free from the destructive grazing of sheep, plants and wildlife alike thrive on a scale unknown elsewhere in the country. Here you can wade knee-deep in meadows of wildflowers, fertilised by the guano of countless breeding sea birds, and listen at sundown for the haunting bark of the arctic fox, unpersecuted and tamer here than anywhere else in Iceland. The Nature Reserve is off limits to all motor traffic, making the only way to explore it by boat or on foot. There is no accommodation and little evidence of the once-flourishing farming community. Traces of bridle paths crisscross the mountain passes, linking the fjords and inlets.

In summer, a ferry operated by Sjóferðir sails daily from Ísafjörður to a number of destinations in Hornstrandir bringing day-trippers, hikers and descendants of the original landowners who now use the remaining old farmsteads as summer cottages. Another ferry also sails south from Hornvík along the Strandir coast to Norðurfjörður (see page 227), making it possible to travel south from Hornstrandir

The Emptying Land

Rural depopulation is known throughout Iceland. However, in the West Fjords it has been a particularly serious problem for decades, threatening the continued existence of many remote communities and totally claiming the lives of others. Human settlement of the Hornstrandir peninsula of the West Fjords, for instance, was always marginal at best: winters came earlier, snow lasted longer and temperatures were always lower than elsewhere in the region. Surprisingly life here, although tough, was prosperous, at least for a while. At Hesteyri in Horstrandir, abandoned houses and a church suggest a once flourishing settlement. A trading place since 1881, Hesteyri was the base for a Norwegian whaling station from until 1912, ruins of which are still clear to see. In the 1920s a herring processing factory was built in the village where about 80 people lived. This closed in 1940 and in 1952 the last inhabitants moved away. Not only was the harsh climate of Hornstrandir an added challenge but the only source of geothermal water in the peninsula is Reykjafjörður, several days' hike away. Elsewhere in the region, poor communications have been to blame for rural depopulation. Still today, travel around the region can be exasperating due to the highly indented nature of the coastline and the fjord system at its heart. Stony, mountain plateaux between the fjords add to the difficulties.

without first backtracking to Ísafjörður in order to continue your journey. All ferry times are available from the tourist office in Ísafjörður.

Scheduled stops include Aðalvík and Hesteyri in the northwest, Hornvík in the north, Hrafnfjörður in the southeast and Veiðileysufjörður in the south. The return voyage itself is an adventure as a day trip, but most people choose to disembark at either Aðalvík or Hesteyri and hike east across to Hornvík. Another option is to take the ferry to Hrafnfjörður and then hike north to Hornvík. Check the times and sailing schedule of the ferry carefully before setting out because not all destinations are served on a daily basis and Hornstrandir is a pretty remote location – it's not somewhere to get stranded.

Sea birds and driftwood

Not far from the Hornbjargsviti lighthouse rise the majestic bird-cliffs at **Hornbjarg 6**, nesting ground for tens of thousands of pairs of noisy guillemots, Brunnich's guillemots, razorbills, puffins, kittiwakes and fulmars. Not for the faint-hearted, **Kálfatindur** peak, the highest point along the cliffs, is a 534-metre

(1,760-ft) vertical drop to the Greenland Sea. From its lofty summit, the noise is deafening and the view simply breathtaking – some claim to have seen the distant Greenland icecap from here.

In view of Kálfatindur is attractive **Hornvík Bay 7**. It has a long sandy beach, some impressive waterfalls, a plentiful supply of driftwood and is a pleasant camping spot. In a rare bout of clear weather (for some reason, more likely in late summer), the place is nothing short of idyllic and makes an ideal base from which to explore the area. Across the bay is **Hælavíkurbjarg**, another impressive bird-cliff. Spring still draws daring Icelanders to lower themselves on ropes down the cliff-face and collect the prized guillemots' eggs.

Besides seal-hunting, coastal farmers of the West Fjords have always harvested something else from the sea: driftwood. These benefits are unevenly distributed as some farms have better driftwood-beaches than others. There has always been a lot of driftwood on Hornstrandir and it was extensively used in the past, as little timber was imported. Dealing in wood was profitable for local inhabitants,

TIP

Given the circuitous nature of many roads in the West Fjords, one of the best ways to get to and around the region is by air. Indeed, there are no fewer than three airports in the area, a sure sign of the difficult terrain: Ísafjörður, Bíldudalur and Gjögur on the Strandir coast. The aerial views of the West Fjords' flat-topped mountains can be breathtaking.

BELOW: a female eider duck on its nest, surrounded by saxifrage.

Icelanders go to great lengths to take Guillemot eggs from their precarious cliff-side nests.

and many of them were also known as skilled craftsmen, making useful items out of driftwood, such as tubs and barrels, and selling them in the West Fjords and other parts of the country. Driftwood is still collected in Hornstrandir, now mainly used for fenceposts, which are sold all over Iceland.

South of Ísafjörður

Route 60 winds over several high passes to link the fjords south of Ísafjörður. A tunnel has been made through the basalt rocks of Breiðadalsheiði, which at 610 metres (2,013 ft) is the highest pass in the area; it was often blocked in the past, cutting off villages for days, sometimes weeks, at a time.

The village of **Suðureyri** ❽, 17 km (10 miles) off the main road, is buried in the shadow of the extremely steep **Súgandafjörður** fjord. The village's main claim to fame is that it lives without direct sunlight throughout the four winter months, longer than any other village in Iceland. The sun's rays first peek over the high mountains and strike the village on 22 February each year, an occasion celebrated, as everywhere else in the West Fjords, with "sunshine coffee".

Önundarfjörður ❾, a fjord between Barði and Sauðanes headlands, is unmistakable because of its sandy beach which almost straddles the fjord in a golden arc. On a rare sunny day the shallow waters heat up and locals from nearby **Flateyri** throng to bathe in the Greenland Sea. The headland, on which the 350 inhabitants of Flateyri live, was probably left there when a large part of a mountain cleaved into the sea. In 1823 Flateyri became an authorised trading place, and fish and fish-processing are still the main industries. There is said to have been a pagan temple on the hill Goðahóll above the village.

Across the fjord, the historical parsonage of **Holt** ❿ was the birthplace of the 17th-century bishop Brynjólfur Sveinsson. The attractive timber church here dates from 1869 and contains artefacts from the time of Bishop Brynjólfur.

Dýrafjörður, the next fjord south, ranks among the most scenic in Iceland – sheer mountains seem to rise straight from the shore, leaving little or no lowland for farming. The inhabitants have made do with other resources and the village of **Mýrar** ⓫ has Iceland's largest eider duck colony, with 7,000 pairs. The first settler at the nearby farm Alviðra was none other than a son of King Harald Fairhair of Norway. Today it offers accommodation to travellers.

National saints and sinners

Across the fjord, **Þingeyri** ⓬ (population 450) was the first trading post in the West Fjords. It takes its name from an ancient assembly whose sacred site was said to be enclosed by walls at either end of the mountain **Sandfell**, rising above the village. The old residents still remember the walls and in the town there are ruins of an ancient booth, used by visitors to the assembly, which are a historical monument. Don't miss the drive up Sandfell – from the top there is a beautiful view of the mountains, separating Dýrafjörður from Arnarfjörður. This mountain ridge is often called the "West Fjord Alps". In the 19th century the French wanted to establish a colony in Þingeyri to support their fishing fleet, but were turned down. In nearby **Haukadalur** valley there is a grave of French seamen. This valley is also the setting for the tragic events of the saga of Gísli Súrsson. Outlawed for a suspected vengeance killing, Gísli spent a gruelling 13 years on the run, but was eventually tracked down and slain. Gísli's farms at Hóll and Sæból (8 km/5 miles along the fjord from Þingeyri) are abandoned.

The village of **Hrafnseyri** ⓭, in Arnarfjörður fjord, was the birthplace of nationalist Jón Sigurðsson *(see panel on page 56)*. There is a small **museum** (open summer daily 10am–8pm; admission charge) and a **chapel** to his memory.

Further along the fjord, an indistinct route leads up Fossdalur valley to **Mount Kaldbakur** ⓮, the highest peak in the region. It is officially 998 metres (3,273 ft) high, but locals have added a cairn to credit the region with its only 1,000-metre peak. In clear weather the full-day hike is worth the effort, with views as far away as the Snæfellsnes icecap.

Dynjandi waterfall ⓯ is located at the head of the northern arm of Arnarfjörður. Also known as Fjallfoss ("moun-

tain falls"), the 100-metre (328-ft) high cascade literally drops off the edge of the mountain, fanning out to a width of 60 metres (197 ft) at its base. Below it, a series of waterfalls cascade: Hundafoss, Strokkur, Göngumannafoss, Hrísvaðsfoss and Bæjarfoss.

Europe's most westerly point

Some kilometres beyond here the road splits. If you head west, Route 63 passes the fishing villages of **Bíldudalur** and **Tálknafjörður** (5 km/3 miles off the main road). From Bíldudalur the difficult, but impressive Route 619 passes the opening of several valleys, before it ends at the **Selárdalur** farm, where the pastor Páll Björnsson (1621–1706) lived, well known for his wisdom and his persecution of witches. He was said to have been an excellent speaker and an unusually good linguist. According to a legend, a black-sailed schooner was once seen off Selárdalur. People feared that pirates were on board. The pastor went out to the vessel, spoke to them in an eastern language and told them the area was full of witches. As a result the pirates

Traditionally the difficulty of a high pass was measured by the number of fish-skin shoes that were worn through to cross it. In the passes south of Ísafjörður a nine-skin pass was not unusual. Nowadays these routes are more of a test of the nerves of the driver and the suspension of the car.

BELOW: the picturesque cascades of Dynjandi waterfall.

TIP

If you're a fan of beautiful golden beaches, you're in luck. The West Fjords have two of Iceland's most enchanting sandy strands: Breiðavík and Rauðasandur, both within easy reach of each other. Regrettably though, sunbathing is unlikely to be an option even on the sunniest of days since the air remains stubbornly chilly. Breiðavík is also accessible by public transport from Ísafjörður.

BELOW: a pristine beach at Patreksfjörd.

exchanged gifts with him and sailed away. Also on Route 63 is the larger town of **Patreksfjörður**, which has a small guesthouse, although little of real interest to the visitor. Across the fjord, **Hnjótur** ⑯ has a small **Fishing and Farming Museum** (open mid-May–mid-Sept daily 10am–6pm; admission charge) which is worth a stop. The museum's exhibits are neatly presented and on the walls there are original drawings showing how the old tools and equipment were used. All this is the work of Egill Ólafsson, the curator.

The real lure of the area is the bird-cliffs at **Látrabjarg** ⑰, at the westernmost point of Iceland – and thus Europe. Extending for 14 km (9 miles) and rising to 444 metres (1,465 ft) at their highest point, the cliffs are home to one of Iceland's greatest concentrations of sea birds. The hundreds of thousands of puffins are happy to let visitors approach to within a few feet of their cliff-top perches.

A weekly bus service links the cliffs with **Breiðavík** 12 km (7 miles) away, which offers the nearest accommodation. This only allows a short stay, however: to reach the highest point of the cliffs

involves a long, full-day hike from Breiðavík. The bird-cliffs have also been the scene of human dramas. When the British trawler *Dhoon* ran aground below the cliffs in the winter of 1947, a remarkable rescue operation by the local farmers saved all 12 crew members. Lowering themselves by ropes as if they were collecting eggs, they hauled the exhausted men up the 200-metre (650-ft) cliff-face to safety. Southeast of Látrabjarg is Iceland's most magnificent stretch of golden sand, **Rauðasandur**.

Another first settler

At the head of Patreksfjörður fjord, Route 62 crosses over to the southern coast of the West Fjords – **Barðaströnd** – a region that gets more than its share of foul weather. This entire stretch of coast has little over 500 inhabitants, largely because the shallow waters of Breiðafjörður bay do not attract the valuable cod and haddock. This was where the Viking Hrafna-Flóki made one of the first settlements in Iceland, long before Ingólfur Arnarson arrived. The *Landnámabók (Book of Settlements)* relates that the fishing was so good that Flóki neglected to make hay for his livestock, and they perished over the winter. In spring he climbed a high mountain and, looking north, saw ice-filled fjords. It was this drift ice, and not the glaciers, that prompted him to name the land "Iceland" on his eventual return to Norway. However, it is said that he came back some years later and spent the rest of his life in Iceland.

The village of **Brjánslækur**, at the entrance to Vatnsfjörður, is the terminal for the Breiðafjörður ferry, which connects twice daily with Stykkishólmur on the Snæfellsnes peninsula.

Route 60 continues south around the fjords, a long and winding drive. There is a chance of spotting the rare white-tailed sea eagle here, though only 30 or 40 pairs of this now protected species remain after centuries of hunteuing. The main settlement here is **Bjarkalundur** ⑱, the unofficial gateway to the West Fjords, with a hotel and camping facilities within sight of the twin peaks of Vaðalfjöll.

The Strandir coast

The rugged eastern flank of the West Fjords is one of the least visited parts of Iceland. The population of the area has been steadily declining, and now the only town of any size is **Hólmavík**, which has basic facilities. Farming is hard and good harbours few: **Djúpavík**, for example, a once-bustling herring station, is now virtually abandoned, but has a wonderfully situated summer hotel.

The village of **Norðurfjörður** is the end of the road. Beyond here, a hiking trail follows the coast to Hornstrandir. Allow between 10 and 14 days, expect all kinds of weather, take double the normal rations – and don't count on meeting another soul.

From Norðurfjörður, there's also a summer ferry connection to Hornvík in Hornstrandir which sails twice a week via Reykjafjörður. ❏

Bird-watching at Hælavíkurbjarg cliff.

RESTAURANTS & BARS

Café Riis
Hafnarbraut 39, Hólmavík
Tel: 451 3567
There's a nautical theme to the decor inside this tasteful cafe-cum-restaurant which also serves a fine selection of freshly caught fish. Ask too to sample their rotten shark – considered something of a delicacy in these parts. **$$**

Faktorshús
Austurvegur 7, Ísafjörður
A fine selection of cakes and sweets inside this handsome old wooden structure which once was home to the local trading manager. **$**

Fernando's
Hafnarstræti 12, Ísafjörður
Tel: 456 5001
Pizzas and the occasional fish dish at Ísafjörður's most popular and busiest restaurant. **$$**

Gistiheimilið
Breiðavík. Tel: 456 1575
Personal service with a smile and fish suppers which are known for miles around. **$$**

Hótel Djúpavík
Djúpavík village Tel: 451 4037
A superb location to enjoy fish as fresh as you will ever taste at this friendly hotel and restaurant on the Strandir coast of the West Fjords. **$$**

Hótel Flókalundur
Flókalundur. Tel: 456 2011
An upmarket choice for fish dishes at the hotel restaurant, which is popular with people heading to and from the ferry at nearby Brjánslækur. **$$$**

Posthús
Strandgata 38, Tálknafjörður
A simple cafe in the town centre which has a limited selection of sandwiches and cakes available. **$**

Thai Koon
Hafnarstræti 9, Ísafjörður Tel: 456 0123
Spicy and authentic Thai food, quite a rarity in Iceland, at this simple cafe-cum-restaurant inside Ísafjörður's main shopping mall. **$**

Tóki Munkur
Hafnarstræti 1, Þingeyri
Tel: 456 8466
The place for pizzas and pasta dishes. **$$**

Vagninn
Hafnarstræti 19, Flateyri
Tel: 456 7751
Freshly caught fish is always on the menu. A good stop on your way to and from Ísafjörður. **$$**

Þorpið
Aðalstræti 73, Patreksfjörður
Tel: 456 1295
A selection of salads, fish dishes and lamb. Great views over the fjord. **$$**

● ● ● ● ● ● ● ● ● ● ● ● ● ● ● ●
Categories are for an average-priced dinner per person, without wine. $$$ over ISK 4,000, $$ ISK 2,000–4,000, $ under ISK 2,000.

Observing Iceland's Sea Birds

One of the most unforgettable sights in Iceland is that of a huge, cliff-side sea bird colony – a common and noisy occurrence in breeding season

Sea birds can be seen and heard everywhere in Iceland – circling overhead or offshore but, most often, stacked in vast, raucous colonies on steep cliffs and island coastlines. By the million they live, winter, or come to breed here – some 25 species in all, plus a few more on passage north or south. No wonder the great aim for many human visitors to Iceland is to watch these birds, sometimes by walking and climbing long distances to see the colonies without disturbing them. Watching sea birds is easiest by boat or from a nearby cliff, where the gap in between gives the birds a sense of security.

The northernmost island of Grímsey, on the Arctic Circle, is home to about 100 shepherds and fisherfolk. But great breeding colonies of birds outnumber them by their thousands – fulmars, including the rare blue fulmar, guillemots, including the Brunnich's sub-species, gannets and many others.

Even Reykjavík, with 190,000 inhabitants (over half of Iceland's population), also has its own colonies of auks, gulls such as kittiwake – easily distinguished by the cry that gives it its name – eiders and many other ducks. Near the golf course, a colony of Arctic terns use the golfers for diving practice.

Iceland's many great peninsulas, the West Fjords, Snæfellsnes and islands such as the Vestmannaeyjar offer much to discover. Pointing the binoculars at the ever-changing sea or the steadfast cliffs, you do not have to be an expert to feel the thrill of finding a species that, to you at least, is new.

Above: The razorbill's chunky beak, with its vertical white stripe, can be part of the mating ritual – a bird attracts a mate by using its beak to make a castanet-like rattle.

Below: A vivid red beak and short red legs make the arctic tern easy to spot among other birds – and its noisy cry is unmistakeable.

Right: The fulmar. Among all the gull-like birds to be seen flying over sea and cliffs, the fulmar is easily identified by its stiff-winged flight.

THE LAST OF THE GREAT AUKS

The great auk was once the king of the auk species – black and white seabirds with short, stubby necks, including guillemots, razorbills, little auks and puffins. At one time, there were great auk colonies in Iceland, North America, Greenland and the Faeroes. But the great auk had one major disadvantage. It was flightless. Sitting stolidly on a rock, the great auk was easy prey for hunters in remote areas. The colonies grew smaller until, by the start of the 19th century, few remained except on St Kilda and on Iceland's islands. Still, they were hunted. In 1844, two hunters visiting Eldey island, southwest of the Rejkjanes peninsula, spotted a single great auk. They were swift – one stroke of the club and the great auk was gone forever.

ABOVE: Thousands of sea birds sit calmly as the waves pound against the great sea cliffs on the west of the Snæfellsnes peninsula to the north of Reykjavík.

ABOVE RIGHT: Many species of gull are found in huge numbers in Iceland. One of the best known is the kittiwake, with its easily recognised call.

BELOW: The modestly sized puffin, with its distinctive curved red, blue and yellow beak in summer, is everyone's favourite. Pairs of puffins breed and raise their young in burrows on clifftops.

ABOVE: Brunnich's guillemot is an Icelandic speciality, overlapping in many places with its more southerly cousin, the guillemot.

BELOW: Large, strong-flying gannets, which make spectacular steep dives for fish, come to Iceland's cliffs during the breeding season.

HÚNAFLÓI AND SKAGAFJÖRÐUR

This rugged region of mountains, waterfalls, cliffs and islands has been largely bypassed by tourism – few turn off the Ring Road to find the coast's remote attractions

Jutting into the icy Arctic Ocean, the Skagi peninsula divides the northern coast of Iceland into the Húnaflói bight and Skagafjörður fjord. It is well worth taking the time to follow the narrow dirt roads, often little more than graded tracks, into a windswept wilderness of basalt cliffs crowded with nesting sea birds, black volcanic sand spits and beaches inhabited only by seals.

Rural backwater

The Ring Road runs through some rich agricultural land here, its alluvial soil weathered from some of Iceland's oldest rocks. The entry point to the area is **Brú** ❶ ("bridge") – a tiny hamlet which is really little more than a petrol station. It is dominated by the huge bulk of **Tröllakirkja**, a hill that stands over 1,000 metres (3,300 ft) from the flat surrounding farmland. Brú is at the head of the narrow **Hrútafjörður** fjord formed by the extensive glacial moraines (deposits) which dominate the area. The land in this region is rich in minerals and this, coupled with the high rainfall, encourages the establishment of many rare alpine and arctic plants, particularly gentians.

The farmstead of **Ósar** lies 18 km (12 miles) north along Route 711 on the **Vatnsnes** promontory. From here are superb views across the **Húnafjörður bay** to Blönduós. In the foreground is the moraine-dammed inlet of **Sigríðarstaðavatn**, with the Hóp lagoon beyond. Grey seals bask on the sand spits at low tide while eider duck and terns nest among

the lyme grass. A short distance along the shore are several basalt stacks eroded and awash with the ocean swell. The first, **Hvítserkur**, has a hole through its base. White guano flecks the ledges of the black rock like icing. According to folklore this 15-metre (49-ft) high stack was a troll turned to stone by the sun.

Hóp ❷ is the largest saltwater lagoon in Iceland, virtually cut in half by a narrow sand spit and almost isolated from the sea by **Þingeyrasandur**, a low-lying, black sand dune with great swards of lyme grass on its seaward side. This was

LEFT: Hvítserkur arch with nesting sea birds.
BELOW: yellow lady's bedstraw.

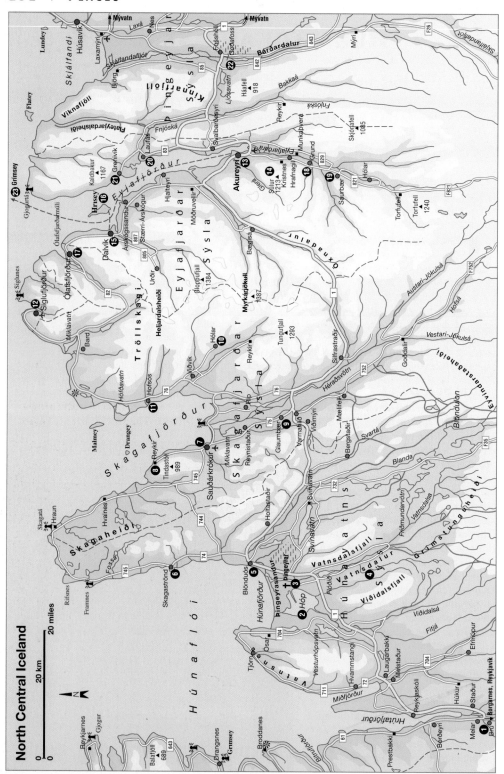

North Central Iceland

0 km 20 km

0 20 miles

used in the past as a seed crop to mill for flour. Over the centuries, the dune has expanded seaward as more sand has been deposited by the ocean. Tundra plants have then colonised the older dunes to provide great flashes of colour: purple thyme, yellow lady's bedstraw, white northern orchid, deep blue gentians, and parnassus grass and silverweed. Overhead, arctic skuas wheel about attacking arctic terns; below, running free across the sands, are Icelandic horses, which are particularly common in this area.

Medieval centre of learning

On the way to the dunes, the dirt track (Route 721) passes one of Iceland's greatest historical sites, **Þingeyrar ❸**. The local bishop Jón Ögmundarson built Iceland's first Benedictine monastery here in 1112. It quickly became a literary hotspot, with monks working full-time transcribing the Bible and the sagas. The name reflects the site's original function as a þing (district assembly). All that remains today is a solitary church erected over 100 years ago.

Near to where Route 721 meets the Ring Road is **Þrístapar**, the hilly site of Iceland's last execution which occurred on 12 January 1830, when the murderers Agnes and Friðrik were beheaded. Across the road is the **Vatnsdalur valley ❹**, a geologist's dream dotted with steep mounds of ground moraine. Just as striking is evidence of the largest known landslip in Iceland that occurred here in October 1720. The side of the huge ridge, **Vatnsdalsfjall** (800 metres/2,624 ft high), collapsed and dammed the river below to create a new lake – **Flóðið**.

With a population just over 1,000 the town of **Blönduós ❺** is the best base for exploring this region. Situated where the River Blanda enters the Húnaflói, it is an important fishing community. The town's bright houses contrast with the local green fields and grey screes.

The Ring Road crosses a bridge that spans the **River Blanda** (where a salmon fishing permit can cost a small fortune) and there is a turn-off to the heart of Blönduós, with a large modern hospital,

garage and hotel. Near to the bridge is the high school, which has a swimming pool and an open-air jacuzzi in the grounds. All smell distinctly sulphuric due to the natural hot spring water.

In the middle of the river, to the east of Blönduós, is the island of **Hrútey**, reached via a small footbridge from the north bank. There is a circular path through the tundra scrubland and it is a good place for birdwatching. The river torrent slows as it passes into the tidal stretches of Blönduós, where rare ducks and divers congregate. From Blönduós, the Ring Road runs directly to Akureyri, passing eventually through the **Öxnadalur** valley, considered the finest scenery on the highway from Reykjavík. Alternatively, Akureyri can be reached following the rougher roads along the wild northern coast.

Remote wilderness

The **Skagi** peninsula lies to the northeast of Blönduós. The dirt highway that hugs its western edge passes through a narrow band of agricultural land overshadowed by the mountains behind. **Skagaströnd ❻**, with a population of barely 600, is the only settlement of any size. Established as

Moss gathers on the glacial moraine characteristic of this area of northern Iceland.

BELOW: the stone church at Þingeyrar.

Basalt rocks near Vogurviti, formed in a series of extensive hexagonal lava steps. An unmanned lighthouse looks over the small lakes, sand spits and rocky shores, the habitat for countless birds.

BELOW: the bishopric of Hólar, once north Iceland's religious centre.

an important trading port in the 16th century, today it is a quiet fishing centre built on a rocky outcrop joined to the peninsula by good alluvial soil. Brightly coloured wooden houses edge a sweeping bay with the snow-splashed mountain peaks of **Spákonufell** as the towering backdrop.

North of Skagaströnd sand dunes and shingle bays give way to cliffs. The ever-deteriorating road climbs upwards and across the top of the **Króksbjarg** and **Bakkar** cliffs – home to a large number of sea birds. Rows of sandstone outcrops contrast with the black basalt lava, usually hexagonal in section. Thousands of kittiwakes vie for nesting space on ledges whilst fulmars nest on the tops of the columns. Near to where the River Fossá cascades over the cliff there is a small grassy headland almost completely undermined by the sea – a great place from which to observe the sea birds. Beyond Bakkar is a temporary respite in the high cliffs. **Vogurviti** is an unusual outcrop of basalt rock (*see margin, left*).

Saudárkrókur

Within the Skagafjörður fjord lie several small islands rich in birdlife. The most

famous of these is **Drangey**, once a hide-out for outlaws, including the saga figure of Grettir the Strong. The island can be reached from **Sauðárkrókur 7**, the region's administrative centre at the head of the fjord. First settled by Scotsmen from the Hebrides, today Sauðárkrókur has a population of over 2,700, making it second only to Akureyri in size on Iceland's north coast. As a result, it has many amenities including swimming pool, cinema and even a gliding club. Thermal springs supply hot water to the town's inhabitants and a natural hot pool, Grettislaug, can be visited just to the north, at **Reykir 8**. In Glerhallavík Bay, near the pool, thousands upon thousands of exquisitely beautiful quartz stones, polished by the pounding surf, have been washed up on the beach. It's forbidden to remove any of them from the bay, and, indeed, access is only possible at low tide on foot from Reykir.

Another mountain track (Route 744) with superb views of the area runs over **Þverárfjall** into moorlands of cottongrass. South of Sauðárkrókur, at **Glaumbær 9**, is a finely maintained turf house **museum** (open June–late Sept daily 9am–6pm;

admission charge). The several wood-fronted buildings have thick turf walls and roofs. Below the old turf farmhouse there is a coffee-shop, where you can get Icelandic pancakes. This is in **Áshús**, a house in the building style that supplanted the turf house in the 19th century.

East of Skagafjörður

The eastern flank of Skagafjörður is lined with steep mountains barring all roads through to the interior beyond. This region can be penetrated only by backpackers: at an altitude of 1,300 metres (4,265 ft) are the remnants of an ancient icecap, consisting today of three main glaciers. Accessible by car is the ancient bishopric of **Hólar ⓾**, founded in 1106 and for over 600 years the religious centre of the North. The high-towered "cathedral", from 1763, is charming. The altarpiece, believed to be Dutch, from the early 16th century, was donated by Jón Arason, the last Catholic bishop of the area who was put to death in the Reformation. A difficult hike, from Hólar to the Urðir valley and Dalvík, crosses the snow fields of Heljardalsheiði through some of north Iceland's finest scenery.

Further north is the little fishing village of **Hofsós ⓫**, with the **Icelandic Emigration Centre** (open June–early Sept daily 11am–6pm; admission charge). The Centre, on the sea-front by the harbour, houses an exhibition tracing the history of Icelanders who emigrated to America; there is also an information service, an interesting library and a souvenir shop. Another small exhibition, "Hunters and Fishers", is located in one of the oldest warehouses in Iceland, built in 1777 in the style of a log cabin.

Visitors driving north around Skagafjörður towards Siglufjörður, will find their eyes drawn to the island of **Málmey** offshore. This concave-shaped outcrop of lava is 4 km (2½ miles) long and rises at either end into high cliffs. **Siglufjörður ⓬** is at the end of its own road, set in a beautiful fjord. Amidst a range of glaciated mountains, the town's current population of 1,800 is its lowest in recent history, but a generation ago this was the centre of the herring industry. An increase in tourism has helped the economy, particularly the growing popularity of winter skiing, but Siglufjörður remains a shadow of its former self. ❑

The English poet W.H. Auden visited Sauðárkrókur during his travels in 1937. He was unimpressed, noting that the town "might have been built by Seventh Day Adventists who expected to go to heaven in a few months, so why bother anyway?"

BELOW LEFT: most small settlements in Iceland have a café and/or a bar.

RESTAURANTS & CAFÉS

Bíó Café
Aðalgata 30,
Siglufjörður
Pizzas, burgers and lamb chops all at reasonable prices in this simple but pleasant cafe on the main street. **$$**

Kaffi Krókur
Aðalgata 16,
Sauðárkrókur
Tel: 453 6299.
Very popular café and restaurant serving the likes of baked salmon as well as the usual

selection of pizzas and burgers. **$$**

Ólafshús
Aðalgata 15,
Sauðárkrókur
Tel: 453 6454.
Another good choice – prices are a little less than across at Kaffi Krókur though the range of dishes is similar and equally tasty. **$$**

Sigtún
Suðurbraut 6, Hofsós
Tel: 453 7393.

This simple restaurant is the best that tiny Hofsós has to offer. The usual selection of fish dishes is on the menu. **$$**

Við Arbakkann
Húnabraut 2, Blönduós.
A basic cafe with a limited selection of sandwiches and cakes down by the waterfront. **$**
● ● ● ● ● ● ● ● ● ● ● ●
Categories are for an average-priced dinner per person, without wine.
$$$** over ISK 4,000, **$$** ISK 2,000–4,000, **$ under ISK 2,000.

AKUREYRI AND SURROUNDINGS

Akureyri is Iceland's second city, and makes an ideal base for trips to the nearby fjords and some of the country's most photographed attractions

By Icelandic standards, Akureyri is a thriving metropolis: with a population of only 17,000, it is the country's largest town outside of the Greater Reykjavík area. Sitting squarely on the Ring Road, a hub for bus and air transport, it has grown in recent years into the undisputed centre of the North.

Despite being only 100 km (60 miles) from the Arctic Circle, it enjoys some of the warmest weather in the country in summer, when it is not unusual to see day after day of 20°C (68°F) temperatures and clear skies, bringing flowers into the streets and turning Akureyri into Iceland's version of the tropics.

The setting is spectacular: at the base of Eyjafjörður fjord, Akureyri has a backdrop of sheer granite mountains tipped with snow all year (in winter, an even layer of snow usually makes this Iceland's premier skiing spot). And, while Akureyri's modern architecture leaves a lot to be desired, there are enough older wooden buildings around town to give it some provincial charm.

Gateway to the North

The first settler to claim the Eyjafjörður region was the Norwegian Helgi the Lean (named after a stint on the Orkney Islands as a child, when he was poorly fed by foster parents). Helgi had indiscriminate religious habits: in traditional pagan fashion, he tossed the high-seat pillars from his longship into the sea, allowing the god Thor to choose the site of his new home. But when they washed up 7 km (4 miles) south of modern-day Akureyri, Helgi named his farm Kristnes (Christ's Peninsula), just in case.

The Viking farmers who ended up around Eyjafjörður were relatively peaceful, to judge from their low profiles in the sagas. A notable exception was Víga-Glúmur. A morose and gangly youth regarded as a buffoon by his peers, Víga-Glúmur surprised everyone on a journey to Norway by slaughtering a berserk warrior in combat. He became a worshipper of Odin and returned to Iceland to make the lives of his former tor-

PRECEDING PAGES: the church at Laufás and Eyjafjörður. **LEFT:** Akureyri from Eyjafjördur. **BELOW:** fishing at Dalvík.

Today Akureyri has one of the most active fishing fleets in Iceland and is home to the country's largest canning factory. It also accounts for some 30 percent of Iceland's manufacturing output.

BELOW: the steep climb to Akureyrikirkja.

mentors a misery, becoming chieftain of the Eyjafjörður region by trickery and intimidation. However, he offended the goddess Freyja by butchering one of his in-laws in the goddess's sacred cornfield. After 40 years, Freyja had her revenge – in old age, Víga-Glúmur lost Odin's protection and had to abandon his estates. He died blind and alone.

The profit motive

The town of **Akureyri** ⓭ did not come into existence until the 16th century, when a trading post was set up as a meeting place for local farmers. In the 1770s, the first permanent house was built, and in 1862, with a grand total of 286 inhabitants, it was made a municipality. An excellent harbour soon made this the centre of the new co-operative movement among Icelandic farmers *(see page 116).*

By the early 20th century, grandiose wooden mansions had filled the southern part of Akureyri. The spit at the northern part of town, **Oddeyri**, became the port and warehouse area, and it remains so to this day (the name Akureyri is a blend of *Akur*, meaning field, and *eyri*, spit, after the land that projects into the fjord). Akureyri has a university and a modest local flourishing of the arts, with several theatre groups, plus a number of nightspots and cinemas.

The residents have a mixed reputation in the rest of Iceland. The town is seen as the bastion of middle-class values and, despite the good weather it enjoys, its people are considered closed, traditional and even somewhat dour. Icelanders say that you can't get to know the people of Akureyri unless you are born and raised there – being conceived in the town while your parents were on holiday doesn't count. Even being raised there may not be good enough: tales are told of Akureyri neighbours who accidentally meet in Reykjavík and have long, friendly conversations, only to act like virtual strangers once they return home. Whatever the truth of this, Icelanders have no qualms about flocking to Akureyri, especially at weekends: flights from Reykjavík are packed with holidaymakers, while people from every cor-

Akureyri

0   300 m
0   300 yds

ner of the North drive in to their figurative "big smoke" for a taste of the action.

Exploring the town

Akureyri is compact enough to explore on foot, and the most logical place to start is the partly pedestrianised shopping mall of **Hafnarstræti**. This is the commercial centre of the town, if not its most attractive point: the buildings are the classic, characterless slabs typical of modern Icelandic towns, and, to top it off, loud piped music sometimes echoes through it in summer. The saving grace is an Akureyri institution, the **Bautinn restaurant ⓐ** (tel: 462 1818) across the road at no.92 Hafnarstræti (*see page 247*). One of the most reasonably priced eating spots in Iceland, it has justly been elevated to one of Akureyri's tourist attractions – ask to eat in the glassed-in pergola, which is brightly lit on the numerous sunny days.

The fjord **waterfront** is only a short hop from the mall, usually with a few picturesque trawlers sitting in port. From here, there is a good view of the basalt **Akureyrarkirkja ⓑ** that has dominated the town since its construction in 1940.

Designed by the architect Guðjón Samúelsson, the church can look distressingly unattractive in most lights. Even so, it is Akureyri's pride and joy, and worth the five-minute walk uphill for a visit. Inside, the stained-glass windows show scenes from Icelandic history and the life of Christ in a style that can only be described as cartoon-book. There is an organ with 3,200 pipes, while the centre window in the chancel was donated by England's Coventry Cathedral – it was one of the only parts that survived the bombing during World War II. Most curious is the model ship hanging from the ceiling, a tradition in Iceland, Greenland and the Faroe Islands to protect the parish's fishermen at sea.

A short climb up **Eyrarlandsvegur** leads to the **Botanical Garden ⓒ** (Lystigarðurinn; open June–Sept Mon–Fri 8am–10pm, Sat & Sun 9am–10pm), famed for its 2,000 species of local and foreign flowers blooming outside in Akureyri's warm microclimate. The park was set up by a local women's association in 1912, then taken over by the town in the 1950s – two of the voluntary managers are commemorated by statues.

TIP

It can be extremely difficult to find a hotel room in Akureyri on summer weekends. Make a booking at least a week in advance, or try to visit on weekdays.

BELOW: Akureyri from the eastern side of Eyjafjörður.

With benches and well-kept lawns, the gardens are a perfect place to relax on a sunny afternoon.

Historical tour

Starting back down in the pedestrian mall, a stroll south along Hafnarstræti follows the waterline through the oldest part of Akureyri. There is a plethora of small museums located in this area.

The **Mattías Jochumsson Memorial Museum** (open June–Aug daily 1.30–3.30pm; admission charge) at Eyrarlandsvegur 3, in the building known as Sigurhæðir, is easily reached from the main street by following a footpath up around the church. This is now the restored home of one of Iceland's most revered poets and dramatists. Jochumsson penned the lyrics for Iceland's national anthem, *Iceland's 1,000 Years*, in 1874.

Continuing on past the combined **tourist information office** and **bus terminal**, Hafnarstræti runs into Akureyri's old business district. The area still has many fine mansions in the so-called Icelandic frame-house tradition – to the uninitiated, they look like Swiss chalets. The last was built in 1911, when

other styles came into vogue, including the use of metal sidings pressed into a brick pattern and painted over to look like stone and mortar. Near the intersection with Lækjargata is Akureyri's oldest house, **Laxdalshús** ⓓ. Built in 1795, this tiny restored wooden building (open summer daily 11am–5pm) was occupied until 1978, mostly as home to some 30 people from three or four families.

South along the waterfront following Aðalstræti is **Friðbjarnarhús** ⓔ (open July–Aug Sat and Sun 2–5pm; admission charge), the museum of the International Organisation of Good Templars (a chapter opened in Akureyri in 1884), then the more appealing **Nonnahús** ⓕ (open June–Sept daily 10am–5pm; admission charge). This is the restored home of Reverend Jón Sveinsson, nicknamed Nonni, author of the Nonni series of children's books that are still well loved in Iceland and continental Europe. The house, where Nonni spent some years of his childhood, was built in 1850 and has been maintained in its original form – even the kitchen still has its old implements – making this the most interesting of Akureyri's old homes. Finally, the

BELOW: the pedestrian mall of Hafnarstræti.

KEA

The people of Akureyri joke that virtually everything in their town is owned by KEA. Whilst this wry comment may not reduce the average visitor to unstoppable fits of laughter, it is certainly true that KEA (incidently, nothing to do with the well-known Swedish furniture store, IKEA) is omnipresent in this small town of 17,000 people. KEA, or the Kaupfélag Eyfirðinga, was founded in June 1886 by a group of farmers from around Eyjarfjörður, to strengthen their hand in the negotiation of export prices for their sheep being sent to England. Ten years later the cooperative opened its first store and a slaughterhouse for cows soon followed. Throughout the twentieth century things really boomed for the cooperative which grew in size and become involved in numerous ventures. Indeed, a short stroll around Akureyri today, reveals the KEA logo emblazoned on everything from fishing boats to hotels. KEA has been proud of its northern roots and has concentrated its business in and around the Akureyri region. However, recently there have been attempts to enter the Reykjavík market by building a shopping centre at the BSÍ bus station. As in most countries, there's intense rivalry in Iceland between the capital and its closest rivals. Whether Reykjavíkers will ever agree to real estate development on their doorstep being carried out by their country cousins remains to be seen.

Akureyri Museum ⑥ (Minjasafn; open June–mid-Sept daily 11am–5pm; mid-Sept–May Sun 2–4pm; admission charge) has an exhaustive collection of local memorabilia, from old farming tools to milk cartons, as well as some excellent 19th-century photographs. Outside, a small church, which was moved from Svalbard across the fjord, sits beside Iceland's first nursery.

Anyone still not sated by museums can head back into town to the **Akureyri Art Museum** ⑪ (Listasafn Akureyrar; open Tues–Sun noon–5pm; admission charge) and **Daviðshús** ① (open 15 Jun–1 Sept: daily 4–5.30pm) on Bjarkarstígur, the 1944 home of poet Davíð Stefánsson left as it was when he died. A short walk away, on a rock between Glerárgata and Þógrunnarstraeti, is a statue of **Helgi the Lean** ① *(see page 239)*, with an impressive view over Eyjafjörður.

Short excursions

Pleasant as strolling around Akureyri can be, the real attraction is the surrounding area. A few short trips are very close to town. Only an hour on foot or 10 minutes' drive south is **Kjarnaskógar forest**, one of Iceland's few wooded areas, and a popular picnic place. Hikers can head for the symmetrical, Fuji-like **Mount Súlur** ⑭, visible on clear days from Akureyri. Drive west on Súluvegur (past the rubbish dump) to the small creek – look out for a wooden ladder over the barbed wire, then follow the yellow markers. You should allow several hours of hard (and not very inspiring) walking to reach the 1,213-metre (3,980-ft) summit looking out over the **Glerá** valley. In winter, skiing fans head for the Skidastadir Lodge at **Hlíðar-fjall**, offering the best slopes in the area only a 10-minute drive from town. Many non-skiers also head there for the view of the **Vindheimajökull** glacier.

Exploring the fjord

Perhaps the most popular day trip from Akureyri – and one that can be driven alone or organised through the tourist office – is along the western flank of Eyjafjörður fjord. The well-paved Route 82 offers sweeping views over the rich farming land of the area, with glacier-scoured mountains to the west (their peaks are often buried behind a steady line of grey cloud) and steely blue waters to the east. The district here is known as **Árskógsströnd**. As in the rest of the North, the fields are dotted in summer with hundreds of gigantic white plastic rolls containing hay for the winter – a high-tech innovation that has quickly replaced the more poetic but inefficient methods of traditional hay-gathering. Cows, sheep and geese wander at will, and it is not unusual for traffic to be stopped while a farmer leads a line of cattle over the road to pasture.

Although Route 82 can be followed directly north, a turn-off at Route 816 leads to a ruined port area, called **Gásir**, for many centuries the biggest port in northern Iceland. Many overgrown ruins of the old port can still be seen in the grass. Another short side road (Route 813) leads to the farm **Möðruvellir**, birthplace of the writer Jón Sveinsson. There is a much-photographed farmhouse at **Stærri-Árskógur**, flush against a steep mountain backdrop.

Woollen goods can be a good buy in Iceland.

BELOW: downtown Akureyri.

Skiers enjoying the snow around Akureyri.

Dalvík N (population 1,500) is the dominant town on this side of the fjord. A prosperous fishing village today, Dalvík's claim to fame in Iceland is the 1934 earthquake measuring 6.3 on the Richter scale that brought rocks crashing down from the nearby mountainside and destroyed about half of the town's homes.

Hrísey Island

These days, travellers call in at Dalvík mainly to catch the ferry over to Grímsey and **Hrísey island** N (ferries also run from nearby Árskógssandur). Hrísey is, in fact the second largest island off Iceland's coast, giving Eyjafjörður ("island fjord") its name. On a fine day, the 15-minute trip is well worthwhile – on weekends, there are usually some well-dressed folk from Akureyri making the excursion solely to dine on the island's speciality, Galloway beef, served up at the **Brekka restaurant**.

Hrísey is the only place in the country where Galloway cattle are raised, and it is prohibited by law to remove them to the mainland. It is also the location of Iceland's quarantine centre: when it opened in 1974, all animals on the island

BELOW: the mountains of Eyjafjörður looming on Hrísey's horizon.

had to be killed to minimise the risk of cross-infection. The result has been that Hrísey now supports some of the lushest vegetation in the entire country.

There is a small village here with a church for the 300 or so inhabitants, which during World War II was the billet for five British servicemen whose job was to check up on all trawlers entering the fjord, with only a broken machine gun to back them up. Much of Hrísey is a nature reserve and so off-limits to hikers, but there are still plenty of trails across the flat moorlands, covered in purple heather and full of birdlife.

North from Dalvík

Back on the mainland, a popular side trip from Dalvík is into **Svarfadardalur** valley, entering on Route 805 and returning along Route 807. From the end of Route 805, hikers and horseriders can head into the wilderness of **Heljardalsheiði** for camping trips in some of the finest mountain country in Iceland.

North of Dalvík, a nerve-wracking and treacherous gravel road winding along the steep coastline was made more bearable by the opening in 1991 of a 3.5-km (2-

mile) tunnel. This one-lane passage through the mountainside has become something of a tourist attraction in itself, although claustrophobes might prefer to risk the old road around the headland of **Olafsfjarðarmúli** – which, incidentally, is a good place to see the midnight sun in July, with views on a clear day to Grímsey island, on the Arctic Circle.

Ólafsfjörður ⑰ is a fishing village of 950 people nestled amongst a ring of snow-capped, 1,200-metre (3,900-ft) high peaks. Despite the setting, it has little more of interest than fishing boats and factories.

Points south

Heading south from Akureyri, Route 821 runs along the Eyjafjarðará river valley. The pretty farm **Kristnes**, built on the site where Helgi the Lean first settled, is 7 km (4 miles) along on a hill with a strategic view of the fjord. A few minutes further south is another farm, **Grund** ⑱, with one of the most unusual churches in Iceland – with its several Romanesque spires, it looks transplanted from St Petersburg. The farmer Magnús Sigurðsson built it to his own design in 1906 to serve the whole river valley. The

church broke a nearly millennium-old tradition by being built on a north-south axis instead of east-west.

A good example of a more traditional church, made of turf and stone, is at the farm of **Saurbær** ⑲, which is situated 27 km (17 miles) south of Akureyri on Route 821. The quaint interior is open to visitors. At this point, the road continues to the farm of **Torfufell** (offering farmhouse accommodation), or across the river valley to return to Akureyri on Route 829. En route is the historic farm of **Munkaþverá**. Originally known as Þverá, this was the birthplace in the 10th century of the notorious Odin-worshipping Viking Víga-Glúmur. In the 12th century, a Benedictine monastery was built on the site, although none of it remains. Finally, at **Ytri-Hóll**, look out for a classic turf house that is still in use: the tiny chimney poking out from the grassy roof only makes it look even more like a hobbit's hole.

Eyjafjördur's eastern shore

The Ring Road runs east of Akureyri – giving some of the best views of the town – before running north and heading into the **Grýtubakkahreppur** district. Turn

Boarding the ferry to Hrísey Island. Ferries operate from Árskógssandur every 2 hours for the 15-minute journey, and there are also departures from Dalvík which stop en route to Grímsey (for more details see page 316).

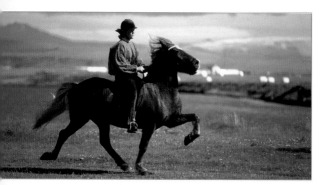

of the rugged Fjörður peninsula, which has been uninhabited since World War II.

The Ring Road continues east towards Lake Mývatn, but first passes the small lake **Ljósavatn** ("lightwater") and a turn-off to the farm of the same name. This was the Saga Age farm of the chieftain Þorgeir Þorkelsson, Law-Speaker in the Alþingi in AD 1000, who was forced to decide whether Iceland should be pagan or Christian. As the *Kristni Saga* tells it, Þorgeir spent 24 hours under his cloak before deciding for the Christians. Riding back from Þingvellir to his home at Ljósavatn, he passed a giant waterfall and decided to toss all his carved images of pagan gods into its waters. This powerful waterfall, **Goðafoss** 22 ("fall of the gods"), is virtually beneath the Ring Road a few kilometres further on, and is the easiest of Iceland's major falls to visit. Most cars and buses en route to Mývatn stop here at the small petrol station/store at **Fosshóll**.

The surrounding area of the **Bárðardalur** valley is a 7,000-year-old lava flow, through which the Skjál-fandafljót river has cut a path to form Goðafoss. ❑

Horse-riding expeditions into the remote Fjörður peninsula are offered by Polar Horses (tel: 463 3179; e-mail: polarhestar@ polarhestar.is; www.nett.is/polar) at Grytubakki II farm 4 km (2½ miles) outside Grenivík.

BELOW: the church at Grund.

off at Route 83 for **Laufás** 20, a beautifully situated farm looking out over Eyjafjörður with a small white church and 19th-century turf farmhouse **museum** (open mid-May–mid-Sept daily 10am–6pm; admission charge). Built in the 1860s, the dirt-floored building was a vicarage and upper-crust home, and is now crowded with antiques. A famous touch is the carved woman's face and duck placed over the middle segment of the farmhouse. Just 22 km (14 miles) from the Ring Road turn-off is the picturesque but somnolent fishing town of **Grenivík** 21 (population 300). Only founded in 1910, Grenivík is at the edge

RESTAURANTS, CAFÉS & BARS

Restaurants

Akureyri

Bautinn
Hafnarstræti 92, Akureyri
Tel: 462 1818
An Akureyri institution which is always busy with locals and visitors alike. A good central location for burger and fries as well as a couple of more substantial meat dishes. **$$**

Café Karolína
Kaupvangsstræti 23, Akureyri
Attracts a select gathering of Akureyri's young and bohemian. With tasteful artwork adorning the walls, this is a pleasant place to while away an hour of two with a cappucino and a slice of delicious homemade cake. **$**

Friðrik V
Kaupvangsstræti 6, Akureyri
Tel: 461 5775
Undoubtedly the finest place to dine in Akureyri. Owner and chef, Friðrik, trained at London's River Cafe and also worked in Reykjavík's Hótel Holt before opening this elegant first floor restaurant serving creatively prepared fish dishes blending the freshest Icelandic ingredients with a subtle hint of the Mediterranean. **$$$**

Glaumbær
Ægisgata 10, Ólafsfjörður
Popular with local fishermen who come here after tieing up their boats in the harbour right outside the door. Serves tasty fresh fish as well as more mainstream burgers and pizzas. **$$**

Greifinn
Glerárgata 20, Akureyri
Tel: 460 1600
The most popular Italian restaurant in Akureyri with lots of different pizzas and pasta dishes to set your tastebuds tingling. Popular with locals so it's worth ringing ahead to book a table. **$$**

La Vita è Bella
Hafnarstræti 92, Akureyri
Tel: 461 5858
A good choice for well prepared Italian fare in the centre of Akureyri. Although the pasta and pizzas are good value, the meat dishes on the menu seem overpriced. **$$–$$$**

Strikið Brasserie
Skipagata 14, Akureyri
Tel: 462 1700
There are great views of the fjord from this pleasant brasserie which has tasty lamb and fish mains. Worth seeking out at midday for their special-offer lunches. **$$–$$$**

Peng
Strandgata 13, Akureyri
Tel: 466 3800
One of the few Chinese restaurants outside Reykjavík, this place has a superb value eat-as-much-as-you-want lunch buffet, as well as all various popular Chinese dishes on an extensive menu. **$$**

Out of town

Brekka
Hrísey island Tel: 466 1751
There are superb views from this hillside restaurant inside the Brekka guesthouse on Hrísey island. There's generally a chicken and a fish dish on the menu, as well as a range of burgers. **$$**

Kaffi Sogn
Goðabraut 3, Dalvík
A limited choice of pizzas and a couple of fish dishes in the centre of Dalvík close to the town hall. **$$**

Bars

Akureyri

Café Amour
Ráðhústorg 7
A great spot for an early evening drink right on the main square.

Græni Hatturinn
Hafnarstræti 96
This basement pub is the closest thing Akureyri has to a British pub. It's located beneath a café.

Sjallinn
Geislagata 14
The place to come for the cheapest beer in Akureyri, this pub is attached to the town's main club.

PRICE CATEGORIES

The price guide is for the average price of dinner per person, without wine:
$$$ Over ISK 4,000
$$ ISK 2,000–4,000
$ Under ISK 2,000

RIGHT: an Icelandic buffet lunch.

Icelandic Hauntings

One in every 500 inhabitants of Iceland is a ghost. According to *Vættatal*, the spiritual *Who's Who* of Iceland by folklore historian Árni Björnsson, more than 500 ghouls, trolls, and paranormal beings haunt the island, making a substantial – or perhaps insubstantial – addition to its quarter of a million human population. This high ghost quotient is not entirely unexpected, as Iceland is the perfect home for any spook, with long periods of darkness in winter and an abundance of grotesque rock and lava formations providing perfect camouflage for monsters and ogres.

Flesh-and-blood Icelanders, it seems, enjoy excellent relations with their neighbours from the other world. In a survey on the supernatural in Western Europe, Icelanders topped the league for ghostly experiences, with 41 percent claiming contact with the dead, compared to the European average of 20 percent.

Traditionally, however, ghosts were not harmless visitations from the dear departed. They usually took the form of an *afturganga*, a dead man turned zombie, and were capable of killing people or (worse) taking them to hell. Only the spiritual powers of a priest or the physical prowess of a strongman could exorcise such a nightmarish spook.

A very uncomfortable characteristic of the *afturganga* is his tendency to walk again before anyone knows he has died. One such was the Deacon of Dark River, who drowned on his way to pick up his girlfriend to take her to a dance. Nonetheless, he turned up, a little late, and the unsuspecting girl got on the back of his horse. As they rode through the night, she overheard him muttering:

The moon hides, as death rides,
Do you not see the white mark
On my brow, Garun, Garun.

Fortunately, this ditty held two clues to his true nature: firstly, ghosts always repeat things, and secondly they cannot say "God." The girl's name was Guðrún, and Guð is "God" in Icelandic. The terrified Guðrún managed to jump off – seconds before the ghostly rider and horse disappeared into an open grave leading straight to hell. She was never the same again, and some say she lost her mind completely.

Other forms of ghost are the *fylgja* or familiar spirit, and its close relations the *móri* or the *skotta*. These are shadowy, malevolent spirits, and when they are ill-wished onto a man, they will follow him and his descendants unto the ninth generation.

Then there are the trolls – elemental beings who, fortunately, turn into stone if they are caught outside in daylight. All of Iceland is dotted with trolls who stayed out just that little bit too long – including the great stone troll-cow, Hvítserkur, caught having a drink of sea-water just off the northwest coast.

All things considered, Icelanders probably prefer their more attractive other-worldly neighbours, the elves. Like Hollywood filmstars, they look like humans – but are richer, more glamorous and usually completely amoral. According to one legend, the elves were the children that Eve hadn't finished washing when God came to visit – they were not fit to be seen, so she had to hide them. Thus, they are also known as the Hidden People, and with good reason – only 5 percent of Icelanders have actually met one. Nevertheless, elves are held in the highest regard, with 53 percent of the population either believing in, or not denying, their existence.

In legend, those who visit the elves and survive the experience return to the human world laden with riches but often strangely changed. In nearly all cases, the elves decide when and where they will be seen by humans. Usually it is when they need their assistance. Human women, it is said, are sometimes fetched by distraught elfen husbands to act as mid-wives to elf-mothers who are having difficulties in childbirth.

One 20th-century figure to have had an encounter with the Hidden People was trade-union leader Tryggvi Emilsson, who, as a young man, was saved from death by an elf-maiden after he had fallen down a gully. Her beauty, he said, haunted him the rest of his life. Elf-women have been known to have even more intimate physical relations with human men, and are obviously more liberated than their human counterparts, often leaving their lovers holding the baby, as it were.

It is of some consolation that these semi-supernatural offspring are usually highly talented and handsome. Elf-men, on the other hand, make conscientious and kind lovers, according to the tales told by the few women who have been lucky enough to have tried one out.

The elves of Iceland are treated with great respect. The rocks and hills in which they make their homes are diligently preserved, for great harm traditionally comes to those that tamper with these elusive neighbours. Roads skirt round well-known elf-hills. One such is the road that runs from Reykjavík to the suburb of Kópavogur, which is actually called Álfhólsvegur, or Elf-Hill Road. On the main street of the town of Grundarfjördur, a rock stands between the houses numbered 82 and 86 – the elves live at number 84.

LEFT: an elf-maiden rising from her grotto.
ABOVE: Christmas trolls.
RIGHT: two rowdy trolls.

Despite these superstitious gestures, Dr Árni Björnsson says that true believers in elves and ghosts comprise only a very small minority in Iceland. "Most of us do not actively believe in these things, but on the other hand we are reluctant to deny their existence," he says. "It is really a form of scepticism. We live in a land which is highly unpredictable – what is grass and meadow today could be lava and ash tomorrow. So we have learnt not to rely too much on the factual evidence of our senses."

And, of course, the existence of elves in our modern world is such a nice idea. "People think it would be fun if they did exist, so they pretend to believe in them. Unlike other nations, we aren't in the least ashamed of it. In fact, we are rather proud of our elves." He adds: "Iceland is a big country for such a small population. We've plenty of room for neighbours of all kinds."

Indeed, this laissez-faire attitude is ensconced in folk tradition and the sagas. The medieval bishop, Guðmundur the Good, once set off to consecrate Drangey, to drive away the multitude of ghouls, fiends and devils that haunted this island. As he went about his holy work, a voice rang out from the rocks. "Consecrate no more, Guðmundur," it cried. "The wicked need some place to be." The bishop sensibly took the point and quickly returned to shore. ❑

GRÍMSEY

Situated on the Arctic Circle, the island of
Grímsey is a remote outpost, home to huge
colonies of sea birds and just under 100 islanders

T he folk on the remote, weather-beaten island of **Grímsey** ㉓ tell the tale of a local minister who discovered that the Arctic Circle ran right through his house. He decided that it not only bisected his bedroom, it bisected his bed: the minister slept on one side of the Arctic Circle, his wife on the other, and rarely did either cross the great divide.

The apocryphal story is told and retold in various forms (sometimes it's a minister, sometimes an old magistrate), but it sums up the tongue-in-cheek attitude the Grímsey islanders have to the Arctic Circle – an imaginary line which, to the outside world, puts Grímsey on the map. They can only regard with some bemusement anyone who makes the pilgrimage all the way to their remote polar outpost just to say that they've walked across a geographical abstraction. "How did it feel?" someone might ask with good-natured concern. "Have your feet turned blue yet?"

But, although its location on latitude 66°30' N may still be Grímsey's claim to fame, a steady stream of travellers are finding out that the island has more concrete attractions to offer. The sheer isolation of this tiny piece of land, with a population of only just over 100, has its own peculiarly Icelandic appeal: the scenery is wild and beautiful, the birdlife extraordinary, while the people remain beguilingly eccentric. And Grímsey has one of the strangest histories in Iceland, settled by chess-playing Vikings and supported by a 19th-century American mil-lionaire. (And, frankly, it is quite fun to know that you're standing on the Arctic Circle.)

Island of chess players

Grímsey was first settled in the 10th century by a Viking named Grímur (hence the name Grím's island), whose descendants took the Icelandic obsession with chess to new extremes. Tradition has it that long summers and longer winters were spent devoted to the game, with some players spending weeks confined to their beds devising new stratagems.

PRECEDING PAGES:
fish-drying the
traditional way.
LEFT: the Grímsey
road sign. **BELOW:** a
portrait of Willard
Fiske, Grímsey's
benefactor, in the
island's library.

EYJARBÓKASAFNIÐ II.

Taking a boat trip off the shores of Grímsey. Scheduled services from the mainland sail from Dalvík, north of Akureyri, three times per week. The trip takes 3½ hours. See page 316 for details.

BELOW RIGHT: the last of Willard Fiske's donated chess sets.

Chess was more important than life itself: it was not unknown for a player to fling himself into the sea rather than bear the shame of defeat.

Perhaps not surprisingly, Grímsey did not prosper as a fishing port. On one occasion in the 18th century, the entire male population except for the minister was lost in a single fishing accident (perhaps they were exhausted from playing chess). According to folklore, the minister took responsibility for repopulating the island himself.

Then, in the late 19th century, the island's eccentric reputation was brought to the attention of a wealthy North American named Daniel Willard Fiske – prominent journalist, Old Icelandic scholar, friend of both the Icelandic independence hero Jón Sigurðsson and the writer Mark Twain, and, in 1857, chess champion of the US. Although Willard Fiske only glimpsed the shores of Grímsey as he passed it in a steamship, the island fired his vivid imagination and he decided to take its local population under his wing.

First Fiske sent the essentials: a gift of 11 marble chess sets to each of the farms on the island. These were followed by masses of firewood and a bequest to finance the island's first school and library. Finally, on his death in 1904, Fiske left the inhabitants of Grímsey $12,000 – at that time the most money anyone had ever given to Iceland. Today, Fiske is still revered on Grímsey as a sort of secular saint. His birthday on 11 November is celebrated with a meeting and coffee in the community hall. Fiske's portrait still hangs in the library, while a large number of male islanders sport the decidedly un-Icelandic name of Willard. Unfortunately, Grímsey hasn't kept up the love of chess. Hardly anybody plays it – these days, the favourite game is surfing the internet.

Last stop before the Pole

Until the 1930s, the only way to reach Grímsey was on the mail ship that left Akureyri once every six months (you could return six months later, provided bad weather didn't prevent the ship from running).

Today, there is a year-round ship service, taking about six hours each way from Dalvík, while daily light aircraft

A Nation of Chess Players

Probably introduced by the first settlers in the 9th century, chess was a common pastime in Iceland through the Middle Ages, as shown by numerous old expressions from the game which have been preserved in everyday speech. When Willard Fiske visited towards the end of the 19th century, he found eager players all over the country. Fiske published Iceland's first chess magazine, providing a theoretical training ground that soon guided the game into the realms of organised sport. In 1959, Friðrik Ólafsson became the nation's first grandmaster. The next generation was inspired by the "Match of the Century" which took place in Reykjavík in 1972, when Bobby Fischer wrested the world championship from Boris Spassky. Among the enthusiasts were Helgi Ólafsson and Margeir Pétursson, then in their teens and now both international grandmasters. In their wake came two other grandmasters, later joined by a further five. Still a star in Iceland, Fischer returned in 2005 – having been controversially offered Icelandic citizenship to avoid facing criminal charges in the US resulting from having played an international match in the former Yugoslavia, thus breaking sanctions regulations.

flights from Akureyri take only 25 minutes to cover the 41 km (25 miles). Arriving by plane in Grímsey is a truly memorable experience since, more often than not, the plane flies low over the runway before attempting to land, in an effort to chase away the hundreds of birds which gather here to feed. The aircraft then comes round a second time to land. However, sometimes the birds are so stubborn that one of the island's tractors has to be driven up and down the landing strip as well to encourage the birds to take to the air. Indeed, on departure from Grímsey, it's not uncommon for birds to strike the aircraft's wings as they and it take off at the same time.

Both the plane and the ferry allow travellers to return from the island on the same day – which, until 1991 when a new guesthouse opened, was just as well, since the only accommodation was on the floor of the community centre. (Camping is permitted if you site your tent discreetly.)

Getting acquainted with the island is not difficult. There are 10 old farms on the island, but most of the inhabitants live in the "village" of **Sandvík** – the name for the 15 houses lined up along the harbour.

After World War II, Grímsey still didn't have electricity, there was little fresh water and the occasional case of scurvy was reported among the islanders. Modern fishing techniques have brought Iceland's new affluence here – the township may have a rather scruffy look, but the houses are modern, there are satellite dishes to pick up television, greenhouses to grow vegetables and a large indoor swimming pool. Although there is only one road on Grímsey – 3 km (2 miles) long – the island boasts a handful of private cars and several tractors.

The Grímsey **community centre** can be identified by the mural on its walls. Built on the site of the old school financed by Fiske, it still contains the library, original photographs of the benefactor and the only one of the 11 marble chess sets still in existence. Nobody seems to know where the rest have gone.

A short walk west of the village is the whitewashed, late-19th-century wooden **church**. Above the altar is a replica of Leonardo da Vinci's *Last Supper*, painted by a mainland artist, Arngrímur Gíslason.

TIP

The island is only 4 km (2½ miles) by 2 km (1¼ miles) in size, and can be circumambulated in about 5 hours. A hiking trail begins from the airport and strikes out across some especially tussocky grass towards the island's west coast and a number of sheer birdcliffs. Winding its way along the clifftops, the path gradually descends towards the islands's harbour where it joins the main road. It's now a straightforward stroll past the church and the village store back towards the airstrip.

BELOW: Sandvík, the main settlement on Grímsey.

The nearby **parsonage**, which was built in 1909, is now run by a layman – Grímsey pays for a minister to come every three months from Akureyri (if he wants to come more often, he has to pay for the journey himself). It's long been rumoured on the island that the Arctic Circle runs right through the middle of the priest's bed, putting an icy division between him and his wife. However, in reality, this is extremely unlikely since the Arctic Circle is not constant but is currently creeping northwards, due to the earth's uneven orbit, at a rate of 15 metres (50 ft) or so every year. It won't be for another 10,000–20,000 years that the northward movement will stop, by which time the Circle will have reached 68 degrees north, well to the north of Grímsey's geographical position, and will then start moving slowly south again.

Along the coast are the traditional fish-drying racks. There are four fish processing plants on the island, concentrating on salted fish and dried cod-heads (which are sold to Nigeria). Sheep used to wander the island until 1988, when an outbreak of the stock disease scrapie forced them all to be put down.

In 1973, an unexpected addition to the island's wildlife appeared in the form of a polar bear that had floated over from Greenland on an iceberg. It was promptly hunted down and shot and is now stuffed in Húsavík Museum on the mainland.

BELOW: arctic terns wheeling overhead.

Dive-bombers of the Arctic Circle

Heading back to the eastern end of the island, the road runs straight into the bitumen runway of the airport (where the Básar guesthouse, one of two places for formal accommodation, is also to be found). The runway is carpeted by resting sea birds – before some landings or take-offs, a car is driven up and down in an attempt to shoo away these potential hazards to aircraft.

Usually that's the end of the matter. Should you be visiting in June or July, however, the scene is more like something from Alfred Hitchcock's *The Birds*. That's when the arctic terns are nesting all over the island, and anyone coming near a bird's young is fair game for a divebomb attack. The screeching call *kría! kría! kría!* (which is actually the bird's name in Icelandic) is the prelude to a possible peck on the back of the head – which is why, in this season, everyone wears a thick hat (a leather glove under a beany or beret is recommended) and carries a big stick (the Básar Guesthouse will lend out plastic rods to guests for self-defence).

On the northern side of the runway is the Grímsey road sign, theoretically marking the location of the Arctic Circle. Arrows point to various world highlights (including New York: 4,445 km/ 2,763 miles; Sydney: 16,137 km/10,027 miles; London: 1,949 km/1,225 miles), although for some reason the North Pole doesn't get a mention.

A path leads away from the airport towards 100-metre (330-ft) cliff faces, which can be followed completely around the island. Soon the trail disappears beneath a bed of thick, matted grass, which seems to glow green against the blue of the sea. The polka-dot of yellow weeds finishes off the colourful effect (there are a total of some 100 species of flowering plant on Grímsey).

The cliffs on the north and east sides of the island are also where the most spectacular birdlife can be found, creating a din that is little short of cacophonous. Thirty-six species of bird nest on the island, including 11 different types of sea bird. There is a large puffin community, and it is quite possible to come within a few metres of these birds (but don't walk too close to the edge of the cliffs, since underground puffin nests can be accidentally crushed). There are fulmars, kittiwakes, gulls and arctic terns, and Grímsey is the last place in Iceland where the little auk breeds (only two or three pairs are left, the rest all staying closer to the Pole).

Although it is located on the Arctic Circle, Grímsey's summers and winters are never as extreme as one would imagine: the June midnight is bright but never blinding, and there are about four hours of vague light in December (provided the weather isn't very cloudy, that is, in which case it stays dark).

Even so, life on the island is still tough, and it says something for the islanders' spirit that they have kept their numbers at around 100 while other tiny Icelandic islands have lost their wealth and population. Schoolchildren, who spend their last three years studying on the mainland, almost always return to Grímsey. Even though not many play chess here now, the island still shows the eccentric, indomitable spirit that inspired the old benefactor Daniel Willard Fiske. ❑

EAT

There are only a couple of places to eat on Grímsey. The **Básar Guesthouse** (Tel: 467 3103), attached to the island's guesthouse, is a pleasure: fresh fish straight from the ocean accompanied by boiled potatoes and salad. Simple but tasty. The **Krían** is a greasespoon café down by the harbour serving something-and-chips and other fry-ups.

BELOW LEFT: the light of the midnight sun. **BELOW:** midwinter aurora.

LAKE MÝVATN

This outstandingly beautiful area has the twin attractions of the serene lake at Mývatn, one of Iceland's major breeding grounds for birds, and spectacular volcanic activity

Sitting just to the west of the Mid-Atlantic Ridge that is slowly tearing Iceland apart, the Lake Mývatn district is one of the most volcanically active regions on earth. Created by a powerful basaltic lava eruption 2,300 years ago, the lake and its surrounding landscapes are dominated by curiously shaped volcanic landforms such as pillars of lava, while the surrounding wetlands are a favourite breeding and feeding spot for many varieties of waterfowl, especially ducks, attracted here by a plentiful supply of food in the form of the countless insects which congregate here in the summer months. In this respect, Mývatn is unusual: Iceland's relatively low summer temperatures and strong winds do not provide a ready habitat for insects.

In the mid-1970s, earthquakes centred here were felt in the entire north of the country, with lava erupting from nearby Mount Krafla over several years to spectacular effect. Activity continued through the early 1980s and today there are almost daily subterranean rumblings (although they are mostly too small to be noticed except by scientific instruments). Nowhere else in Iceland can you see the same combination of craters, fresh lava fields, hot springs, geysers and bubbling mud pools.

Meanwhile, the lake's natural beauty and role as a wildlife breeding ground led to it being set aside as a national conservation area in 1974 – a status that actually gives it more protection than a National Park. The lake is a veritable oasis on the fringes of Iceland's bleak northern deserts, supporting, among other things, the world's largest population of breeding ducks. As a result, Mývatn has established itself as Iceland's number one tourist attraction outside of the "Golden Circle" and a place that has been known to keep nature lovers occupied for weeks. And while offering plenty to explore in its own right, it also makes a good base for trips to the Northeast and to Askja in the interior.

Main attractions
REYKJAHLIÐ
HÖFÐI
HVERFELL
JARÐBÖÐIN NATURE BATHS
HVERARÖND
MOUNT KRAFLA

PRECEDING PAGES:
Route 87 from Húsavík to Mývatn. **LEFT:** Mývatn in autumn. **BELOW:** a bubbling mud pool near Námafjall.

Bird-watching devotees swear that the bridge on the Ring Road over the Laxá River is Iceland's premier location, bar none, for spotting birds.

In search of sulphur

Although the winters are long and cold, covering the lake with ice for seven months of the year, Mývatn enjoys more sunshine and receives less rain than almost anywhere else in the country. As a result, it has been popular with settlers from the Saga Age onwards: in 1908, archaeologists dug up a Norse longhouse whose wall was over 40 metres (130 ft) in length, and may have contained a temple of Thor.

Dating their ancestry back to those days are the Reykjahlíð family, whose farm covers the whole surrounding area – at some 6,000 sq. km (2,300 sq. miles) in size, it is the biggest farm in Iceland and more than twice the size of Luxembourg. The family's days of glory were in the 14th century, when sulphur was mined from Námaskarð on their land and sent to Europe to be made into gunpowder. This remote corner of Iceland helped keep the world's wars rolling until the 19th century, when other sulphur sources were found.

Farming in the area also prospered despite the devastating eruption of the Leirhnjúkur crater (10 km/6 miles north-east of Reykjahlíð). The "Mývatn-fires" lasted for five years, from 1724 to 1729, wiped out three farms and wrecked Reykjahlíð's buildings – but created some of the bizarre lava formations which now make the area so fascinating.

Today the farm is still working, although the owners have invested in the tourist business and allow visitors access to almost every part of the property. Travellers started arriving in numbers to see Mývatn and its surroundings in the early 20th century, and the family built the first hotel, the **Hotel Reykjahlíð**, in the 1940s – it has since housed everyone from Prince Harald of Norway to a steady stream of backpackers. In 1968, a diatomite plant was opened at Bjarnarflag near Mývatn, and a small village, also known as **Reykjahlíð ❶**, sprang up around the hotel northeast of the lake to become the service centre of the area.

With hotels, camping grounds, supermarkets and snack bars, Reykjahlíð is a functional base for travellers. It does boast the local **church** – although it was rebuilt in 1972, it is on the site of the original church that was in the path of the lava flow in 1729 and seemed cer-

BELOW: a lone bather among the pseudo-craters to the south of Lake Mývatn.

Lake Mývatn map

Husavík
Hólasandur
Viðidalshnjúkar
87
Leirhnjúkur 609 — Víti
Krafla ❶❶ 818
Grímsstaðaheiði
Hlíðarfjall 771
863
Grímsstaðir
Eldhraun
Reykjahlíð ❶
Bjarnarflag ❾
Hverarönd
Sandvatn
Vindbelgjarfjall
❷
Námafjall 432
Jarðböðin Nature Barhs ❿
❸ 529
Syðri-Neslönd
Grjótagjá ❽
Mývatn
Hverfell ❼
Hrutey
Haganes
Geiteyjarströnd
Hraunbunga 490
Mikley
❻ Dimmuborgir
Höfði ❺
Kálfaströnd
Álftagerði
Skútustaðagígar
Skútustaðir ❹
849
1
Lake Mývatn
Grænavatn
0 — 3 km
0 — 3 miles
N

tain to be destroyed. Miraculously, the lava parted literally at the church door and flowed on either side of the wooden building, an event that the devout ascribed to divine intervention. In the school building at Reykjahlíð, beside the swimming pool, is a **visitors' centre** run by the Icelandic Nature Conservation Agency. It has information on routes around the area and its natural history, with some excellent lava exhibits.

Circuit around the lake

A road – most of which amounts to no more than a dirt track – circles Lake Mývatn, connecting the various points of interest. The lake itself is 37 sq. km (14 sq. miles) in area, making it the fourth-largest in Iceland, but unusually shallow – the average depth is only 2 metres (7 ft), with the deepest point only 4½ metres (15 ft). This shallowness allows the sun's rays to reach the bottom to create a thriving growth of algae and plankton. There are 50 islets.

The name Mývatn actually means "midge lake" and, for long stretches of the summer, clouds of these tiny flying insects can make any visit a misery. Bil-lions usually emerge in June and August to dive into eyes, noses and ears with relentless energy. They are often joined by biting blackflies, so make sure you bring some insect repellent. (Head nets are, not surprisingly, sold in most shops.) It is cold comfort to learn that the midges are crucial to the lake's ecosystem: their corpses fertilise the lakeside and the larvae are a staple for birds and fish.

The surfeit of midges as fodder has also made the River Laxá, which flows through Mývatn, the source of Iceland's biggest salmon (they spawn in the lower part of the lake). Mývatn offers the best trout fishing in the country.

The fields of fire

Heading north from Reykjahlíð, Route 87 crosses the lava flow from the 1720s that dominates the topography of the village and the northern landscape of the lake. Called **Eldhraun** ("fire lava"), this barren landscape gives a glimpse of the desert that Route 87 runs into – so devoid of life that NASA sent its Apollo 11 crew for training missions here in the late 1960s. Keep an eye out on the left-hand side for a giant bubble of dried lava,

TIP

A great way to get to grips with the land-scapes around the lake is to take a sightseeing flight from the airstrip at Reykjahlíð with the Mýflug airline. Flights operate during the summer and require a minimum of two passengers. Tours vary in duration from twenty minues to two hours, with the longer flights also taking in Krafla, Dettifoss, Ásbyrgi and the Jökulsárgljúfur canyon. There are full details of the options available at www.myflug.is where prices range from ISK 5,000 to 20,000.

BELOW: the Hverfell crater overshadowing Reykjahlíð.

In winter local farmers still cut holes through the ice to lower their hooks – part of a ritual that dates back to the Middle Ages, when fish were the only winter food and could mean the difference between life and death.

where the surface layer has been cracked like a huge egg.

Turning left onto Route 848, the landscape becomes much greener and quickly reaches the marshes of the **Conservation Area**. This is the main breeding ground for the lake's birds, and during the nesting season its shoreline is off-limits (15 May to 20 July). Fifteen species of duck have been recorded on the lake, and up to 100,000 birds can be gathered here at once. Most of the birds are summer migrants, arriving from late April onwards. The tufted duck and the greater scaup are the most prolific species, but the beautiful Barrow's goldeneye, red-breasted merganser and the teal are also common. The Barrow's goldeneye is one of the few birds to spend the winter at Mývatn, carefully choosing ice-free areas of the lake which are kept open by warm currents. Virtually the entire European population of the species breeds here. In addition to ducks, the unusual red-necked phalarope, Slavonian grebe and whooper swan are common visitors, as are the great northern diver and red-throated diver. Incidentally, there is a long tradition in the

BELOW: lava formations at Dimmubórgir.

Mývatn area of collecting birds' eggs for private consumption. However, local people are sure to follow the age-old tradition of always leaving at least four eggs in the nest for incubation. The view overlooking the bird-dotted lake from **Neslandatangi peninsula ❷**, which almost cuts the lake in two, is particularly serene at dusk.

South of the conservation area, the 529-metre (1,735-ft) peak of **Vindbelgjarfjall ❸**, seen to the right, can be climbed in a couple of hours for views of the lake. Beyond that, another smaller lake, **Sandvatn**, is probably the best place in the area to see gyrfalcons.

South of here, the road now runs into the Ring Road. On the southern shore of the lake is Mývatn's secondary service centre of **Skútustaðir ❹**, with a petrol station, church and snack shop.

From here, there is an easy hour-long path around the **Skútustaðagígar pseudo-craters**. These were formed when water was trapped beneath flowing lava, boiled and burst up through the surface, creating what looks like volcanic cones. Some were formed so recently that their sides are still charred.

Picnic promontory

One of the most sheltered and relaxing spots on the lakeside is **Höfði ❺**, a forested promontory that has been turned into a reserve, with a small admission fee. There is a vaguely fairy-tale atmosphere to the place, with paths running through flower-covered lava outcrops and forests of birch trees. Large rocks by the lakeside rocks also provide ideal picnic hide-aways.

A turn-off to the right leads to **Dimmuborgir ❻** ("black castles"), a vast, 2,000-year-old field of contorted volcanic pillars, some extending as high as 20 metres (65 ft). There is a viewing platform over the expanse, and visitors can wander about among the haunting arches, caves and natural tunnels. The most famous formation is **Kirkjan** (the Church), a cave that looks like the interior of a Gothic cathedral, and a 3-metre (16-ft) hole that provides an amusing opportunity to take a photograph.

Further along the same road is the looming crater of **Hverfell ❼**, formed in an eruption 2,500 years ago and these days likened to a giant football stadium. A steep path runs up the side of the crater

which is made entirely of loose volcanic rubble, or tephra. Hverfell's rim provides one of the most sweeping views of the Mývatn area. Inside the 1,000-metre (3,280-ft) wide crater, hikers have written messages in huge letters of light-coloured stone.

En route back to Reykjahlíð, by the left side of the road is **Grjótagjá ❽**, an underground hot spring made by a buckle in the earth (the site is unmarked but a space for it has been cleared beside it). The green waters feel tepid to the touch but below the surface can be scalding, so swimming is forbidden.

Volcanologists' paradise

The Ring Road running east of Reykjahlíð immediately leads to a completely different landscape, a desolate, sandy plain of mixed orange and brown hues known as **Bjarnarflag ❾**. Further on is

A common scoter, a species of diving duck common to Lake Mývatn but rare elsewhere in Iceland. Bird-spotters can see numerous other species of waterfowl, including the Barrow's goldeneye, one of the few North American species that breed in Iceland, as well as birds of prey including short-eared owls and gyrfalcons.

BELOW: studying the moss.

The continuous volcanic activity can make for rough and tortuous roads.

BELOW: the hissing and steaming mud pools of Hveraönd.

the site of Mývatn's former diatomite plant which once processed the microscopic fossils called diatoms that were taken from the lake floor; on the right is a brick factory, putting the local excess of tephra to good use. However, of more interest to visitors, the **Jarðböðin nature baths** (open June–Aug daily 10am–midnight, rest of the year daily noon–10pm; admission charge) are the north's answer to the Blue Lagoon. This sublime open-air geothermal pool lies just off the Ring Road and is an altogether more agreeable experience than its more famous cousin on the Reykjanes peninsula. There are far fewer bathers here, giving you the opportunity to loll undistrubed in the aquamarine waters as long as you like. The water comes from a local geothermal source and is cooled to around 38–40°C (100–104°F) to make it pleasant for bathing. In addition to the main pool, there's a hot pool and a couple of steam saunas.

An overwhelming stench of sulphur greets travellers as the road climbs over the ridge of **Námafjall**, whose series of cracks – the largest appeared as recently as 1975 – betray its location plumb on the Mid-Atlantic Ridge. The Námafjall geothermal field has been drilled, revealing temperatures over 290°C (554°F) at a depth of 1¾ km (1 mile). Steam and mud craters formed in this field during the Mývatn-fires of 1724, and new fissures spread south into the area in April 1728. At the pass is a parking area with views over the lake, and, stretching out on the other side is the famous boiling mud pit of **Hveraönd ⑩** – perhaps one of Iceland's most infernal and fascinating sights. Walkways run across the multi-coloured clay of the area, through dozens of bubbling pits and steaming vents. The surface here is particularly thin, and at some places likely to crumble, so to avoid being boiled alive in a mud pot, keep well within the marked paths.

Man-made disaster

A rough dirt road leads 7 km (4 miles) north to the **Krafla area ⑪**, named after one of the mountains at the centre of the region, and heart of the most recent volcanic activity. Pipes from the Krafla geothermal power plant form a metal doorway to the area, which is strangely appropriate: the construction of the plant in 1973, with its many bore holes into the earth's crust, is considered by some scientists to be responsible for triggering the eruptions that began here in 1975 – the first since the 1700s. Between 3 and 8 km (2–5 miles) beneath the Krafla field lies a magma reservoir which is the source of the volcanic activities in the area. Magma builds up in the reservoir, causing the earth to rise, until it is released as rock intrusions or in the form of volcanic eruptions, resulting in the earth's surface sinking again.

The activity in the early 1970s, known as the "Krafla-fires" began with a dramatic spurt of molten lava that lit up Reykjahlíð by night. Some 15 eruptions followed in the next decade, but luckily the lava all flowed away from the small village and no major damage was done. Even so, the earth's thin crust has regularly risen and fallen several centimetres as magma moves through underground chambers. Volcanologists are expecting Krafla to blow again any time.

A stern warning sign (volcanic hazard zone – do not enter) at the first parking area here was put up in the 1980s to keep tourists away, but had the opposite effect: hundreds gathered here to see what would happen. The warning sign has now been removed, and during the summer there is still a stream of visitors who go out to the black, partly warm lava field of the Krafla caldera that was spat up from the earth during the 1970s and 1980s, and the crater of **Leirhnjúkur** (formed during the explosions of the 1720s). If you can forget the disconcerting possibility of being blown to kingdom come, this whole lifeless, primeval area gives as good a glimpse of the freshly formed earth as anyone is likely to get.

Further on, a second parking area sits at the base of **Víti**, a colourful explosion crater (not to be confused with the other Víti crater further south – *see page 307*), about 320 metres (1,050 ft) wide, which is now thought to be inactive. This is close to Mount Krafla itself, which, far from being a classic volcanic cone, is the rim of a larger caldera that has been worn and exploded almost beyond recognition. A walking trail leads around the crater rim. Víti was the initial source of the 1725 volcanic eruptions which blighted crop production for years afterwards. The name Víti means "hell". ❏

EAT

Whilst in the Lake Mývatn area be sure to sample some locally produced geothermal bread, *hverabrauð*. Making use of the plentiful supply of free heat and power, the sticky, sweet loaves are baked in an underground oven heated by geothermal steam rising from deep underground. A less appetising local dish is fermented duck eggs; these tend to be foul-smelling and only for the more adventurous.

RESTAURANTS

Gamli Bærinn
Reykjahlíð village Tel: 464 4170
A dependable choice for soups and filling lunches as well as more substantial dinner dishes of fish and lamb. A pleasant, cosy interior makes this the premier choice for eating at Lake Mývatn. $$

Hótel Reynihlíð
Reykjahlíð village
Tel: 464 4170

Fine dining in the hotel restaurant beside the lake with expertly prepared fresh fish and meat dishes, and a good choice for a special occasion in this part of the country. $$$

• • • • • • • • • •
Categories are for an average-priced dinner per person, without wine. $$$ over ISK 4,000, $$ ISK 2,000–4,000, $ under ISK 2,000.

THE GREAT OUTDOORS

The vast open spaces and wild landscapes of Iceland offer a wealth of opportunities for all who love the great outdoors.

Iceland is an adventure holiday destination *par excellence*. Mountains, glaciers, lakes and thundering waterfalls are all here in abundance, and with its expansive wilderness areas and clear air, this northern land makes an intoxicating change from the usual run-of-the-mill destinations. Ever increasing numbers of visitors want to get out and experience all that wild nature for themselves. And there is a great deal on offer, from gentle hikes and horse-riding excursions to more demanding pursuits such as ice-climbing, white-water rafting and enough wilderness adventures to satisfy the most demanding free spirit.

One of the advantages of a rugged, sparsely populated country (about two people per sq. km) is that you can *really* get away from it all. If you want peace and solitude, this is where you can be sure of finding it. Trekking holidays – usually undertaken as an organised group through a specialist agency – are the classic way to experience remote and roadless regions. Iceland's glaciers and icecaps are another major draw for those in search of a different kind of experience, be it skidooing, ice-climbing, cross-country skiing or simply walking in the pristine environment.

A great way to reach places where no vehicle (even a 4x4) can easily take you, is on horseback. Riding all day among deserted valleys and mountains, fording rivers, leading your second mount which carries supplies and bedroll, you will gain real insight into the way Icelanders used to live. *For more details on what's available and a list of tour operators, see Travel Tips pages 332–5 and 341–2.*

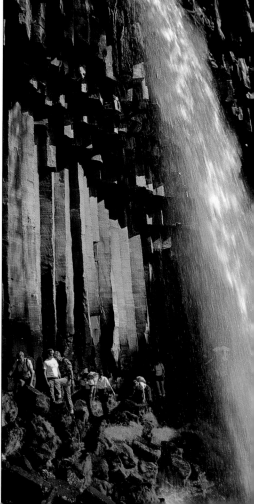

LEFT: skidooing is an exilharating way of exploring Iceland's icecaps. A trip is easily arranged through any one of the numerous tour operators *(see page 341).*

RIGHT: Trekking possibilities are endless. One of the most popular areas is Skaftafell National Park in the south of the country, with Svartifoss waterfall an awe-inspiring highlight.

ABOVE: White-water rafting on the Vestari-Jökulsa River in the Skagafjörður region.

ABOVE LEFT: Cycling can be hard going in Iceland, with rough roads and often poor weather. All the better for the intrepid enthusiast…

BELOW: An adventure of the less demanding kind is provided by a boat trip around the dramatic Jökulsarlón lagoon off the southeast coast.

BELOW LEFT: The Icelandic horse is ideal for inexperienced riders. Farms all over the country offer horse-riding from one-hour excursions to longer trips which can last several days.

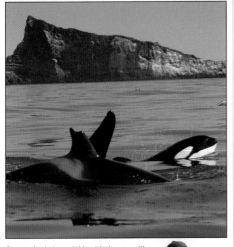

ABOVE: A whale-watching trip is an exciting experience, with various species regularly encountered including minke, humpback, sperm and kiler whales. Prime areas are accessed from Húsavík in the north and Ólafsvík in the west.

THE NORTHEAST

In this remote and little-visited region you can see sea birds and whales in their natural, unspoilt environment, and visit the unexpectedly lush Jökulsárgljúfur National Park

PRECEDING PAGES: the Ásbyrgi canyon in Jökulsárgljúfur National Park. **BELOW:** the church at Húsavík.

ypassed by the Ring Road and its stream of regular traffic, the North-east is one of Iceland's most isolated areas. Only the growing fame of the Jökulsárgljúfur National Park usually brings travellers here, with very few continuing on to explore the rugged coastline – largely because of poor transport services, bad roads and few good hotels.

However, if you're looking to explore off-the-beaten-track Iceland, this is one of the best places in the entire country to make for. True, tourist attractions as such are few and far between, but the real draw of this corner of Iceland is to experience nature in the raw and to see a side of Icelandic life which is rarely glimpsed in some of the more cosmopolitan centres of the country. Here, life goes on much as it has for decades with little thought for tourism; travel here and you're guaranteed a rare insight into what it's like to live in an almost forgotten part of Iceland, as obscure to most Reykjavíkers as it is to foreigners, on the very edge of the Arctic.

Yet the coastal route has a number of attractions for those with their own transport and an interest in finding out what lies off the beaten track. Dozens of atmospheric fishing towns cling precariously to this shore just south of the Arctic Circle. Exploring these quiet, conservative outposts and the craggy cliffs and wilderness areas around them reveals the harsh seafaring world that is in many ways Iceland's backbone.

Gateway to the northeast

The transport artery of the region, following the whole coastline, is Route 85. Approaching from either Akureyri or Lake Mývatn, this road runs through the Aðaldalur valley right down to the shoreline of Skjálfandi ("shivering fjord"), an expanse of sand dotted by small lakes with an impressive wall of mountains as a backdrop.

Rows of picturesque fish-drying racks by the roadside fittingly announce the main town in the region, **Húsavík ❶** (population 2,500). The name "house bay" was given by the Swedish Viking Garðar Svavarsson, who journeyed to Iceland in AD 850 after his mother had seen it in a dream.

Long before the official First Settler, Ingólfur Arnarson, set foot on the island, Garðar spent a winter at Húsavík – and, when he left, an unfortunate fellow named Náttafari was left behind with two slaves. The trio settled down permanently across the bay from Húsavík (the site can be seen from town), but have been disqualified from being considered Iceland's first settlers because their presence was involuntary.

Húsavík today is a tidy and agreeable town set above the first-rate harbour that provides for its existence: nearly everyone who lives here is involved with fishing or fish-processing. The view of the colourful trawlers, murky black waters and snow-spattered granite mountains across the bay is particularly impressive. Near the docks is the headquarters of the Þingeyjarsysla Co-operative Society, which was established in 1882, the first of its kind in Iceland and a landmark in Húsavík's growth.

Dominating the town is an unusual cross-shaped **church**, with a 26-metre (85-ft) spire and modern sculptures in the garden. The church, built in 1907, was designed by the Icelandic architect Rögnvaldur Ólafsson and made from Norwegian timber. It is counted among Iceland's most attractive churches and seats about 450 people. When it was built there were only 500 people living in the parish. The impressive altarpiece, depicting Lazarus raised from the dead, was painted in 1931 by Sveinn Þórarinsson from the nearby farm of Víkingavatn.

Diagonally opposite the church, the **Icelandic Phallological Museum** (open late May–early Sept daily noon–6pm; admission charge) is the country's most off-beat museum and an absolute must (it has replaced a similar museum in Reykjavík). Inside, there are examples of the penises of virtually every mammal found in Iceland or its offshore waters. Although the museum doesn't yet have a human specimen, it does have a certificate from a local farmer who agreed to donate his to the museum on his death.

Húsavík's other museum, **Safnahúsið** (open June–Aug daily 10am–6pm; Sept–May Mon–Fri 9am–5pm, Sun 4–6pm; admission charge), is the best in

A mountain hut at Þeistareykir, southeast of Húsavík. These huts offer basic accommodation in hiking areas across Iceland –see page 321 for details.

BELOW: Husavík's Phallological Museum.

Whale-watching tours, operated by two different companies, run from Húsavík several times daily during the summer months. Trips can be booked with Gentle Giants (tel: 464 1500) and North Sailing (tel: 464 2350) at their offices by the harbour. Should you fail to see whales, both companies offer a free second trip.

the northeast: prize exhibits include a replica of the 1584 Guðbrandur's Bible (the first translation of the Old and New Testaments into Icelandic, still considered the most ambitious publishing project ever undertaken in Iceland); and the polar bear that floated from Greenland to Grímsey island in 1973 only to be greeted by a bullet in the skull and then stuffed.

Húsavík is best known as a base for **whale-watching tours**, and there are a huge variety of cetaceans off the coast, including humpback, minke and fin whales, killer whales, dolphins and porpoises. Both companies operating *(see margin, left)* claim a 99-percent success rate for sightings.

Arctic vista

For a panoramic view over the whole Húsavík area, drive a kilometre north of town to the unmarked yellow gate on the right, then continue as far as your car can take you (only a four-wheel drive should attempt the full distance on this dangerously slippery road). There is a viewfinder

at the top, from which you can spot two small islands in the bay: **Flatey** had over 100 inhabitants 50 years ago but has now been abandoned, while **Lundey** is crowded only with puffins.

From this point, the roads become dustier and road signs fewer. Lying north along Route 85 is the squat peninsula of **Tjörnes** ❷, whose 60-metre (200-ft) cliff faces are renowned among geologists for their ancient fossils and easily visible geological strata. Non-geologists can get an idea of what is going on at a well-known but difficult-to-find site by the seashore, turning off on a dirt road to the left at the **Ytri-Tunga** farmhouse (the farm is unmarked but the road is before the **Hallbjarnarstaðir** farm, and crosses an electric fence). At Hallbjarnarstaðir there is a small **mineral-and-fossil museum** (open June–Aug daily 10am–6pm; admission charge; tel: 464 1968). This was once the home of the farmer Kári Sigurjónsson, who helped scientists to research shells. The exhibition tells the story of the prehistoric fossils from the Tjörnes layers in the cliffs below.

The road reaches the coast, then steeply descends the alarming cliff face

The Northeast

at **Hallbjarnarstaðakambur Crest**, a dip on either side of the river where the layers of geological deposits are obvious to the naked eye and fossils of molluscs can be picked from the earth. At the shore, look out for a large greenish slab of rock, not native to Iceland, thought to have arrived from Greenland on sea-ice.

East of Tjörnes, the plain of **Kelduhverfi** is made up of sandy glacial wash (similar to the larger *sandur* in the South), and is at the northern point where the two halves of Iceland are splitting apart. Volcanic activity in the 1970s here was related to the eruptions at Krafla near Lake Mývatn, with fissures appearing that are still visible. The whole area is at the mouth of the **Öxarfjörður** fjord. To the north of the highway is **Lake Víkingavatn** ❸, and two farms of the same name; the newer offers farmhouse accommodation, while the older has been occupied by descendants of the same family since the 1700s.

Giant hoof print

The great attraction of the Northeast, and one that has become increasingly popular in recent years, is the **Jökulsárgljúfur**

National Park ❹ (the full name, meaning "glacial river canyon", is difficult for non-Icelanders to pronounce but can be referred to as Jökulsá Canyon – pronounced *yer-kool-sar*). Once private property within the huge Ás estate, the park was formed in 1973 and extended later to cover approximately 150 sq. km (58 sq. miles).

One of the park's gems is the great horeseshoe-shaped canyon of **Ásbyrgi**, located almost immediately at the turn-off from Route 85. It's not hard to see why the first Viking settlers decided that the canyon had been formed by Sleipnir, the god Odin's flying horse, crashing a giant hoof into the earth. A 100-metre (330-ft) cliff-face makes a smooth, 1 km-(⅝-mile) wide ring around a profuse carpet of greenery, while a smaller outcropping of cliffs (suitably called Eyjan or "island") rises in the middle.

A lonely road in the Raufarhöfn district of the far northeast.

BELOW: trekking to the Jökulsá canyon.

Geologists believe that the canyon was formed relatively recently by a gigantic *hlaup* or glacial flow from an eruption under the faraway icecap of Vatnajökull. The best view is from the furthest part of the canyon, which can be reached after a 100-metre (330-ft) walk west from the parking area. Turning east from the car park leads to a natural spring for drinking water, while taking the trail straight ahead ends up at a small lake full of ducks – their quacks echo around the natural amphitheatre.

Camping is permitted in the canyon near its entrance, where a park ranger keeps an **information office** and sells small brochures giving detailed descriptions of some of the main hiking routes in the park. From here, a path also leads to the top of the cliffs, climbing the canyon at its easiest point (although a rope is provided to help in the ascent). Once up, walkers can follow the cliffs, with excellent views over the whole canyon, or even take the trail as far south as Dettifoss – two days' walk away.

No matter whether you walk for an hour or a day, this is one of the most pleasant hikes in Iceland, and if you get tired, just lie on the heather and eat some of the wild berries that grow abundantly in the canyon's summery climate.

Towards Dettifoss

The rest of the park follows the powerful **Jökulsá á Fjöllum**, Iceland's second-longest river. Two roads run down the length of the park, one on either side of the river: the western road runs across some classic highland heather to **Vesturdalur** walking trails and the mysterious natural columns of **Hljóðaklettar** ❺ (echoing rocks), which form a sort of ghostly stone forest that can be explored for hours. Further on, the road heads to **Hólmatungur**, a lush stretch along the river canyon, before crossing a suddenly barren desert landscape to Dettifoss.

Unfortunately, the western road is deeply corrugated and, while two-wheel drives can make the journey, they need to crawl along at a gruelling 15 kph (10 mph). The eastern road is better, but after Dettifoss it becomes a jeep track.

Either way, it's worth the effort: **Dettifoss** ❻ is Europe's largest waterfall, and the effort needed to reach it only seems to add to the excitement. There is nothing contained or artificial about Dettifoss, no wooden boardwalks or viewing balconies installed to detract from Nature. Clouds of spray can first be seen several kilometres away; from the car parks, visitors scramble over square blocks of grey lava, hearing the thunderous drumming before getting a glimpse of the falls. Some 500 cubic metres of water spill over its ledges every second: although it is just 44 metres (145 ft) tall, the sheer hypnotic volume of the flow makes this arguably Iceland's most awesome sight.

For those who want to see more falls, **Hafragilsfoss** is 2 km (1½ miles) downstream, and **Selfoss** about the same distance upstream. A four-wheel-drive road heads from Dettifoss south to Lake Mývatn, but other cars will have to track back to Route 28.

Cod coast

Heading north from the entrance of the National Park leads to Iceland's least

TIP

If you are planning to camp in the National Park, stock up at the Ásbyrgi petrol station and supermarket at the Ásbyrgi farm outside the park. This is the only place selling supplies within about 25 km (15 miles).

BELOW: the canyon of Hólmatungur.

visited area. Tourist officials say that even the uninhabited centre of Iceland attracts more travellers than the Northeast coast.

The first village, **Kópasker** ❼, with a population of 140 souls almost all involved in the fishing of shrimp, can seem like a ghost town on most days. Like the other villages of the area, Kópasker thrived on the herring boom until the late 1960s when herring migration patterns changed.

Beyond Kópasker is the flat, exposed peninsula of **Melrakkaslétta** ("fox plain"), where winds howl straight from the North Pole in winter and, on a bad day, summer can seem almost as dismal. The cliffs at **Rauðinúpur** are the only place in the world where it is possible to watch gannets nesting on land from below and the side rather than just from above. The northernmost part of mainland Iceland (and, incidentally, the spot where the saga character Þorgeir Hávarsson was finally brought down after he had slaughtered 14 attackers), **Hraunhafnartangi**, is marked by a lighthouse – the Arctic Circle lies just 2.5 km (1½ miles) offshore.

Even so, the remoteness of the barren plain, which can support very little agriculture, is perversely appealing. The coastline is covered with driftwood from as far away as Siberia and supports a good deal of birdlife.

Although **Raufarhöfn** ❽ made the transition from herring to cod fishing in the 1970s, it has never recaptured the great days when thousands of seasonal workers came to its factories. Today there are many more buildings and jetties than the population of 250 can use, and Raufarhöfn is losing more young people to the cities. In an attempt to keep people in this economically important area, the Icelandic government built an airstrip though it is no longer profitable to fly here (during long winters, the town had been completely cut off except by sea). Even so, the isolation of this town – which over long periods has not even had a local doctor – is extreme. However, in an attempt to attract tourists to the town and boost the flagging economy, local hoteliers have built an Arctic version of Britain's famous Stonehenge. The Arctichenge, as it's known, will be over 50 metres (160 ft) in diameter and will act

Drying fish the traditional way.

BELOW: Dettifoss waterfall swathed in spray.

Just south of the Arctic Circle, this area is never truly dark between May and early August.

BELOW: fish dishes dominate the menu in most Icelandic restaurants.

as a giant sundial, catching and training the long hours of sunshine in this part of Iceland during the summer months. The structure is located on top of the hill which overlooks the village.

Lying south of Raufarhöfn is the **Langanes** peninsula, whose marshy, cliff-bound expanses are the last word in Icelandic remoteness – it can really only be visited with a four-wheel drive or on foot. At the peninsula's tip is a monument to some shipwrecked English sailors who managed to climb the 100-metre (330-ft cliffs) only to die subsequently of exposure.

Heading south, the village of **Þórshöfn 9** is a pretty, little fishing village where it's worth breaking your journey around the coast. Although there's little in the way of specific sights, the busy harbour provides a focus to the village which enjoys a regular air link with Akureyri. One of the best hiking trails in the northeast is now within easy reach. From Þórshöfn, an unmade road heads northeast past the airstrip across the windswept Langanes peninsula heading for the youth hostel and farm, Ytra Lón. From here you can hike out to the tip of

the peninsula, Fontur, marked by a lighthouse, and there's a good chance you'll spot gyrfalcons on the way.

Back on the main road heading south, Bakkafjörður is an uneventful and very small fishing village that is typical of the area which most visitors bypass en route for the more rewarding **Vopnafjörður 10**, set in a picturesque location at the head of the eponymous fjord. The snow capped mountains behind the town seem to trail down into huge rocks broken into the sea, complemented by the granite range across the fjord. Here the weather is better and the atmosphere more optimistic – the feeling is closer to the East Fjords than the northeast. The village had its 15 minutes of fame in 1988, when local girl Linda Pétursdóttir became Miss World.

From Vopnafjörður, the highway runs away from the coast, passing **Burstarfell 11**, an excellent **Folk Museum** (open mid-June–mid-Aug daily 10am–6pm; admission charge) in a 19th-century farmhouse. The road now climbs into the northeastern desert, passing a viewing platform over **Lake Nykurvatn**, before rejoining the Ring Road in some of Iceland's most barren landscape. ❑

RESTAURANTS

Eyrin

Eyrarvegur 3, Þórshöfn
Tel: 468 1250
A real local's favourite for pizzas and freshly caught cod. **$$**

Gamli Baukur

Hafnarstétt 9, Húsavík
Tel: 464 2442
Popular with visitors who come to Húsavík to go whale-watching. The fish

here is truly delicious and is served with creative sauces, including a tangy basil pesto. **$$**

Hótel Norðurljós

Aðalbraut 2, Raufarhöfn
Tel: 465 1233
A superb location for the hotel restaurant overlooking the pretty harbour and the accompanying fishing boats (also has an outdoor terrace). The food here is predictable – mostly fish dishes – though they are always fresh and tasty. **$$**

Hótel Tangi

Hafnarbyggð 17, Vopnafjörður
Tel: 473 1840

Perfectly acceptable, though none-too exciting fare at this modern hotel on the main drag. **$$**

Salka

Garðarsbraut 6, Húsavík
Tel: 464 2551
More café than restaurant, the emphasis here is on pizzas. It's easy to find beside the main road running through the town and is useful if you need to dine and dash. **$$**

• • • • • • • • • • • • • • • •

Categories are for an average-priced dinner per person, without wine. **$$$** *over* ISK *4,000,* **$$** ISK *2,000–4,000,* **$** *under* ISK *2,000.*

The Most Useful Servant

One of the incidental advantages of Iceland's almost total isolation over the centuries is that the Icelandic horse, the stocky breed introduced by the first Nordic settlers, has survived almost unchanged for over 1,000 years. Today, it is protected by strict regulations which forbid the import of horses into Iceland, and which state that an Icelandic horse sent out of the country can never return to Iceland, for fear of importing diseases to which the local breed would have no immunity.

"Elegant" is not an adjective which springs to mind to describe the Icelandic horse. These chunky, thick-set, muscular animals bear little resemblance to their leggier European relatives, though they can put on a fine turn of speed. They have adapted to the cool climate by growing a thick, shaggy overcoat for winter, which is shed in the spring. In summer, their coats can be groomed to shining smoothness.

In spite of their relatively small stature (13 hands on average), Icelandic horses are famed for their strength and stamina. They have played a vital role in Iceland's history, for centuries a roadless, bridgeless land. Known affectionately as Þarfasti Þjónninn ("most useful servant"), the horse was the sole form of overland transport in Iceland until the 19th century. In many remote regions, the horse's supremacy has continued, and even today has a vital role to play during the autumn round-up when sheep are herded from remote mountains.

Surefooted, intelligent, affectionate, home-loving and sometimes headstrong, the horse is also known for its five gaits. In addition to the conventional walk, trot and gallop, it has two additional steps in its repertoire: the *tölt* or running walk, and the *skeið* or pace. Some can't manage the *skeið*; these are known as four-gaiters. The *tölt*, almost unknown in other breeds of horse, is a smooth run, which (unlike the trot) does not shake the rider about in the saddle and is understandably very popular for overland travel, particularly for those who are not used to horseback travel.

Horse-riding is now Iceland's number-one leisure activity. Riding clubs flourish all over the country, and various competitions, races, shows and meets are held throughout the summer months. Iceland's equine population numbers in the region of 50,000. Horse breeding and trading, on a fairly modest scale compared to many other countries, is becoming an important business.

Fifteen national organisations in Europe and North America are affiliated to the International Iceland-horse federation (FEIF), and international Iceland-horse championships are held annually. Iceland always sends a team of horses and riders to the world championships, and invariably that team carries off many of the prizes – although, frustratingly, the top local-bred Icelandic horses can never be sent to the international contests. Since horses taken overseas are not re-admitted, no devoted rider would think of taking their best horse to compete in Europe only to leave it behind. ❑

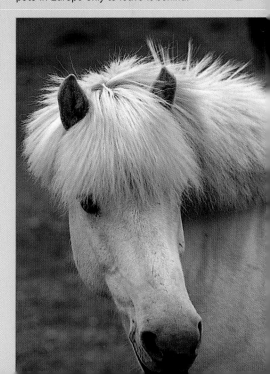

ABOVE & RIGHT: the shaggy-haired Icelandic horse.

THE EAST FJORDS

This region of Iceland, often overlooked by
tourists, offers peace and tranquillity – from the
long, thin lake Lögurinn, surrounded by forest, to
remote farms and small fishing villages

Reykjavík

For travellers arriving from mainland
Europe, Scotland and the Faroe
Islands by ferry, the jagged, snow-
capped profile of the East Fjords provides the first glimpse of Iceland. It's a
breathtaking sight as the boat edges into
Seyðisfjörður fjord towards the town's
ornate wooden buildings strung out
along the seaboard. But not many stay to
see what else this region has to offer. Iceland's eastern coast has a reputation of a
place to be passed through quickly en
route to somewhere else.

This is a pity, and not just because the
East enjoys the sunniest weather in the
country. The rugged coastline and dry
interior here are full of wilderness areas
rarely visited by foreigners, although
they are well known among Icelanders.
And along the way are remote farms and
fishing villages that, unusually for Iceland, have still hung on to a degree of
old-world charm.

The region is at the centre of the greatest environmental debate Iceland has
ever known. An aluminium smelter
opening in Reyðarfjörður is set to transform the local economy, creating scores
of new jobs yet its power is supplied by
a dam that has been built in an environmentally sensitive part of the interior
causing outrage across the country.

Hub of the east

Whether arriving by ferry, car or bus,
travellers use as an orientation point the
East's most important urban crossroad,
Egilsstaðir ❶ (population around

1,600). The first houses were built here
less than 50 years ago, and Egilsstaðir
still has an unfortunate prefabricated feel.
Egilsstaðir doesn't have a town centre to
speak of and is instead composed of a
small number of suburban streets, seemingly striking off in different directions
from the Ring Road which slices through
the settlement. As a result it's unlikely
you'll want to linger and Egilsstaðir is
best used as a staging post. Like many
smaller towns in this part of Iceland, its
social and economic life seems to hinge
around the Esso petrol station. Flanking

Main attractions
SEYDISFJORDUR
BORGARFJÓRDUR-EYSTRI
LOGURINN LAKE
HALLORMSSTADARSKÓGAR FOREST
REYDARFJORDUR
ESKIFJORDUR MARITIME MUSEUM

PRECEDING PAGES: a
house at the fishing
village of Reyðar-
fjörður. **LEFT:** typical
East Fjords scenery.
BELOW: Seyðis-
fjörður from the
ferry.

Arctic skuas are common in the East Fjords region.

the station are the camping ground, tourist information office and a huge supermarket – a place that can turn into an elbows-only feeding frenzy on days when the ferry arrives in nearby Seyðisfjörður.

Still, Egilsstaðir also has a number of hotels, among them a brand new one with all modern facilities, which makes a convenient base. Its sister-settlement, the tiny village of **Fellabær** ❷ (population 50) lies across a long bridge – at 301 metres (990 ft) this was the longest bridge in Iceland for many years – and enjoys a picturesque setting. Try for lakeside accommodation in huts on the Skipalækur farm, although they are often booked up months in advance.

The port of **Seyðisfjörður** ❸, where

the ferry from mainland Europe docks, lies directly east along the mostly paved highway Route 93. The journey is worth making even for those not taking the boat: in complete contrast to Egilsstaðir, Seyðisfjörður is full of Scandinavian character, a town that approximates to one's mental image, so rarely fulfilled, of an Icelandic fishing town. However, the harbour has recently been rebuilt in order to accommodate the new super-ferry owned by Smyril Line, which now operates year-round linking Seyðisfjörður with points south. There's now an impressive new terminal building incorporating a café and a tourist office beside the extended berth which is occupied by the new *Norröna* when she arrives on Thursdays.

Set on the fjord of the same name and surrounded by sheer mountains, it was founded in the 1830s and soon became the largest and wealthiest town in the East of Iceland – resulting in the construction of many wooden homes in an elegant Norwegian style.

Most of Seyðisfjörður's 800 or so inhabitants are involved in fishing in some way, and the arrival every autumn of herring schools in the shallow waters of the nearby fjords is still a cause for mass mobilisation, bringing everyone from schoolchildren to the aged out to the fish factories. (The autumn herring catch is from different stock to the summer catch, which between the 1930s and the 1960s turned Iceland's northeastern outposts into Klondike-style boom towns, before overfishing wiped out the population.) In summer, the frequent ferry traffic keeps much of Seyðisfjörður busy, and on Wednesday evenings and Thursday mornings an arts and crafts market is held to coincide with arrivals and departures. Classical music and light jazz concerts are held in Seyðisfjörður church every Wednesday in summer. There is a fine view of the town and fjord from the highway, which winds up past small waterfalls into the **Fjarðarheiði** mountains. The best spot for taking photos is a columnar basalt monument to the first postman of the region, who regularly made this journey on horseback when it was decidedly more dangerous than it is today.

Haunted highway

Another spectacular excursion from Egilsstaðir is to Borgarfjörður-Eystri, following Route 94 north. The highway passes the Edda Hotel at **Eiðar** before entering an expanse of marshland bordered to the north by the Jökulsá á Dal river. The whole area is crowded with birdlife.

Over a high pass, **Dyrfjöll**, one of Iceland's most dramatic mountain ranges, comes into view. Watch out on the left for the bridge of a fishing trawler sitting in a field – it was dragged there on truckback by a local, Fitzcarraldo, who wanted to piece together a boat in Borgarfjörður. He gave up half way, leaving a surreal vision for passers-by. This is an unnerving stretch of highway, with dramatic drops down into the sea and

A turf-covered house in Borgarfjörður-Eystri.

BELOW: Dyrfjöll towers above Borgarfjörður-Eystri.

TIP

One of the most enjoyable ways to reach Borgarfjörður Eystri is to hitch a ride with the postman. The mail van leaves Egilsstaðir every weekday at 11am for the switchback ride over the mountains to the village. The truck also serves as the local post office once it arrives.

BELOW: a remote farm at Húsey.

graphic evidence of recent landslides. A wooden cross records that the road was once said to be haunted. Fatal accidents were so common here in the Middle Ages that they were attributed to a ghost named Naddi, supposed to live in a scree called Naddagil. In the early 1300s, a priest was dragged out here to perform an exorcism, and just to make sure, locals erected a cross in 1306. The cross has been replaced innumerable times, but each bears the Latin inscription, *Effigiem Christi: qui transis pronus honora* – "You who are hurrying past should honour the image of Christ."

The town of **Borgarfjörður-Eystri** ❹ (East Borgarfjörður, to distinguish it from the bigger Borgarfjörður in western Iceland) is also known as **Bakkagerði**. It is ringed by dramatic mountains: the ochre range to the east, past the black sand beach, is made from an acidic form of lava called rhyolite. This black rock, along with pieces of jasper and agate, is polished into everything from paperweights to gravestones at the **Álfasteinn art shop** (open Mon–Fri 11am–8pm, Sat & Sun noon–6pm), at the north end of the village.

Ask at the shop for the key to the local **church**, with an altarpiece painted by the renowned artist Jóhannes Kjarval, who was born in Borgarfjörður and made the area famous in his paintings. He was said by one critic to have "taught the Icelanders to experience the beauty of their own landscape". A monument to the artist can be seen by the main road, just outside the village. Across the street from the church is a colourful turf house that is still inhabited and, towards the beach, a stone hillock called **Álfaborg** ("elf hill"), held to be inhabited by the hidden people (*see also* Icelandic Hauntings, *pages 248–9*).

Eastern isolation

A second road north of Egilsstaðir (Route 925, via the Ring Road) leads to **Húsey** ❺, a farm that has earned a measure of fame for its remoteness and serenity – representing, as one traveller put it, "the real Iceland." Lying in the flatlands just south of the Jökulsá á Dal river, in the shadow of the Dyrfjöll mountains, Húsey's gaily painted corrugated-iron buildings date from the 1930s. The farm is still operational and until recently was one of the few in Iceland to still engage in the controversial practice of sealing. Walks can be made across the heather to the black sand beach nearby, where the Iceland's two species of raptor – gyrfalcons and merlins – can often be seen hovering overhead; horse-riding trips can also be made into the surrounding wilderness. Húsey's utter peacefulness is seductive, and many visitors stay much longer than planned. The old-style guesthouse accommodation offered is simple but comfortable, and lying in bed at night listening to the howling wind, one gets a vivid idea of just how isolated pioneering Icelandic farmers have been through the centuries.

Inland from Húsey, the Ring Road follows the **Jökulsá á Dal** river valley before hitting the central deserts en route to Lake Mývatn. The bridge across the river was held to be haunted by a monster who would occasionally dine on unsuspecting travellers. There has been a bridge here since 1564. In 1994 a new bridge was built about 1 km (½ mile) south of the old one. It is the highest in the country, 40 metres (130 ft) above the river. Farmhouse accommodation is available at a space-age concrete building at **Brúarás**. Further west, look out for the rise of Goðanes overlooking the river south of the highway: this supposedly once a temple of Thor, and sacrifices were held nearby. Today there are ruins below the hill, of indeterminate age.

The rough Route 923, which turns south off the Ring Road along the Jökulsá á Brú, heads for the farm of **Aðalból** ❻ and country related to the much-beloved *Hrafnkels Saga*. The story tells of Hrafnkell Hallfreðarson, an unsavoury chieftain who lived at Aðalból and worshipped Freyr, the Norse god of war. Hrafnkell swore to Freyr that he would kill anyone who rode his favourite horse, Freyfaxi, and when one of his shepherds innocently did so, felt obliged to hunt him down and chop open the poor fellow's skull. A blood feud resulted in Hrafnkell being outlawed at the Alþingi and ambushed by the victim's cousin, Sámur – who, rather than killing Hrafnkell, maimed him horribly by stringing him up with a rope through the Achilles tendon and seizing his lands. The horse that had caused all the trouble was flung into a pond and drowned.

At this stage, Hrafnkell decided that Freyr was little practical use as a deity and abandoned his worship. Appearing to turn over a new leaf, he slowly rebuilt his fortune at a nearby farm. Of course, Hrafnkell was only biding his time: six years later, he took his revenge, descending on Sámur with a band of warriors and driving him from the East. According to the Saga, Hrafnkell then lived happily ever after. Some ruins from Viking times have been found at the farm Aðalból, but fans of the sagas will mostly have to use their imaginations.

The great Icelandic forest

South of Egilsstaðir stretches the pencil-shaped lake of **Lögurinn** ❼. Over 100 metres (330 ft) deep, the lake is said to be home to the Lagarfljót serpent. Sightings of this strange creature have been

If you wish to explore the woods of Lögurinn, there is a network of footpaths, and both individual trees and groups are labelled. A small descriptive booklet is also available.

BELOW: camping by the banks of Lögurinn.

Reindeer were introduced to Iceland from Norway in the 18th century.

BELOW: a bike ride at dusk near Valþjófsstaður.

recorded since the 14th century. It appears on the lake, according to written documents and eyewitnesses, in different forms – as a snake, dragon, seal, horse or even in the shape of a house.

Lögurinn is also famed as the site of the country's largest wooded area, **Hallormsstaðarskógur**. Nearly all of the woods were protected from grazing animals between 1905 and 1927. The wood is now 740 sq. km (285 sq. miles), the total fenced-in area being 1,850 hectares (around 4,500 acres). In 1903 a nursery, called Mörkin, was established to grow different kinds of native and foreign trees. Since then it has distributed some 12 million plants. An arboretum was formally opened in 1993, with a total of 54 tree species – 31 coniferous and 23 broadleaved. The reafforestation programme here (using tough plants from Alaska and Siberia among others) has created optimism that other parts of Iceland might return to their pre-Viking state of being "covered by woods from mountain to shore".

On the lake, **Hallormsstaður** is a popular spot for Icelandic vacationers (there is a camping ground and an Edda hotel).

A little further towards the end of the Fljótsdalur valley is the farm Hrafnkelsstaðir, where Hrafnkell, the hero of *Hrafnkels Saga*, went after he had been maimed. At the southern end of the lake, **Valþjófsstaður** ❽ farm is where the beautiful carved wooden church door, dating back to AD 1200 and on display in the National Museum in Reykjavík, was found. The box-like modern church now on the site sports a shiny new replica. Nearby **Skriðuklaustur** was the site of a monastery from 1493 until the Reformation (1550). In 1939 the author Gunnar Gunnarsson, who was well known for his novels in Denmark and Germany, settled at Skriðuklaustur and built a large, quirkily designed house, which he later presented to the Icelandic state. North of Lögurinn, a steep hour-long walk leads to the "hanging falls" of **Hengifoss** ❾, 120 metres (393 ft) high.

Hiking country

A rough four-wheel-drive road runs south of Lögurinn to **Mount Snæfell** ❿, the 1,833-metre (6,013-ft) peak that dominates the valley. Further on are the

Kverkfjöll mountains at the northern edge of the icecap. Special buses run from Egilsstaðir to the hut at the base of Snæfell in the summer. The mountain is in fact an ancient primary volcano, surrounded by colourful rhyolite. If you are in good shape you can hike up to the peak from the hut, which stands about 800m (2,600 ft) above sea-level. The hike to the top takes about 4–6 hours. The warden at the hut will provide all the necessary information.

For those who want to spend more time exploring the area, a popular long-distance walk is between Snæfell and Lónsöræfi – taking up to 7 days, depending on how long is spent at each stop. This is a spectacular hike in an uninhabited wilderness. Multicoloured rhyolite rocks can be found in many places, while impressive canyons and ravines cut through the land from time to time. There are plenty of flowers in early summer, and reindeer herds can sometimes be seen along the way. It is essential to have a good, up-to-date hiking map and to contact the local tourist information centre (in Egilsstaðir), to obtain all the necessary information on the route,

especially concerning the state of rivers and streams, and not least, the expected weather in the area. Do not attempt the walk alone – much of it is remote and can be misty and icy.

Starting from Snæfell hut it is best to organise a lift in a four-wheel-drive towards Vatnajökull glacier. From here is is possible to walk over the **Eyjabakka-jökull** glacier, a tongue of Vatnajökull (you will need crampons) towards the hut at **Geldingafell**. From there the next hut to head for is at **Kollumúli**. The hut here is run by the local Travellers' Association and situated by the tranquil lake **Kollumúlavatn**. It is a good idea to spend two nights here and use a whole day for exploring the surroundings, perhaps hiking down into the **Víðidalur** valley. The next stage of the walk is down to **Nes**, where you may also need a day to explore the magnificent scenery. The last day's hike takes you to the crest of **Illikambur**, where you can catch a ride on the daily bus to Höfn.

Following the fjords

The Ring Road runs directly south of Egilsstaðir, although many prefer to take

A farmer in the East Fjords outside her painted house.

BELOW: a lone trawler plies an eastern fjord.

TIP

Boat trips (tel: 478 8119) to Papey island run from Djúpivogur in the summer. Papey is about 40 minutes away, and the whole trip, including a guided walk on the island, usually takes about 4 hours. This undulating island of tussocky grassland and marshes is just two square kilometres in size and a favourite breeding spot for many species of bird, especially puffins who are drawn here by the low sandy cliffs in which they make their burrows.

BELOW: Lón lagoon, backed by snow-capped mountains, near Stafafell.

the slower but better-paved and more scenic route hugging the coast. The start of the coast road runs through a steep river valley lined by pencil waterfalls at regular intervals – each would be a marvel in other countries but in Iceland is just part of the backdrop. **Reyðarfjörður ⑪** is the first of many quiet fishing villages along this part of the coast, magnificently situated at the base of the steepest fjord in the East. The town's old streets give it an unusually authentic, human feel: small plants are neatly lined up in the windows of corrugated-iron buildings and, on a fine day, old fishermen promenade along the split-level streets.

From Reyðarfjörður, Route 92 runs north along the coast, passing the new aluminium smelter which has caused the biggest environmental row in Icelandic history *(see page 106)*, to **Eskifjörður ⑫** (population 1,000), noted for its **Maritime Museum** (open June–Aug daily 1–5pm; admission charge) with exhibits on fishing and whaling dating back to the 18th century. Among the many interesting items in the museum is a model of the whaling-station that was in nearby Hellisfjörður between 1904 and 1913. At

this time there were five whaling-stations in the East Fjords. The museum is housed in the oldest building in Eskifjörður. Built in 1816 as a shop, it was later used as a warehouse, fish-processing house and storage space for fishing-tackle.

Further along Route 92, **Neskaupstaður ⑬**, with a population of 1,500, enjoys a remote position at the end of the narrow, winding highway. In the summer boat trips go from Neskaupstaður to the site of the former whaling-station in the deserted **Hellisfjörður**. On the trip you visit the highest sea-cliff in Iceland, along with some inlets for birdwatching.

Heading south along the fjords from Reyðarfjörður, the road is squeezed between the choppy North Atlantic and steep mountains – their twisted peaks are usually shrouded in a haunting mist, making this look like troll country. The small villages of **Fáskrúðsfjörður**, **Stöðvarfjörður**, **Breiðdalsvík** and **Djúpivogur ⑭** all pass in quick succession, but it is worth making a stop in Stöðvarfjörður to visit the interesting stone collection of Petra Sveinsdóttir, which is signposted from the main road towards the end of the village. About 5 km (3 miles) northwest of Djúpivogur lies the farm **Teigarhorn**, known for the most beautiful and varied zeolites in the world. The cliffs at the coast, where the zeolites are found, are now a nature reserve, but you can walk down to the farm and have a look at the farmer's private collection, which is on display in a small cottage below the farmhouse.

On the Ring Road southwest of Djúpivogur, heading towards Höfn, is the farm of **Stafafell**, which offers accommodation to travellers and has become a popular base for hikers making day trips into the surrounding river valleys. It has a small church with some interesting artefacts. Nearby is the large and peaceful **Lón** lagoon.

The surrounding area of **Lónsöræfi** is renowned for its wild and dramatic landscape, where deep valleys and chasms have been carved among the mountains by the glacial river Jökulsá. There are plenty of fine hiking trails throughout the area. Using Stafafell as a base, there is a relatively easy day hike, taking about four to six hours. It starts by taking the path up the mountain above the farm, and from there through the Selárdalur valley down to the colourful Hvannagil gorge. The trail carries on along the stream at the bottom of the gorge, towards the river Jökulsá, and ends on a track, passing a few summer-cottages, before returning to Stafafell.

Papey Island

Clearly visible from Djúpivógur, the departure point for summer boat trips from the mainland *(see margin, left)*, the uninhabited island of **Papey** 🅖 is visible out to sea from Djúpivogur, named after Irish monks, who are said to have lived here before the settlement. It was later colonised by farmers, and an old house, built at the beginning of the 20th century, is still here, along with the smallest and oldest wooden church in the country, believed to date from 1807. The building is chained to the ground to prevent it from blowing away in the fierce winds. ❏

The church at Stafafell.

RESTAURANTS & CAFÉS

Café Nielsen
Tjarnarbraut 1, Egilsstaðir
Tel: 471 2626
A snug little cafe and restaurant serving a good choice of light lunches, including the usual fish and lamb dishes. There is additional seating upstairs. **$$**

Egilsbúð
Egilsbraut 1, Neskaupsstaður
Tel: 477 1321
Perenially popular with local fishermen, this down-to-earth restaurant is known for its large pizzas and is without question the best place to eat in Neskaupsstaður – though don't expect great sophistication and haute cuisine. **$$**

Hótel Framtíð
Vogaland 4, Djúpivogur
Tel: 478 8887
Housed in an old timber building dating from the early 1900s, this cosy and intimate restaurant is a good choice for fresh fish. Ask about the excellent value dish of the day, which includes a hearty helping of soup and bread. **$$**

Hótel Herað
Miðvangur 5, Egilsstaðir
Tel: 471 1500
Top-notch cuisine in an elegant restaurant attached to the main hotel in Egilsstaðir. The Herað is a popular place, so it's a good idea to book a table in advance. This is one of the few places in Iceland where you'll find reindeer meat on the menu. **$$$**

Hótel Seyðisfjörður
Austurvegur 3, Seyðisfjörður
Tel: 472 1460
Renowned for miles around for the quality and tastiness of its freshly prepared fish dishes, this chi-chi restaurant inside the hotel is a must. Be sure to reserve a table, though, since the restaurant is inordinately popular with locals and visitors alike. **$$$**

Kaffi Lára
Norðurgata 3, Seyðisfjörður
A good choice for cakes, coffee and sandwiches at this pleasant café down by the Seyðisfjörður waterside. **$**

• • • • • • • • • • • •
Categories are for an average-priced dinner per person, without ISK 2,000–4,000, $ under ISK 2,000.

THE INTERIOR

**Home to Iceland's wildest, most extreme scenery,
the vast, empty interior can be accessed
by a number of routes suitable for
four-wheel-drive vehicles**

D uring the Age of Settlement few
Viking colonists braved the desolation of the interior. Only outlaws, banished from their society and the
fertile coast, took refuge in its chilly
expanses. By the 13th century, some
paths had been created through the Central Highlands for short cuts from north
to south. Today, 800 years later, the vast
region of the interior is still almost totally
uninhabited.

This large, empty region is Iceland's
premier attraction for adventurous travellers. Nowhere else in Europe is so
remote from civilisation, or offers such a
range of scenery, the most dramatic Iceland has to offer: broad icecaps which
split their sides into great glacial tongues;
volcanoes of every size with extensive
fields of block lava and pumice; freezing deserts and endless outwash plains
of black sand. There are two main routes
that go right across the interior: the
Kjölur and the Sprengisandur. Other
routes offer further opportunities for
exploring this unique area.

In the southeast of the interior in the
pristine land immediately to the north of
Vatnajökull icecap, the recently constructed dam at Kárahnjúkar has divided
public opinion and led to the biggest
debate Iceland has ever seen on environmental protection *(see page 106)*.

Challenge of the wild

There are serious logistical problems to
be overcome before visiting the interior.
Roads are reduced to mere tracks, most

passable only in four-wheel-drive vehicles. Many of the interior routes are open
only in the middle of summer and even
then snowfalls and blizzards can still
occur. There are years when some tracks
never open due to the severe weather.

The weather is unpredictable and
camping is the main form of accommodation, although there are exceptions in
the form of a few huts operated by the
Icelandic Touring Club (Ferðafélag
Íslands). Located in key areas, like the
Sprengisandur and Kjölur, facilities are
very basic but useful in emergencies.

Main attractions

HVERAVELLIR
ALDEYJARFOSS
LANDMANNALAUGAR
ÓFÆRUFOSS
HERÐUBREIÐ
OSKJUVATN / VÍTI CRATER
KVERKFJÖLL MOUNTAINS

PRECEDING PAGES:
a winter drive
through remote
Landmannalaugar.
LEFT: Herðubreið.
BELOW: Kerlingarfjöll.

The Interior

Modes of transport through the interior vary from the buses that operate between Reykjavík and Akureyri via the Kjölur route in summer *(see pages 300, 306 and 315–6 for details)* to the latest high-tech 4x4 or beaten-up Land-Rover, to mountain bikes and walking. If you are bringing your own transport, extreme care is required in preparation. You must take everything you will need with you, including all food and water, and in some cases fuel, and to be aware of how to deal with the punishing terrain and weather conditions *(see also pages 103–4, 317–19)*. Because of the dangers, many travellers opt to embark with one of the adventure-tour operators based in Reykjavík. These use short wheelbase, four-wheel-drive coaches for tours ranging from day excursions to longer-term camping trips. For the latter, the vehicles are heavily modified, often to include a kitchen and a full complement of picnic tables and chairs. An alternative form of adventure tour is traversing the interior on horseback.

THE KJÖLUR ROUTE

The Kjölur route, based on an ancient byway used in Saga times, is one of the main links across the interior, passing between the Langjökull and Hofsjökull icecaps. A four-wheel drive is advisable but other vehicles are sometimes seen on the southern part of the main track which begins at the majestic **Gullfoss** waterfall in the southwest *(see page 179)* and runs northwards to the **Blöndudalur** valley. The first part of the journey, to the hot springs of Hveravellir, is on a road of gravel, stones and rock, with the occasional small river to be forded. Beyond Hveravellir, the route deteriorates as the track becomes muddy with several extended river crossings. Nonetheless, in comparison with other interior routes, the Kjölur is relatively well travelled.

Into the interior

Leaving Gullfoss, the grassland on the plain above the falls soon changes to lichen-dotted stones. There is a steady drop in temperature as the landscape

looks increasingly bleak and uninviting. On the skyline the only relief is the snow-sprinkled mass of **Mount Bláfell** (1,204 metres/3,950 ft).

Before Bláfell there is a ford across the **River Sandá** and a track branching off to the left. This detour from the main route, taking several hours as a round trip, goes to the large glacial lake **Hagavatn** ➊ and the icecap of **Langjökull**. As the track winds and bumps its way towards the edge of the ice, it crosses a once volcanically active fissure several miles in length. All that remains today is a high ridge of black rock with a narrow break that allows access through to the edge of the glaciers. The final approaches to the icecap are very steep due to huge deposits of glacial moraine, and vehicles should be left below. Water gushes out from the top of the moraine where lake Hagavatn has formed. Standing on the edge of the moraine, buffeted by the cold wind, there is a view of the lake, edged in ice, and, way below, the sweeping plains of black sand that are blown southward and enrich

Wading through one of the many glacial streams.

BELOW: in a four-wheel-drive across the interior.

Fittingly, given its distinctly alien landscape, NASA scientists have found a plausible model for Martian conditions underneath the barren surface. The existence of microbes, surviving in extreme conditions at Grimsvotn, a volcano beneath the Vatnajökull icecap, bolsters the theory of life on the red planet.

BELOW: Hveravellir.

the agricultural land beyond Gullfoss.

Back on the main Kjölur route you head towards a second, even larger glacial lake, **Hvítárvatn ❷**. Skirting around the bulk of Mount Bláfell to the east, the track descends to the **River Hvítá**, plunging through four or five tributary streams and small rivers. A spectacular view opens up across desolate dark tundra towards the distant blue glaciers of Langjökull icecap and Hvítárvatn lake.

On the horizon lies another icecap, **Hofsjökull**: the conflicting winds from the two icecaps create swirling dust clouds in between. From the bridge over the Hvítá, there is a clear view to the lake. Small icebergs can usually be seen

in the water, and on the far shore towers the outlet glacier from which they originated. A good base for a more extended exploration of the area is the Touring Club hut at **Hvítárnes**. Beyond here, the brown dusty plain gives way to expanses of gravel and then great black stretches of volcanic clinker, with mountains and glaciers always on the horizon.

The track soon crosses the southern stony slopes of the small mountain, **Innri-Skúti**. As well as affording a panoramic view over the **Jökulfall** river valley to the Hofsjökull icecap and Kerlingarfjöll mountains, the slopes are particularly rich in tundra plants. Most are no more than tiny specks which eke out an existence sheltered between the rocks. Small pink cushions of moss campion compete with white mountain avens and other alpines for space. In common with other tundra life, such plants have to cope with long, severe winters, followed by short, relatively warm summers. This ensures that any growth is very stunted. Stunted willows grow barely centimetres above the ground; as soon as they grow above this height, they become bent over by the constant wind.

The track detour to **Kerlingarfjöll** ❸ is well signposted as it dips down into the Jökulfall river valley. The river can become a raging torrent when it rains, making it difficult to cross. Nearby is a small airstrip. These are dotted throughout the interior for emergency use but this one also allows access to the summer ski school of **Árskarð**. The Kerlingarfjöll region is an excellent climbing area with superb views of Hofsjökull, many deep ravines and well-vegetated slopes. The mountain peaks, rising to 1,400 metres (4,600 ft), are made of rhyolite, making a stark contrast to the dark plains of Kjölur. In a succession of small gorges, sulphur and boiling water vent to the surface – which looks particularly eerie when there is a mild drizzle in the air and great clouds of steam rise out of the myriad small fissures in the ground. Boiling pools have splashed mineral-laden waters across rocks, colouring them green, red and yellow. These mountains can be a very cold place to camp and there are occasional snowfalls even in August. At the end of the track, near to the ski school, is a touring hut which operates a small café in season. It makes a delightful refuge, even if only for a brief coffee.

Returning to the main Kjölur route, you will see the table-mountain **Kjalfell** (1,008 metres/3,307 ft). To the northeast of it, on a low lava ridge, is **Beinahóll** ("hill of bones"). In 1780 four men from Reynistaður farm in Skagafjörður perished here in bad weather with a flock of sheep. Because of this incident most travellers over Kjölur for the hundred years afterwards passed on the west of Kjalfell, instead of using the main track to the east of the mountain.

A warm oasis

Hveravellir ❹, 100 km (60 miles) from Gullfoss, is an oasis within the cold desert. The hot springs here are very different from those at Kerlingarfjöll. Deep pools of brilliant, near-boiling blue water, are lined with white silica; all around are small mud pools of black, brown and red minerals. Hissing jets of steam emerge from tall rocky cones, while a number of springs cascade water which runs gently down the slopes. The deposits of silica and sulphur cover the ground like great sheets of glass with fine traces of yellow.

The Icelandic playwright Jóhann Sigurjónsson (1880–1919), a resident of Copenhagen, wrote a very successful play about the lives of the outlaw Eyvindur and his wife Halla, who lived at Hveravellir. In 1917 the play was turned into a film.

BELOW: crossing steaming ground on a walkway at Hveravellir.

TIP

Scheduled buses run between Reykjavík and Akureyri via the Kjölur route daily between mid-June and early September. Departures from both cities is at 8am. From Reykjavík, buses arrive at Hveravellir at 1.10pm, and then on to Akureyri for 5pm. Heading south from Akureyri, Hveravellir is reached by 11.15am. All buses stop at Gullfoss and Geysir. See www.sba.is for more information.

BELOW: perfect reflections in a Landmannalaugar lake.

Hveravellir is close to being classified as the interior's only settlement due to the presence of a touring hut, campsite and weather station. Some of the blue pools are as near as the natural world comes to a jacuzzi. With the air temperature near freezing, bathing is possible in one of the outlet pools located by the car park. Among the peculiar hot springs in the area are **Bláhver** and **Öskurshólshver**, the latter being so noisy in earlier times, that it reminded 18th-century travellers in Hveravellir of a screaming lion. Another is **Eyvindarhver**, named after the 18th-century outlaw Fjalla-Eyvindur, who is said to have boiled his meat in the spring. Ruins of the outlaw's shelter can be found on the edge of the lava, near the spring. Born in 1714, Eyvindur became a thief. In his early thirties he went into self-imposed exile in the mountains, for over 20 years. He met and married Halla Jónsdóttir. They settled in the beginning at Hveravellir, where they lived rather comfortably, gradually joined by a gang of thieves. On one occasion, though, Halla was captured and taken away. One night, as the kidnappers camped in Borgarfjörður in West Iceland, the exhausted

guards fell asleep. Next morning Halla was gone. The swiftest horse was also missing and so were the provisions. Clear footprints of two horses led to the mountains – Eyvindur had come in the night to free his wife.

North from Hveravellir runs 70 km (43 miles) of rough track until the hard road at the Blöndudalur valley. The winding **River Seyðisá** has several fording places which frequently change: great care is needed when crossing. The shallower parts attract water birds, such as phalaropes, which churn up the bottom by walking in circles to dislodge small animals for food. Much of the water comes from the two icecaps and on a clear day the views are magnificent

SPRENGISANDUR AND LANDMANNALAUGAR

The route through the Sprengisandur area can be reached in several ways from the north of Iceland. Although it is easier to reach than the Kjölur route, a four-wheel drive is still necessary. There are three main ways to reach the start of the route proper, all of which converge at or near Laugafell at the edge of the Sprengisandur. After making the crossing through the interior the main route reaches the beautiful and remote area around Landmannalaugar, where it is well worth taking the time to go hiking, before continuing down to the south coast.

Reaching the Sprengisandur

The most easterly way into the interior takes Route 842 then F26 through the Bárðardalur valley via Goðafoss. A scraped road soon degrades into a rough track, which climbs past the beautiful waterfall of **Aldeyjarfoss** with its tall basalt columns. On clear days there are spectacular views across the Ódáðahraun towards Askja. The shield volcano of Trölladyngja, part of the Gæsavatnaleið route, is clear on the horizon to the south.

A more central route on the F821 goes from the end of the Eyjafjörður valley. Passing the abandoned farm of Nýibær, where there used to be a weather station, the road continues to Laugafell. The third, most westerly route to the Sprengisandur is via Route F752 through the Vesturdalur valley which starts in Skagafjörður. The jeep track begins by

the farm of **Þorljótsstaðir** which was abandoned in 1944. The track crosses **Orravatnsrústir**, wet grasslands covered with cottongrass and sedge, around the two lakes of **Reyðarvatn** and **Orravatn**. The area is extremely marshy, with large hillocks covered with low-growing bushes. In the centre of the area is a small hill, **Orrahaugar**, where there is a refuge hut. Shortly before this route joins Route F821 near Laugafell it crosses the river **Austari Jökulsá**, a huge glacial river fed by several streams and rivers from the Hofsjökull glacier. The river used to be a great obstacle to those travelling this route, but there is now a bridge at **Austurbugur**.

A cold desert

At **Laugafell** ❺, on a ridge leading northwest from the mountain of the same name (890 metres/2,900 ft) there are several warm springs, which reach 40–50°C (104–120°F), and a warm bathing pool. Various kinds of grass flourish around the springs. Close to the tourist hut, which was built in 1948, there is a small trough, most likely man-made, containing warm water. According to an old story a woman named

Motorcycling, with a suitable bike and equipment, can be a good way of seeing the interior.

Flowers among the Lava

Most unfairly, Iceland is often called "barren". True enough, it's hardly a riot of flowers, fields and forests from coast to coast – in fact, well over half the country's area is wasteland. Visitors arriving at Keflavík Airport often think they could be on the moon when they look out on the treeless lava fields and the dark mountain slopes beyond. This impression is, however, misleading. While Iceland has next to no trees (a waggish visitor once remarked, "if you're lost in an Icelandic forest, stand up"), there is plenty of compensation. Mosses, lichens and flowering plants flourish all over the country. And even in the barest highlands sections, an occasional bloom takes root.

Birch, Iceland's most widespread tree, generally takes the form of a relatively low-growing shrub, often in dense copses and thickets. In the rare locations where it can grow straight and tall, the birch may reach 10–12 metres (30–35 ft). Afforestation efforts have introduced many foreign tree species, particularly evergreens. Some have flourished in their new environment, so mixed glades and woods are seen in many parts of the country today. Iceland's largest forest is at Hallormssta»ur, in the east.

Botanists believe that half of Iceland's plant species are survivors of the Ice Age, while around 20 percent have been introduced, deliberately or by chance, since humankind's arrival in the 9th century.

The local vegetation has been characterised as oceanic sub-arctic in character. About one-third of the plant species are of the arctic-alpine type. Many species of sedges and rushes are found in marshes and bogs; cottongrass (common and Schewchzer's), which flourishes in wetlands all over the country, was formerly used to provide wicks for fish-oil lamps which were the main form of lighting.

In addition to its 470 vascular plants (30 of them rare enough to be protected by law), Iceland has no fewer than 500 different mosses and liverworts. Mosses are generally the first plants to take root on lava fields, preparing the ground for later colonisation by grasses, ferns and later trees. One of the most interesting species among Iceland's flora is the misnamed *Bryoxiphium norvegicum*, sword moss. Though named "norvegicum," sword moss has never been found in Norway, and was first identified at Lake Kleifarvatn in 1928. Found in the US, Mexico and parts of Asia, it is unknown elsewhere in Europe.

About 450 lichens and 250 fungi are known in Iceland. Very few of Iceland's mushroom species are harmful to eat (though some do not taste very nice), and none is deadly poisonous, so mushroom-picking is a popular autumn pastime. Courses in mushroom identification are held from time to time, generally culminating in field trips to gather mushrooms under expert supervision.

Berry-bearing plants such as the crowberry, blueberry and bog whortleberry are common on heathlands, and after a good summer they give abundant berries for jam-making. Families often travel out in the autumn into the country in search of the biggest, juiciest berries. ❏

ABOVE AND LEFT: an unlikely splash of colour in an otherwise barren lava field.

Þórunn, daughter of Jón Arason, Iceland's last Catholic bishop, brought her family to stay here in the 15th century during the Black Death, and made the pool with her own hands. Near Laugafell the gravel expanse of the **Sprengisandur** truly begins with magnificent vistas eastwards to **Vatnajökull** and the smaller icecap of **Tungnafellsjökull** and westwards to Hofsjökull. A number of river crossings later, the blue tongues of glaciers come into view. A track forking to the east leads off the gravel plain to **Gæsavötn**, a small yellow-green oasis and crystal-clear lake amid the dark dramatic landscape. Beyond lie the Gæsavatnaleið and Askja routes.

At **Nýidalur ❻**, close to the geographical centre of Iceland, stand several huts – invariably a welcome sight. There is a small campsite on the only patch of green in the area, but even in the middle of summer high winds and near-freezing temperatures make camping a desperate option. The better choice is to stay in the huts which offer both warmth and hospitality. Wardened during the summer months, they have occasionally been cut off for a few hours by snow and bad weather. But, whatever the climate out-

side, the atmosphere inside these huts is always congenial, with travellers habitually swapping tales and sharing food. The next stop on the route is shortly after the mountain of **Kistualda** (790 metres/2,600 ft) which offers panoramic views, There is a petrol station and a cosy little coffee-shop at **Versalir** where one can get delicious home-made Icelandic waffles.

The dusty track south to **Þórisvatn ❼** (Iceland's second largest lake) continues the landscape of glaciers and black gravel plains. Just beyond the lake and on the main track is the tiny settlement of **Hrauneyjafoss**, where there is a petrol station, a coffee-shop and a small guesthouse. With the development of new hydroelectric schemes several lakes, not shown on all maps, can be seen close to the fork in the main track southeastwards to Landmannalaugar.

After a relative absence of vehicles, there is a steady increase in traffic south of Hrauneyjafoss en route to Landmannalaugar. The greatest change here is in the colour of the scenery. Instead of the dark Sprengisandur gravel, gaudy green mosses now coat the ancient rhyolitic rocks. The hills are bright yellow, green

Cycling can be extremely hard going anywhere in Iceland, let alone in the interior. Poor surfaces, strong winds and rain make these routes challenging for even the most experienced cyclists.

BELOW LEFT: lichens form patterns at Landmannalaugar. **BELOW:** a rainbow over the barren interior landscape.

Characteristic reddish volcanic rock at Eldgjá.

and red, dotted with deep blue lakes, creamy brown outwash plains and snow patches lying on grey Rhacometrium mosses. Shortly before Landmannalaugar a side road to the east leads to the edge of **Ljótipollur** (the "ugly puddle"), a picturesque explosion crater which has colourful sides and some greenish water at the bottom.

Exploring Landmannalaugar

Hot springs form the nucleus of **Landmannalaugar ❽**, and steam rises from every corner of the valley. Volcanic activity in the last 10,000 years has been restricted to a few northeast to southwest fissures. The youngest, the **Veiðivötn** fissure, created lava formations and other craters, including Ljótipollur, extending about 30 km (21 miles) to the north.

This is a popular centre for tourists and there are several camping areas but in midsummer the main site near to the hot pools, used for swimming, tends to become crowded. Landmannalaugar lies near the outskirts of the **Torfajökull** volcanic district. Warm and cold springs at the foot of the lava flows make it a

true "paradise in the desert". **Laugahraun**, the lava above the tourist hut, was deposited in a relatively recent eruption, probably at the end of the 15th century. The streams of geothermal and spring water, coming from under the lava-wall, mix to make streams and pools of an ideal temperature for bathing. There are trout in most of the lakes around Landmannalaugar, including Ljótipollur and Frostastaðavatn. Arctic char have also been added to some lakes in the area.

Landmannalaugar is a part of the **Fjallabak Nature Reserve** and forms a good base for the many walks in the area. With the cold climate and frequent sandstorms, vegetation is scarce, although least willow grows on the dry sands and lava, and cotton grass in the marshes.

The bedrock of Fjallabak dates back about 8–10 million years. The volcanoes in the area have been most active in the last 2 million years, during the last Ice Age. The varying and delicate colours of the mountain peaks that predominate in Fjallabak are due to their composition of rhyolitic rock. Interglacial rhyolite lava can be found in **Brandsgil**, which is only about an hour's walk from the hut at Landmannalaugar. Other popular hikes are to the summit of **Bláhnúkur** (940 metres/3,100 ft), formed by sub-glacial rhyolites (erupted under ice or water), and to the fumaroles of **Brennistein-salda** – these walks take between one and two hours each. Sub-glacial activity has also produced some hyaloclastite ("móberg") mountains such as **Loð-mundur** and **Mógilshöfðar**.

Slightly longer walks in the area include a five or six hour hike to the summit of **Háalda** (1,090 metres/3,600 ft) and a walk around Frostastaðavatn taking two to three hours. The major trek in this area is down to Þórsmörk in the Southwest, which takes four or five days if you are reasonably fit. It is best attempted only between mid-July and early September. The scenery encompasses lava flows, rhyolite hills and spectacular views over glaciers. Along the way there are overnight huts at Hrafntinnusker, Álftavatn and Emstrur.

Returning to the coast

Travellers are faced with several routes from Landmannalaugar. It is possible to take a track southwestwards on Routes

26 or 32 to join up eventually with the Ring Road near the south coast. Perhaps the most dramatic, however, is southeast to **Bláfjall** and eventually the coast. Although improved, the track here still provides adventure in the form of numerous river crossings, many of which require long periods of wading down the rivers to check their depth. Again only four-wheel drives should attempt these crossings due to the depth of the water and the possibility of quicksand.

Before Bláfjall there is a track off to the gorge and waterfall of **Eldgjá ❾** (the

Crossing a river in a four-wheel-drive. For a list of do's and dont's see page 318,

BELOW: colourful rocks on the Ljotipollur crater, in the Fjallabak Nature Reserve, Landmannalaugar.

*The Landnámabók
(Book of Settlements),
compiled probably in
the 12th and 13th cen-
turies, tells of a num-
ber of settlers from
the British Isles, some
of whom may actually
have been themselves
descendants of Nor-
wegians. The exact
numbers will never be
known but of signifi-
cance is the virtual
absence of words of
Celtic origin in the
language. These are
limited to a few place
names, such as Papey
and Dímon and per-
sonal names such as
Kjartan and Njáll*

BELOW: natural
patterns in the
Fjallabak Nature
Reserve.

"Fire Fissure"). Eldgjá is the most extensive explosion fissure in the world. It is
a 40-km (25-mile) long volcanic rift,
reaching from the Mýrdalsjökull glacier
to the mountain **Gjátindur** (950
metres/3,100 ft). The most impressive
part is the northern end, where it measures 600 metres (2,000 ft) wide and 200
metres (660 ft) deep. A part of it is supposed to have been formed in a violent
basalt eruption around AD 934. There
are indications that the fissure is related
to the volcano Katla, which is under the
ice of Mýrdalsjökull glacier.

Cascading into the rift is the famous
waterfall of **Ófærufoss**. It used to have a
much-photographed natural arch of
basaltic rock which formed a footpath
over the lower cascades. The arch, which
featured in the Icelandic film *In the
Shadow of the Raven*, has since collapsed due to heavy snow and flooding.
The hilly region around Bláfjall is a popular walking area. Ancient lava flows are
carpeted with mosses and lichens, while
innumerable streams and small waterfalls pour out of rocky fissures only to
disappear again under broken lava and
cushions of moss

THE ASKJA ROUTE

This track through the interior is more
difficult than the Sprengisandur and
Kjölur routes, and four-wheel drives are
sorely put to the test. Most tracks are
marked by yellow poles or cairns of
stones and, with reference to good maps,
navigation is fairly straightforward.

The track that leads off Route One (the
Ring Road) to the east of Lake Mývatn is
marked by several makeshift signs warning against two-wheel drive vehicles
attempting to go any further. The track
travels for some 64 km (39 miles), following close to the glacial river **Jökulsá á
Fjöllum**, before reaching the mountain of
Herðubreið. To begin with, the view west
across the Ódáðahraun plain is quite intim-
idating. A flat expanse of black gravel and
pebbles (called *grjot* in Icelandic), which
is made up from the country's largest lava
flow, stretches almost to the horizon.

The going is hard due to the severe
corrugations in the track. A small range
of black hills has to be negotiated, giving
from the summit a spectacular view of
the Jökulsá – a vast braided glacial river.
Patches of black sand become more frequent with pockets of stabilising lyme

grass. In this desert, few plants survive. The ancient and twisted frames of dwarf willow are testimony to the harshness of the environment. Among the dark gravel lie balls of primordial-looking grey lichens. Under stones protected from the wind sit small brown moths, barely moving, the only visible sign of animal life.

The track twists and turns eventually towards the edge of the River **Lindaá**, a tributary of the Jökulsá. This is the first major river crossing and along the river banks are great carpets of the pink-flowered arctic river beauty, contrasting against the black sand.

A black landscape

The track undulates considerably for the next 20 km (12 miles) as it climbs and descends an extensive lava field. The bare rock is covered at times with patches of sand and pumice. The mountain of **Herðubreið** ❿ gradually comes to dominate the view as it rises some 1,060 metres (3,500 ft) above the surrounding plain. On a cloudy day the upper reaches of Herðubreið are often hidden from view, which only adds to the mountain's gloomy splendour.

For centuries Herðubreið was held to be impossible to climb. The first attempt was made by the English traveller Richard F. Burton in 1872. Accompanied by a local farmer from the Mývatn-area, Burton had to turn around, because of rockfalls, shortly before they reached the top. First to get to the top of the mountain were the German geologist Hans Reck and the Icelander Sigurður Sumarliðason in 1908. Those who intend to climb the mountain should contact the warden in the hut at **Herðubreiðarlindir**, in order to get thorough information about the best route.

Herðubreiðarlindir is a wonderful oasis in the middle of black sands and lava fields. It is rich in vegetation and water springs, which appear from under the lava. In the lava, ruins of an ingeniously fashioned shelter made by the 18th-century outlaw Fjalla-Eyvindur can be found. He spent one winter here, which was, according to him, the worst time of his long exile, since he had no warm water and was forced to live on raw horse-meat all winter long. The Jökulsá á Fjöllum nearby becomes a violent glacial torrent, creamy brown with rock flour and

TIP

Between early June and September the Askja route can be accessed by buses from Lake Mývatn. There are 3 departures weekly. There are also summer-only buses from Mývatn all the way down to Landmannalaugar via Sprengisandur, with connections on to the southwest and Reykjavík. Be warned that buses travel very slowly (far slower than a jeep). Mývatn to Askja takes around 8 hours, and the bumpy terrain makes for an uncomfortable ride.

BELOW: the icy summit and steep, ridged sides of Herðubreið.

Extreme winter conditions on the northern flank of Vatnajökull.

running between banks of dark lava.

The journey from Herðubreið to Askja is another 35 km (21 miles), much of which is across the yellow pumice fields of **Vikursandur**. The soft honeycombed segments of pumice, originally produced by the eruption of Víti in 1875, have been blown by the wind into small yellow dunes, contrasting with the dark block lava beneath. Storms in this area can make travelling very hazardous.

To the north of Askja lies the centre of the vast **Ódáðahraun** ("ill deeds lava field") which, at over 3,000 sq. km (1,080 sq. miles), is the world's largest. This vast area remained unexplored for centuries and was thus seen as mysterious, giving rise to tales of extensive outlaw settlements. Organized travel and exploration did not begin until the early 19th century.

A forbidding caldera

Mount Askja ⓫ is not the neat cone that it appears on the horizon. Seen from closer up, it is a 45 sq. km (16 sq. mile) caldera of black lava, cream pumice screes and white snow. Low cloud often clings around the summit, which is located amid the sprawling **Dyngjufjöll**

massif. A narrow track winds around the base of Askja, through the **Öskjuop** pass to a small parking area. A walk leads through the outer walls of Askja into the huge crater, where the great jagged **Vikraborgir** lava field was created as recently as 1961. A deep inner crater is partially flooded with steaming water and marks the site of the 1875 eruption.

Öskjuvatn, a lake several kilometres across, is the deepest in Iceland at 217 metres (715 ft). The water of the lake has collected in a deep depression that developed following a tremendous volcanic explosion in the Askja caldera in 1875. This eruption was the first in the Dyngjufjöll mountains that was subjected to scientific research. At the beginning of 1875 powerful and consistent earthquake shocks were felt in the surrounding area. At the same time an increasing volcanic cloud was seen over the mountains. Four men from the Mývatn district then took it upon themselves to venture in the middle of the winter south to Dyngjufjöll, where they discovered craters in the southeastern corner of Askja. They found three slag cones, two of them active, little or no new lava, but the ground had subsided a good deal, and deep cracks had developed in the vicinity of the craters. After the men returned, the eruptions continued and came to a climax at Easter. Then there was an enormous volcanic explosion that spread a thick layer of grey pumice over a great part of the eastern countryside, devasting many farmsteads and damaging others. This explosion has been traced to the Víti crater, but others in the area were probably also active at the same time.

First to arrive at Askja after the eruption was an Englishman, W.L.Watts, accompanied by two guides. The same spring Watts had trekked across the Vatnajökull icecap, reaching Askja on 14 July. He discovered a deep depression with a circumference of about 8 km (5 miles), and down in it gaping fissures and seething hot springs, spewing steam and water high into the air. A black column of smoke was rising out of the Víti crater, scattering clay dust in all directions. Because of the tremendous volume of smoke, it was difficult for Watts and his guides to get a clear view of the crater. Throughout the summer of 1875 there were considerable outbursts in Askja, causing volcanic dust or ash to fall in the closest rural districts.

Several travellers, most of them Englishmen, visited Askja during the following decades. In the early 20th century, German scientists began making expeditions into the area. One of the first was the Knebel expedition of 1907, which came to a tragic end. Two members of the expedition, Walter von Knebel and Max Rudloff, disappeared, and were probably drowned in the lake, for their companion, Spetmann, who was collecting samples in a different part of the mountains, found no trace of his friends. The next year, 1908, Knebel's fiancée, Ina von Grumbkow went to Askja, accompanied by the geologist Hans Reck. Their attempts to throw light upon the disappearance of Knebel and Rudloff proved fruitless.

The last eruption of Askja began at the end of October 1961 and lasted for a little more than three months. The lava flowed from five craters, now named Vikraborgir, covering a great part of Öskjuop, the entrance to the caldera.

Onward from Askja

From the route between Herðubreiðarlindir and Askja there is a signposted

BELOW: reindeer crossing barren ground in the interior.

The 120-km (72-mile) track from Askja to Tómasarhagi was immortalised in Desmond Bagley's thriller Running Blind. The way that the book's hero Alan Stewart drove in his Land-Rover has changed little since then except for the bridging of the River Tungnaá at the end. It may be difficult, but at least you're unlikely to have a hail of bullets at your back, as Stewart had.

BELOW: a sight-seeing plane flies over the deep crevasses of the Vatnajökull icecap.

side track to the magnificent **Kverkfjöll** ⑫ ("Nook Mountains") at the northern edge of Vatnajökull. Close to the centre of the range is the second-highest volcano in Iceland, rising to 1,860 metres (6,102 ft). It is split from north to south by a steep and rugged glacier named **Kverkjökull**, which has burrowed out a deep valley, leading to an almost entirely ice-filled caldera. Kverkfjöll has erupted several times in recorded history, although it is less notable for its volcanic activity than for its geothermal nature. A valley named **Hveradalur** ("hot spring valley") cuts southwestwards into the mountains at a height of 1,600 metres (5,250 ft). The traveller who hikes into the valley will be rewarded with the entire spectrum of yellow, red and green nuances that characterise *solfatara* areas. Vapours rise everywhere from fumaroles and bubbling mud pits, and in the northeast where the valley is at its narrowest, it is almost blocked off by vapours from the largest vent. The valley is more than half-way surrounded by a brilliant white névé glacier, and at its southwest end there is an oval lake with greenish-blue ice walls. On a clear

day, there is a magnificent view over the wasteland of Ódáðahraun and to the mountains rising up above the high plateau. Beautiful ice caves have also been discovered in the area. A tourist hut can be found north of Kverkfjöll, and another one high in the mountains.

THE GAESAVATNALEID ROUTE

Running southwest from Askja there is a hazardous track, connecting the Askja route with the more westerly one that runs through the Sprengisandur. Known as the Gæsavatnaleið route, it passes very close to the Vatnajökull icecap.

Since this route is particularly hard going in places, it is essential to have a tough four-wheel-drive vehicle with an experienced driver. It should take about four or five hours from start to finish. Spring meltwater brings a flood from the Vatnajökull icecap and, with it, black volcanic sand. This outwash plain runs for many kilometres towards Askja and offers the first major obstacle on the track. Late on warm summer days and after heavy rain meltwater comes roaring out of Dyngjujökull creating wide rivers that flow all over the sands east of Urðarháls, an old glaciated volcano. These rivers are called Síðdegisflæður ("Evening morasses") and can be dangerous for all motor vehicles – avoid them at times when water levels are likely to be high. Marked at intervals with yellow poles, the track reaches the icecap at the forbidding black glacier of **Dyngjujökull** ⓭. Close inspection reveals that the ice is covered in black volcanic ash. Up above is the tufa mountain **Kistufell** (1,450 metres/4,750 ft). In September 1950 the Icelandic aircraft "Geysir" crash-landed on Bárðarbunga in Vatnajökull. The successful rescue operation had its headquarters on Kistufell.

Navigation becomes more treacherous as the route crosses the difficult boulder-strewn sides of **Trölladyngja**, the greatest shield volcano in Iceland, measuring 10 km (6 miles) in diameter and rising to about 600 m (2,000 ft) above the surrounding area. Lava flows from Trölladyngja are thought to have run all the way down to the Bárðardalur valley, which comes out on the north coast, just to the east of Akureyri. The weather here can be cold and wretched, and blizzards are commonplace in summer, but the solitude of the wilderness is awe-inspiring.

After hours of slow driving across block lava spewed out by a succession of volcanic craters, the track emerges above a ridge of cairns high on the edge of the Mid-Atlantic Ridge. Below lies the Sprengisandur plain. This is also where the meltwater from the icecaps collects in a succession of rivers, many of which are bisected by the track.

The Gæsavatnaleið route ends at the small oasis of **Tómasarhagi** ⓮, with a junction of braided rivers, beneath the glacier **Tungnafellsjökull**. ❑

Admiring the view from Dyngjujköll across to Kverkjökull.

BELOW: glacial streams flowing through the vast gravel plain of Sprengisandur.
FOLLOWING PAGE: an East Fjords landscape.

INSIGHT GUIDES
TRAVEL TIPS

ICELAND

TRANSPORT

GETTING THERE
AND GETTING AROUND

GETTING THERE

By Air

All international flights arrive at Keflavík airport, 50km (31 miles) from Reykjavík. After every flight arrival a bus transports passengers to the BSÍ bus station about 1.5 km (1 mile) from the centre of Reykjavík; the journey takes about 45 minutes and costs ISK 1,200 (pounds sterling and US dollars accepted); from the bus station, minibuses continue to various hotels in Reykjavík.

Icelandair is the main airline serving Iceland, operating from both Europe and North America. The airline sells its tickets as singles, so to buy a return ticket you simply put two single tickets together. When booked in advance, a single ticket from the UK (see below for departure airports) to Iceland costs from £70. In summer it is essential to book well in advance to secure the lowest fares. Icelandair regularly reviews its destinations and although the following list was correct at the time of publication, it is well worth checking that your airport is still served by the airline when planning your trip. In the UK, Icelandair serves London Heathrow, Manchester and Glasgow; in mainland Europe, Amsterdam, Copenhagen, Frankfurt, Helsinki, Oslo, Paris and Stockholm; and in North America, Baltimore, Boston, Halifax, Minneapolis, New York, Orlando and Washington. Book online at www.icelandair.co.uk or www.icelandair.com.

Iceland Express, currently the only budget airline operating flights to Iceland, has daily departures from London Stansted, as well as Alicante, Basel, Berlin Schönefeld, Billund,

Copenhagen, Eindhoven, Frankfurt Hahn, Friedrichshafen, Gothenburg, Oslo, Paris CDG, Stockholm and Luxembourg. Some routes are, however, seasonal and only operate during the summer months. The airline reviews its destinations every year and looks set to continue adding new routes to its ever expanding network. Book online at www.icelandexpress.com. Iceland Express operates fluctuating pricing and fares are generally cheaper the earlier you buy. Latest details are available on the airline's website.

British Airways flies all year round from London Gatwick to Reykjavík four to five times per week. Prices start at £45 single.

Icelandair
Iceland: Ticket office, Hotel Loftleiðir, Reykjavík. Reservations, tel: 50 50 700, email: sales@icelandair.is, www.icelandair.is
UK: Adam House, 2nd floor, 1 Fitzroy Square, London W1T 5HE. Reservations, tel: 0870 787 4020, email: uk@icelandair.is, www.icelandair.co.uk
US: 5950 Symphony Woods Rd, Suite 410, Columbia, MD 21044. Reservations, tel: 1-800 223 5500,

email: america@icelandair.is, www.icelandair.com

Iceland Express
UK call centre, tel: 0870 240 5600, www.icelandexpress.com

British Airways
Reservations, tel: 0870 850 9850, www.ba.com
Air Iceland, the domestic airline *(see page 315)* also operates flights from the Faroe and Greenland Islands.

Stopovers
Icelandair offers a free stopover in Iceland for people travelling between Europe and North America. This may not always apply to the cheapest internet fares; if in doubt check with the airline. Maximum stay is 72 hours.

By Sea

The Faroese shipping company, Smyril Line, operates a year-round ferry service to Seyðisfjörður in eastern Iceland. Routes, ports and schedules change according to the season, though there is always one weekly departure for Iceland at any time of year. Smyril Line's new superferry, *Norröna*, operates a zig-zag route across the North Atlantic which takes in the ports of Tórshavn (Faroe Islands), Bergen (Norway), Hanstholm (Denmark), Seyðisfjörður (Iceland), Scrabster (Scotland) and Lerwick (Shetland Islands). Scrabster and Lerwick are only served during the summer months. Timetabling is complicated and departure times depend on both the week and the season. For the latest information see the Smyril Line website. During the winter months, when the ferry doesn't call at either Scrabster or Lerwick, it is possible to connect with the *Norröna* by first travelling to the Shetland Islands from Aberdeen. Passenger and vehicle fares, though, are expensive and it is almost always cheaper to fly to Iceland and then hire a car.

Faroe Islands: J Broncksgøta 35, PO Box 370, FO-110 Tórshavn, Faroe Islands, tel: 298 345900, email: office@smyril-line.fo, www.smyril-line.com
UK: Scantours, 73 Mornington St, London NW1 7QE, tel: 020 7554 3530, email: info@scantours.com, www.scantours.com

Iceland: Smyril Line Ísland, Stangarhylur 1, 110 Reykjavík, tel: 570 8600, email: info@smyril-line.is, www.smyril-line.is.

If you are planning to bring your own car to Iceland by ferry, *see "Bringing Your Vehicle" on page 318.*

GETTING AROUND

For the independent traveller, a first visit to Iceland can seem a daunting prospect. Getting to Iceland, both by air and ferry, can be a major expense, although for travellers from the UK flights have become significantly cheaper in recent years, and domestic air travel is relatively inexpensive. When you get there, however, car hire is expensive – four-wheel drive is even more costly but a necessity for the highland routes.

Many independent travellers opt for a travel package. Tour operators offer a wide range of options from a simple fly-drive or flight and bus or air pass deal to a week in Reykjavík or a full-board hotel, farmhouse or camping tour. It is often cheaper to take a package of some sort.

Arrival and Departure

Almost all travellers arrive in Iceland at Keflavík Airport. All Faroe Islands

Domestic Air Routes and Prices

So-called "Net offers" are available on most Air Iceland flights which, when booked in advance, help to secure the best price for any particular flight. It is always worth checking with the airline before paying for a full-price ticket since they may be able to offer an alternative fare or departure.

The cheapest internet fares are as follows: **From Reykjavík to:** Akureyri ISK 6,200; Egilsstaðir ISK 6,600; Ísafjörður ISK 6,100; Heimaey ISK 4,600; Höfn ISK 4,190; Sauðárkrókur ISK 3,590; Bíldudalur ISK 3,590; Gjögur ISK 3,590. **From Akureyri to:** Grímsey ISK 2,500; Vopnafjörður ISK 2,500; Þórshöfn ISK 2,500.

and Greenland flights land at Reykjavík Airport and the odd international flight lands at Akureyri, in the north of Iceland, or Egilsstaðir, in the east. Arriving by sea you will dock either at Seydisfjörður, in the east of the country, or Reykjavík.

The "flybus" transfer coach meets all incoming flights and takes about 45 minutes to cover the 50km (31 miles) by road from Kelflavík to BSÍ bus station. From here, an onward transfer service is provided to the major hotels. Buses 1, 3 and 6 to the centre of town operate regularly throughout the day and evening.

For returning to the airport, the flybus leaves the bus station two hours and fifteen minutes before flights leave Keflavík. Arrange pick up at the reception desk; buses are provided from other major hotels to connect with the flybus. Many people flying out of Iceland combine their journey to Keflavík with a visit to the Blue Lagoon. Most tours to the Reykjanes peninsula let you get off at the airport for afternoon flights.

By Air

Air Iceland, also known in Icelandic as Flugfélag Íslands, is Iceland's main domestic airline, although it also operates flights between Iceland and Greenland. Most of Iceland's main towns are linked by air to Reykjavík. Currently, there are flights from Reykjavík to Akureyri, Ísafjörður, Egilsstaðir and the Westman Islands. From Akureyri flights operate to Grímsey, Þórshöfn and Vopnafjörður. The smaller Ernir Air operates flights to Reykjavík, to Bíldudalur and Gjögur in the West Fjords, Sauðárkrókur and Höfn. All domestic flights to and from Reykjavík use the central city airport, rather than the international airport at Keflavík. In winter, when many roads are blocked by snow, flying is simply the only way to get around. Needless to say, flight schedules can be disrupted by weather, even in summer. Icelandic pilots are reputed to be among the most experienced in the world because of the variety and

frequency of extreme conditions that they fly in. Reservations are advisable on all routes, especially in the summer months:
Air Iceland (Flugfélag Íslands): Reykjavík Airport, tel: 570 3030, fax: 570 3001, e-mail: vefstjori@airiceland.is, www.airiceland.is
Ernir Air: Reykjavík Airport, tel: 562 2640, email: ernir@ernir.is, www.ernir.is

By Bus

Bus travel in Iceland is efficient but not cheap. It can in fact work out more expensive than flying on most of the longer routes. From Reykjavík, long-distance buses depart from the **BSÍ Bus Terminal** at Vatnsmýrarvegur 10. In summer, buses depart daily for destinations around Route 1 (the Ring Road) and elsewhere. On some routes, brief stops are made at tourist attractions en route.

Because of road conditions and distances, some destinations, such as Egilsstaðir in the east, require an overnight stop in Akureyri or Höfn. On other routes, for example to the West Fjords, services are less frequent. BSÍ also operates scheduled **bus tours** in summer, some with a guide

Main Bus Routes

Below are the scheduled main BSÍ bus routes, frequency, journey times and approximate cost during summer months:
Reykjavík–Akureyri: daily (6 hours), ISK 7,300.
Akureyri–Mývatn–Egilsstaðir: daily in summer, otherwise Mon, Wed, Fri (4 hours 30 mins), ISK 5,300.
Egilsstaðir–Höfn: daily in summer only (4 hours), ISK 5,000.
Höfn–Reykjavík: daily in summer only, ISK 8,800.
Reykjavík–Stykkishólmur: daily (2 hours 30 mins), ISK 3,700.
The BSÍ website, www.bsi.is, provides full details of all bus routes in English and is a good starting point for planning journeys.

but mostly unguided, to places of interest, including Þingvellir, Gullfoss and Geysir, Þórsmörk, Landmannalaugar and Eldgjá (all daily) and across the central highlands over the Kjölur (daily) and Sprengisandur routes (2–3 weekly).

Full details of routes and schedules are available online and in the BSÍ Iceland Summer booklet, published each year, available from tourist offices and tour operators.

Timetables and prices are available from **BSÍ Travel**, Vatnsmýrarvegur 10, 101 Reykjavík, tel: 562 1011, e-mail: bsi@bsi.is, www.bsi.is

Bus Passes

For information on bus tickets and passes, contact BSÍ *(see above)*.

BSÍ offers several bus passes that are well worth considering. The best is the **Full Circle Passport** (ISK 23,800; ISK 35,300 if the West Fjords are included) which allows one full circuit around the Ring Road following the same direction, with no time limit other than those set by road conditions (this particularly applies to routes to/from the West Fjords). You can stop off as often as you like, and both offer discounts on tours, accommodation, bike hire and ferries. Another useful pass is the **Highlights Passport** which offers unlimited travel to some of Iceland's top attractions, including Gullfoss, Geysir, Þingvellir, Landmannalaugar, Þórsmörk, Skaftafell, Akureyri and Mývatn. It

also includes transport across the interior by both the Sprengisandur and Kjölur routes. The price of the pass depends on the length of its validity; it is available from 7 days (ISK 28,000) to 15 days (ISK 48,500).

Combined bus and air travel tickets – **Air/Bus Rover** tickets – permit a round trip including some of the highland bus routes and offer a small discount. You can purchase them abroad through many of the tour operators.

Hitchhiking

If you have unlimited time and patience and are prepared to carry a tent and plenty of food, and walk where necessary, then hitchhiking will get you round the Ring Road and on some of the more travelled minor roads. However, bear in mind that the sparse traffic on Icelandic roads often consists of visitors and locals on holiday, with little space to spare in their vehicles. There is hardly any long-distance commercial traffic, and you may find that most rides are from locals on a trip to the nearest shop.

Hitchhiking is reasonably safe, and though quite reserved, most Icelanders do speak some English. Once the ice is broken they may go out of their way to help and provide fascinating snippets of information about their country. If you plan to hitch on the highland routes be prepared for a long wait – on some routes you may only see one or two vehicles a day.

Cycling

For the mountain-bike enthusiast, Iceland might seem an obvious choice. There are miles of rugged mountain tracks empty of traffic, and even the main roads can hardly be called busy. However, there are snags: accommodation and shops are far apart and virtually non-existent in the highlands, so carrying a heavy load is unavoidable; high winds, sandstorms and driving rain can make the cyclist's life a misery; if you damage your bike, you may have to resort to a bus to get you to a repair shop. It is fair to say that most Icelanders regard foreign cyclists as clinically insane.

But Iceland is growing in popularity for cyclists, and a number of tour operators offer biking holidays with support vehicle back-up.

Airlines can carry your bike free, providing it forms part of your 20 kg (45 lb) luggage allowance. When booking, make sure you specify that you are taking a bike and preferably pack it in a box. Around Iceland you can transport your bike on the buses, if there is space available, but you may be asked to remove pedals and wheels. Iceland does not have many specialist cycle shops, but for repairs most villages have a *verkstæði* (workshop).

Useful Addresses

Icelandic Mountain Bike Association, P.O. Box 5193, 125 Reykjavík, tel/fax: 562 0099,

---

Scheduled Ferry Services and Prices

Þorlákshöfn–Heimaey: (Vestmannaeyjar): twice daily 8.15am and 4pm from Heimaey, noon and 7.30pm from Þorlákshöfn. 2 hrs 45 mins each way. There are bus connections to Reykjavík for each sailing through BSÍ, tel: 525 7700. Price: one way, ferry only ISK 2,000 for adults, ISK 1,000 for children (12–15 years; under 12s go free) and seniors, ISK 2,000 per vehicle up to 5m (15ft). Reservations are essential for vehicles, at least 30 mins prior to departure. Information from Herjolfur, tel: 481 2800; www.herjolfur.is

Árskógssandur–Hrísey: Sævar sails daily every 2 hours each way between 9am and 9pm. The journey takes 15 minutes. Price: ISK 700 one way. A special bus service is available from Akureyri. For information and bookings contact

tel: 695 5544 or see www.nat.is. **Dalvík–Grímsey (via Hrísey):** Mon, Wed and Fri, leaving Dalvík at 9am, arriving in Grímsey 3 hours 30 mins later and departing from there at 4pm. There is a special bus service from Akureyri, leaving at 7.30am and picking up passengers when the ferry docks on its return. Price: one way, ferry only ISK 2,000. Contact Landflutningar-Samskip, Ranarbraut 2b, 620 Dalvík, tel: 458 8970, email: jonarnar@samskip.is, www.nat.is. **Stykkishólmur–Flatey–Brjánslækur:** twice daily in June, July and August from Stykkishólmur at 9am and 3pm, returning from Brjánslækur at noon and 6pm respectively. Once daily in other months, departing from Stykkishólmur at 2pm (9am on Sat). The journey takes 2½ hours, and all sailings call at Flatey Island. If you wish you can stop over in Flatey and catch a later sailing.

Price: ISK 2,400 for children 12–15. Cars up to 5 m (15 ft) long pay ISK 2,400 one way. Reservations must be made for cars. For details, tel: 433 2254. Connecting buses run from Brjánslækur to various places in the West Fjords in summer only. For information and bookings, contact Sæferðir, Smiðjustígur 3, 340 Stykkishólmur, tel: 433 2254, email: seatours@seatours.is. www.seatours.is.

Ísafjarðardjúp–Jökulfirðir–Hornstrandir: from Ísafjörður there are regular scheduled ferry services to various locations in this part of the West Fjords in the summer. They vary in departure days and length, and each leg of the journey has a different price: for schedules and prices, call Vesturferðir, tel: 456 5111, e-mail: vesturferdir@vesturferdir.is; www.vesturferdir.is

e-mail: ifhk@mmedia.is; www.mmedia.is/ifhk

Bike shops in Reykjavík:
- GÁP, Faxafeni 7, tel: 520 0200.
- Hvellur, Súðarvogur 6, 104 Reykjavík, tel: 577 6400.
- Útilif, Kringlan 4–10, tel: 545 1580.

Repairs in Reykjavík:
- Borgarhjól, Hverfisgata 50, 101 Reykjavík, tel: 551 5653.
- Verslunin Markið, Ármúli 40, 108 Reykjavík, tel: 553 5320, www.markid.is

Mountain bike hire:
- BSÍ Travel, at the main bus terminal, tel: 562 3320.
- Borgarhjól, Hverfisgata 50, tel: 551 5653.

Many places around Iceland hire out normal bikes; make enquiries at hotels and campsites. Both Akureyri Bus Station and Lake Mývatn by Hotel Reynihlíð also have a reasonable selection.

By Ferry

Iceland has a number of small offshore islands dotted around its highly indented coastline. Many are inhabited because in past centuries they offered easy defence against enemies as well as good fishing. Sea birds too were an important supplement to the diet and their droppings fertilised the grassy soil, making the land ideal for farming. Scheduled ferry services link many of these islands with towns on the mainland; services are less frequent from September to May *(see panel, opposite)*.

Reykjavík Transport

Reykjavík's city centre is tiny in comparison to its sprawling suburbs. You can easily wander around on foot through the narrow streets clustered around the harbour and lake and cover most points of interest in a morning.

By Bus

Many hotels and guesthouses, as well as the main youth hostel and camping site, are all outside the centre, so it makes sense to use the excellent public bus system run by the Reykjavík bus company SVR. Most services operate 6am–midnight Mon–Sat with a reduced service on Sunday. At peak times buses run at 10–20 minute intervals and at 30-minute or one-hour intervals in the evenings and at weekends. Bus stops are marked "SVR" and a flat fare is charged with no change given. If you need to change buses, ask for a transfer ticket *(Skiptimidi)*, which is

Reykjavik Tourist Card

The Reykjavík Tourist Card is valid for unlimited travel on city buses, and admission to swimming pools and municipal museums (including the National Gallery, Culture House and Nordic House). It is available for 1, 2 or 3 days and costs ISK 1,200, 1,700 and 2,200 respectively. The cards may be purchased at the Tourist Information Centre at Aðalstræti 2, at the Reykjavík City Hall, hotels and guesthouses, bus terminals, museums and swimming pools.

valid for 45 minutes. If you plan to use the buses a lot, it is worth buying either a Reykjavík Card *(see panel)* or pre-paid tickets, which give a small discount, available along with a route map from the two terminals at Lækjargata and Hlemmur. For bus information, tel: 540 2700.

By Taxi

Hailing taxis on the street is a hit and miss affair. It is easier to go to one of the taxi ranks around town or ring the taxi firms directly:

Hreyfill, tel: 588 5522.
BSR, tel: 561 0000.
Bæjarleiðir, tel: 553 3500.
Borgarbílastöðin, tel: 552 2440.

The majority of taxis seat four passengers but some larger vehicles seating up to seven people are available on request. If you have unusually large or long items of luggage, ring **Sendibílastöðin**, tel: 552 5050, and ask for a minibus *"Sendibíll"*. These are often less expensive than a taxi but are only licensed to carry one or two passengers plus the luggage.

Tipping taxi drivers is not customary in Iceland. All taxis are metered and if you require a receipt ask for a *nóta*. Most drivers speak some English. The busiest time for taxis is after midnight on Friday and Saturday nights, when it can be virtually impossible to find one.

Driving

Rules of the Road

Iceland drives on the right. It is mandatory to drive with headlights on at all times; the use of seat belts,

both front and rear, is also mandatory. Drink driving is a serious offence – just one can of lager takes you over the legal limit. Priority, unless otherwise indicated, is given to traffic from the right – when in doubt, give way.

Speed limits are 50kph (30mph) in urban areas and 30kph (20mph) in residential areas. On gravel roads outside urban areas the limit is 80kph (50mph), and 90kph (60mph) on paved roads.

From November–May, snow tyres or studded tyres are mandatory; all rental cars will be fitted with them.

By law, driving off marked roads and tracks is prohibited. The high latitude and cool climate means the growing season is very short: four months in the lowlands but only two months in the highlands. As a result, damaged vegetation takes years, sometimes decades, to recover. Particularly at risk are marshlands and mossy areas where deep ruts caused by vehicles leave huge scars. The very fine, loose soil is vulnerable to erosion and damage is likely to accelerate the process.

Driving Conditions

Though road conditions in general fall below the standard of their European and North American counterparts, Route 1, also known as the Ring Road, which goes around the island, together with minor roads in settled districts, present no major problem to the normal two-wheel drive car in summer. Most of Route 1 is now paved, as are many of the minor country roads, particularly in the south and west of Iceland. A tunnel under the Hvalfjörður fjord, near Reykjavík, was opened in 1998 and markedly improved communications in the southwest of the country. The price for passing through is somewhat steep: ISK 1,000 one way for a normal family car.

Unpaved sections of road can become pot-holed and rutted, unpleasantly dusty in dry weather and muddy when it rains, but are still perfectly passable. Where the surface is loose gravel, it is vital for vehicles to slow down for oncoming traffic. In fact, you should always drive on gravel surfaces with great caution; there have been a number of fatal accidents involving tourists in the past few years.

For travelling around the coast, a two-wheel drive is perfectly adequate. Anyone contemplating a trip to the interior is entering a different league. Four-wheel drives are essential, and even then you should travel in teams of two or more cars (note that insurance companies will not cover hire cars taken into the interior).

For the jeep enthusiast Iceland is a playground of unbounded delights, its many rugged mountain tracks and unbridged rivers a challenge for even the most experienced. Travel through the uninhabited highlands also requires extreme caution; year after year unwary visitors (and Icelanders) undergo the unpleasant and sometimes fatal experience of their vehicle overturning in a seemingly innocuous river or the less serious but still frequent occurrence of getting stuck in sand. Fording rivers requires the utmost care.

Highland routes generally open the first week in July and close at the end of August, but this varies from year to year and route to route. A map is published every summer showing which highland routes are open and is constantly updated throughout the season. It is forbidden to attempt these routes before they are opened. The Ministry of Tourism publishes a brochure on travels in the Iceland highlands which is available free from many travel agencies and tourist information centres. Details of road conditions, updated every few minutes for all routes in Iceland, can be found on the internet at www.vegagerdin.is (tel: 354 1777).

For more information about mountain roads and the best routes to travel in the highlands, tel: 522 1000.

Motorcycling in Iceland

The weather is rarely perfect but, nonetheless, Iceland – in summer at least – is a magnificent destination to explore by motorbike. If you are staying on the main roads then a standard road bike is fine; however a trail or enduro machine will open up the interior and the numerous gravel or dirt roads elsewhere. It is important to realise, though, that there are no fuel stations away from the main settlements and the Ring Road: if you are venturing into the interior you will need to plan accordingly. The gravel and dirt roads can be treacherous, and fast-flowing rivers need to be forded (see panel below). For this kind of adventure, it is advisable to avoid travelling alone.

There is currently no motorcycle rental available in Iceland, so you'll either have to bring your own bike (on the ferry or by air) or sign up for a tour. www.ktm-tours.net operate one hour, half-day and full-day motorcycle tours as well as longer trips around the island. North Enduro (www.northenduro.is) offer 7-day tours across the interior along the Askja route.

Bringing your Vehicle

Given the high cost of hiring vehicles in Iceland, it may seem an obvious choice for Europeans to bring their own vehicle. However, remember that road conditions are not good, and unless you drive only at low speed, your suspension may suffer. Flying stones from passing vehicles are likely to damage your paintwork, whatever speed you drive. The constant vibrations from rutted and potholed roads may also damage your vehicle, not to mention the copious quantities of dust that will enter every nook and cranny. Nevertheless many visitors do bring their own car, year after year, without suffering major damage. See page 316 for details on car ferries to Iceland.

On arrival in Iceland your vehicle may be inspected to ensure that it is roadworthy. You will need to produce the following documentation: a passport, driving licence, car registration document and a green card or other proof of auto insurance while in Iceland. A temporary importation permit will then be issued for the duration of your stay, which may not exceed three months. Other conditions for temporary import of vehicles are that the vehicle must be imported by the owner only or anyone having legal possession of it (eg through hiring), the vehicle must be brought to the country when the owner arrives, or within one month of arrival the vehicle must be used by him, his spouse or a hired chauffeur, the vehicle must not be lent, sold or hired and the vehicle must be re-exported within the stipulated time period.

Crossing Rivers by Four-wheel Drive

Many rivers, particularly if glacial, can vary enormously in flow. Heavy rainfall or a warm sunny day can treble their flow in hours. Generally, in warm weather, the flow is highest in late afternoon and lowest in early morning.

If the river looks deeper than knee height, stop before crossing and look for the best place to ford, checking the flow in several places. With sediment-laden glacial rivers it is difficult to judge the depth. Narrow crossings are the deepest, wider crossings will be shallower, especially on straight stretches. On bends, the deepest water is usually on the outside. Where there is an obvious fording place, where the water enters a calm phase forming a pool, the water will be shallower on the downstream side.

Watch out for large boulders, swept down into the fording place by strong flow, or sand – both should be avoided. If it is necessary, and safe to do so, wade first, using a safety rope. If in doubt, do not cross. Wait for another vehicle, get a second opinion, and help each other through. Keep in first gear, in low ratio if available, and drive slowly and steadily without stopping. If there is a strong current, try to cross by heading downstream to avoid fighting against the current.

Fuel may only be imported in the vehicle's fuel tank. If your vehicle uses diesel, it will be subject to a special tax on arrival in Iceland. This is because diesel fuel is very much cheaper than petrol and normally this tax is built into the purchase price of the vehicle. The amount will depend on the make of vehicle and intended length of stay. Full details can be obtained from Icelandic embassies abroad.

Use of mudguards is compulsory to minimise stones being thrown onto oncoming vehicles on gravel roads. It is advisable to buy a grille for the front of the car to protect headlights from damage. Before leaving home try to make sure your vehicle is completely dust-proof and ensure that any luggage stored on the roof is adequately protected against both dust and water.

Hiring a Vehicle

You can hire anything from a small car to a 40-seater coach in Iceland, depending on your needs and group size, but prices are high (less so outside the peak tourist season). Four-wheel drive vehicle hire is very expensive. It is often better to arrange vehicle hire with one of the tour operators abroad who offer a package that includes flights and car hire.

When arranging your rental, check what the rates include. The majority of rates advertised are for up to 100 km (65 miles). Prices double for unlimited mileage, if that is available. Many hire companies do not even offer unlimited mileage, nor do they include the hefty 24.5 percent VAT or the highly recommended fully comprehensive insurance in their daily rental price. Rental charges do include basic third-party insurance but not a collision damage waiver,

which is always payable locally.

If you wish to hire locally, the following companies offer a full range of vehicles:

ALP Car Rental, at Reykjavík City Airport, Reykjavík, tel: 562 6060, e-mail: alp@alp.is, www.alp.is
Atak Car Rental, Smiðjuvegur 1, Kópavogur, tel: 554 6040, e-mail: atak@atak.is, www.atak.is
Avis, Knarrarvogur 2, Reykjavík, tel: 591 4000, or at Keflavík Airport, plus other sites (see website), e-mail: avis@avis.is, www.avis.is
Hertz/Icelandair, Reykjavík Airport, 101 Reykjavík, tel: 522 4400, e-mail: hertz@hertz.is, www.hertz.is
National Car Rental, Skeifan 9, 108 Reykjavík, tel: 568 6915m Tryggvabrant 12, 600 Akureyri, tel: 461 6000, e-mail via website www.nationalcar.is

Many hire companies offer one-way rentals, allowing you to drive from Reykjavík to Akureyri, for example, and then return by air. Provided you stick to roads designated for the category of vehicle, assistance will be provided in the event of breakdown. Hire nothing but a four-wheel drive for a tour across the highlands. It is worthwhile going over your intended route with the rental company to check what roads are allowed for your type of vehicle.

Petrol

Petrol is quite expensive in Iceland, and is roughly the same price everywhere across the island. Regular, super and unleaded petrol and diesel fuel are available in towns, villages and even in remote country districts, but not always at frequent intervals.

Before leaving a town or village it is always a good idea to check how far it is to the next petrol station. In

uninhabited areas there is no petrol available and you will need to take spare fuel tanks with you. Remember that petrol consumption is particularly heavy on the rough interior routes. Petrol stations also stock basic spare parts and most have toilets and either a cafeteria or a restaurant available.

Petrol stations usually open daily at 7.30, 8 or 9am and close any time from 7.30–11.30pm. On Sundays they generally open between 10am–1pm. Shell petrol stations marked "Select" are open 24 hours. After-hours petrol can be bought at station pumps – these are labelled *sjálfsali* (self-service) and they usually accept both cash and credit/debit cards.

Driving in Reykjavík

Reykjavík is still small enough for drivers not to experience serious traffic jams, though the city centre – particularly Miklabraut – can often get congested during rush hour. Negotiating the inner city by car can also be tricky since there are a lot of narrow and one-way streets. The best compromise is to park in one of the numerous car parks on the fringe of the inner city, and then walk into the centre.

Most car parks close during the night; their hours are clearly stated on the ticket machine upon entering. Note that you must pay at the vending machine before returning to your car. Prices are generally ISK 80–150 per hour.

Payment at parking meters and in metered parking lots is mandatory from 10am–6pm on weekdays and 10am–1pm on Saturdays. Parking meters cost ISK 80–150 for an hour. Parking fines are a hefty ISK 1500 if paid within 14 days, ISK 2,250 if paid after that.

A CCOMMODATION

HOTELS, GUESTHOUSES, HOSTELS & CAMPING

Making Bookings

Although accommodation in Iceland is expensive, facilities are generally good and the overall standard is high. The growth in tourism heralds an increasing number of hotels. Most accommodation outside Reykjavík and other towns is only open in the summer months, from June–September. It is advisable for visitors to reserve accommodation, especially during the peak summer months of July and August. You should be able to find dormitory sleeping-bag accommodation and space to bed down at camp sites but even youth hostels are usually fully booked during the peak summer period.

Most forms of accommodation, except camp sites, can be booked through tour operators in your own country, and better rates can often be obtained this way. Links to hotels, guesthouses and camp sites can also be found on the website of

the Icelandic Tourist Board (www.visiticeland.com).

There are several useful publications listing accommodation. For an overview, try *Hotels and Guesthouses in Iceland*, available from The Icelandic Travel Industry Association, Borgartún 35, 105 Reykjavík, tel: 511 8000, www.saf.is, e-mail: info@saf.is

Other more specific publications are mentioned below under the relevant sections.

Hotels usually accept payment by credit card, but payment for guesthouses, farms, hostels and camp sites is generally by cash only.

Hotels

International-style hotels with a full range of facilities are mainly found in the Reykjavík and Akureyri areas. Elsewhere they are few and far between. Top prices are over ISK 25,000 for a twin room in a luxury hotel, with en-suite shower or bath, and breakfast included. Most

international-style hotels have good facilities for disabled people. Thirteen top-quality hotels have formed the **Foss Hotel** chain and have hotels in various locations around the country. Prices for a double room with en-suite bath/ shower and breakfast range from ISK 12,600–21,500 in high season. They do not generally have facilities for the disabled.

Tourist-class hotels offer fewer facilities but most have rooms with private shower/bath and a restaurant. They are to be found in Reykjavík and in towns around the country and are open all year round. Prices are usually somewhat less than those of the international-style hotels and facilities for the disabled tend to be lacking.

In summer Iceland's country boarding schools open as "summer hotels", most operating under the **Hotel Edda** chain. They offer comfortable accommodation, generally in rooms with a basin but without a private shower/toilet. Prices start from ISK 7,100 for a twin room with shared facilities. Breakfast costs around ISK 900. Most have their own restaurant.

Guesthouses

These are usually small, often family run, and offer basic bed-and-breakfast accommodation. Prices vary, depending on the range of facilities and location, but start as low as ISK 5,500, including breakfast, for a twin room. Guesthouses are good bet for those travelling on a budget, with facilities generally of a high standard, and invariably clean. In most cases, however, the rooms do not have private baths, nor special facilities for the disabled. In the peak season book well in advance.

Private Homes

Because of the shortage of hotel space in the height of the summer, some families offer bed-and-breakfast accommodation in their own homes, mostly in the Reykjavík area. Bookings can be made through local tour operators. Private lodgings in Reykjavík can be booked via Tourist Information at Reykjavík Complete, Aðalstræti 2, tel: 590 1550, e-mail: info@ visitreykjavik.is. Prices for private homes are similar to those given for guesthouses.

Farm Guesthouses

Over-dependent on sheep-farming, many farmers have been encouraged to branch out into tourism. Farms around the country offer a variety of services to visitors from bed-and-breakfast and sleeping-bag accommodation to self-catering holiday cottages (or summer houses as they are known locally), rented on a weekly basis. Excursions on horseback, fishing and other activities can be arranged. Not all are working farms.

Farm guesthouses are listed in the Icelandic Farm Holidays booklet, available through tourist offices across the country, tour operators, which also handle bookings, or directly from **Icelandic Farm Holidays**, Síðumúli 13, tel: 570 2700, e-mail: ifh@farmholidays.is, www.farmholidays.is

Prices start at around ISK 2,000 per person for sleeping-bag accommodation, ISK 3,500–4,500 per person in a twin (an extra ISK 900 with breakfast). There is an extra fee of ISK 1,100 for a single. Cottages cost ISK 30,000–60,000 per week in summer, depending on the facilities and number of people they sleep; they cost less in winter.

Travelling via farmhouses is highly recommended for anyone interested in really getting to know Iceland. Many of the farms are in unique, sometimes remote locations, and staying on a working farm gives an insight into the country's ancient rural lifestyle.

Booklets of 10 pre-paid nights at farms can be bought either in Reykjavík or from tour operators, giving some discount. If you opt for sleeping-bag accommodation you may get your own room, although not all farms provide this service. Many farms offer kitchen facilities for

cooking, and almost all will cook guests' meals. Prices for meals vary from farm to farm.

Each farm has its own character and range of services, so careful perusal of the Icelandic Farm Holidays booklet is recommended. Reservations at the individual farms can be made by telephone, or you can simply drop in at any farm where the IFH sign is displayed.

Youth Hostels

There are 25 youth hostels around Iceland, situated in towns, villages and farming districts. Offering dormitory sleeping-bag accommodation with cooking facilities, many hostels also provide meals. Some prohibit sleeping bags, providing a duvet or blankets, but you will need to hire or use your own sheet lining. Hostels are open to people of all ages and in Iceland you do not have to be a member of the IYHF (International Youth Hostels Federation) though prices are slightly lower for members.

In July and August it is advisable to pre-book hostels through tour operators or directly with the **Icelandic Youth Hostels Association**, Sundlaugavegur 34, P.O. Box 1045, 121 Reykjavík, tel: 553 8110, e-mail: info@hostel.is; www.hostel.is. The association also provides a booklet listing hostels and the facilities they offer. Sleeping-bag accommodation costs ISK 2,100 per person a night at the hostels, or ISK 1,700 for association members. Breakfast costs around ISK 900.

Mountain Huts

Marked on maps by a triangle, you find mountain huts in uninhabited areas. Mountain huts are owned and maintained by:
Ferdafélag Íslands (The Touring Club of Iceland), Mörkinn 6, 108 Reykjavík, tel: 568 2533, e-mail: fi@fi.is, www.fi.is
Útivist, Hallveigarstíg 1, 101 Reykjavík, tel: 562 1000, fax: 562 1001, e-mail: utivist@utivist.is, www.utivist.is

Some huts are accessible by road but others are intended solely for hikers. Some are small, sleeping six to eight persons and have no facilities – others sleep over 100 and offer cooking facilities and flushing toilets. It is always wise to pre-book the huts, as some are kept locked with no resident warden. For these a key is obtained from the Touring Club's office. All huts are uncatered, so please bring your own supplies.

Camping in Reykjavík

Reykjavík Campsite
Laugardalur, Sundlaugavegur 34
Tel: 568 6944
Located behind the youth hostel at the edge of Laugardalur valley, next to the city's largest swimming facility. The camp site offers cooking and laundry facilities. Things get busy in the summer and pre-booking is advisable for larger groups. **$**

Non-members are charged a fee of about ISK 1,500–2,200.

Sheep Round-up Huts

These are basic huts, owned by farming communities and used during the annual sheep round-up in September. Often marked on maps as *Kofi*, many will be kept locked at other times of the year and are not intended for use by tourists.

Emergency Huts

Located on mountain passes, remote stretches of road and along uninhabited coasts, these orange-painted huts are stocked with food, stove, blankets and a radio. They are, by law, only for emergency use.

Camp Grounds

Camping is allowed in most places in Iceland, though on private or farming land it is subject to the owner's permission. Within national parks and conservation areas, it is only allowed at designated areas.

Official camp sites are found in most towns and villages, at national parks, nature conservation areas, places of natural beauty and some farms and community centres. The standard varies. Expect to pay about ISK 600 per person per night depending on facilities. A leaflet listing camp grounds is published by the **Icelandic Tourist Board**, Lækjargata 3, 101 Reykjavík, tel: 535-5500, fax: 535-5501, e-mail: info@icetourist.is, www.visiticeland.com

Sleeping Bags

Anyone interested in saving money should bring their sleeping bag with them. As well as being essential for mountain huts and some hostels, many farmhouses and guesthouses offer "sleeping bag accommodation" at a reduced rate.

Hotels are listed in alphabetical order within price categories.
Towns and cities are listed in alphabetical order.

REYKJAVÍK

City Centre

Hótel Borg
Pósthússtræti 11
Tel: 551 1440
Fax: 551 1420
E-mail: hotelborg@hotelborg.is
www.hotelborg.is
The city's first hotel, right
in the old town centre.
Beautifully renovated in Art
Deco style, with a very
popular restaurant. **$$$$**

Hótel Holt
Bergstaðastræti 37
Tel: 552 5700
Fax: 562 3025
E-mail: holt@holt.is
www.holt.is
Luxury hotel in central
Reykjavík, tastefully
decorated throughout
with Icelandic works of art.
It is also well known for
having one of the finest
ranges of whiskies in the
country. **$$$$**

Hótel Klöpp
Klapparstígur 26
Tel: 595 8520
Fax: 595 8521
E-mail: info@grand.is
www.centerhotels.is
Pleasant hotel right in the
middle of town. The nearby
Hótel Skjaldebreið
(Laugavegur 16, tel: 595
8510, fax: 595 8511) is
run by the same company.
$$$$

Hótel Óðinsvé
Óðinstorg 11
Tel: 511 6200
Fax: 511 6201
E-mail: odinsve@hotelodinsve.is
www.hotelodinsve.is
A charming hotel on a quiet
street in the heart of the
city. Tasteful decor. A
restaurant on the premises
was rated one of the 100

best new restaurants in the
world by Condé Nast. **$$$$**

Fosshótel Lind
Rauðarárstígur 18
Tel: 562 3350
Fax: 562 3351
sales@fosshotel.is
A modern hotel on the
outskirts of the old centre,
close to Hlemmur bus
terminal. There are very
good facilities for the
disabled and the central
non-smoking
rooms are available. **$$$**

Hótel Leifur Eiríksson
Skólavörðusígur 45
Tel: 562 0800
Fax: 562 0804
Attractive and comfortable
hotel, centrally located
opposite Hallgrímskirkja
church. **$$$**

Metropolitan
Ránargata 4a
Tel: 511 1155
Fax: 552 9040
E-mail: bookings@metropolitan.is
www.metropolitan.is
On a quiet street in the
city's west end, very close
to the centre. Modern
facilities and small but
comfortable rooms. **$$$**

Guesthouse Adam
Skólavörðustígur 22
Tel: 896 0242
Fax: 551 1506
E-mail: adam@adam.is
Good location close to the
Hallgrimskirkja; open all
year. Breakfast is ISK 800
extra. **$$**

Guesthouse Aurora
Freyjugata 24
Tel: 899 1773
book@aurorahouse.is
On a quiet tree-lined street
near Hallgrímskirkja church,
about a 10-minute walk
from the centre. One of the
best places at this price. **$$**

Guesthouse Baldursbrá
Laufásvegur 41
Tel: 552 6646
Fax: 562 6647
E-mail: baldursbra@centrum.is
One of the best
guesthouses in the city, run
by a German-Icelandic
couple. The service is
friendly and hospitable and
there is a hot tub in the

back yard. **$$**

Guesthouse Svala
Skólavörðustígur 30
Tel: 562 3544
Fax: 562 3650
This guesthouse is housed
in a stately old residence in
the heart of the city.
Several unique shops on
the same street sell
everything from designer
gear to quirky toys. **$$**

**Salvation Army
Guesthouse**
Kirkjustræti 2
Tel: 561 3203
Fax: 561 3315
The cheapest guesthouse
in Reykjavík. There are no
frills but the place is neat
and clean and the central
location is excellent. There
are facilities for cooking on
the ground floor. **$**

South of the Centre

Radisson SAS Hótel Saga
Hagatorg
Tel: 525 9900
Fax: 525 9909
E-mail: reservations.saga.reykjauik@
radissonsas.com
A top-class hotel not far
from the city centre and
next door to the University
Theatre, home of the
Iceland Symphony
Orchestra. Excellent
facilities and one of the
best restaurants in the
country on the top floor,
with a wonderful view over
Reykjavík and beyond. **$$$$**

Hótel Loftleiðir
Reykjavíkflugvöllur
Tel: 444 4500
Fax: 444 4501
www.icehotel.is
Owned by Icelandair and
located at Reykjavík
airport. Modern and
comfortable with an
excellent restaurant.
Situated close to the
Öskjuhlíð nature reserve
and the Perlan, with a
panoramic view of the city
and surroundings, but a
bracing 25-minute walk to
the centre of town. **$$$**

East of the Centre

Hótel Reykjavík
Rauðarárstígur 37
Tel: 514 7000
Fax: 514 7030
www.hotelreykjavik.is
A modern hotel with a
friendly atmosphere to the
east of the centre. The
Hlemmur bus terminal only
a short distance away.
$$$$

Hótel Cabin
Borgartún 32
Tel: 511 6030
Fax: 511 6031

PRICE CATEGORIES

Prices are for a double
room per night in high
season. Rates can be 30
percent lower Sept–Apr.
$$$$ ISK Over 16,000
$$$ ISK 11,000–16,000
$$ ISK 7,000–10,000
$ Under ISK 7,000

TRANSPORT

ACCOMMODATION

ACTIVITIES

A – Z

LANGUAGE

E-mail: booking@hotelcabin.is
A modern hotel with small but comfortable rooms, about a 20-minute walk from the town centre. Has good views of the ocean and mountains beyond. **$$$**

Guesthouse 101
Laugavegur 101
Tel: 562 6101
Fax: 562 6105
E-mail: guesthouse101@simnet.is
This is one of the few guesthouses offering good facilities for the disabled. On the main shopping street just a short distance from the Hlemmur bus terminal. **$$**

Laugardalur

Grand Hótel Reykjavík
Sigtún 38
Tel: 514 8000
Fax: 514 8030
E-mail: reservations@grand.is
Comfortable hotel with full facilities, located close to the Laugardalur swimming

pool. Spacious rooms and excellent service. **$$$$**

Park Inn Island
Ármúli 9
Tel: 595 7000
Fax: 595 7001
A modern, comfortable hotel with the largest nightclub in Iceland on the premises. The location is not very picturesque but is close to a number of attractions, such as the Laugardalur geothermal pool. **$$$$**

Youth Hostel
Sundlaugavegur 34
Tel: 553 8110.
Fax: 588 9201.
Well-run hostel with good facilities. Situated on the fringe of Laugardalur, next to the open-air swimming pool. Good bus connections nearby. **$**

Suburbs

Guesthouse Hólaberg
Hólaberg 80

Tel: 567 0980
Fax: 557 3620
A very good bet for those on a budget. Located in the Breiðholt suburb with good bus connections to the city centre. Free pick-up from Reykjavík air or bus terminals. Good walking and cycling paths nearby. Bike rental and free use of bike if staying more than four nights. Breakfast costs ISK 700 extra. **$**

Self-catering Apartments

Fosshótel Barón
Barónsstígur 2–4
Tel: 562 3204
Fax: 552 4425
E-mail: sales@fosshotel.is
Self-catering apartments for rent close to the main shopping street and the Hlemmur bus terminal. Sizes and prices vary but start at ISK 12,600 per

night. Apartments with two bedrooms are ISK 19,100.

Room with a View
Laugavegur 18, 6th floor
Tel: 552 7262
Fax: 552 1485
E-mail: info@roomwithaview.is
www.roomwithaview.is
Luxurious furnished apartments, which sleep up to seven people. In accordance with the name, most of the rooms have a balcony and a great view. Sizes and prices vary, starting from ISK 9,900 per night for an apartment sleeping two.

Luna Hotel Apartments
Spítalastígur 1
Tel: 511 2800
Fax: 511 2801
E-mail: luna@luna.is
www.luna.is
Restored 1920s' town house in a quiet central part of town. Studio apartment at ISK 12,900; up to three-room apartment at ISK 20,900.

THE REYKJANES PENINSULA

Blue Lagoon

Northern Light Inn
P.O. Box 13, 240 Grindavík
Tel: 426 8650
Fax: 426 8651
E-mail: welcome@northernlightinn.com
Located at the Blue Lagoon, mainly serving transit passengers en route to or from the nearby airport. **$$$**

Hafnarfjörður

Hafnarfjörðus Guesthouse

Hjallabraut 51, by Víðistaðatún park, Hafnarfjörður
Tel: 565 0900
Fax: 555 1211
A quieter alternative to the busy hostel and camp site in Reykjavík. The trip to the capital takes about 30 minutes by bus. **$**

Keflavík

Flug Hótel
Hafnargata 57, Keflavík
Tel: 421 5222
Fax: 421 5223

Up-market hotel, mainly for airport passengers, with restaurant and bar. All rooms are en-suite. **$$$**

Hótel Keflavík
Vatnsnesvegi 12–14, Keflavík
Tel: 420 7000
Fax: 420 7002
Comfortable hotel near the airport with various services on-site and restaurants nearby. The hotel runs a much cheaper guesthouse ($$) across the street at No. 9. **$$$**

Njanðvík Youth Hostel
Fitjabraut ba
Tel/fax: 421 8889
Newly renovated hostel; perfectly located for Keflavík international airport. **$**

THE SOUTHWEST

Fluðir

Guesthouse Syðra-Langholt
845 Flúðir
Tel/fax: 486 6674
Based in a farm south of Flúðir and open all year. **$**

Hella

Guesthouse Árhús
Rangarbakkar, 851 Hella
Tel: 487 5577

Fax: 487 5477
Open year-round, with 21 cottages and camping on the banks of the Ytri-Ranga River in the village of Hella. **$**

Hveragerði

Hótel Eldhestar
Vellir, Hveragerdi
Tel: 480 4800
Fax: 480 4801

E-mail: info@eldhestar.is
www.hoteleldhestar.is
Iceland's premier "eco-hotel", a lovely one-storey wooden building surrounded by greenery. The rooms are comfortable and there are log fires in the communal areas. The hotel has full disabled access and all rooms have computer connections and direct

access to the garden. The hotel also arranges horse riding and golfing packages. **$$$**

Hótel Örk
Breiðumörk, 810 Hveragerði
Tel: 483 4700
Fax: 483 4775
One of the Key group of
hotels, with comfortable
rooms and a pool.
$$–$$$

Hvolsvöllur

Hótel Hvolsvöllur
Hlídarvegur 7, 860 Hvolsvöllur
Tel: 487 8050
Fax: 487 8058
Comfortable small hotel
near the Saga Centre. **$$$**

Hótel Edda
Skógar, 861 Hvolsvöllur
Tel: 444 4830
One of 13 Edda hotels in
Iceland. Close to the

Skógafoss waterfall.
Sleeping-bag
accommodation is
available. Summer only.
$$–$$$

Selfoss

Hótel Geysir
Haukadal, 801 Selfoss
Tel: 480 6800
Fax: 480 6801
Small hotel just a stone's
throw from the famous
geysers. Self-catering
accommodation also
available. **$$**

Vík

Hótel Edda Vík
Klettsvegur, 870 Vík

Tel: 487 1480
Fax: 487 1302
An all-year hotel offering
good facilities, with
sleeping bag
accommodation available.
$$

Youth Hostel Norður-Vík
Suðurvíkurvegur 5
Myrdal, 870 Vík
Tel: 487 1106
Just outside Vík, this is a
basic hostel and
guesthouse. **$**

Þingvellir

Hotel Valhöll
Þingvellir
Tel: 480 7100
Fax: 480 7101
Dating from 1898, this is a

rare opportunity to stay in
a period building in the
Icelandic countryside.
Situated next to the
historic sights, with views
across the Þingvellir plains.
$$$$

Þórsmörk Valley

Þórsmörk Hut
Ferðafélag Íslands, Mörkinn 6,
108 Reykjavík
Tel: 568 2533
Fax: 568 2535
A busy hut and crowded
camp site in summer, but
empty in winter. Sleeps
75 people in bunks.
Makes a good base for
walks in the Þórsmörk
valley. **$**

VESTMANNAEYJAR

Heimaey

Hotel Þórshamar
Vestmannabraut 28
Tel: 481 2900
Fax: 481 1696
A fairly up-market hotel. A
lower-priced guesthouse is
attached. **$$–$$$**

Hótel Eyjar
Bárustígur 2
Tel: 481 3636
Fax: 481 3638
Hotel with well-appointed
apratments right in the
centre of Heimaey. **$$**

Guesthouse Heimir
Heiðarvegur 1

Tel: 481 2929
Fax: 481 2912
Guesthouse/sleeping-bag
accommodation. **$**

Guesthouse Hvíld
Höfðavegur 16
Tel: 481 1230
A very good-value budget
guesthouse. **$**

THE SOUTHEAST

Höfn

Fosshótel Vatnajökull
Lindarbakki, 781 Höfn
Tel: 478 2555
Fax: 562 4001
Good facilities in a wonder-
fully convenient location for
Vatnajökull, 10 km (6 miles)
from Hofn. **$$$**

**Guesthouse
Hrollaugsstaðir**
Suðursveit, 781 Höfn

Tel: 478 1057
Fax: 478 1905
Located between Jökulsárlón
and Höfn. Sleeping-bag
accommodation available.
$–$$

Nýibær Youth Hostel
Hafnarbraut 8, 780 Höfn
Tel: 478 1736
Fax: 478 1965
An old house on two
floors near Hofn harbour.
Rooms with bunks. **$**

Smyrlabjörg Hostel
Suðursveit, 781 Hornafjörður
Tel: 478 1074
Fax: 478 2043
Old farmhouse hostel
and guesthouse near
Höfn. **$**

Kirkjubaejarklaustur

Hótel Klaustur
880 Kirkjubæjarklaustur
Tel: 487 4900

Fax: 487 4614
A comfortable all-year
hotel in the village of
Kirkjubæjarklaustur. **$$$**

SNÆFELLSNES AND THE WEST

PRICE CATEGORIES

Prices are for a double
room per night in high
season. Rates can be 30
percent lower Sept–Apr.
$$$$ Over ISK 16,000
$$$ ISK 11,000–16,000
$$ ISK 7,000–10,000
$ Under ISK 7,000

Arnastapi

Guesthouse Snjófell
Arnarstapi, 356 Snæfellsbær
Tel: 435 6783
www.snjofell.is
A value-for-money
guesthouse with good
cooking facilities for
guests. Tours onto

Snæfellsjökull glacier leave
from here. **$**

Borgarnes

Hraunsnef
Bifröst 311 Borgarfjördur
Tel: 435 0111
Located just off Route 1, 3
km (2 miles) north of

Borgarnes. A busy and pleasant summer-only guesthouse. **$**

Hamar Youth Hostel
310 Borgarnes
Tel: 437 1663
Set in a beautiful farmhouse at the golf club northeast of Borgarnes, with views over nearby Borgarfjörður and the Skarðsheiði mountains. **$**

Buðir

Hótel Buðir
Buðir
Tel: 435 6700
Destroyed by fire in 2001, the hotel was rebuilt a couple of years later and

offers stylish, well-appointed accommodation – and a fine restaurant. **$$$$**

Reykholt

Fosshótel Reykholt
320 Reykholt
Tel: 435 1260
Fax: 562 4001
A former boarding school converted into a hotel with its own restaurant. **$$**

Stykkisholmur

Hótel Stykkishólmur
Borgarbraut 12, 340 Stykkishólmur
Tel: 430 2100
Comfortable hotel with

tremendous views over the pretty town of Stykkishólmur. **$$$**

Hótel Breiðafjörður
Aðalgötu 8, Stykkishólmur
Tel: 433 2200
E-mail: hotelbreidafjordur@prinsvaliant.is

A friendly hotel located in the town centre, close to the harbour. **$$**

Sjónarhóll Hostel
Höfðagata 1, 340 Stykkishólmur
Tel: 438 1417
Large, comfortable hostel in the old town. **$**

THE WEST FJORDS

Breiðavík

Gistiheimilit Breiðavík
Breiðavík
Tel: 456 1575
www.breidavik.net
Cosy guesthouse in Iceland's most westerly village, with sweeping views over Breiðavík bay. Handy for the Látrabjarg bird cliffs. **$$**

Djúpavík

Hótel Djúpavík
Djúpavík, 522 Árneshreppur
Tel: 451 4037
Fax: 451 4035
In the remote village of Djúpavík, this former hostel for women workers (Djúpavík was once a fish-processing centre) has

been renovated and is now a comfortable hotel. **$$**

Hólmavík

Gistiheimilid
Borgarbraut 4, Hólmavík
Tel: 451 3136
Fax: 451 3413
Guesthouse with self-catering and sleeping-bag accommodation available. Wonderful views. **$**

Isafjörður

Hótel Ísafjörður
Silfurtorg 2, 400 Ísafjörður
Tel: 456 4111
Fax: 456 4767
E-mail: info@hotelisafjordur.is
A rather characterless hotel in the middle of town. Also runs a cheaper summer

hotel, Torfnes, in the boarding school at the western end of town. **$$–$$$**

Guesthouse Áslaugar
Austurvegi 7, 400 Ísafjörður
Tel: 456 3868
Fax: 456 4075
E-mail: gistias@snerpa.is
A guesthouse/homestay in the middle of the old town, next to the indoor swimming pool. Also has sleeping-bag accommodation. **$**

Reykjanes

Hótel Reykjanes
Tel: 456 4844
Fax: 456 4845
www.mes.is
Spectacular views across the fjord in a fully equipped

Reykjavík

hotel; swimming pool, sauna and steam baths fed by hot spring waters. **$$**

Flókalundur

Hótel Flókalundur
Flókalundur, Vatnsfjörður
Tel: 456 2011
Fax: 456 2050
Close to Brjánslækur (ferry to Stykkishólmur), with a good restaurant and rooms with facilities. **$$$**

HUNAFLOI AND SKAGAFJORÐUR

Blönduós

Geitaskarð Farm
Langadal, 541 Blönduós
Tel: 452 4341
Fax: 452 4301
Farmstay just outside Blönduós, near the ring road. **$–$$**

Hofsos

Sunnuberg Guesthouse
Suðurbraut 8, 565 Hofsós

Tel: 453 7310
Offers basic rooms, some of which are en-suite. **$–$$**

Hvammstangi

Ósar Youth Hostel
Vatnsnesi, 531 Hvammstangi
Tel/fax: 451 2678
Farmhouse hostel located in a peaceful spot by the sea; good for bird life. **$**

Sauðarkrókur

Hólar i Hjaltadalur
Hólar i Hjaltadalur, 551 Sauðárkrókur
Tel: 455 6333
Cabins and rooms are available during the summer. **$–$$**

Siglufjörður

Hótel Lækur (Hvanneyri)
Aðalgata 10,

Reykjavík

Siglufjörður
Tel: 467 1506
Basic guesthouse. Rooms with shared facilities. **$**

AKUREYRI AND SURROUNDINGS (INCLUDING GRÍMSEY)

Akureyri

Hótel Akureyri
Hafnarstræti 67, 600 Akureyri
Tel: 462 5600
Fax: 462 5601
In a quiet spot just outside the town centre, with views out to the fjord. $$$$

Hótel Kea
Hafnarstræti 83–85, 600 Akureyri
Tel: 460 2000
Fax: 460 2060
E-mail: kea@hotelkea.is
www.hotelkea.is
A very reliable hotel in the centre of town. Shares restaurant and reception with the Hótel Harpa. $$$$

Guesthouse Gula Villan
Brekkugata 8, 600 Akureyri
Tel: 461 2860
Fax: 461 3040
Comfortable guesthouse

in the town centre; also has sleeping bag accommodation. $–$$

Guesthouse Sólgarðar
Brekkugata 6, 600 Akureyri
Tel/fax: 461 1133.
Small but comfortable guesthouse in the town centre, which also has sleeping bag accommodation. $–$$

Akureyri Youth Hostel
Stórholt 1, 603 Akureyri
Tel: 462 3657
Fax: 462 5037
Busy hostel, a fair distance from the centre of town. It's advisable to book ahead in summer. $

Hrísey

Guesthouse Brekka
Brekkugata 5, 630 Hrísey

Tel: 466 1751
Fax: 466 3051
E-mail: brekkahrisey@isl.is
Comfortable but small guesthouse with restaurant. $–$$

Dalvík

Sóley
Skíðabraut, 620 Dalvík
Tel: 466 3395
Rooms with or without bathroom in a modern block painted bright yellow. $$

Syðri-Hagi Farm
Árskógsströnd, 621 Dalvík
Tel: 466 1961
Fax: 466 1903
Farm accommodation near the ferry to Hrísey. Wonderful views over the fjord. $–$$

Grímsey

Guesthouse Básar
Tel: 467 3103
Next to the airstrip, with standard rooms and sleeping-bag accommodation.
$

Gullsól Guesthouse
Tel: 467 3190
Another simple guesthouse on Grímsey, well located by the harbour.
$

LAKE MÝVATN AND THE NORTHEAST

Reykjahlíð / Mývatn

Hótel Reynihlíð
Reynihlíð, 660 Reykjahlíð
Tel: 464 4170
Fax: 464 4371
This established hotel forms the hub of most activities in the area. Also has sleeping bag accommodation. Essential to book ahead – it gets very busy in high season. $$$

Eldá
Halluhraun 15, 660 Mývatn
Tel: 464 4220
This guesthouse operates at three more locations around Reykjahlíð with a choice of comfortable rooms. $$

Skútustaðir Farm
Mývatnssveit, 660 Reykjahlíð
Tel: 464 4212,
Fax: 464 4322
Slightly away from the crowds. $$

PRICE CATEGORIES

Prices are for a double room per night in high season. Rates can be 30 percent lower Sept–Apr.
$$$$ Over ISK 16,000
$$$ ISK 11,000–16,000
$$ ISK 7,000–11,000
$ Under ISK 7,000

Hlíð
Hraunbrun, Kytrur, 660 Reykjahlíð
Tel: 464 4103
Fax: 464 4305
A busy centre with camping, self-catering huts and sleeping-bag facilities. $–$$

Bjarg
Tel: 464 4240
Camp site and rooms with shared facilities beside the lake. $

Fosshóll / Laugar

Fosshótel Laugar
650 Laugar
Tel: 464 6300
Fax: 562 4001
An old boarding school, well located for exploring the area between Mývatn and Akureyri. Summer only. $$–$$$

Fosshóll Farm Hostel
Bárðardal, 645 Fosshóll
Tel: 464 3108
Fax: 464 3318
In a beautiful setting right next to the Goðafoss falls between Akureyri and Mývatn. Also has camping facilities. $

Húsavík

Fosshótel Húsavík
Ketilsbraut 22, 640 Húsavík

Tel: 464 1220
Fax: 464 2161
Open all year, this friendly hotel has a good restaurant and is centrally located. $$$

Guesthouse Árból
Ásgarðsvegur 2,
640 Húsavík
Tel: 464 2220
Fax: 464 1463
A comfortable old guesthouse in the middle of town. $$

Höll Farm
671 Kópasker
Tel: 465 2270
Fax: 465 2353
Ideally located for visiting Jökulsárgljúfur National Park. $–$$

Þinghúsið Hraunbæ
V. Laxa í Aðaldal, 641 Húsavík.

Tel: 464 3695
Fax: 464 3595
Renovated old community house, which makes a good base. $–$$

Víkingavatn Farm
Kelduhverfi, 671 Kópasker
Tel: 465 2233
Fax: 465 2233
This farm offers a selection of rooms plus sleeping-bag accommodation.
$–$$

THE EAST FJORDS

Borgarfjörður-Eystri

Guesthouse Borg
720 Borgarfjörður-Eystri
Tel: 472 9870
An old building which has
been tastefully renovated;
excellent walks are
possible nearby. **$**

Breiðdalsvík

Hótel Bláfell
Sólvöllur 5, 760 Breiðdalsvík
Tel: 475 6770
Fax: 475 6668
A well-priced and
comfortable hotel, which
also offers sleeping-bag
accommodation – cheaper
than the price of a
standard room. **$–$$**

Djúpivogur

Hótel Framtíð
Vogaland 4, 765 Djúpivogur
Tel: 478 8887
Fax: 478 8187
A well located and
comfortable hotel, with
sleeping-bag accom-
modation available. Camping

is also available nearby. The
hotel organises boat trips to
the offshore island of Papey
and arranges bike hire and
sea-angling trips. **$$–$$$**
Berunes Youth Hostel
Berunes 1, 765 Djúpivogur
Tel/fax: 478 8988
A very comfortable but
small hostel in a renovated
old farmhouse. **$**

Egilsstaðir

Valaskjálf
Skágarlönd 3, 700 Egilsstaðir
Tel: 470 5050
In the middle of town, with
restaurant/bar and
solarium. **$$$**
Egilsstaðir Guesthouse
700 Egilsstaðir
Tel: 471 1114
Fax: 471 1266
Pleasant accommodation
situated on the shores of
Lake Lagarfljót. **$**
Húsum Farm
Ferðaþjónustan Húsum,
701 Egilsstaðir
Tel: 471 2003
Fax: 471 2004
A small farm guesthouse

with great character and
friendly service. **$**

Reyðarfjörður

Fjarðahótel
Búðareyri 6, 730 Reyðarfjörður
Tel: 474 1600
Fax: 474 1601
A modern, comfortable
hotel next to the post
office on the main road
in Reyðarfjörður. **$$**

Seyðisfjörður

Hafaldan Hostel
Ranargata 9, 710 Seyðisfjörður
Tel: 472 1410
Fax: 472 1610
One of the best hostels
in Iceland, brimming with
character. **$**

Stafafell

Stafafell Hostel
Lón, 781 Höfn
Tel: 478 1717
Fax: 478 1601
Over a century old, the
Stafafell has been restored
and refurbished as a basic

hostel. An excellent base
for treks to Lónsöræfi and
Geithellnadalur. Camping
also available. **$**

Mountain Hut

Snæfell Hut
Ferðafélag Fljótsdalshéraðs
(Fljótsdalur touring club) 700
Egilsstaðir
Tel: 853 9098 (summer),
471 1433 (winter)
A comfortable mountain
hut and adjacent camp site
with a full-time warden in
summer, hot showers and
WC. A good base for walks
in the Snæfell area. The
same organisation runs
the Geldingafell and
Egilssel huts on the
Vatnajökull east traverse
route. **$**

THE INTERIOR

The Askja route

Herðubreiðarlindir Hut
Touring Club of Akureyri,
P.O. Box 48, 602 Akureyri
Tel: 462 2720
Fax: 462 7240
An old but comfortable hut,
with room for 30 people. **$**
Kverkfjöll Hut
Ferðafélag Fljótsdalshéraðs
(Fljótsdalur touring club), 700
Egilsstaðir
Tel: 853 9098 (summer),
471 1433 (winter)
A comfortable mountain hut
with a full-time warden in
summer, hot showers and
WC. Ideal base for walks in
the Kverkfjöll area. **$**

The Kjölur route

Hveravellir Hut
Ferðafélag Íslands, Mörkinn 6,
108 Reykjavík
Tel: 568 2533
Fax: 568 2535
E-mail: fi@fi.is

A very busy hut, which is
used by tour groups passing
over the Kjölur route. Club
members have priority. **$**

Landmannalaugar

Hólaskjól Hut
Skaftárhreppur (community office),
Kirkjubæjarklaustur
Tel: 487 4840
Fax: 487 4842
Mountain hut near Eldgjá
on Fjallabaksleið. Basic but
comfortable and not usually
busy. Great walking and
cycling nearby. **$**
Landmannalaugar Hut
Ferðafélag Íslands, Mörkinn 6,
108 Reykjavík
Tel: 568 2533
Fax: 568 2535
E-mail: fi@fi.is
A crowded hut in summer,
with bunkbeds plus a busy
camp site. A good starting
point for treks in the area
and ties in with other huts
on the Laugavegur trail. Club

members have priority. **$**
Sveinstindur Hut
Útivist, Hallveigarstíg 1,
101 Reykjavík
Tel: 562 1000
www.utivist.is
Basic but new hut in a
traditional design, east of
Landmannalaugar. Makes an
excellent base for walks off
the beaten track. **$**

Sprengisandur

Guesthouse Hrauneyjar
Sprengisandi, 851 Hella
Tel: 487 7782
www.hrauneyjar.is
On the Sprengisandur
route, with basic rooms.
Attached service station
and camp site. **$**
Guesthouse Versalir
Sprengisandi, 851 Hella
Tel: 852 2601/487 5078
Basic rooms and cabins on
the Sprengisandur route. A
petrol pump and restaurant
are also available here. **$**

Laugafell Hut

Touring Club of Akureyri
P.O. Box 48, 602 Akureyri
Tel: 462 2720
Fax: 462 7240
Heated hut north of
Hofsjökull ice field.
Accommodates 15. **$**
Nýidalur Huts
Ferðafélag Íslands, Mörkinn 6,
108 Reykjavík
Tel: 568 2533
Fax: 568 2535
E-mail: fi@fi.is
A good base for walks
and cycling in a desolate
location on the Sprengis-
andur route. Camping
available. Room for 120
people. **$**

TRANSPORT

ACCOMMODATION

ACTIVITIES

A – Z

LANGUAGE

A CTIVITIES

THE ARTS, NIGHTLIFE, FESTIVALS, SHOPPING, OUTDOOR ACTIVITIES AND CHILDREN

THE ARTS

Sources of Information

That a country with a population of 310,000 has three professional theatre companies, a thriving film industry, a national ballet, opera and symphony orchestra and hosts an international arts festival every other year is itself remarkable. Add to this the two-dozen or so museums and galleries in Reykjavík and over 50 others throughout the rest of the country, internationally acclaimed opera singers, a jazz band that has made it into the UK charts, world-famous rock bands and a world-class female pop star – can anywhere else match Iceland for variety and intensity of cultural activity in such a small community?

Any tourist information office should have copious amounts of information about the cultural events taking place at any given time. The tourist brochure *What's On in Reykjavík* has extensive cultural listings. Over and above that they are invaluable sources of information for travellers, with maps, bus schedules, descriptions of walking tours and more. These are available just about anywhere tourists go and are free of charge.

Music

Iceland is a nation of music lovers, as witnessed by the vast number of concert recitals given over the course of a year and by the numerous choirs active in the country over the winter months.

The Iceland Symphony Orchestra, which has gained widespread

international acclaim, holds concerts during the winter only. Not to worry: a vibrant music scene kicks in at the beginning of the summer, both in and outside of Reykjavík. Below is a listing of the main musical events and venues, year-round. Please note that cafés and pubs often have live music – check the listings at the back of *Morgunblaðið* or *What's On in Reykjavík* for more details.

Venues in Reykjavík

Iceland Symphony Orchestra, University Concert Hall, Hagatorg (opposite Hótel Saga), tel: 562 2255, e-mail: sinfonia@sinfonia.is, www.sinfonia.is. Weekly concerts in winter with international guest artists.

Iðnó,
Vonastræti 3, tel: 530 3030. This renovated theatre hosts various types of concerts during the summer, anything from jazz to piano and theatre music recitals.

Jazz at Jómfrúin,
Lækjargata 4, tel: 551 0100. This restaurant serves excellent Danish-style open sandwiches and has jazz recitals on Saturdays from 4–6pm during the summer.

Kaffileikhúsið
(The Café Theatre), Vesturgata 3 (rear), tel: 551 9055. This charming old building is a unique venue for performances of various kinds. There is a summer concert series: jazz music, classical and jazz vocalists and more.

Nordic House,
Hringbraut (by the university campus), tel: 551 7030, www.nordice.is. Hosts concert recitals year-round.

Sigurjón Ólafsson Museum,
Laugarnestanga, tel: 553 2906,

fax: 581 4553, www.lso.is. A yearly concert series with recitals every Tuesday evening in summer.

Summer Nights at the Organ, Hallgrímskirkja church. A group of music lovers have formed an association that plans Sunday concerts all year in Hallgrímskirkja church. In summer these feature organ music.

Venues outside Reykjavík

Contact the Tourist Information Centre in Reykjavík for information on dates and bookings for the following events:

Bright Summer Nights, Hveragerði. A three-day concert series, held early each summer, featuring both Icelandic and foreign works.

Kirkjubæjarklaustur Chamber Music Festival, Kirkjubæjarklaustur. This yearly festival takes place for one weekend each August, in beautiful surroundings, with national and international musicians.

North Iceland Concert Series, various churches in northern Iceland. This takes place mostly in and around Akureyri and often features church music.

Reykholt Festival, Reykholt. A three-day concert festival held every summer, with the emphasis firmly on premiering contemporary Icelandic works.

Skálholt Festival, Skálholt Church. The church at this ancient bishopric in the southwest hosts a yearly concert series on weekends in July and August. The focus tends to be on baroque music with musicians from around the world. Admission to all events is free.

Stykkishólmur Concert Series, Stykkishólmur church. A series of six concerts that are held in this modern church over the summer.

Theatre, Ballet and Opera

For information on current productions contact the Tourist Information Centre in Reykjavík, and check the back pages of daily *Morgunblaðið*, or *What's On in Reykjavík*.

Iceland offers up exceptional theatre with actors and directors of international calibre. All productions at the main professional theatres are in Icelandic, but often they are stagings of famous works with which tourists will be familiar.

Opera and dance, of course, transcend the language barrier. The Icelandic Opera is a world-class professional company, featuring top performers. The Icelandic Dance Company has in the past few years focused exclusively on modern dance. It is made up of both Icelandic and international dancers and has toured extensively abroad.

Venues in Reykjavík

Reykjavík City Theatre (Reykjavík Theatre Co.), Listabraut 3, tel: 568 5500, fax: 568 0383, e-mail: midasala@borgarleikhus.is, www.borgarleikhus.is
The Icelandic Opera, P.O. Box 1416, Reykjavík, tel: 511 6400, e-mail: opera@opera.is, www.opera.is
Kaffileikhúsið, Vesturgata 3 (rear), tel: 551 9055. Regular and diverse theatre in a café setting. Dinner can usually be had before the show.
Light Nights, Iðnó, Vonarstræti 3 (by the lake in the city centre), tel: 551 9181, e-mail: info@lightnights.com, www.lightnights.com. A unique theatrical presentation in English of scenes from Iceland's history and literature. Performing early July to the end of August; check local press or the tourist office for days. A synopsis of the show is available at the door in several languages.
The Icelandic Dance Company, National Theatre, Hverfisgata 19,

tel: 588 0900, fax: 588 0910, e-mail: id@id.is, www.id.is
National Theatre of Iceland, Lindargata 7, Reykjavík, tel: 585 1200, fax: 585 1201, e-mail: leikhusid@leikhusid.is, www.leikhusid.is

Venues outside Reykjavík

Venues for cultural events outside the capital include:
Akureyri Theatre Company, Hafnarstræti 57, Akureyri, tel: 460 0200, e-mail: midasala@leikfelag.is, www.leikfelag.is. Open Sept–June.
Hafnarfjarðarleikhúsið, Strandgata 50, Hafnarfjörður, tel: 555 2222, fax: 555 0553, e-mail: theater@vortex.is, www.hhh.is

NIGHTLIFE

Since the early 1990s Reykjavík at night has been transformed from a sleepy provincial city to one of the hottest venues in Europe, with as lively a nightlife as you will find anywhere. Many locales which masquerade as perfectly civilised cafés during the day transform into rip-roaring bar rooms in the evening. But most places don't even start getting lively until after 11pm. If you are intent on serious drinking come prepared – a half litre of draught beer costs around ISK 600–700 in most places.

In most cafés and night spots, the clientele is young and dress is casual. For upmarket Reykjavík establishments you have to dress smartly, as for night clubs.

Drinking

Iceland has strict rules about buying and drinking alcohol. You have to be at least 20 years old to buy alcohol and you may be asked to show proof of your age. Visitors wanting a regular tipple should bring in their full duty-free allowance, because all alcoholic drinks are expensive in Iceland.

Wines, spirits and beers over 2.25 percent alcohol are only sold at

state-controlled outlets, ÁTVR shops. Light beer can be bought in general supermarkets.

Pubs, Bars and Cafés

Opening hours were extended in 2000, with pub/club owners permitted to keep their places open pretty much as long as they liked. This was partly to help alleviate the congestion on the streets that took place when the legal closing hour was 3am. These days Reykjavík's weekend nightlife doesn't really get going until after 1am. Most pubs and bars are open Sun–Thur 6pm–1am and Fri–Sat 6pm–5am, or even later.

For individual listings, *see Places* chapters (Reykjavík, page 161, and Akureyri, page 247).

FESTIVALS

Diary of Events

February
Þorrablót: Although there is no fixed day for Þorrablót, most communities celebrate it in February. Essentially an occasion to eat, drink and be merry, Þorrablot has its roots in a long-forgotten pagan ritual. A feast of Icelandic delicacies, including the dreaded rotten shark *(hákarl)* and singed sheep's heads, is washed down with Brennivin (the local caraway-seed-flavoured spirit) and plenty of song and dance. If you are in Iceland in February it is well worth enquiring if there is a Þorrablót scheduled. Many are private affairs but those in the smaller villages are open to all, though must usually be booked in advance.
Sunshine Coffee: For many of the remote fishing villages situated in the steepsided West Fjords, real winter starts when the sun ceases to rise above the mountains and even in fine weather the village is in perpetual shadow. The sun is often absent for several months but when its first rays hit the village again, everyone celebrates with sunshine coffee.

Cinema

Icelanders are avid cinema-goers and Reykjavík has an amazing number of screens considering its small size. Most films are from the US though a certain number of Icelandic and European films are also shown. All films are advertised in the daily press and shown with the original soundtrack,

sub-titled in Icelandic. There is a large film festival in Reykjavík every two years, as well as the occasional smaller festival of alternative or artistic films. Check *What's On* for details. Other towns throughout Iceland have cinemas and smaller villages show films once or twice a week.

Cultural Festivals

Contact the Tourist Information Centre in Reykjavík *(see page 341)* for details on the following events:

Dark Music Days: Every other year in January. A festival organised by the Composers' Society, with emphasis on new Icelandic music.

Reykjavík Jazz Festival: An annual event in late summer or early autumn, with acclaimed international jazz performers; tel: 862 1402, fax: 843 6300, e-mail: festival@reykjavikjazz.com, www.reykjavikjazz.com.

Reykjavík Arts Festival: First held in 1970, this takes place every other year for two weeks in May or June. It features music, theatre, visual arts, opera and ballet, and attracts national and international artists; tel: 561 2444, e-mail: artfest@artfest.is, www.artfest.is

Festival of Church Arts: Held biannually in Reykjavík, around Pentecost and in Akureyri in early summer. The main emphasis is on music, though visual art, dance and theatre also feature.

International Film Festival: Held every other October. A range of mainstream and experimental works – a must for film buffs.

Reykjavík Cathedral Music Days: An annual November festival featuring organ and choral music, with a guest composer or organist.

Reykjavík Cultural Night: Held on a Saturday in late August. The city centre turns into a cultural mecca, with every venue utilised. Musical events are staged in shops, poetry readings in cafés, street theatre flourishes and self-appointed performers set up wherever they can. The night culminates with a fireworks display; pubs and cafés are open extra late and are packed until the small hours.

March

Bolludagur, Sprengidagur and Öskudagur: The Monday before Shrove Tuesday everyone bakes *bollur*, a kind of pastry eclair filled with cream, hence the name Bolludagur. Shrove Tuesday is called Sprengidagur (Explosion Day) and traditionally a hearty meal of salted lamb and split peas is served. On Ash Wednesday, or Öskudagur, children collect money for sweets and delight in pinning small cloth bags – in the old days, they used to contain ashes – to the backs of unwary strangers.

April

First Day of Summer: In a country where winter seems to drag on interminably, celebrating the first day of summer in April (usually on the third Thursday in the month) seems a little premature. Even so, there are big festivities in Reykjavík.

June

Sjómannadagur (Seafarer's Day): The first Sunday in June is the greatest celebration of the year in many fishing villages. Often a holiday for the whole village and always for seamen, there are rowing and swimming races and a chance for the young and not so young to test their skill and strength in contests from tugs of war to sea rescue. A fun-filled and lighthearted occasion with lots going on.

Independence Day: Iceland's national day is celebrated on 17 June, the day in 1944 when the country declared full independence from Denmark and also the birthday of Jón Sigurðsson who contributed more than any other Icelander to the struggle. The greatest celebrations are in Reykjavík, with parades, street theatre and music, side shows and dancing, but the day is a festive occasion throughout the country.

August

Verslunarmannahelgi: The first weekend in August is a long weekend all over Iceland with everything shut on the Monday. Icelanders by the thousands take to their cars and head out of town to camp in the wilds or join in one of the organised events that are held throughout the country. These range from teetotal family festivities to loud rock festivals. Most visitors will probably want to avoid popular destinations for Icelanders at this time. On the same weekend, Heimaey in the Vestmannaeyjar (Westmann Islands), celebrates its own þjóðhátíð festival commemorating the day in 1874 when Iceland got its constitution. Bad weather prevented the islanders from reaching the mainland so they celebrated independently and have done so ever since. The occasion draws Icelanders from all corners of the country to a huge outdoor camp for a weekend of music, song and dance and a fair amount of drinking.

September

Réttir: During the month of September farmers set off on horseback to round up their sheep, who have grazed freely in the highlands over the summer. When the sheep are brought down to the lowlands they are herded into pens and sorted. The end of this major event in the farming calendar is celebrated with singing, dancing and general festivities. If you are in Iceland around this time it is well worth checking out where Réttir is scheduled to take place. The Tourist Information Centre in Reykjavík will be able to assist.

December

Christmas and **New Year's Eve**: Celebrations begin on 24 December when many people attend mass before going home to a festive dinner, gifts and dancing around the Christmas tree. New Year's Eve's celebrations consist of huge bonfires and an explosion of fireworks at midnight.

SHOPPING

In the past Iceland tended to attract tourists for whom shopping was not on the travel agenda, mostly because the main attraction was the landscape, but also because prices were considered ridiculously high. At best foreign visitors might purchase some woollen goods. But things are changing. Today Reykjavík is actively promoted as an up-market and accessible shopping option, and special shopping trips to Reykjavík arranged for foreign residents have proved popular.

Icelandic taxes remain extremely high – although note that most shops offer a Tax Refund cheque *(see panel, page 331)*, which reduces the price by 15 percent. However, Reykjavík is being marketed at those who believe in paying for style and quality. Geographically, the capital is also very shopper-friendly, with the stores concentrated in a relatively small area.

What to Buy

Woollen Goods

The Icelandic sheep is an almost pure breed descended from the animals brought over by the first settlers. Its fleece is of an exceptional quality and produces a wool that is durable and

How to Pay

Most shops accept payment by credit card or travellers' cheques. Some offer discounts for cash and it is always worth asking.

naturally water resistant, yet soft and warm. It is this wool that is used to make the handknitted sweaters with traditional patterns around the yoke.

A simple cottage industry has grown to create one of the country's major agricultural exports, and though the traditional sweaters are still handknitted, the bulk of woollen goods are now machine-made. For a handknitted sweater expect to pay at least ISK 8,500; however, if you buy the wool, circular needles and pattern (available in several foreign languages) you can knit yourself one for under ISK 4,500.

For handknitted sweaters it is worth trying some of the farms in the Icelandic Farm Holidays network. Sweaters on sale here are usually cheaper than those in the shops and they will be fully homemade and handknitted.

Sheepskin goods

These are expensive but the quality is excellent. Hats, slippers and gloves sell for approximately ISK 2,500–5,000.

Books

There are many fine books on Iceland aimed at the visitor and almost all are available in English. Many can be bought abroad through tour operators who also run a book and map service (see Tour Operators, page 342). Books published outside Iceland will be much cheaper to buy abroad.

Fine Art Cards

Some very attractive yet inexpensive cards depicting the works of some of Iceland's finest painters, such as Johannes Kjarval and Ásgrímur Jónsson, are available at the National Gallery in Reykjavík and at bookshops.

Ceramics

If the rather garish lava ceramics are not to your taste, shop around. Pottery in Iceland tends to be artistic

rather than functional, so expect to pay accordingly. There are some fine potters producing unusual pieces. Often they will sell their own work in their studio, or will be members of an artisans' co-operative (see panel, page 332, for details).

Food

If you can protect your luggage against the smell, pack some dried fish. It weighs nothing, keeps for ever and may amuse your friends. Eat it with lashings of butter. Smoked trout and salmon also keep quite well. If you like skyr, take some home – you can make your own culture in the same way as yoghurt and it freezes well. A wide range of Icelandic foods is sold at the duty free shop at Keflavík Airport for departing passengers.

Music

Two CDs of Icelandic folk songs in particular can be recommended: Íslensk alþýðulög – Icelandic Folk Songs and Vikivaki – Songs from the Saga Island. There are also fine

classical recordings by the Iceland Symphony Orchestra, particularly of works by late composer Jón Leifs (try to listen before buying – his music is intense and not for everyone), as well as by other Icelandic classical musicians. Look out for CDs by Björk, Gling Gló, Múm (electronica), Sigur Ros (indie) and Leaves (guitar).

Where to Shop

There are two main shopping areas in Reykjavík: in the centre of the city, most of the tourist shops are in and around Hafnarstræti and Austurstræti, though Laugavegur, leading out of the centre, is home to the majority of the fashion shops.

The other main shopping area, which houses most of the usual European high-street chain stores, is the Kringlan mall – located outside the city centre but easily reached by bus. The woollen goods and souvenir shop Íslandia is located in the Kringlan mall, as is the Nýkaup supermarket, which offers the most extensive selection of food products in Iceland. Kringlan is also home to a wide variety of attractive boutiques.

Shops in Reykjavík

Try the following for a wide variety of gifts, woollen goods, ceramics, crafts and jewellery:
Íslandia, Kringlan shopping mall.
Rammagerðin, Hafnarstræti 19.
Ullarhúsið, Aðalstræti 4.
Thorvaldsen's Basar, Austurstræti 4. (All sales proceeds donated to charity.)
Víkurprjón, Hafnarstræti 1–3.
There are also a number of good gift and craft shops situated on

Tax-free Shopping

All non-residents (other than Icelandic citizens) are entitled to a VAT refund on goods purchased in Iceland if their value exceeds ISK 4,000 in one shop. You pay the full amount, VAT included, in the shop. Ask for your VAT-refund and the shop assistant will fill out a special "Global Refund Cheque", which you then take to the tax refund desk at the airport. Although the Global Refund is by far the most common system in Iceland, there are other refund systems which may have other rebate procedures – ask at the shop where you buy the goods. The refund (less about 5 percent handling charge) will amount to approximately 15 percent of the purchase price.

As you leave Iceland, show the customs officers the goods you

have purchased and ask for your refund cheque to be stamped. Woollen goods do not need to be shown. Global Refund cheques can be cashed in at your departure point from Iceland or at any Global Refund centre world-wide. You can also mail cheques which have been stamped by customs to the Global Refund office and they will credit any account you specify. If you are leaving Iceland from Keflavík Airport and your refund amount is less than ISK 4,000 you need only show your goods at the airport bank where you cash your cheque.

For more information on refunds see the Shopping in Iceland brochure that is available in most shops, free of charge; www.icelandrefund.is; www.globalrefund.com

Commercial Galleries in Reykjavík

The following galleries mostly feature sales exhibitions:

Gallerí Fold, Rauðarástígur 14, tel: 551 0400; e-mail: fold@myndlist.is Diverse selection of paintings and crafts. Mon–Fri 10am–6pm, Sat 10am–4pm, Sun 2pm–5pm (closed Sun in July and Aug). Also in Kringlan mall, tel: 568 0400. Open in mall hours.

Gallerí Jens, Kringlan Mall, tel: 568 6730. Jewellery designed and crafted by Icelandic artists, the unique styling drawn from the Icelandic landscape. Open in mall hours.

Kirsuberjatréð, Vesturgata 4, tel: 562 8990. Unique and beautiful crafts made from such unconventional materials as fish skin and pig's bladders. Mon–Fri

noon–6pm, Sat 11am–5pm.

Kogga, Vesturgata 5, tel: 552 6036. Ceramics by one of the country's foremost potters. Mon–Fri 9am–6pm, Sat 10am–2pm.

Listvinahús, Skólavörðustígur 41–43, tel: 551 2850. Ceramics, unique in texture and colour; nice designs, woollens. Mon–Fri 9am–6pm, weekends 10am–4pm.

Snegla, Grettisgata 7, Reykjavík; tel: 562 0426. Run by a collective; lovely crafts, paintings and objets d'art. Mon–Fri noon–6pm, Sat 11am–3pm.

Textilkjallarinn, Lokastígur 28, tel: 551 3584. Hand-printed and painted textiles. Bedcovers, sheets, scarves and more, made of cotton, satin silk and wool. Mon–Fri noon–6pm, Sat 10am–noon, or by arrangement.

Skólavörðustígur, near Hallgrímskirkja church.

For books try:
Eymundsson, Austurstræti 18.
Mál og Menning, Laugavegur 18.

For photographic equipment:
Hans Petersen, Bankastræti 4, Laugavegur 82, and Kringlan mall.

Opening Hours

Shopping hours vary in Iceland – some smaller shops in the centre of Reykjavík may open only for a few hours on Saturdays, for example, or not open at all. By contrast some shops stay open late every day of the week, particularly book and record stores. Most shops are open Mon–Thur 9am–6pm, Fri 9am–7pm and Sat 10am–4pm.

Shops in the Kringlan mall are open Mon–Wed 10am–6.30pm, Thur 10am–9pm, Fri 10am–7pm and Sat 10am–6pm. Some shops are open 1–5pm on Sundays, particularly in winter.

Branches of the two main supermarket chains, Hagkaup and Nóatún, stay open until 8pm and 9pm, respectively. The 10–11 and 11–11 supermarket chains stay open until 11pm, as their names imply. Many corner shops, selling sweets and basic groceries, stay open until 10pm or later. In the countryside, some supermarkets in the Kaupfélag (Co-op) chain, notably those attached to petrol stations, may stay open until 8 or 10pm. In the evenings basic groceries, snacks and confectionery are sold at a *sjoppa* (kiosk).

OUTDOOR ACTIVITIES

Hiking

For walking off the beaten track and variety of scenery Iceland is unsurpassed. Hiking in Iceland is very popular with Icelanders and foreigners alike and both facilities and variety of hiking trails have improved tremendously since the early 1990s.

The most popular marked long-distance trail runs from Landmannalaugar south to the coast at Skógar and takes four to five days. Known to the locals as "Laugavegur", which is also the name of Reykjavík's main shopping street, the route is scenically stunning but well trodden, though venture off the track and you are unlikely to encounter another soul. There are huts along the way, owned by Ferðafélag Íslands and Útivist, from whom a key can be

obtained in Reykjavík to gain entry, but it is advisable to take a tent as well in case the huts are full.

In the Jökulsárgljúfur National Park, a two-day walk follows the length of the spectacular gorge from Ásbyrgi to Dettifoss, with camp sites en route. Within the two other national parks of Þingvellir and Skaftafell and protected areas such as Mývatn, there are marked paths suitable for day hikes.

Another area that is attracting growing numbers of backpackers is Hornstrandir, in the extreme northwest. A series of indistinct and mostly unmarked trails link the fjords and bays of this rugged, uninhabited area. Hornstrandir is linked to Ísafjörður by a scheduled boat service.

The East Fjords district from Borgarfjörður-Eystri southwards and Lónsöraefi in the southeast both offer challenging and varied wilderness hiking.

For some the ultimate challenge is to traverse Iceland's interior, following one of the highland tracks that run north to south. In clear weather the views are stunning, but much of the route is over bare sand and stone desert with little variation in terrain or scenery. Far more interesting hiking is often to be found in the areas immediately bordering the settled districts. The Kjölur and Sprengisandur routes are tough but highly rewarding to part hike. Take a map, compass and overstock on food just in case – routes are largely unmarked and it may take you longer than expected.

Hiking Maps

National parks and some nature conservation areas produce leaflets, including maps and hiking times. These are often more accurate and up-to-date than the general map series *(see Maps, page 338)*. Maps of Hornstrandir, Landmannalaugar and Þórsmörk areas mark paths but should be used with caution – the Hornstrandir map, for example, does not mark cliff faces! Always use these maps combined with the general map series.

Bird-watching

Iceland is renowned for its birdlife and is home to some of the largest breeding colonies in the world. A variety of cliff-nesting species can be seen at Látrabjarg in the West Fjords (see page 223), and sea birds, including puffins and arctic terns, can be seen all around the island. Lake Mývatn (see page 261) is a major breeding ground for ducks, while Skaftafell (see page 200) is home to the world's largest colonies of great and artic skuas. Bird-watching tours can be arranged through agencies both in Iceland and abroad (see Tour Operators, page 341).

Horse-riding

The sturdy Icelandic horse is a pure and unique breed, descended from stock brought over by the first settlers from Norway in the 9th century. No horses have been imported for 800 years so the breed has remained pure. It has adapted to the demands of harsh weather and rough terrain and is ideally suited to local conditions.

The Icelandic horse still plays a vital role in the autumn round-up, when farmers throughout the country set off for the highlands on horseback to gather their sheep. Mostly, however,

horses are used for recreation and riding is a popular sport among Icelanders. Farms all over the country offer visitors anything from a one-hour ride to a seven-day trek. The majority of these can be booked in advance through tour operators abroad (see pages 341–2).

Prices start at ISK 3,000 for an hour's ride. On long treks food and lodging is included; price per day is ISK 12,000–15,000. Information on stables can be obtained from the Tourist Information Office, Reykjavík, or from: **Icelandic Farm Holidays**, Síðumúli 13, Reykjavík, tel: 570 2700, fax: 570 2799, e-mail: ifh@farmholidays.is, www.farmholidays.is

White-water Rafting

Rafting has steadily gained in popularity as a sport and there are now a number of tour operators offering a wide variety of such trips (see page 341). Main rafting areas include Skagafjörður in the north and the Hvitá river in the southwest.

Angling

Unlike many countries, Iceland has clean waters, and salmon runs have not been disturbed by sea fishing. Excellent fishing is therefore available but at a very high price. Permits cost ISK 7,000–24,000 per day, and sometimes even more. The other snag is that most rivers have to be booked months, if not years, in advance. For further information contact:
Angling Club of Reykjavík,

Iceland from the Air

Sightseeing flights from Reykjavik airport offer a unique view of areas such as the Tindfjallajökull and Eyjafjallajökull glaciers, Grímsey Island and Vestmannaeyjar (see Sightseeing Air Tours, page 342). Trips can be arranged through **Iceland Guest**, Austurstraeti 17, 101 Reykjavik, tel: 534 4141; e-mail: info@icelandguest.com, www.icelandguest.com

Háaleitisbraut 68, Reykjavík, tel: 568 6050, e-mail: svfr@svfr.is, www.svfr.is
National Angling Association, Hagatorg, 107 Reykjavík, tel: 553 1510, fax: 568 4363, www.angling.is. Trout fishing can often be arranged on-the-spot and at a reasonable price. Many of the farms in the Icelandic Farm Holidays booklet (see Farm Guesthouses, page 321) offer trout fishing. An open voucher system is available for some of the farms in this network.

Sea angling can be arranged from many fishing villages and coastal farms and can be combined with a boat trip to offshore islands, or whale-watching excursions. This is usually best arranged directly with hotels and farms.

Iceland's waters are disease-free, so all equipment coming into the country, including waders and boots, must be disinfected (see Entry Regulations, page 337).

Swimming

If Iceland has a favourite national sport, it has to be swimming. The country's vast geothermal resources account for the selection of great pools throughout the country: just about any place with a population over 500 will have one. These range from the ultra-modern pools in the Reykjavík area to the more primitive examples, such as the mineral-water pool at Lýsuhóll on the Snæfellsnes peninsula, complete with algae-covered bottom.

In Reykjavík, just about everyone will have their own favourite pool. The Laugardalur swimming pool is perennially popular, though many locals complain that it is too big, favouring the smaller-scale Vesturbæjarlaug in the west end of the city, or the small but modern facilities on Seltjarnarnes. Those with small children might prefer the recreation-centre-like facilities of Árbæjarlaug pool, with its hot pots, spouting fountains, water slides and reclining jacuzzi seats.

Safety for Hikers

All safety rules apply, doubly so when hiking in uninhabited areas or crossing rivers: fatal accidents are not uncommon among foreign travellers. Wherever possible seek the advice of local people at farms, mountain huts and national park wardens' offices and leave details of your intended route. Remember to inform people when you have arrived back safely.

Venturing off the beaten track is only for properly equipped hikers with considerable wilderness experience. Many of the BSÍ and other highland bus services will take hikers into remote areas and if pre-arranged, will pick up again further along the route, several days later. Obtain all you need for a trip beforehand, including sufficient food. Water is not always available, particularly in the cold desert region of the

Ódáðahraun. Even if you find water, you may have to filter it to remove the fine particles of rock in the glacial rivers. In case of problems, rescue is often difficult. Wardened huts and most vehicles have radio communications and can summon aid in an emergency.

When crossing rivers on foot face upstream and link arms with other members of the party to steady yourself, forming a wedge shape. Glacial rivers can flood after heavy rainfall or on a warm summer day. They can be very dangerous and if in doubt it is always best to wait until the flood subsides, often in only 12 hours.

Along uninhabited stretches of coastline, at regular intervals, are emergency huts for shipwrecked seamen. These huts are equipped with radios and are not for hikers' use except in a real emergency.

Whale-watching

Whale-watching has been growing steadily in popularity in Iceland in recent years, and a vast number of whale-watching tours are now offered across the country. Some tour operators even promise that you will get your money back if you don't spot a whale.

The most commonly sighted species is the minke, with killer whales, sperm whales, finbacks and humpbacks less often seen. The larger whales can usually be seen in the north, around Húsavík and in the Breidafjörður bay, while dolphins most often appear off the south coast.

The best times for whale sightings are late spring and summer and you do not always have to be on a boat to see them: sometimes just a close look out to sea will reveal a whale's back breaking the surface.

The following agents operate specialist whale-watching tours, while many other groups offer boat tours with the possibility of whale sightings:
Dolphin and Whalespotting, P.O. Box 92, 230 Keflavík, tel: 421 7777, fax: 421 3361; www.dolphin.is
Elding, Ægisgarður, 101 Reykjavík,

tel: 555 3565; www.elding.is
Gentle Giants Whalewatching, Húsavík, tel: 464 1500; www.gentlegiants.is
North Sailing Whale-Watching, Hafnarstétt 9, 640 Húsavík, tel: 464 2350, www. northsailing.is
Seatours, Smiðjustigur 3, 340 Stykkishólmur, tel: 433 2254, www.seatours.is
Sjóferðir ehf, Town Hall, 620 Dalvík, tel: 863 2555; www.simnet.is/sjoferdir
Whale Watching Centre, PO Box 409, Ægisgarður 7, 101 Reykjavík, tel: 533 2660; www.hafsulan.is

Skiing

Facilities and conditions for skiing fall far short of the Alps or North America. Snow is most consistent in the north. In the south, bad weather, even lack of snow, often closes the slopes for days on end.

Downhill Skiing

On a clear, calm weekend the whole of Reykjavík seems to head out of town and there can often be long queues for the lifts. Skiing is one of Iceland's bargains – a day ticket costs around ISK 1,500 and children pay half price. The best facilities are in Reykjavík and Akureyri but other towns also have skiing areas and shorter drag lifts.

Reykjavík

Bláfjöll, one of the main skiing areas,

is about half an hour's drive from Reykjavík. Scheduled buses depart from the BSÍ bus terminal in Reykjavík several times a day. The track to the ski slopes is open to private four-wheel-drive vehicles.

The lifts are open 10am–6pm daily and until 10pm on Tues, Wed and Thur, when the slopes are floodlit. There is one chairlift and several drag lifts and boot and ski hire is available. There is no overnight accommodation but a cafeteria serves snacks and drinks. For up-to-date information (recorded message in Icelandic) on conditions and opening times, tel: 570 7711.

Akureyri

There is more reliable snow and similar facilities at Hlíðarfjall, just above Akureyri, which has one chair lift and three drag lifts. Buses leave

the city bus terminal three times a day and the slopes are open 1–6.45pm, until 8.45pm on Tues, Wed and Thur, and 10am–5pm at weekends. There is a café and sleeping-bag accommodation. For information, tel: 562 7733.

Cross-country Skiing

Both Bláfjöll and Hlíðarfjall have marked cross-country ski trails but most people will probably want to head off on their own. This is safe in the farmed lowlands; venturing into uninhabited areas is only for the properly equipped and fit. Some tour operators offer cross-country skiing excursions (see Tour Operators, page 341, for details).

Summer Skiing

The Kerlingarfjöll Mountains, just off the Kjölur route through the central highlands, offer summer skiing. The season starts as soon as the track opens and goes on as long as the snow lasts (mid-June to late-Aug). There are drag lifts, a campsite and sleeping-bag accommodation. Buses to Kerlingarfjöll are operated through BSÍ (see page 316), who have up-to-date information on departures.

Golf

With over 50 courses, golf is thriving in Iceland. Most of these have just nine holes, however there are 18-hole courses at: Reykjavík, Hafnarfjörður, Garðabær, Hella, Keflavík, Vestmannaeyjar and Akureyri. For further information contact: **Golf Federation of Iceland/ Golfsamband Íslands**, Engjavegi 6, Reykjavík, tel: 514 4050, fax: 514 4051, www.golf.is

The major golfing event in Iceland is the Arctic Open, which takes place in June each year and is open to professional and amateur golfers alike. Hosts to the event are the **Akureyri Golf Club**, P.O. Box 896, 602 Akureyri, tel: 462 2974. A complete package including flights, accommodation and admission charges can be booked through tour operators abroad.

Skidooing

Skidooing (snowcatting) is an exhilarating sport that has to be experienced. An essential means of communication on remote farms in winter, snowcats are increasingly used for recreation.

In summer, trips run daily from Höfn to the Vatnajökull icecap, from where you can join a one- or two-hour guided excursion by skidoo. A full-day trip is also possible but must be booked in advance through **Jöklaferðir** Glacier Tours, 780 Hornafjörður, tel: 478 1000, fax: 478 1901, e-mail:

vatnajokull@vatnajokull.com,
www.vatnajokull.com

If you have a four-wheel-drive jeep, you can take the track up to the glacier (off from the Ring Road at Smyrlabjarg) – an experience in itself.

For excursions onto Snæfellsjökull glacier, contact **Ferðaþjónustan Snjófell**, Arnarstapi, 355 Ólafsvík, tel: 435 6783, fax: 435 6795, e-mail: snjofell@snjofell.is, www.snjofell.is

Ice Climbing

In summer guided day-walks on the glaciers from Skaftafell National Park can be arranged through the park warden's office. For more ambitious expeditions contact the following organisations:
Iceland Alpine Club/Íslenski Alpaklúbburinn, Skutuvógur IG 104 Reykjavík, tel: 868 8754, e-mail: info@isalp.is, www.isalp.is
Öræfaferðir, Hofsnes-Öraefi, 785 Fagurhólsmýri, tel/fax: 478 1682, www.hofnes.com

Spectator Sports

Most Icelanders are avid sports fans and handball, football and basketball are all popular. Football is a summer sport, while handball and basketball, being indoor sports, are played year round. In all three sports Iceland has excellent players under contract to well-known teams abroad. Most international matches take place in Reykjavík and international and national games are advertised in the press. For information contact:
Iceland Sports Association/Íþróttasamband Íslands, Íþróttamiðstöðin, Engjavegur 6, 104 Reykjavík, tel: 514 4040, e-mail: isi@isisport.is, www.isisport.is

Boxing is banned in Iceland, but Glíma, a form of wrestling from

settlement times, is still practised. Contact Glímusamband Íslands at Iceland Sports Association.

Possibly Iceland's best-known spectator event is chess and the country has produced several grand masters in recent years. International chess tournaments are regularly held in Iceland.

Riding clubs hold races and other events throughout the summer.

The Reykjavík Marathon takes place in August each year and includes the marathon, half marathon and a 7½-km (4½-mile) fun run. For information and registration contact the **Athletics Federation of Iceland**, Sports Centre, Engjavegur 6, 104 Reykjavík, tel: 514 4040, e-mail: fri@fri.is, www.fri.is

CHILDREN'S ACTIVITIES

Facilities for Children

In Iceland, children are greeted with enthusiasm and welcomed at hotels, and in restaurants and homes. Many restaurants provide baby chairs and children's portions. Tourist Menus give free meals to children of five and under and a 50 percent discount to those aged 6–12. Hotels, if notified in advance, will provide a cot but families with a baby would be advised to bring their own carry cot. Children aged four and under will often stay free if not occupying a separate bed, but where an extra bed is required a reduction for the child is usually given.

Places to take kids around Reykjavík

There are a number of places of special interest to kids in the

Reykjavík area. Some cost money, others do not; a case in point is the **Tjörn** in central Reykjavík, which on weekends normally attracts hordes of children and their families to feed the ducks and geese.
The Family Park and Farmyard Animal Zoo, Laugardalur Valley, tel: 575 7800. Open summer daily 10am–6pm; winter 10am–5pm. This is a great spot for a family outing. When the kids tire of looking at the seals, foxes, reindeer, horses, cows, pigs and all the other animals, they can head over to the Family Park. There they can try their hand at operating little electric automobiles, pull themselves across a man-made lake on a raft, climb in a Viking-ship replica and much more. There is a large grill, which can be used free of charge for barbecuing hot dogs or whatever else. And the seals are fed twice a day: at 11am and 4pm. Price: children (5–12 years) ISK 350, adults ISK 450, free for under fives.
Harbour Area, Reykjavík Harbourfront. During the summer there are little trampolines and other play equipment. There are also several large tubs with fish, crabs, starfish and so on. Those who dare can hold a crab or starfish. All free.
Natural History Museum, Hlemmur 5, tel: 590 0500, www.ni.is. Open June–Aug Mon, Thur, Sat and Sun 1–5pm; Sept–May same days 1–4pm; free.
Swimming Pools; just about any and all will do. The best ones for kids are the Árbær pool, Fylkisvegur, tel: 567 3933, with its outdoor/indoor pool, hot pots, water slides for big and little kids, whirlpool, sauna and solarium and the Laugardalur pool, Laugardalur valley, tel: 553 4039, which has a very large children's pool and a big water slide.

A – Z

A HANDY SUMMARY OF PRACTICAL INFORMATION, ARRANGED ALPHABETICALLY

A dmission Charges

Although Iceland is an expensive country to visit as a tourist, admission charges for museums and galleries are generally quite reasonable. Expect to pay around ISK 600–700 for entry into most museums around the country. Some attractions, such as the National Gallery in Reykjavík, do not charge admission. In some instances, an entry ticket for one museum will give free entry or reduced entry to another (if they are operated by the same organisation – ask locally).

During the winter months, there is often a charge for checking in a coat when entering a bar or smart restaurant. This is not a strict admission charge but if you refuse to pay you will be denied access.

B udgeting for Your Trip

Iceland is one of the world's most expensive countries to visit. Its small consumer base and high import costs conspire to make most items and services several times more expensive than you will be used to

paying at home. In order to bring costs down, you need to be as self-sufficient as possible and also consider when you will visit since prices outside the main tourist season are around one third lower than during the summer months. Generally, if you visit during the summer, stay in decent hotels, eat out in restaurants most nights and undertake a few activities, you should expect to pay upwards of ISK 20,000 per day. However, it is possible to cut costs by staying in guesthouses or youth hostels and eating the odd meal in a restaurant – for this, you should reckon on about ISK 7,500–10,000 per day. Camping and self-catering will cost around ISK 3,000 per day. Alcohol is extremely expensive, so it's a good idea to either refrain from drinking whilst in Iceland or bring your own with you from home.

Business Travellers

Iceland may be isolated but it has never been insular. From its early days of settlement the nation has relied on trade for survival. Iceland

continues to trade avidly and there is as much enthusiasm for imports as there is energy in establishing markets abroad for its many excellent products. To establish business contacts, the following addresses may be useful:
Federation of Icelandic Trade, Kringlan 7, Reykjavík, tel: 588 8910, fax: 568 8441, e-mail: fis@centrum.is, www.fis.is
Iceland Chamber of Commerce, Kringlan 7, Reykjavík, tel: 510 7100, fax: 568 6564, e-mail: mottaka@chamber.is, www.chamber.is
Ministry of Industry and Commerce, Arnarhuoll, 150 Reykjavík, tel: 545 8500, fax: 562 1289, e-mail: postur@ivr.stjr.is, www.stjr.is/ivr

Weather Information

The Icelandic Meteorological Office provides recorded weather bulletins in English; tel: 902 0600, then choose 1 on a touch-tone phone (this service is not available from all telephones). For a weather forecast on the internet, go to www.vedur.is/english

TRANSPORT

CLIMATE CHART

Reykjavik

☐ Maximum temperature
■ Minimum temperature
〜 Rainfall

Trade Council of Iceland,
Borgartún 35, Reykjavík, tel:
511 4000, fax 511 4040,
e-mail: icetrade@icetrade.is, www.icetrade.is
Doing business in Iceland is
generally informal and always on a
first-name basis. Smart dress is
really only essential if you plan to eat
out at one of the better restaurants
or visit one of Reykjavík's less casual
nightspots. In business, most
Icelanders dress "smart casual".
If you are invited to a business
associate's family home, a gift of
flowers would be most appropriate,
or a bottle of whisky. Both will be
appreciated. But a word of warning –
some Icelanders drink but others
never touch a drop.

C limate

Influenced by the warm Gulf Stream
and prevailing southwesterly winds,
Iceland's temperate oceanic climate
is surprisingly mild for the latitude
(63–66°N). Reykjavík's average
January temperature is similar to that
of Hamburg, -0.5°C (31°F), though
the July average is a cool 11°C
(52°F). Because the Gulf Stream
influences the south and west of the
country, there are marked regional
differences in climate. This is also
due to the prevailing winds and the
position of mountain ranges.
The north, east and interior experience colder winter temperatures
but warmer summers, and markedly
less precipitation. The south side of
Vatnajökull can see up to 10 times
the annual 400 mm (16 inches) of
rain of those areas north of the
glacier. This is quite evident in the
vegetation cover on lava flows. In the
northeast, lava dating back
thousands of years is still bare,
while in the south of the country a
200-year-old flow is covered with
thick spongy moss.
Whatever the weather, you are
likely to experience Iceland's most
ubiquitous natural element – wind.
The Icelandic language allows for at

least eight different degrees of wind,
from *logn* (calm) to *rok* (strong gale),
and you can expect to encounter
most of them during your stay.
Finding shelter is not generally a
problem in the settled lowlands but
for the hiker or cyclist, a storm in the
central highland deserts or glacial
outwash plains may mean hours,
even days, of unimaginable misery.
The soil whipped up by such winds
can blot out the sun, covering the
land in a brown haze.

Customs

Visitors aged 20 and over are
allowed to bring in 1 litre of spirits up
to 47 percent alcohol content and 1
litre of wine up to 21 percent alcohol
content. Six litres of foreign beer or 8
litres of domestic beer may be
brought in instead of either the wine
or spirit allowance.
Visitors aged 18 and over may
bring in 200 cigarettes or 250 grams
of tobacco. As alcohol is expensive, it
is worth bringing your full allowance. If
you do not use it yourself, it will make
a very welcome gift.
You may bring in 3 kg of food up to
the value of ISK 4,000 free of duty,
but the import of uncooked eggs, raw
milk products and uncooked meat,
including salami, bacon and
uncooked ham, is prohibited.

D isabled Travellers

Wheelchair access is available at
most of the major hotels. The rough
terrain and the lack of developed
facilities mean wheelchair access to
Iceland's natural wonders is rare.
There are paved paths at Geysir,
Gulfoss and Þingvellir National Park.
For information on vehicles for hire
suitable for disabled persons,
contact one of the tour operators or
tourist information offices. Highland
buses for wheelchair users are
available on request.
The Icelandic Hotel and Restaurant
Association publishes a leaflet
entitled Hotels and Guesthouses,
which lists establishments that are
accessible to the disabled. Larger
department stores, as well as the
Kringlan Mall, are accessible to
wheelchair users. The ferries Baldur
and Herjólfur also have good facilities
for the disabled. All airlines flying to
and from the country can
accommodate disabled passengers.
Sjálfsbjörg, the Association of the
Disabled in the Capital Area, tel: 550
0300, e-mail: mottaka@sjalfsbjorg.is,
www.sjalfsbjorg.is, has published an
English-language booklet entitled
Accessible Reykjavík, which lists

Emergencies

For police, ambulance, the fire
brigade or other emergency
situations, call 112.

establishments and institutions
accessible to the disabled.

E mbassies

UK: Laufasvegur 31, tel: 550 5100,
www.britishembassy.is
US: Laufasvegur 21, tel: 562 9100,
www.usa.is
Canada: Túngata 14, tel: 575 6500,
www.canada.is
Ireland: Irish Embassy in
Copenhagen, tel: (+45) 3542 3233,
e-mail: irlemb@email.dk
Australia: Australian Embassy in
Copenhagen, Denmark, tel: (+45) 70
26 36 76.
The Icelandic Foreign Ministry has
a full list of diplomatic
representatives on its website:
utanrikisraduneyti.is

Entry Regulations

The normal entry stamp in your
passport is valid for a stay of up to
three months. You may be asked to
produce evidence of funds to support
yourself and an air or ferry ticket out of
the country. Icelandair offices abroad
are not allowed to sell one-way tickets
to non-residents unless in conjunction
with a return ferry ticket. If you wish to
extend your stay after arrival, this can
be done at the main police station in
Reykjavík, at Hverfisgata 115, or at
police stations around the country.
If you intend to work in Iceland,
you will need a pre-arranged job and
a residence and work permit which
your prospective employer applies for
before you enter the country.
Residents of the European Economic
Area (EEA states) may stay in Iceland
for up to three months without having
an air or ferry ticket out of the
country and may also look for work.
Residents of the following
countries may enter Iceland using
their personal identity card: Austria,
Belgium, France, Germany, Italy,
Lichtenstein, Luxembourg, The
Netherlands and Switzerland.
Angling gear that has been used
outside Iceland, including boots and
waders, must be disinfected by a vet
before being taken into the country.
You may be asked to produce a
certificate stating that this has been
done. Your equipment can be
disinfected on arrival at your expense.
It is forbidden to introduce any
animal into Iceland without

ACCOMMODATION

ACTIVITIES

A – Z

LANGUAGE

permission from the Ministry of Agriculture. A lengthy period of quarantine is invariably required for all animals.

Etiquette

Shyness towards visitors may be mistaken for coldness, but Icelanders are by nature hospitable and innately curious about foreigners and their ways. Family ties are strong yet they are great socialisers and many a tale is told around the coffee table. In such a small, closeknit society Icelanders invariably find that they are all related, albeit distantly, to one another and are quick to establish connections when introduced, by delving into their family trees.

If you are invited to an Icelander's home, it will most likely be for coffee, often accompanied by copious quantities of cakes and biscuits. The younger generation may be more likely to invite you for dinner; in this case a small gift – wine or flowers, for instance – is appropriate though not essential. It is customary to shake hands, when greeting and leaving, and Icelanders always remove shoes before entering their home.

Smoking is prohibited in public buildings and the gracious visitor to a private home should always ask for permission before lighting up.

Iceland uses the old system of patronymics, once common throughout Scandinavia. It raises eyebrows when an Icelandic family checks into a hotel abroad – mother, father, son and daughter will all have different last names. Very few Icelanders have surnames. Instead a child takes his father's first name, to which is added son or dóttir (son or daughter) as the case may be. Thus, if a father named Magnús has a son, Jón, and a daughter, Kristín, their full

names will be Jón Magnússon and Kristín Magnúsdóttir. And as Icelandic women never change their names on marriage, their mother too will have a different name. A child may also take the mother's name by law, though this is less common. If the identity of the father is not established the child may take the mother's or grandfather's name.

Icelanders always use first names and visitors will be expected to follow suit. The concept of titles, except for ministers of religion, is unknown. The exception to this is on formal letters when Herra (or Hr.) Magnús Jónsson or Frú Kristín Jensdóttir would be a correct form of address on the envelope.

In the telephone directory, all entries are listed under first names. If the prospect of sifting through pages and pages of Jón Jónsson is daunting, many entries also give the person's profession (in Icelandic) as well as the address.

G ay Travellers

For information and advice contact: **The Gay and Lesbian Association/Samtökin '78**, Laugavegur 3, 101 Reykjavík, tel: 552 7878, e-mail: office@samtokin78.is. Open daily 1–5pm; Monday and Thursday evenings there is a library and a coffee bar. Samtökin '78 also have a website: www.samtokin78.is. There is more information about the gay scene in Iceland at www.gayice.is.

H ealth and Insurance

Iceland is a very healthy country. Nonetheless, all visitors should have adequate medical insurance, though an agreement exists between Iceland, the UK and Scandinavian countries for limited health insurance coverage of its residents. Travellers from those countries should obtain the European Health Insurance Card (formerly the E111 form) before leaving home. No vaccinations are required for visitors, unless you are arriving from an infected area. Tap water is perfectly safe to drink.

For medical help call **The National Hospital** (Landsspítali-Háskólasjúkrahús) on 543 1000, weekdays 8am–4pm. A doctor is on call after those hours, and at weekends. In case of serious illness or accidents, the emergency ward at the **Reykjavík City Hospital** (Sjúkrahús Reykjavíkur) is open around the clock, tel: 525 1700.

For non-emergency medical treatment outside normal hours the

Medical Centre (Læknavaktin), Smáratorg 1 (in Kópavogur), is open 5pm–8am weekdays and 24 hours on weekends and public holidays. Call 554 1770 for help or advice. A nominal charge is made.

A children's doctor is on call at the **Domus Medica Medical Centre**, Egilsgata 3, Reykjavík, tel: 563 1010, evenings until 10pm, Sat and Sun 11am–3pm.

Emergency **dental care** is available, tel: 575 0505 for information about dentists on duty.

Most pharmacies (apótek) are open normal business hours (9am–6pm). However, Lyfja at Lágmúli (daily 8am–midnight) and Lyfja at Laugavegur 16 (Mon–Fri 10am–7pm, Sat 10am–4pm) have longer opening hours.

I nternet

Virtually everyone in Iceland has internet access at home. Hence, there are very few internet cafes across the country. The best place to find internet access is at the local library or in your hotel or guesthouse where it is usually available in the lobby. Libraries may levy a small fee (usually no more than ISK 200–300 per hour) and operate a booking system to use the net, whereas hotels and guesthouses usually provide free, unrestricted access. Tourist offices, where they exist, usually also have one or two terminals for internet use. Once again there's usually a nominal fee, similar to that in libraries.

Useful websites about Iceland include the following: www.icelandinfocus.com A good source of geographic information about Iceland. www.grist.org/news/counter/2005/04/26/iceland Bizarre facts about Iceland. www.iceland.is/history-and-culture//nr/80 An interesting and informative address by Magnus Magnusson about Iceland. http://en.wikipedia.org/wiki/Iceland A brief introduction to Iceland and its people. www.whatson.is The lowdown on cultural events and happenings across Iceland, with emphasis on Reykjavík. www.icetourist.is The definitive travel website of the Icelandic tourist board. www.icelandreview.com A daily news digest of events in Iceland. www.vedur.is/english The all important daily weather forecast for all areas of the country.

L eft Luggage

Hotels, guesthouses and hostels will often store luggage free of charge for guests.

Lost Credit Cards

In case of loss you can cancel your credit cards as follows:
Visa, Álfabakki 16, Reykjavík, tel: 525 2000. Emergency (24 hours): 525 2200. Toll-free number: 800 5252.
MasterCard/EuroCard, Ármúli 28, Reykjavík, tel: 550 1500 (24 hours). Emergency number (in Denmark): (+45) 3673 7373.
American Express, emergency number (in the UK): (+44) 20 7365 4846.
Diners Club, Engjateigur 9, Reykjavík, tel: 568 0050. Emergency number (in Denmark): (+45) 3672 3672.

Lost and Found

The lost and found office in Reykjavík is at Borgartún 33, tel: 569 9018; open weekdays 10am–noon and 2–4 pm.

M aps

Visitors can obtain a useful (and free) tourist map of the country and city plan of Reykjavík, which is adequate for general planning purposes and orientation but not for actual touring, from tourist information centres, airports, bus terminals and accommodation throughout Reykjavík and the rest of the country.

More detailed maps can be bought from most tourist offices and all larger bookshops in Iceland, as well as at many fuel stations. For general touring purposes the Insight Fleximap (1:910,000) has a laminated finish ideal for withstanding Iceland's wind and rain. The 1:500,000 touring map Ferðakort is excellent, as is the Kortabók Road Atlas. Greater detail is on the nine sectional maps in the Landmælingar 1:250,000 series but for most visitors the cost precludes the purchase of a full set. Large-scale 1:100,000, 1:50,000 and 1:25,000 maps of areas of particular interest to visitors, such as Þórsmörk/Landmannalaugar, Mývatn, Skaftafell, Hekla, Vestmannaeyjar and

Banking Hours

Banks are open Mon–Fri 9.15am–4pm, but rural branches may have limited opening hours. All banks have a few branches with extended opening hours, particularly in shopping malls such as Kringlan. All offer foreign exchange services.

Hornstrandir, are also available. But a word of warning: the accuracy of such maps, especially when marking footpaths and cliff faces, falls far short of maps in other countries. A general map series on the same scales also covers all areas of the country but some sheets are still under preparation or out of print. Highly recommended is the excellent geological map 1:500,000, with a key in English and Icelandic.

Media

Newspapers and Magazines

English language newspapers and magazines are on sale in Reykjavík, one or two days after publication. They can also be found in public libraries. A daily news-sheet, *Icelandic Review*, is available at some newsagents and hotels.

Two magazines, *Iceland Review* (www.icelandreview.com) and *Icelandic Geographic* are published in English with informative articles and magnificent photographs *Morgunblaðið*, the longest-established daily, has excellent coverage of foreign affairs, reflecting an isolated nation's desire to keep pace with the world. *DV*, the other major daily, has a more popular appeal but is still based on serious news coverage. *Fréttablaðið*, published Mon–Fri, is free and relatively lightweight in both content and size.

Pick up a copy of the free listings magazine *What's On in Reykjavík* at the tourist office; www.whatson.is

Television

That a nation of 310,000 should have no fewer than six television channels is surprising, with a number of locally produced programmes. Channel 1 is state-run, Skjár 1 is independently run, Omega is a Christian station and the others are pay-TV, by subscription; these feature a fair number of foreign films, serials and documentaries that are usually undubbed, save for children's programmes. Satellite TV is available by subscription in Iceland, giving direct access to the usual international news and

entertainment channels including CNN and the BBC.

News in English

A summary of world news in English can be found on Teletext page 130 on the national television channel, Sjónvarpið.

Money

The monetary unit is the Icelandic króna (plural: krónur), divided into 100 aurar. Notes are in denominations of ISK 5,000, 2,000, 1,000 and 500. Coins are in denominations of ISK 100, 50, 10, 5 and 1.
In late 2007 the exchange rate was ISK 123 to the pound sterling, ISK 61 to the US dollar and ISK 85 to the euro.

You can bring in unlimited foreign currency in the form of travellers' cheques or bank notes and up to ISK 14,000 in Icelandic currency. It is generally not worth purchasing large amounts of Icelandic króna abroad as a poorer rate of exchange is given. Similarly you should change back all unused króna before leaving Iceland (this can be done at the airport departure lounge) and you may need to produce receipts of exchange transactions from foreign currency or travellers' cheques to króna.

Exchange Facilities

The simplest way to obtain Icelandic króna is to find an ATM cash machine – plentiful in Reykjavík and other Icelandic towns. Banks will change foreign currency or travellers' cheques – US dollars, sterling and euros are all easily exchanged. Many hotels, local shops, even roadside restaurants and taxi drivers will accept pounds sterling, euros and US dollars.

Hotels usually exchange travellers' cheques and banknotes for guests, at a rate slightly below the bank rate, depending on the availability of cash in the till.

Outside normal banking hours 24-hour exchange facilities are available at Keflavík Airport:
Landsbankinn on the second level, for departing and arriving passengers.

Change Group on the lower level of the arrivals hall, past customs control.

Credit Cards

Credit cards are used everywhere in Iceland, with the most ubiquitous being Visa and MasterCard/EuroCard. American Express, JCB and Diners are far less common.

Cash advances are available on Visa and MasterCard/EuroCard from all banks, savings banks and automatic cash machines displaying the respective logos.

Debit Cards

Visa, Delta, Maestro/EDC and Electron debit cards are widely accepted. Cash may be obtained against these cards in all banks and automatic cash machines displaying the relevant logos.

VAT refunds

Foreigners making purchases in excess of ISK 4,000 are entitled to a partial VAT refund when they leave Iceland. For full details, *see Tax Free Shopping on page 331.*

P hotography

Crystal-clear air and long hours of daylight create ideal conditions for photography, and enthusiasts may go through more film than they plan to. Note that you should always use a UV/skylight filter when photographing outdoors. All photographic equipment, film and processing is very expensive (think of a number and double it), so bring your own or purchase it at the Duty Free Shop at the Keflavík airport. If you do have to buy film in Iceland, bear in mind that outside Reykjavík slide film, in particular, may be hard to obtain.

Postal Services

Post offices *(Íslandspóstur)* are found in all major towns and villages and some country districts. The postal system is efficient with letters taking 3 to 5 days to reach Europe or North America. Air-mail letters or postcards to Europe cost ISK 70; to other areas they are ISK 90. You can buy stamps from post offices though it is often worth checking at shops that sell postcards, as some also stock stamps. The Central Post Office, Posthússtræti 5, Reykjavík, has a philatelic section, but stamp collections are also sold at souvenir shops. Icelandic stamps often show birds and natural phenomena and many are inexpensive, perhaps making an unusual and affordable gift to take home.

Poste Restante is available at post offices throughout the country. Mark letters clearly with the surname in capitals or underlined.

Post offices are generally open Mon–Fri 9am–4.30pm. The post office on Posttíusstræt 5 (near Laugardalur) in Reykjavík is open Mon–Fri 9am–6pm, June, July and August Sat 10am–2pm.

Public Holidays

January New Year's Day/ *Nýársdagurinn* (1st).
March/April Maundy Thursday, Good Friday, Easter Monday; First Day of Summer/ *Sumardagurinn fyrsti* (third or fourth Thursday in April).
May Labour Day (1st); Ascension (sixth Thursday after Easter); Whitsun (eighth Monday after Easter).
June Independence Day (17th).
August *Verslunnarmannahelgi* (first Monday).
December Christmas Day (25th), Boxing Day (26th). Christmas Eve and New Year's Eve are half-day holidays.

R eligious Services

Just over 90 percent of Icelanders belong to the Lutheran Church, about 1 percent are Roman Catholics and various denominations account for the remaining 9 or so percent of the population.

Reykjavík has a number of churches which hold regular services on Sundays and in the week. Churches in central Reykjavík include: **Hallgrímskirkja**, Skólavörðuhott, tel: 510 1000; **Dómkirkjan** (the cathedral), Kirkjustræti 16, tel: 520 9700; **Catholic Church**, Túngata, tel: 552 5388 (celebrates Holy Mass in English on Sundays at 8pm); **Fríkirkjan** (Free Church), Fríkirkjuvegur 5, tel: 551 4579.

Outside Reykjavík there are Lutheran churches in all towns and villages and on many farms as well, though services may not be held every Sunday in rural districts. Apart from main **Akureyrikirkja**, Akureyri also has a Catholic church at Eyrlandsvegur 26.

S ecurity and Crime

Iceland is one of the world's safest countries. Of the few people in prison most are drugs offenders. Public places are well lit. Violent crime is virtually non-existent, bar the odd domestic dispute and drunken brawl. The latter is most likely on Friday and Saturday nights, when the city's youth takes to the streets of central Reykjavík on a (mostly good-humoured) drunken spree.

Though Icelanders are relaxed when it comes to security, for the visitor all normal precautions apply. Pickpocketing and street crime are rare, although Reykjavík has a number of drug addicts and alcoholics who steal to fund their habits, so some caution is always sensible. Petty theft does occur in swimming-pool changing rooms (always leave valuables at the pay desk) and in bars and nightclubs. In the event of theft or loss, contact the nearest police station, where you will be required to fill in a statement. A copy is invariably required to claim on insurance.

Student Travellers

Student discounts are rarely, if ever, advertised. It is worth asking at museums. Icelandair offers a standby youth fare, which may help students planning on spending longer than the standard one and three month apex tickets allow.

T elecommunications

The Icelandic word for telephone is *Sími*. Public telephone kiosks are something of a rarity in Iceland so making a telephone call demands ingenuity and perseverance. Restaurants, roadside service stations, swimming pools and hotels often have coin-box telephones, taking ISK 10, 50 and, usually, 100 coins. Most call boxes will also accept phonecards – available from post offices. Calls made between 7pm and 8am are charged at a reduced rate. Try to avoid calling from your hotel room – hotels often charge three times the official rate.

Direct dialling is available to most countries – to call internationally from Iceland, first dial 00 followed by the country code. Country codes and international dialling procedure in English are listed in the telephone directory. Alternatively, you can dial 114 to enquire about the correct country code. For international directory enquiries dial 115.

All Icelandic telephone numbers have seven digits, with no area codes. The international code for calling Iceland from abroad is 354.

Fax services are available from post offices around the country and many hotels also offer this service to guests and sometimes to non-residents. The main tourist information office in Reykjavík also has good telephone and fax facilities which are available to visitors.

Tipping

Tipping is not customary in Iceland and is not expected.

Toilets

Public toilets are a rarity. It is better to make use of the facilities at your accommodation or at a bar or cafe.

Tour Operators

A wide range of travel packages are offered by tour operators in Iceland and abroad. Itineraries range from short coach-based sightseeing tours to longer camping tours and activity holidays – including horse-riding, whale-watching, hiking, river rafting, snowmobiling and mountain biking. Those who prefer a roof over their head but do not mind roughing it a little could try sleeping-bag accommodation holidays. Winter packages offer cross-country skiing, snowmobiling and jeep touring.

Outside main towns with tourist offices, it is worth asking at your hotel for details of local tours. Some operators offer a special service for schools and universities. Local Tourist Offices usually offer sightseeing tours ranging from one morning to several days.

For more detailed information contact the Icelandic Tourist Board or Tourist Information Offices.

Tour Operators in Iceland

Arinbjörn Jóhannsson, Brekkulækur Farm, 531 Hvammstangi, tel: 451

Tourist Offices

Reykjavík: Tourist Information, Aðalstræti 2, 101 Reykjavík, tel: 590 1550, e-mail: info@visitreykjavik.is, www.visitreykjavik.is. Open 1 June–15 Sept: daily 8.30am–7pm; 16 Sept–31 May: Mon–Fri 9am–6pm, Sat & Sun 10am–2pm.
Iceland Visitor Travel Center, Lækjargata 2, tel: 511 2442, www.icelandvisitor.com. Open June–Aug daily 9am–10pm, Sept–May Mon–Sat 10am–6pm.
Akureyri: Tourist Information Centre, Hafnarstræti 82, 600 Akureyri, tel: 462 7733, fax: 461 1817, e-mail: info@eyjafjordur.is; www.eyjafjordur.is. Open June–Aug: Mon–Fri 7.30am–7pm, Sat & Sun 8am–5pm; Sept–May: Mon–Fri 7.30am–4pm.

2938, fax: 451 2998, e-mail: brekka@nett.is. A company offering unique holidays in northwest Iceland. Especially notable are a 10-day Icelandic-style Christmas/New Year celebration and a spring hiking tour in May to observe nature's awakening. Also does horse-riding *(see page 342)*.
Eldá Travel Service, Bjargi, 660 Reykjahlíð, tel: 464 4220, fax: 464 4321, e-mail: info@elda.is, www.elda.is. Based next to Lake Mývatn, Eldá offers a wide variety of tours in the northeast including the "Grand Mývatn Tour", tours to Gjástykki and Dettifoss, and whale-watching. Many run daily during the summer months.
Gudmundur Jónasson Travel, Borgartún 34, Reykjavík, tel: 511 1515, fax: 511 1511, e-mail: gjtravel@gjtravel.is, www.gjtravel.is. A diverse variety of tours including horse-riding and river rafting.
Iceland Excursions Allrahanda, Höfðatún 12, 110 Reykjavík, tel: 540 1313, fax: 540 1310, e-mail: allrahanda@allrahanda.is, www.icelandexcursions.is. Day tours from Reykjavík to the southwest of the country, including whale-watching, the Blue Lagoon and glacier tours.
Iceland Total, Skútuvogur 13A, 104 Reykjavík, tel: 585 4300, email: info@icelandtotal.com, www.icelandtotal.com. Part of the Icelandair group, this company seemingly offers every kind of tour imaginable: everything, from whalewatching to glacier tours, is available.
Iceland Travel Ltd, Lágmúli 4, 128 Reykjavík, tel: 585 4300, fax: 585 4390, e-mail: it@icelandtravel.is, www.icelandtravel.is. Well established agency, with a full range of tours to all parts of Iceland – including a variety of adventure tours.
Icelandic Farm Holidays, Síðumúli 13, Reykjavík, tel: 570 2700, fax: 570 2799, e-mail: ifh@farmholidays.is, www.farmholidays.is. A variety of tours, including farm holidays and farmhouse accommodation.
Nonni Travel, Brekkugata 5, Akureyri, tel: 461 1841, fax: 461 1843, e-mail: nonni@nonnitravel.is, www.nonnitravel.is. Offers trips around Akureyri and nearby areas including Mývatn, and Grímsey, by boat or air.
Reykjavík Excursions, BSÍ Bus Terminal, 101 Reykjavík, tel: 562 1011, e-mail: main@re.is, www.re.is. Organises day trips and sightseeing tours in and around Reykjavík.
Snæland Grímsson, Langholtsvegur 115, 104 Reykjavík, tel: 588 8660, fax: 588 8661, e-mail:

Tourist Offices Abroad

USA: tel: 212-885 9700, fax: 212-885 9710, mailing address: 655 3rd Ave, New York, NY 10017, www.goiceland.org
UK: There is no tourist office in the UK; for information on the internet, visit www.icetourist.is

snaeland@snaeland.is; www.snaeland.is. Hiking, group tours, day excursions, winter excursions, jeep safaris and more.

Adventure Tours

A number of tour operators specialise in adventure tourism, such as river rafting, glacier tours, kayaking, winter excursions and mountain climbing. Many larger tour operators may also offer such trips as part of their regular programme.
Activity Tours, Vegamót, 560 Varmahlíð, tel: 453 8383, fax: 453 8384, e-mail: hestaact@isholf.is, www.rafting.is. White-water rafting in the Skagafjörður region of north Iceland. Three rivers, graded according to difficulty.
Blue Biking, Stekkjarhvammur 60, 220 Hafnarfjörður, Iceland, tel/fax: 565 2089, e-mail: bluebiking@ simnet.is, www.simnet.is/bluebiking. Made-to-measure bicycle tours, designed to suit your needs. All the necessary equipment is provided.
Glacier Tours, Alfaheidi 1E, 200 Kopavogur, tel/fax: 564 6452, e-mail: vatnajokull@vatnajokull.com, www.vatnajokull.com. Snowmobiling onto the Vatnajökull ice-cap, seafood buffet on the glacier for groups, and sailings on Jökulsárlón glacial lagoon. Protective gear provided.
Ice Travel, Álftaland 17, 108 Reykjavík, tel: 588 5555, e-mail: ice@icemail.is, www.icemail.is. Individual/group tours, expeditions. Snowmobile and jeep safaris, glacier tours including popular seafood buffet on a glacier, helicopter tours, river rafting etc.
Iceland Excursions Allrahanda *(see previous column)*. Jeep tours combined with hiking, snow scooting, ice climbing and more. Designed for fit people of all ages. Small groups and relaxed ambience. Their pride and joy is a Hummer jeep, which seats nine people.
Icelandic Mountain Guides (Íslenskir Fjallaleiðsögumenn), Vagnhöfði 7b, 110 Reykjavík, tel: 587 9999, fax: 587 9996, e-mail: mountainguide@mountainguide.is, www.mountainguide.is. An association of mountain and trekking guides with

years of experience, which offers tours with a difference. Also custom tours for individuals and groups.
Mountaineers of Iceland, Krókals 5A, 110 Reykjavík, tel: 581 3800, fax: 581 3810, www.mountaineers.is. Offers super-jeep tours off the beaten track.
Öræfaferðir, Hofsnes-Öræfi, 785 Fagurhólsmýri, tel: 894 0894, e-mail: info@hofsnes.com, www.hofsnes.com. Located in south Iceland, specialising in glacier and coastal tours. Bird watching, ascent onto Hvanndalshnúkur (Iceland's highest mountain), ski mountaineering expeditions, ice climbing and more.

Horse-riding Tours

The Icelandic horse is a delightful creature: small, sturdy, sure-footed and good-natured. It also has five different gaits, including the *tölt*, a fast, smooth trot. Since the 1980s the Icelandic horse has been gaining in popularity throughout the world and many foreign Icelandic-horse lovers come to Iceland especially to be able to ride the horse in its natural environment. Besides, experiencing Iceland on horseback is utterly exhilarating. A number of tour operators specialise in horse-riding tours of long or short duration. *(See also page 333)*
Arinbjörn Jóhannsson, Brekkulækur Farm, 531 Hvammstangi, tel: 451 2938, fax: 451 2998, e-mail: brekka@nett.is. Based in the northwest of Iceland. A variety of longer and shorter horse-riding tours, including winter excursions to observe the northern lights and starry night sky.
Eldhestar (Volcano Horses), Vellir, Ölfus, P.O. Box 90, 810 Hveragerði, tel: 480 4800, fax: 480 4801, e-mail: info@eldhestar.is, www.eldhestar.is. Offers short and long riding tours, riding camps, lessons, and special holidays including tours to the National Equestrian Meets.
Íshestar (Icelandic Riding Tours), Sörlaskeið 26, 220 Hafnarfjörður, tel: 555 7000, fax: 555 7001, e-mail: info@ishestar.is, www.ishestar.is. Íshestar organises diverse riding tours of various lengths, including visits to the annual sheep round-up, driving herds of horses, and historical trekking routes across the beautiful Icelandic interior.
Polar Horses, Grýtubakki 2, 601 Akureyri, tel: 463 3179, fax: 463 3144, e-mail: polarhestar@ polarhestar.is, www.nett.is/polar. A family-run outfit offering tours with such intriguing names as "Elves and Trolls Trail". Also organises tours to the National Equestrian Meet and farm holidays with daily riding tours incorporated.

Hiking Tours

Two local outdoor organisations – the Icelandic Touring Association (Ferðafélag Íslands) and Útivist – offer guided backpacking tours and day walks. For more on hiking, *see page 332*.
The backpacking tours are graded according to level of difficulty and accommodation is usually in mountain huts. The tours and walks both generally depart from the BSÍ bus terminal in Reykjavík.
Both organisations are practically national institutions and are extremely popular with Icelanders. Consequently, these tours provide an excellent way to meet the natives. The downside is that the tours are guided in Icelandic, though the majority of guides do speak English as well.

Iceland Touring Association (Ferðafélag Íslands) Mörkinn 6, 108 Reykjavík, tel: 568 2533, fax: 568 2535, email: fi@fi.is, www.fi.is. Founded in 1927, offers various hiking and cross-country skiing tours with mountain hut accommodation. Also operates bus tours.
Útivist, Laugavegur 178, 105 Reykjavík, tel: 562 1000, fax: 562 1001, e-mail: utivist@utivist.is, www.utivist.is. Hiking tours to Þórsmörk and other south Iceland locations, with camping and mountain hut accommodation.

Sightseeing Air Tours

Flugfélag Vestmannaeyja, (Westman Islands Airline), Vestmanneyjar airport, Vestmannaeyjar, tel: 481 3255, fax: 481 2652, e-mail: eyjaflug@eyjar.is, www.eyjaflug.is. Aerial sightseeing around Vestmannaeyjar.
Mýflug Air Service, Reykjahlíð airport, tel: 464 4400, fax 464 4401, e-mail: myflug@myflug.is, www.myflug.is. Offers sightseeing flights around Lake Mývatn from the airfield behind the campsite. On a clear day the 20-minute flight over the lake is stunning. They also fly over Krafla, the Jökulsá Canyon, and the central highlands to Askja and Kverkfjöll. A minimum of four persons is usually needed to go ahead with the flight.

Tour Operators Abroad

UK
Discover the World, Arctic House, 8 Bolters Lane, Banstead, Surrey SM7 2AR, tel: 01737 218800, www.discover-the-world.co.uk. A comprehensive travel and information service for Iceland. Hotel tours, camping and sleeping-bag accommodation tours, activity

holidays including mountain biking, hiking, river rafting and snowmobiling, fly drive and independent travel arrangements, bus and air passes. Also offers winter activity holidays and a book and map service. Special arrangements made for school and university groups.
Dick Phillips, Whitehall House, Nenthead, Alston, Cumbria CA9 3PS, tel: 01434 381440, www.icelandic-travel.com. Iceland specialist with backpacking and coach tours and independent arrangements. Information and book and map service. Special arrangements made for school and university groups.
Icelandair, Adam House, 2nd floor, 1 Fitzroy Square, London W1T 5HE, tel: 0870 787 4020, fax 020 7874 1001, email: uk@icelandair.is, www.icelandair.co.uk. Icelandair's in-house travel agency. Offers a broad range of escorted and unescorted programmes for groups and individuals year round, including fly-drive packages and stopovers.
Sherpa Expeditions, 131a Heston Road, Hounslow, Middlesex TW5 0RF, tel: 020 8577 2717, fax: 020 8572 9788, e-mail: sales@sherpa-walking-holidays.co.uk, www.sherpa-walking-holidays.co.uk. 9- or 15-day escorted walking tours through the Markaflót valley in the Torfajökull region.

USA
Icelandair Holidays, 5950 Symphony Woods Road, Suite 410, Columbia, MD 21044, USA, tel: 1 800 779 2899 ext. 4, e-mail: holidays@icelandair.is, www.icelandair.com. Icelandair's in-house travel agency *(see UK entry, above)*.
Distant Journeys, P.O. Box 1211, Camden, Maine, 04843, USA, tel: 888-845 5781, fax: 207-236 0972, e-mail: djourney@midcoast.com, www.distantjourneys.com. Hiking and walking tours.

W hat to Bring

Iceland is expensive: the 24.5 per cent VAT on most goods means that many items are double the price you would pay elsewhere. Bring everything you are likely to need for your stay in the way of clothing, medicine, camera film and other equipment. If you plan to backpack around the country it is worth bringing in your duty-free food allowance (3kg/6.6lb, up to ISK 4,000 in value) in the form of dried foods. Freeze-dried products are very costly and virtually unavailable outside specialist shops in Reykjavík.

Iceland's freak wind gusts have been known to wreak havoc at campgrounds – a summerweight tent will not survive these winds. If you bring your own tent, make sure you are able to repair bent poles, broken guy ropes and holes in canvas. Bring heavy-duty tent pegs; lightweight aluminium pegs may not be enough.

What to Wear

In summer, light woollens or a fleece, and a wind- and rainproof jacket or coat are essential, along with something for warmer days (wearing layers works best in Iceland's changeable summer weather). If you plan to travel around the country, go walking or head into the uninhabited interior, you must dress accordingly. Your best investment for Iceland will be a quality rain/wind jacket and leggings together with a thick sweater (or a fleece, which will still insulate when wet), scarf, hat and gloves. For footwear, bring a thick-soled pair of walking shoes or trainers. Even if you don't plan to do any serious hiking, a pair of lightweight hiking boots is a good idea – many of Iceland's most visited sights are reached on foot via uneven paths.

Bring swimwear – even the most confirmed non-swimmers will enjoy Iceland's geothermal bathing pools.

Icelanders are very clothes-conscious, which is reflected in the range of styles in Reykjavík's fashion shops. If you plan to eat out at one of the city's better restaurants, you should dress up. Although most pubs and clubs are casual, a few clubs maintain a policy of no jeans or trainers.

For travel in Iceland between October and May, conditions can be severe. Although prolonged cold spells are rare, thanks to the warming effects of the Gulf Stream, temperatures as low as -20°C (-6°F) can occur and, with the wind chill factor, it can feel very much colder than that. So, any visitor planning to travel outside the Reykjavík area in winter must be well kitted out, for example with thermals, a down jacket and a good-quality windproof jacket and hat.

When to Visit

Spring

April and May can be good times to visit Iceland – although it is still cold early in the period and most highland and interior routes are closed to standard vehicles. Long daylight hours, few tourists and the beginning of the whale-watching season are all reasons to visit at this time of year.

Summer

Summer in Iceland is a brief affair. By June the lowlands are snow-free and the land bursts into colour. Between mid-May and the end of July there is almost perpetual daylight. July signals the opening of the highland routes and travellers take to their vehicles in a frenzy of activity. By mid-August the nights are cooler, and the tourist season draws to a rapid close.

Mid-June to mid-August, the high tourist season, sees the warmest, though not necessarily the best, weather. Most people visit at this time and accommodation can be hard to find. However, if you travel off the beaten track, you will still find plenty of open space.

The first half of June and last two weeks in August see less tourist traffic and often have fine weather, though nights can be chilly. Most campsites, summer hotels, tours and excursions only operate from June to the end of August.

For birds and flowers the first half of summer is undoubtedly better, but if you want to get into the highlands don't travel before mid-July. You can catch the midnight sun in June in the north of Iceland but the northern lights do not start to appear until the cooler and darker nights of late August.

Autumn

The first of September signals the end of summer and many tourist operations start winding down, and many of those who work in the travel business during the summer go back to college. The Edda chain of hotels are boarding schools during the winter, so they have to return to their normal operations.

However, farms and other hotels will welcome business and if you have brought a tent, camping presents no problems. Many of the highland routes are passable with care throughout September – the added dimension of autumn colours and a dusting of snow on the mountain ranges can make this one of the most beautiful months.

Winter

Reykjavík is increasingly gaining in popularity as a winter-break destination, and a number of tour operators offer bargain packages out of season. Hotels, most museums and some excursions operate all year in Reykjavík. The winter has its own rewards for independent travellers. Some bus routes and most flights operate year-round but schedules can be disrupted by weather. If you plan to hire a vehicle in winter, a four-wheel drive is a must. Car rental firms and hotels have special winter rates.

Some tour operators offer winter activity holidays with travel by jeep, snowmobile or on cross-country skis (see Tour Operators, pages 341–2).

L ANGUAGE

UNDERSTANDING THE LANGUAGE

About Icelandic

Icelandic is one of the Nordic family of languages and most closely resembles Norwegian and Faroese. Remarkably, the Icelandic spoken today has not changed greatly from the language of the early Norse settlers *(see page 91)*.

For the foreigner, Icelandic is daunting. The good news is that most Icelanders, particularly the young, speak English fluently, as well as Danish, Norwegian or Swedish. German and French are less widely spoken, but also taught at school. Icelanders are by nature quite reticent with foreigners. It may take a while to draw them into conversation but it will be worth it. If you can pick up a few phrases of Icelandic, it will be appreciated.

Pronunciation Tips

Stress falls naturally on the first syllable of a word. The following examples of pronunciation are for guidance only – many Icelandic sounds do not exist in English.

Vowels and Consonants

Two common Icelandic consonants, used throughout this book, are unique, and subtly different from each other:

Ð / ð pronounced 'th' as in *the*
Þ / þ pronounced 'th' as in *thing*

a as in *hard*
á as in *how*
e as in *get*
é as in *yet*
i or **y** as in *thin*
í or **ý** as in *been*
o as in *ought*
ó as in *gold*

ö as in *first*
u as in *hook*
ú as in *fool*

ae as in *fight*
au between the sounds in *fate* and *oil*, as in the French *feuille*
ey/ei as in *day*

fn is pn as in *open*
g when followed by i (except at the start of a word) is y as in *yet*
hv is kf as in *thankful*
j is y as in *yet*
ll is tl as in *bottle*
r is always lightly rolled
rl is rtl as in *heartless*
rn is tn as in *button*
tn and **fn** when at the end of words are almost silent.

Geography

The following lists show common elements in place names, the English translation and an example.

Á	river
Hvítá	white river
Borg	rocky crag
Dimmuborgir	dark crags
Brekka	slope
Brekkulækur	slope stream
Dalur	valley
Fljótsdalur	river valley
Drangur	column
Drangavík	rock bay
Eldur	fire
Eldfell	fire mountain
Eyja	island
Flatey	flat island
Fell	mountain
Snæfell	snow mountain
Fjall	mountain
Bláfjöll	blue mountains
Fjörður	fjord
Hafnarfjörður	harbour
	fjord

Foss	waterfall
Gulfoss	gold falls
Gígur	crater
Lakagígar	cow stomach craters
Gil	ravine
Jökulgil	glacier ravine
Heiði	heath
Hellisheiði	cave heath
Hellir	cave
Sönghellir	song caves
Hlíð	hillside
Reykjahlíð	steamy hillside
Hóll	hill/hillock
Vatnsdalshólar	lake valley hills
Holt	hill
Brattholt	steep hill
Hraun	lava
Ódáðahraun	ill deeds lava
Höfði	cape
Höfðabrekka	cape slope
Höfn	harbour
Þórshöfn	Thor's harbour
Jökull	glacier
Vatnajökull	lake glacier
Lækur	stream
Varmilækur	warm stream
Laug	hot spring
Laugarvatn	hot spring lake
Lind	spring
Hvannalindir	angelica springs
Lón	lagoon
Jökulsárlón	glacier river lagoon
Mýri	marsh
Mýrdalsjökull	marsh valley glacier
Nes	peninsula
Snæfellsnes	snow mountain peninsula
Reykur	steam
Reykjanes	steam peninsula
Sandur	sand
Mýrdalssandur	marsh valley sand
Skarð	pass

Kerlingarskarð	troll wife's pass
Skógur	wood
Skógafoss	wood falls
Staður	place
Egilsstaðir	Egil's place
Strönd	coast/beach
Hornstrandir	horn peak coast
Tindur	peak
Tindfjöll	peak mountains
Tjörn	pond
Störu-tjarnir	big ponds
Vatn	lake
Hvítárvatn	white river lake
Vík	small bay
Reykjavík	smoky bay
Vogur	inlet
Kópavogur	seal pup inlet
Völlur	plain
Þingvellir	assembly plains

At the Restaurant

Most restaurant staff speak some English or other Scandinavian languages. The words and phrases below will help you order from simpler menus.

Ég ætla að fá... **I would like...**

Numbers

Núll	zero
Einn	one
Tveir	two
Þrír	three
Fjórir	four
Fimm	five
Sex	six
Sjö	seven
Átta	eight
Níu	nine
Tíu	ten
Ellefu	eleven
Tólf	twelve
Þrettán	thirteen
Fjórtán	fourteen
Fimmtán	fifteen
Sextán	sixteen
Sautján	seventeen
Átján	eighteen
Nítján	nineteen
Tuttugu	twenty
Tuttugu og einn	twenty one
Þrjátíu	thirty
Fjörutíu	forty
Fimmtíu	fifty
Sextíu	sixty
Sjötíu	seventy
Áttatíu	eighty
Níutíu	ninety
Hundrað	one hundred
Tvö hundrað	two hundred
Þúsund	one thousand
Milljón	one million

Áttu til...? **Have you got any...?**
Meira... **More...**
Ekki meira takk **No more thankyou**
Mjög gott **Very good**
Ég er grænmetisæta **I am vegetarian**
Reikninginn, takk **The bill, please**

Matseðill **Menu**
Forréttir **Starters**
Súpa **Soup**
Brauð **Bread**
Smjör **Butter**
Sósa **Sauce**

Kjötréttir Meat Dishes

Kjöt **Meat**
Lambakjöt **Lamb**
Nautakjöt **Beef**
Svínakjöt **Pork**
Kjúklingur **Chicken**
Hangikjöt **Smoked lamb**

Fiskréttir Fish Dishes

Fiskur **Fish**
Ýsa **Haddock**
Lúða **Halibut**
Rækjur **Prawns**
Lax **Salmon**
Silungur/Bleikja **Trout**

Grænmeti Vegetables

Kartöflur **Potatoes**
Franskar **Chips**
Blómkál **Cauliflower**
Grænar baunir **Peas**
Rauðkál **Red cabbage**
Sveppir **Mushrooms**
Gulrætur **Carrots**
Rófur **Turnips**
Salat **Salad**

Eftirréttir Desserts

Ís **Ice-cream**
Kaka/Terta **Cake**

Drykkir Drinks

Te **Tea**
Kaffi **Coffee**
Mjólk **Milk**
Sykur **Sugar**
Appelsínusafi **Orange juice**
Bjór **Beer**
Pilsner **Low-alcohol beer**
Hvítvín **White wine**
Rauðvín **Red wine**
Vatn **Water**

Useful Words and Phrases

The Icelandic language does not have an equivalent to "please". The phrase *Gerðu svo vel* is employed to invite a person into a house, to the table or to begin eating. It also translates to "here you are" when giving something to somebody. On a public notice "please" is

vinsamlegast. For example, "please take your shoes off", a common request when entering a home or changing room is *vinsamlegast farið úr skónum.* When leaving the table or saying goodbye after a meal or drinks it is customary to thank the host by saying *Takk fyrir mig.*

Hello/good morning *Góðan dag*
Good evening *Gott kvöld*
Goodnight *Góða nótt*
What is your name? *Hvað heitir þú?*
My name is... *Ég heiti*
How are you? *Hvað segirdu gott?*
Fine, and you? *Allt fínt, en þú?*
Fine *Allt fínt*
Alright *Allt í lagi*
Goodbye *Bless*
Yes *Já*
No *Nei*
Thanks *Takk*
Thank you very much *Takk fyrir*
Yes please *Já takk*
No thank you *Nei takk*
May I have... *Má eg fá...*
When? *Hvenær?*
Today *Í dag*
Tomorrow *Á morgun*
Yesterday *Í gær*
In the morning *Fyrir hádegi*
In the afternoon *Eftir hádegi*
Cheers! *Skál!*
How much does this cost? *Hvað kostar þetta?*
Come! *Komdu!*
Excuse me *Afsakið*
Sorry *Fyrirgefðu*
I do not understand *Ég skil ekki*

Signs

Toilet *Snyrting*
Gents *Karlar*
Ladies *Konur*
Open *Opið*
Closed *Lokað*
Danger *Hætta*
Forbidden *Bannað*
Campsite *Tjaldstæði*
Entry *Inngangur/Inn*
Exit *Útgangur/Út*
Parking *Bílastæði*
Schedule *Áætlun*
Airport *Flugvöllur*
Blind summit (road sign) *Blindhæd*
Jeep track *Jeppavegur*
Police *Lögreglan*
Hospital *Sjúkrahús*
Health Centre *Heilsugæslustöð*
Doctor *Læknir*
Dentist *Tannlæknir*
Bank *Banki*
Post Office *Póstur og Sími*
Chemist *Apótek*
Co-op store *Kaupfélag*
Swimming pool *Sundlaug*
Mechanic/garage *Verkstæði*

FURTHER READING

General

A Guide to the Birds of Iceland by Þorsteinn Einarsson, Örn og Örlygur, Reykjavík, 1991. A practical guide to identifying nearly all species of Icelandic birds.
A Guide to the Flowering Plants and Ferns of Iceland by Hörður Kristinsson, Örn & Örlygur, Reykjavík, 1987.
Cod: A Biography of the Fish that Changed the World by Mark Kurlansky, Vintage, London 1999. Highly-acclaimed, fascinating account of a fish and an industry so vital to Iceland.
Ring of Seasons by Terry Lacy, University of Michigan Press, 2001. A good all-round overview of Icelandic history and culture from the perspective of a foreign resident.

Literature

Angels of the Universe by Einar Már Guðmundsson, Mare's Nest, London, 1995. This acclaimed novel won the Nordic Council's Literary Award in 1995. It tells the story of mental disintegration and features a host of colourful characters whose world is at odds with social convention.
The Atom Station by Halldór Laxness, Second Chance Press, New York, 1982. A wonderful dark comedy with a political slant by Iceland's late nobel laureate.
Independent People by Halldór Laxness, Vintage (Random House), USA, 1997. A classic story of a man's struggle for independence, symbolic of the Icelandic nation. The novel won the Nobel Prize.
Treasures of Icelandic Verse by various authors, Mál og Menning, Reykjavík, 1996. An anthology of various Icelandic poems, with both the original and the translation.
Troll's Cathedral by Ólafur Gunnarsson, Mare's Nest, London, 1996. The story of a family beset by violence.
Tainted Blood by Arnaldur Indriðason, Vintage, London 2005. A fascinating murder mystery featuring Reykjavík detective, Erlendur, and his team who investigate a man's murder with

help from Iceland's Genetic Research Centre.
Angels of the Universe by Einar Már Guðmundsson, Mare's Nest Publishing, 1995. A disturbing and moving account of a young man's slide into schizophrenia, based on the true life story of the author's brother. Also released as a film.

Many of Iceland's **Sagas** have been translated into English and other languages; particularly readable are Egils Saga, Laxdæla Saga and Njáls Saga, which are all published under the Penguin Classics label.
   The Sagas of the Icelanders, translated by Robert Kellogg and (appropriately) published by Viking includes 12 sagas.

Other Insight Guides

Apa Publications has more travel guides in print than any other

Feedback

We do our best to ensure the information in our books is as accurate and up-to-date as possible. The books are updated on a regular basis, using local contacts, who painstakingly add, amend and correct as required. However, some mistakes and omissions are inevitable and we are ultimately reliant on our readers to put us in the picture. We would welcome your feedback on any details related to your experiences using the book "on the road". Maybe we recommended a hotel that you liked (or another that you didn't), as well as interesting new attractions, or facts and figures you have found out about the country itself. The more details you can give us (particularly with regard to addresses, e-mails and telephone numbers), the better. We will acknowledge all contributions, and we'll offer an Insight Guide to the best letters received.

Please write to us at:
Insight Guides
PO Box 7910
London SE1 1WE
United Kingdom
Or send e-mail to:
insight@apaguide.co.uk

guide-book publisher, with over 200 **Insight Guides**, more than 100 **Pocket Guides** and over 200 **Compact Guides**.

Insight Guides

Insight Guides provide the reader with the full cultural background to a destination, accompanied by high-quality colour photography. Titles to Northern European destinations include **Denmark, Norway, Sweden, Finland** and **Scandinavia**.

Pocket Guides

Insight Pocket Guides are written by host authors, who show you the best of the places they know well. The books are designed in a series of day trips and excursions, and are particularly useful for people with only a short time in which to make the most of a destination. Each title comes complete with a pull-out map that can be used independently of the guide. The series includes guides to **Oslo/Bergen, Denmark** and **St Petersburg**.

Compact Guides

Insight Compact Guides are handy quick-reference books, packed with essential information for the visitor. The text is arranged around a series of routes, and cross-referenced to maps and colour pictures, making these guides ideal for on-the-spot use. Titles include **Denmark, Finland, Iceland** and **Norway**.

FlexiMaps

Insight FlexiMaps are durable, easy-to-use laminated maps. Essential travel information and a detailed list of top attractions combine with clear and comprehensive mapping. Street maps are indexed. Titles in the series include **Iceland** and **Norway**.

Art & Photo Credits

AKG London 111, 125
Alamy 2, 322, 325, 326
Bryan and Cherry Alexander 95, 122, 179, 196, 201B, 223, 254, 261, 262, 294
John Arnold Images 142
Art Archive 28TL, 57
Asdis Asgeirsdottir/Morgunbladid 215T
Ragnar Axelsson/Morgunbladid 71, 75, 76, 81, 171, 178B, 230, 256, 262T, 290, 301T, 307, 309, 310
Axiom 78, 150T
Mick Barnard/Nore-Ice 124, 170, 209, 213B, 303L
Bodo Bondzio 17T, 18, 202, 277, 279B
John Buckingham/NHPA 284T
Corbis 4, 7, 14–15, 29MB, 65L, 102R, 216/7, 224, 240T, 243, 249T, 260, 273
Julian Cremona 128R, 44, 263, 297
Mary Evans 26BR, 45, 177B, 211B
Getty 28B, 186, 257R, 312, 314
Bragi Gudmundsson 20, 63, 189B
Hrafn Gunnlaugsson 36
Catherine Harlow 10/11, 175, 194/195, 199, 206/207, 221, 224, 234, 265, 275, 287, 292/293, 303R
Blaine Harrington 22, 74, 143, 155T,
Rudy Hemmingsen 9, 197b, 183T, 200, 201T, 202T, 208, 213T, 219, 226, 242, 244, 274, 278B, 279T, 287, 298T&B, 300, 302T, 305
Icelandic Tourist Board 73, 80, 104, 106TB, 120, 157, 162, 165, 166, 172B, 178T, 182, 197, 246T, 303T, 305T, 318, 319 332, 333, 335, 343
Britta Jaschinski 3, 72, 118, 121, 148T 149BL&T, 152, 153T&B, 155, 158T&B, 159, 161, 164, 183, 191, 235, 247, 317, 331, 338
Rich Kirchner/NHPA 128L
Hans Klüche 146T, 149, 151, 154T, 163T, 167T, 182T, 189T, 198T, 231, 233T, 240, 266T, 270/271, 278T, 285, 295, 297T, 304T

Bob Krist 12/13, 64, 65R, 66, 67, 68, 79, 82/83, 84, 85, 86, 90R, 91, 102, 103, 108/109, 110, 113, 114, 119, 148, 188, 190, 192, 193, 218, 221, 241, 257, 266, 304, 306
Kristinn Ingvarsson/Morgunbladid 99
Tom Le Bas/APA 172T, 210
Leonardo 320
Ljósmyndasafn Reykjavíkur 27
National Museum of Iceland 5, 53, 89, 147
Cathleen Naundorf 60, 62, 184/5, 276, 285, 289T, 299, 327
NHPA 123, 126
Nikos Photography 181
Tony Perrottet 16, 26BL, 26TR, 51, 54, 55, 70, 77, 87, 98, 101, 154, 156T, 168/169, 173, 175T, 177T, 194T, 187T, 190T, 191, 222B, 236/237, 245T, 246, 250/251, 252, 253, 254, 255, 264, 272, 290T, 275, 180/281, 286, 288, 289
Photographer's Direct 6, 105, 308T
PhotoLibrary.com 28R, 115, 238, 265, 277, 283, 339
Eckart Pott/NHPA 308
Lance Price 32R, 34, 151T, 154, 193, 233, 282, 288, 334
Arni Saeberg/Morgunbladid 156, 163, 214, 225,
Hasse Schröder 21, 24/25, 88, 96/97, 112, 180, 211T, 258/259, 302
Julius Sigurjonsson/Morgunbladid 150B
Sigrun Sveinbjornsdottir/ Morgunbladid 291
Kjartan Thorbjornsson/ Morgunbladid 146, 239, 244T
Thorkell Thorkelsson/ Morgunbladid 21, 222T
Tom Till/Imagestate Cover
Topfoto 61
Werner Forman Archive/ National Museum Reykjavík 38
Werner Forman Archive/Stofnun Árni Magnússon Institute 37
World Picture News 107T

Map Production: Cosmographics
©2008 Apa Publications GmbH & Co. Verlag KG (Singapore branch)

Production: Linton Donaldson

INDEX

Bold type indicates principal entries